God in the Landscape

Also Available from Bloomsbury

Space, Place and Religious Landscapes, Darrelyn Gunzburg and Bernadette Brady
Shinto, Nature and Ideology in Contemporary Japan, Aike P. Rots

God in the Landscape

*Studies in the Literary History of
Australian Protestant Dissent*

Kerrie Handasyde

BLOOMSBURY ACADEMIC
LONDON • NEW YORK • OXFORD • NEW DELHI • SYDNEY

BLOOMSBURY ACADEMIC
Bloomsbury Publishing Plc
50 Bedford Square, London, WC1B 3DP, UK
1385 Broadway, New York, NY 10018, USA
29 Earlsfort Terrace, Dublin 2, Ireland

BLOOMSBURY, BLOOMSBURY ACADEMIC and the Diana logo are trademarks of
Bloomsbury Publishing Plc

First published in Great Britain 2021
Paperback edition published 2023

Copyright © Kerrie Handasyde, 2021, 2023

Kerrie Handasyde has asserted her right under the Copyright, Designs and
Patents Act, 1988, to be identified as Author of this work.

For legal purposes the Acknowledgments on p. xiii constitute an extension
of this copyright page.

Cover design: Toby Way
Cover image: Mountain Ash Forest, Victorian Central Highlands, re-growth
from the 1939 bushfires © L. Maher

All rights reserved. No part of this publication may be reproduced or transmitted
in any form or by any means, electronic or mechanical, including photocopying,
recording, or any information storage or retrieval system, without prior permission
in writing from the publishers.

Bloomsbury Publishing Plc does not have any control over, or responsibility for, any
third-party websites referred to or in this book. All internet addresses given in this
book were correct at the time of going to press. The author and publisher regret any
inconvenience caused if addresses have changed or sites have ceased to exist, but can
accept no responsibility for any such changes.

A catalogue record for this book is available from the British Library.

Library of Congress Control Number: 2021935684

ISBN: HB: 978-1-3501-8148-9
PB: 978-1-3502-5212-7
ePDF: 978-1-3501-8149-6
eBook: 978-1-3501-8150-2

Typeset by Newgen KnowledgeWorks Pvt. Ltd., Chennai, India

To find out more about our authors and books visit www.bloomsbury.com
and sign up for our newsletters

For Eloise, Aidan, Susannah, and Lachlan

Contents

List of Figures	viii
Preface	ix
Acknowledgments	xiii
Map	xiv
1 Looking Out Across the Terrain	1
2 Landscape of Dissent: Dissent's British Origins and Colonial Australian Experience	13
3 Landscape of Skepticism and Belief: Churches of Christ Travel Literature from the Holy Land to Australia, 1889–96	21
4 Landscape of Urban Transformation: Salvation Army Publicity and Performance in the Parish of the Streets, 1890–1909	39
5 Landscape of Here and Elsewhere: Congregational Poetry at Home in War and Peace, 1914–30	65
6 Landscape of Adventure: Methodist Novels and Imagination on the Mission Fields, 1910–48	89
7 Landscape of Timeless Beauty: Quaker Essays on Beauty in Art and the Painting of Nature, 1922–63	109
8 God in the Landscape	133
Notes	141
Bibliography	191
Index	215

Figures

1. Old Chapel, Coolgardie, Western Australia, 1894 — 6
2. Balcatta Gospel Hall, Western Australia — 8
3. Sanitarium Health Food Company factory, Warburton, Victoria — 10
4. *Map Showing the Liquor Shops of Melbourne City*, August 3, 1901, *The War Cry* — 53
5. *Sowing the Wind, 10. Gave a shame-faced recognition* — 54
6. *At Noonday and Midnight in Gaol, Slum and Opium Den* — 57
7. *Cross Series, Christians in Valley, 38b. The Arrest by the Soldiers* — 62
8. Olive Crane, *O, Sydney!* — 77
9. Arch Webb, *From his elevation on the ridge he watched the round-up* — 99
10. Ernest Ewart Unwin, *Quamby Bluff*, c. 1930s — 123
11. Mary P. Harris, "The Timeless Time," c. 1949 — 127
12. Mary P. Harris at Bundilla with "Billy and Tjikalyi" by William Ricketts — 130

Preface

When Gilbert Handasyde established a nursery in early colonial Melbourne, his 1864 catalog listed not only fruit trees and vegetables essential to the new city's survival but also ornamental plants including roses, verbenas, and nearly sixty Australian native species. Even as the land was cleared for Melbourne's rapid gold-rush expansion, nurserymen hoped it would be reclothed in the beauty of banksia, melaleuca, and *Xanthorrhoea australis*, the native grass tree.[1] The plants' provenance would have been mixed. Many of these Australian species could have been propagated in the nursery near Gardiners Creek, but others, particularly the *Xanthorrhoea*, were likely uprooted from their natural habitat and potted up for sale. This was an age of plant collectors and Australia's landscape yielded treasures to shovels and trowels. Nearly a hundred years later and twenty-five miles to the east, my grandfather, another Gilbert Handasyde, paid a deposit on thirty-four acres of degraded, cattle-grazed creek flats for his youngest son to plant an orchard. Around the dam and along the creek, with the cattle now gone, the scrubby sclerophyll forest quietly returned. This was my childhood wonderland—and a scene in the long backstory to this book. We write from where we are, with the past just over our shoulders.

My family were not the only newcomers to these shores who simultaneously changed the land forever and delighted in its flora and form; generations of Australians have experienced the landscape as a place of spiritual nurture and wonderment, and traveled abroad in search of vistas that bring meaning to life on the road. Many have written in response to what they found. Landscape has long inspired writers, and revelation and epiphany could apply as well to the surrounding scenery as to the inner landscape of the soul. In the nineteenth and early twentieth centuries, newcomers to Australia overlaid this ancient land of sacred stories and Dreaming with their own narratives born of belief and upbringing. They looked out across the terrain through a biblical lens that was tinted with the tales of *Pilgrim's Progress*, geographies of the Holy Land, and a rich mix of rationality and Romanticism. In Australia's broader literary history, countless writings on landscape contribute significantly to understandings of place and spirituality.[2] Histories of the churches are almost silent on the matter. Occasionally they mention annual Harvest Thanksgiving services, prayers for rain, and Sunday School songs about "things wise and wonderful," all of which were vitally important to the people.[3] But the histories of the churches have considered these things incidental. The evidence of the people's religious engagement with landscape is elsewhere. It can be seen in travel literature, missional publicity and performance, poetry, adventure novels, essays on beauty, and more. With a broad range of texts in view, this book reads religious writings of Australian Protestant Dissent for their concern with landscape. It asks how the landscape altered the new arrivals to Australian shores, how the faithful traveled across the landscape and through time, and what presence or absence they perceived. It asks how Australian Protestant Dissent experienced God in the landscape.

Australian Protestant Dissent, or Nonconformity, comprises those denominations, and their ecclesial descendants, that dissented from or did not conform to the established Church of England in the years after the Protestant Reformation. It encompasses denominations that developed in the seventeenth century such as Congregationalists, Quakers, Baptists, English Presbyterians, and, in the eighteenth and nineteenth centuries, Methodists, Brethren, Disciples/Churches of Christ, Adventists, and The Salvation Army.[4] They interest me for three reasons. First, and most importantly for the discussion of landscape, Dissent has a complex history of belonging in British religion, society, and politics, and this has played out in interesting ways when relocated to this other place. Leaving the cultural landscape of Britain, and the United States in the case of some Adventist and Churches of Christ evangelists, Dissenters arrived in Australia with a heritage of tenuous belonging and an exaggerated sense that their identity was forever elsewhere: in heaven, the mission field, or "kingdom come." Some of this sense is shared with all of Christianity, which believes itself to be unfixed: belonging nowhere in particular, for Christ is "with you always" (Mt. 28:20).[5] But for Catholics there is a sense in which holiness also lies in the relics of the saints and, along with Anglicans, within the sanctuary housing the altar.[6] By contrast, in demystified Dissent a table is just a table, a space just a space, and earthly remains are vacated by the soul. The sacred is not to be found in the things of this earth.

Dissent is especially otherworldly, even though it is defined by the historical politics that saw it come into being—the politics of this world. Despite this otherworldly orientation, Australian Protestant Dissent forged a sense of belonging in the landscape through both crossing the land and writing. New memory was made in places that held ancient memory, the landscape's signposts came to make sense, and identities shifted as Dissenters looked out from their new vantage points.[7] They wrote from these places, with the past still in view. A people unused to political power and with uncertainty around belonging, they nevertheless took part in the displacement of First Nations' peoples, and their literature *sometimes* reveals their awareness of this injustice. While these studies focus on the Australian experience, Protestant Dissent also traveled to the United States, Canada, New Zealand, South Africa, and the many other places of the British Commonwealth. The intersections between the lives of Dissenters around the world often come to light. The literary histories of each of these places may prove equally revealing.

Second, writing from where we are, the Dissenting tradition reminds the churches that faith's alliance with human power is always fraught. Even in another hemisphere, removed in time and place from Nonconformity's origins, memory of a long and lively history of protest against the control of the state is timely in this age in which other powers seek alliances with and within churches. Australian Evangelicalism, which overlaps with some but not all of Dissent, and includes parts of Anglicanism, has been studied in considerable depth in recent years.[8] But Dissent's heritage offers its churches something else, something they have begun to forget about themselves and their historical relationship to power.

Third, the many small denominations of Protestant Dissent are neglected in Australian historiography. It is not enough to point to Dissenters (and Evangelicals) as "moral policemen," wholly focused on personal piety and divine judgment and without political or civic consequence.[9] The intersection of politics and religion needs to be taken seriously as a part of Australian history.[10] Protestant Dissent constituted nearly 20 percent of the population at Australia's Federation, a small but influential percentage. The precise percentage of the population is not what is important here, however, but the position on the periphery. The study of the periphery informs our reading of the center and, thus, of the whole. The detail matters. There is variety in Australian religious experience and variety within Protestant Dissent, and too often the experience of one church has been accepted as representative of another without care for the particular theological and political perspectives of each. The particularities of local landscapes matter to historians of the Australian environment, and the same attentiveness should be applied to religion. Histories should not elide one denomination with another—after all, each established denominational presses to persuade the world of their distinct and particular views.

The observation of uncommon detail gives us insight as to how the world looked from these places in the physical and the religious landscape. Other religious groups encountered the landscape in their own ways, and there is no doubt much to explore, but this book is concerned with five distinct Dissenting denominations neglected in Australian historiography: Churches of Christ, The Salvation Army, Congregationalists, Methodists, and Quakers.[11] Each study or micro-history examines a different theme and genre of literature, and a different denomination in the 1880s–1960s. As it observes the particularities of place and perspective, evidence of the denominations' interrelatedness emerges.

The terrain of this history has not been explored before and so this book goes some way to filling a significant gap in the story of Australian Protestant Dissent. The questions it asks and the evidence it explores offer a new angle in the telling of Australian religious history in general, and Dissent in particular. I began my search for literary evidence of relationship with landscape, certain that I was not alone in experiencing more spiritual nurture in nature than the pews. Retired church historians told me the search would be futile. "You won't find much," they said, having spent a lifetime surrounded by the types of documents the churches used to define and defend their institutional identities. These denominational defenses—preacher biographies that sought to prove the importance of the man to the institution, and official church records with their modernist claims of measurable success in people, properties, and programs—were not written to reveal their relationship to the land (though they sometimes do).[12] But the landscape's literary sources were in fact plentiful and easily located in published texts on the shelves of public libraries and church archives. They were fairly evenly divided between male and female authors, a much more representative expression of lived faith than traditional church history sources. In this way, these creative writings challenge patriarchal and institutional assumptions about what constitutes a historical source within Australian Protestant Dissent, and they enable insight into belief and practice in ways that institutional sources frequently do not.

Finally, the literature of landscape has something to say in this era of rapid climate change. Australians, by all reports, care less now for the church as an institution—something that Dissenters have, at some level, always understood—but they still care for the landscape as a place of sacred encounter. Biblical memory still colors their outlooks.[13] Increasingly they tread the soil with awareness that First Nations peoples walked here for millennia, and without causing ecological devastation. This book recalls that there is a lineage of like-minded concern and a backstory to contemporary Christian environmentalism. With the present in mind, this book offers these five focused historical views across the terrain. It is a beginning. There remains a great deal more territory to explore in the understanding of Australian Protestant Dissent and the writing of God in the landscape.

Acknowledgments

I respectfully acknowledge the Wurundjeri people of the Kulin Nation on whose traditional lands, never ceded, this work was written. First Nations' stories of sacred presence and sacred land have been told for millennia in this place and all the places mentioned in the book.

I am grateful to Katharine Massam and Judith Raftery: two wise, generous, insightful scholars whose advice, example, and confidence in my work have made all the difference. I am also thankful to David Bebbington, Anne Elvey, Helen Gardner, David Hilliard, John McDowell, Hugh Morrison, Marita Munro, Glen O'Brien, Claire Renkin, and Russell E. Richey for their perceptive readings and advice, and to all the faculty and students of Pilgrim Theological College and the University of Divinity who have provided feedback on the research over the last several years. Special thanks for the enduring encouragement of Merryl Blair, Graeme L. Chapman, Alan Matheson, and Janet Woodlock.

I acknowledge the contribution of the Australian Government Research Training Program Scholarship. Thank you to Lalle Pursglove and Lily McMahon at Bloomsbury for their support in bringing the book to publication. I appreciate receiving permission to reprint portions of my articles that first appeared in *Colloquium: The Australian and New Zealand Theological Review*, *Melbourne Historical Journal*, and *Australian Garden History*, and to reproduce images from collections of The Salvation Army Australia Museum, the Art Gallery of South Australia, and The Friends' School, Tasmania. Special thanks to Eloise Maher for contributing the map. Every effort has been made to trace copyright holders and to obtain their permission for the use of copyright material. If there are any errors or omissions I would be grateful if notified of any corrections that should be incorporated in future reprints or editions of this book.

Much of the research has relied on the resources of the National Library of Australia, State Library of Victoria, State Library of South Australia, Dalton McCaughey Library, and the Sugden Library at Queen's College, Parkville. I am grateful for their long-term vision in preserving rare texts. I would also like to acknowledge the assistance of archivists, curators, genealogists, and historians: Lynne Chivers at the Bootham School in York; Lindsay Cox and Donna Bryan at the Salvation Army Museum in Melbourne; The Friends' School Archive and Heritage Collection; Caryn Kneale, Darren Hastings, Stephanie Cocks, and Charles Stevenson.

My family have been along for the ride, helping in many different ways, and I am deeply grateful for their good company and their indulgence of my research interests. Finally, thanks to Geraldine and Russell for their unwavering confidence and support, and for instilling in me their love of the Australian landscape.

Map

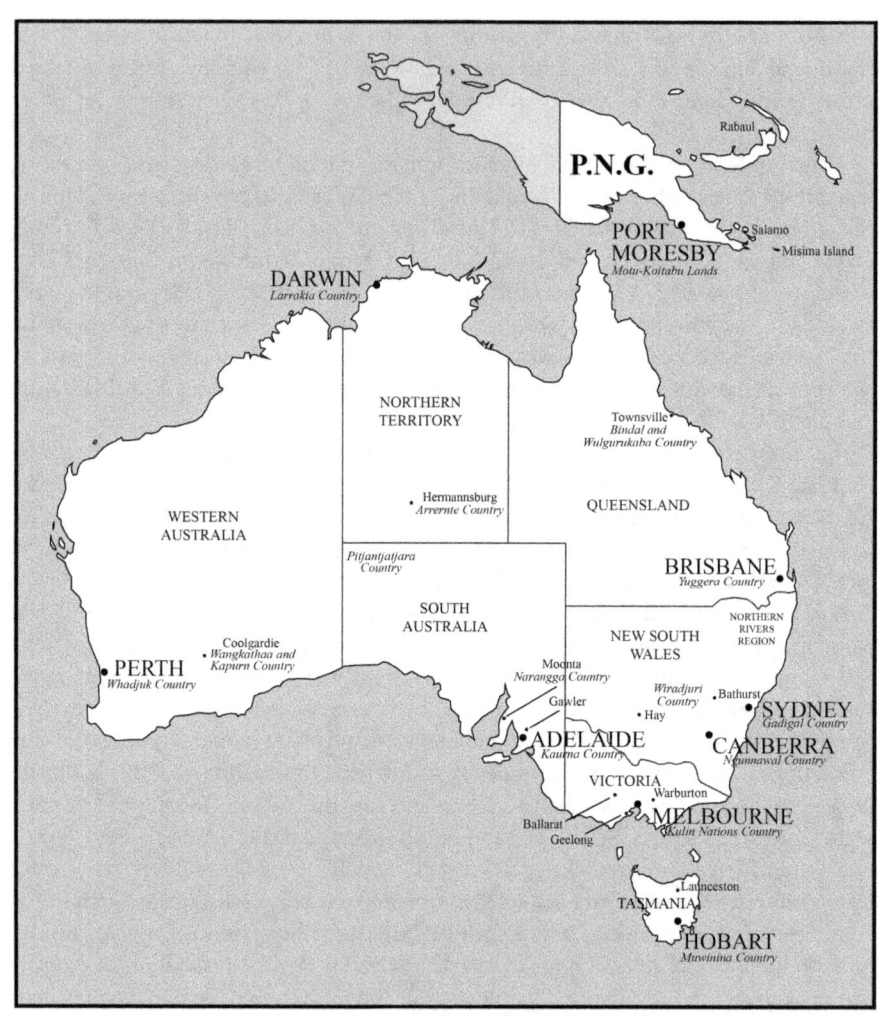

Map 1. Map of Australia and Papua. Created by Eloise Maher.

1

Looking Out Across the Terrain

On the granite outcrops of the You Yangs, two friends surveyed the scene.

"And that is Geelong in the distance. My stars, what a view!"
"And few climb up here to see it … Plains, rivers, bays, mounts, city, village, and headland, all in one swoop."[1]

Christopher Mudd, who was equal parts author, botanist, and Methodist evangelist, considered the observation of nature to be a spiritual discipline. For those who had eyes to see, God would be found in the landscape. His fictional mountain-climbers echoed Ezekiel, bemoaning those who would not look: "There are many such in this world. Having eyes and seeing not."[2] Later, camped by a creek, the two seekers see "Paradise" before them.[3] Their "bush wanderings" lead them along Australia's east coast as pilgrims and as students of nature, for "Without a doubt there is a Presence in the wilds."[4]

Australian Protestant Dissent was attuned to stories of wilderness and Promised Land, and its authors viewed the landscape through the lens of scripture. In a place that held no memories for them, no familiar landmarks where the self could be located,[5] they turned their imaginations to old stories to make new homes in strange lands. The land already had stories, of course. Stories, extending into deep time, connected people and places—the Warlpiri to *manangkarra*, the Tiwi to *timani*, hundreds of nations to hundreds of places across the continent.[6] The newcomers had ears but did not hear First Nations' stories, so many millennia old. Instead, feeling acutely their own lack of connection as they occupied the land, they inscribed the vast landscape with tales from another world and time.

Dissenters in Australia wrote and published all manner of creative works. They described lands real and imagined, putting in words their travels abroad, around the cities, across the countryside, and in the mind's eye. They established presses and opened bookshops; the printed page has always been part of Protestant Dissent. As a religious movement, Dissent or Nonconformity was born in the age of the printing press and religious reform, dissenting from the authority of England's Established Church during the Reformation and not conforming to the Act of Uniformity in 1662.[7] Instead Dissent responded to calls to return to the biblical text as authoritative. Ritual, tradition, and majesty were no rivals for the power of words and the scriptural Word in the life of the individual. Because Dissent or Nonconformity has long been concerned with the Word over the grounded reality of religious ritual and place, landscape and Dissent might seem, at first, to be an unnatural pairing. Dissent's historic separation from the Church of England entrenched its apparent disconnection from the concerns of nation and power and land. Itinerancy among its preachers and sermons about the life beyond have reinforced the idea of Dissenters as "only passing through": citizens of the Kingdom of God and not the kingdoms of this earth. Yet this peculiar heritage is what makes Australian Protestant Dissent's relationship with landscape (in Australia and abroad) especially intriguing. The story of nation and land are entwined, and Dissent's apparent historical disconnection from both makes all the more vivid the attempts by religious Dissenters to write about God in the landscape.

In the beginning, the words of Deut. 32:10 provided a vocabulary. Living in what seemed like the far end of the earth, some early colonists wrote of exile in a howling wilderness.[8] Talk of drought often pitched the hopes of pioneers against a howling wilderness in myths of an inhospitable land. The newspapers carried biblically inspired headlines: in 1893 Queensland's central west was "Simply a Howling Wilderness," and, six years later, the same was said of the land from Bourke to Menindie in northwest New South Wales.[9] Deuteronomy's imagery was powerful and commentators voiced their frustration at the story's hold on the colonial imagination: in South Australia in 1890 it was "very difficult to convince a large section of the community that the greater portion of the northern part of the colony is anything but a howling wilderness."[10] In other times and places the land was seen as a place of bounty and new beginning.[11] In the patriotic years before Australia's Federation, appreciation of the beauty of the distinctive landscape grew, and it became a symbol of identity.[12] Widespread interest in natural history fed both patriotism and spirituality, and Christopher Mudd confidently declared that the "'howling desert' has yet to be found."[13] Not only was there "a Presence in the wilds," but agriculturalists also were the "best missioners ... in league with God the Creator."[14] Protestant Dissent responded to the nation's hopes *and* to a theological shift away from otherworldly thinking and toward a practical application of the gospel. In 1893, Cornish Methodist Joseph Hocking's story of hope for a heaven on earth was serialized in a South Australian newspaper. As he tells it, only an ill-educated old preacher could say, "This world is nothin' ... or rather it is a howlin' wilderness."[15] Increasingly, theology, spirituality and patriotism combined to see the good in this world.

The 1880s to the 1960s saw a transformation of Australia's natural and civic landscape. The colonies became a federated nation in 1901 and, with patriotism and the social gospel in mind, Dissenting churches increasingly engaged with government. They took up a place in the land, made visible in the construction of chapels. On the high street, the hill, and a corner of the paddock there were chapels, halls, and meetinghouses built as a witness and a gathering place. The buildings often harked back to another land even as they left their mark in this new (and ancient) place. Without recognition of First Nations' sacral mapping, colonists proceeded to clear the land with its prior signs and meaning and, in the process, to clear up any doubt as to ownership. Supposing themselves in a spiritually silent land, the noise of colonists' axes and hammers, organs and bells, songs and sermons rapidly reconstructed the landscape in the familiar tropes of European architecture and rhetoric.[16]

For some, their buildings and grounds signified a sacramentalization of land.[17] Palings or post and wire picked out the narrow line between the sacred and secular. But those church traditions furthest from the Establishment resolutely spurned the thought of sacred land. Their chapels, tents, and factories speak of their moral vision and their sense of where God was, or was not yet, to be found. The variety evident illustrates not only a diverse climate and architectural heritage but also the multifarious nature of a term that defines in the negative: "Nonconformity … was only 'one' in the fact of its Nonconformity."[18] Dissent's architecture reflects the dynamic interaction of history, situation, and theological conviction: each denomination's reason for being is written in brick, stone, iron, and weatherboard.[19]

The Churches in the Landscape

Fully imported from England, the Quakers' timber meetinghouse in North Adelaide arrived, in prefabricated parts, on the *Rajasthan* in 1840. It was a gift from the Religious Society of Friends Yearly Meeting in England, sent to the few Quaker families who had recently come to South Australia seeking economic prosperity. Domestic in scale—it is a meeting*house*—the plain rectangular room with slate-tiled roof sits quietly behind the Anglican cathedral. It has neither altar nor pulpit, the building exemplifying the simplicity of the movement's practice and its English origins. The meetinghouse was deposited in colonial Adelaide, on Kaurna Country: a construction from afar in both material and spatial rhetoric. The verandah, with its supporting iron posts, provided a concession to the climate and a liminal space between the sacred interior and the vastness of what seemed, to British eyes, to be the surrounding secular.[20]

Many chapels built by Methodists were fully imported in style, if not in substance. A hundred miles nor-nor-west of Adelaide, on Narungga Country, in a place named for the landscape's "impenetrable scrub,"[21] the Wesleyan Methodists of Moonta built a chapel among the copper mines in 1865. It replaced an earlier and smaller wooden chapel of 1861 in which the Cornish mining families were "packed like herrings in a barrel."[22] Wesleyan Methodists were by far the largest of the four Methodist groups, which also included Primitive Methodists, Bible Christians, and New Connexion, that had arrived in the Australian colonies in the early 1800s.[23] In communities such as Moonta the various denominations within Methodism built chapels close by one another. By 1875 there were twenty-four Methodist churches in Moonta and the surrounding area, just like Cornwall where the different Methodist groups built in the same street.[24] Despite their evangelical revivals, the various churches each remained quite homogeneous communities.[25] In most cases, including Moonta and the nearby Moonta Mines, the Wesleyan Methodists were the most numerous and their buildings reflected this.

Confident of their continuing presence in Moonta Mines, the Wesleyans' second building was made to last. The plans were drawn up by a local man and it was constructed from local stone with brick quoins. However, the building's local heritage ended there as, in deference to the miners' origins, it was closely modeled on a Wesleyan Methodist chapel in Truro, Cornwall.[26] South Australian newspaper reports at the time said that Wesleyan Methodism was so much a part of a Cornishman's life that "no matter in what clime he may establish his home, there will soon be an edifice, in which are promulgated the teachings and doctrines of the Church."[27] Both the buildings and the ceremonies were recognizably those of Cornish Methodists, even in this very different place.[28] The walls were whitewashed with not even a cross; such was the iconophobia of the movement. Instead, the high pulpit dominated and a large, elaborately decorated organ set the chapel apart from other less affluent local Methodist churches. Affluence was relative, however, and, while the Wesleyan Moonta circuit's membership was significantly higher than the central city church in Pirie Street, Adelaide, or than the inner suburban churches in Norwood and Kent Street combined, income was always less.[29]

At the laying of the foundation stone the people processed through the flat dirt streets "headed by the Moonta Mines Brass Band" just as they might have done in hilly green Cornwall.[30] While "clime" may have been ignored, engagement with colonial government was inevitable. At the opening service the choir sang "The Earth is the Lord's," an apparently innocuous choice until one considers the difficulties the congregation had overcome in building on a government mining lease.[31] Likewise, having raised the funds without the tainted grant-money of government, which was sometimes desired by Wesleyans but at the time unavailable,[32] the choir also sang "I will wash my hands in innocency" (Ps. 26:6).[33] The Word remained authoritative.

Notions of purity were also manifested in aesthetics. Not only iconography, but also material display nagged at Nonconformist identity, especially in those denominations whose origins lay in fierce independence and whose congregations identified with the working classes. In their minds, building for outward appearance rather than practical purpose was a betrayal of Dissent's prioritization of scripture and preaching, too much like a second-rate Establishment.[34] So it was that autonomous congregations of working people made do with the materials they had to hand. Galvanized iron chapels, or "tin tabernacles" as the English congregations called them, sufficed in many communities. Iron shared a common materiality with the shearing shed, shop roof, and verandah. A long way from the permanence of sacred stone, they sat modestly, as a temporary shade from the elements, in the everyday industrial and domestic landscape. Yet ready materials did not necessarily last, not even with the addition of buttresses to the Methodist's "tin tabernacle" in Cobar, New South Wales.[35] Or, as in the case of the still-standing galvanized-pipe buttresses on the weatherboard chapel in Johnsonville in Victoria's east Gippsland, the materials endure as the rural congregations dwindle.[36]

Smaller, newer denominations tended to establish themselves with less confidence in the Australian landscape. Many rented rooms from other Dissenting churches and private landlords until their cause was well established and their future was assured. Arriving in Hobart, on Muwinina Country, in the 1880s, just a few years after their movement's formation, a group of Salvation Army members found a civic landscape already well populated with churches. Lacking funds and facing resistance from other denominations who resented their rowdily public missionary methods, the Salvationists initially met in a tent "which grew monthly more battered by the wind and rain."[37] Their transitory beginnings became part of their story, a story that was told, as they grew in number and acceptance, in the city's newspaper. The Hobart *Mercury* reported in 1905 that the Salvationists had rented a chapel from the Primitive Methodists in 1888, then the Exhibition Building in Macquarie Street, the Free Methodist Church, the Tasmanian Hall, then used a tent on land in Elizabeth Street before finally purchasing a hall in Harrington Street.[38] Their arrival in Hobart was not announced by the erection of grand edifice or modest chapel, but by temporary signage and sound: "The peaceful quiet of this Sabbath morning is broken … and presently one becomes aware of the distant blast of wind instruments and the boom of a sufficiently incongruous drum."[39] The story of the movement's homelessness and marginalization spoke of their reason for being. This long list of buildings mattered, not for their architectural significance but for the story—the story of earthly impermanence that reflected the otherworldly imperative of their missionary message and linked the Salvationists with the people to whom they ministered.

Some years later, a postcard told the story of the reopening of The Salvation Army's citadel on Wiradjuri Country in Bathurst, New South Wales, in 1934.[40] The postcard depicts a substantial brick building styled like a public hall or cinema. Many Salvation Army citadels featured embrasures from which metaphorical gunshot might be fired across the rooftops, but this citadel looked less like a fortified stronghold and more like a place of entertainment. Perhaps this was apt, given the Army's love of theater. Girls in uniform with sashes and flags stand in formation outside. Somewhat at odds with the quasi-military and hierarchical nature of the Army, the anonymous note on the reverse side of the postcard is revealing. The writer points out that the alterations to the building cost over £1000 and it was opened by "'some big guns' from Sydney and Melbourne" despite the fact that they "were going strong when I first came to Bathurst in 1884." There is discomfort with the trappings of the movement's seemingly successful establishment, and its hierarchy too.

Without the firm foundations of brick and stone, nor the confident aspirations of towering spires, the stories of early Churches of Christ congregations were also told with a theological intent peculiar to the beliefs of the movement. On Kapurn or Wangkathaa Country, in the low-treed sand plains of Western Australia during Coolgardie's gold-mining boom of the 1890s, a group of miners from Churches of Christ in Victoria took it upon themselves to come together, "breaking bread" under cloudless skies. They met for the Lord's Supper at Dyke's Camp, the denomination needing neither ecclesiastical building nor synod to form new congregations.[41] They did not even require a minister. The breaking of bread among the baptized and simple reading of the Word was enough. The Churches of Christ movement was officially constituted in Britain in 1842 as a loose conference of old and new independent congregations, some of which were previously Scotch Baptist and some seventeenth-century independents. They had united under the writings of former Presbyterians Thomas and Alexander Campbell, who had migrated from the north of Ireland to the United States in the early 1800s, and kept in touch with one another through frequent publications and occasional meetings. The movement's congregational autonomy and simple faith practices were central to their identity and are reflected in the Coolgardie narrative.

Moving on from the Dykes' ragged canvas home, in late 1894 the congregation at Coolgardie purchased a makeshift structure: "a camp, 14 x 12, made of hessian sides and iron roof." The photo reveals a sign, "Church of Christ Meets Here." The "camp" and its rocky soil dominate the scene and the men's spiritual world. Cycling would have been a challenge. An evangelist arrived at the little hessian church in April 1897 and reported, "There were 18 brethren present and three sisters. It was very primitive; no cloth on the table, and an enamel cup and plate used for the breaking of bread. Planks were nailed on blocks in the ground for seats. It was a splendid meeting."[42] Primitivism, both theological and architectural, was something of which to be proud.

However, scripture allowed the congregation to imagine another space. After reading the biblical imprimatur, "Enlarge the place of thy tent, and stretch forth the curtains of thine inhabitation" (Isa. 54:2),[43] the Church of Christ at Coolgardie felt authorized to raise funds for a less remarkable but more lasting single-gabled weatherboard chapel with rectangular windows that they "opened free from debt" in late 1897.[44] The Temple of the Lord, be it hessian or timber, would not be in debt to earthly powers.

Figure 1. Old Chapel, Coolgardie, Western Australia, 1894.

Source: A. B. Maston, *Jubilee Pictorial History of Churches of Christ in Australasia* (Melbourne: Austral Printing and Publishing Company, 1903), 91–2.

Similarly self-reliant, one Brethren congregation in Western Australia moulded their own concrete blocks with which to construct a Gospel Hall. It was a building on a domestic scale among the houses in suburban Balcatta, on Whadjuk Country. A hundred years after the movement arrived in Australia, with British immigrants who met in homes and business premises for "the Breaking of Bread," the congregation at Balcatta also first met in a home. The work grew and the municipal "tin hall" was rented for a time until their brick and breezeblock Gospel Hall was completed. Opening in 1954, building took four years and required a "special appeal" for further volunteer laborers to complete the work.[45]

Just as there were no paid builders at Balcatta, the Brethren movement was not governed by a paid centralized authority and the congregations were led not by paid clergy but by locally appointed lay elders in accordance with their understanding of the New Testament example.[46] Congregational autonomy and resistance to ecclesial structures was reflected in the names given to buildings—Assembly or Gospel Hall or, less often, Bible Chapel—and to the denomination itself. Once popularly known as Plymouth Brethren, having found numerical success in that English town after originating in Dublin in the 1820s, there has been little lasting consensus on denominational naming. Most congregations now sit under the umbrella of Christian Community Churches of Australia.[47] Yet it is the absence of denominational marking that identifies the Balcatta Gospel Hall as Brethren. Set in an expanse of asphalt, the Hall is not a local parish building but one that anticipates that the believers will travel by car from the neighboring sandy suburbs north of Perth. The painted breezeblocks, plaque, and black iron lettering suggest a postwar council facility. Putting aside the civic façade, the modest scale and material is outwardly reminiscent of a 1950s cream brick home: thrifty and unostentatious, centered on the hospitality of the table, and a potential haven of purity in a world of sin.

Contrasting with the newer denominations' make-and-make-do constructions, there was a broad move among older Nonconformists to embrace the ancient-and-modern grandeur of Neoclassical architecture. The choice was largely the preserve of city churches whose location in the center of civic life and of their respective denominations allowed them to build with confidence in their own endurance. The option for Neoclassicism had both economic and theological underpinnings. Harking back to ancient Greece and the Greek texts of New Testament scriptures, Neoclassicism suggested an inheritance that was at once older than that of the Established Church with its Gothic spires and yet fashionably up-to-date. The fact that Nonconformists built in stone when bricks were cheaper suggests that the need for architectural distinction was strong.[48] It was also advocated by influential evangelists. Charles Spurgeon, at the laying of the City Temple's foundation stone in London, 1873, famously claimed that "every Baptist place should be Grecian, never Gothic."[49] The chapel of the Baptist church in Melbourne, located in Collins Street, is an elegant Grecian example dating from 1862.[50] The Grecian preference among Congregational and Baptist churches, denominations that both date from the years following the English Reformation, also suggests ambivalence to the English state's style of churches.[51] Anglicanism and Methodism, which had grown out of Anglicanism despite John Wesley's intentions to stay within, inherited and adopted Gothic architecture as England's "natural

Figure 2. Balcatta Gospel Hall, Western Australia.
Source: Photograph courtesy of G. Parker.

embodiment of Christian worship."[52] But Gothic styles were resisted by churches whose long history placed them at odds with the state. Congregationalists articulated this with moral force, arguing that "a refined and well-educated Congregationalist must reject Gothic, just because if it pleases his eye it will violate his convictions."[53] The Congregational Church on Eora Country, Sydney, had both the funds and the street frontage to make their statement in stone with the construction of the Pitt Street chapel in 1846.[54] Convictions intact, behind the ionic columns and sandstone façade, the rest of the building is in budget-conscious brick.

Congregationalists, having developed from independent churches into England and Wales' third-largest denomination, first came to Australia as missionaries in the late 1700s.[55] Preaching was a priority, and is a focus visible in the Pitt Street Congregational Church interior.[56] It had a high central octagonal pulpit in polished Australian native cedar that was reported as "equal in appearance to mahogany," lest its locally sourced materials be deemed of lesser quality than European equivalents.[57] The congregation's focus on the pulpit was further ensured with "an elevation of four inches at each pew, an arrangement favourable for conveying the sound to all parts of the spacious building."[58] This was a building for the purpose of preaching, presaging the later words of visiting English Congregationalist Dr. Robert William Dale: "Their services were not spectacular, nor did they need any long aisles for religious processions. They wanted a hall in which every person could see the minister and the minister could make every person hear without difficulty ... A Congregational Church was utterly ruined if placed in a building in which it was hard to preach."[59]

Such defiant and distinctive architecture seemed unlikely when the Congregational and Baptist denominations joined with the Presbyterians to form the United Evangelical Church in Moreton Bay (now Brisbane), Queensland. The new united church was a bold experiment in Calvinistic ecumenism involving five hundred passengers who sailed from England on the *Fortitude* in 1849. Modeling the idea on a united church in Connecticut, the Presbyterian minister John Dunmore Lang hoped to overcome the sectarianism that so blighted Christian witness in the nineteenth century and avoid "*three such sentry-boxes of chapels* as these denominations could have the means of erecting separately in each petty locality."[60] The experiment failed and in 1855 the Baptists proclaimed their separate identity by building a Neoclassical chapel in Wharf Street.[61] Nearby, the Presbyterians built in the customary Gothic style, as did the Congregationalists, evidently ignoring the advice that such architecture would "violate ... convictions."[62]

Over the next few decades, convictions favoring Neoclassicism softened among Baptists too as their weatherboard chapels began to reflect less distinctive styles. Some chapels, like the 1887 Sandgate Baptist Church on the coast just north of Brisbane, on Yuggera Country, visibly bridged the ecclesiastical and domestic. The ecclesiastical features included cruciform construction, a "light handsome steeple," and rose windows with "plain cathedral glass" rather than stained glass with its obscuring ecclesiasticism. Echoing local domestic Queensland construction, the Sandgate chapel also had high louvre ventilation, a tin roof, and graceful white painted fretwork.[63] The cheerful practicality of the "Queenslander"-style home became evident in chapel architecture, no doubt assisted by the practice of using church members as builders. Baptists built similar chapels at Toowong, Maryborough, and Graceville. Timber fretwork was also used to pretty effect on simpler single gable chapels built high on stumps for ventilation and flood mitigation in Townsville, Geebung, Coorparoo, and Rosalie.[64] An Australian-styled "Carpenter Gothic" became very popular, just as it did in the United States from whence the term originates. Ease and economy of construction overrode concerns about ecclesiastical appearance.

As chapels proliferated and populations increased across the continent, Church Extension Committees formed. Halls and manses were built. Earlier chapels were enlarged or replaced. Sometimes the rebuilds were in the old style: theology has a material memory. Other buildings in other denominations were built or rebuilt in bold twentieth-century styles that repudiated tradition. Modernist architecture curiously coincided with the theological rejection of memory in favor of the eschaton and a conversionist mindset in which the old life is forever negative and the new, the revolutionary, is ever hoped for.

In the Victorian timber-milling town of Warburton, on Kulin Country, the Seventh-day Adventists were forced to leave their past behind when they lost several buildings to fire and flood. Well established in the district, they rebuilt boldly and, in the 1930s, produced a veritable sacred-industrial complex surrounded by steep hills and towering eucalypts. While their school and hospital continued at existing sites, they erected a brick chapel behind a neat, low fence on the main road. On the other side of the street, the Signs of the Times printing works produced religious literature and, next door, the Sanitarium Health Food factory manufactured vegetarian foods to cater for the scripturally based dietary restrictions of the church and the growing commercial popularity of health foods.[65] The movement had come to Australia for mission work in 1885, and the hospital, print works, chapel, and food factory were all necessary parts of their vision.[66] As a church they were recently formed and eschatologically minded: their founder William Miller, an American and former Baptist, first predicted the end days in 1844.[67] Accordingly, the future-oriented Seventh-day Adventists were unconstrained by a heritage of denominational architecture. They pursued their vision in the European Modern style with buildings that featured light-colored bricks and geometric contrasts in landscaped gardens.[68] Their workers, all church members, enjoyed factory facilities not afforded elsewhere. A worship room was included as part of the design with rows of tubular steel stackable chairs arranged to focus on a lectern, the walls bare but for a clock. Another larger clock on a tower above the Sanitarium factory marked time for the township. This was a place of efficiency, civic-mindedness, and expectation of the end-times. The city-based architect, Edward Billson, won a Royal Victorian Institute of Architects award for his work there in 1940.[69] These Dissenters were theologically and socially set apart from the broader society and yet built in a style that most resembled that of the secular world.

The Adventists were clearly aware of how their buildings impacted positively on Warburton's prosperity and the civic aesthetic at the east end of town. Nestled in

Figure 3. Sanitarium Health Food Company factory, Warburton, Victoria.
Source: Photograph by K. Handasyde.

the valley, they were also conscious of the benefits of rural isolation in maintaining their separation and hence their denominational distinctiveness. However, when the devastating Black Friday fires of 1939 threatened the town, the Adventists threw open the doors of their hospital to all-comers and sheltered "a dozen mothers with young babies in arms" on the factory floor along with many others, including a cat and his 9-year-old owner, the auspiciously named Frank Tempest.[70] While a "refugee train" sat in the station all day long, "with steam up" ready to leave the threatened town at a moment's notice, plans were made to shelter more people in the Adventist's modern factory for, "with its brick walls, self-contained electric light and water plants, [it] is a natural harbour from the fires."[71] Truly a haven was found in the "howlin' wilderness."[72]

Dissenting churches in Australia built in a range of styles and orientations outside the range available to Anglican and Catholic traditions.[73] They sought no consistency of style, no single voice. Many prioritized the preaching of the Word and announced their presence with distinctive street frontage and signage. Others rested silently in the landscape, bringing theology and climate into dialogue through a verandah. Significant numbers self-funded their buildings rather than compromise their spiritual independence by accepting government grants. Building materials and their origins mattered enough to report in congregational histories. As a result of all these factors, their chapels were products of the independent communities that built them; communities that varied across the vast new horizons of the Australian landscape.

A Map for the Journey

With such variety in Australian Protestant Dissent, the case studies in this volume do not set out to look for a single story, but for many. Sometimes they intersect. They begin with Carlo Ginzberg's premise that "reality is fundamentally discontinuous and heterogeneous."[74] The particular matters and generalization does not always follow.[75] Considering the vastness of the historical territory to explore, and keeping in mind the need to be specific, each chapter will be defined by a single genre of writing and the publications of a single denomination. In this way each study, in its own particularity, casts light on the bigger picture of the literature of landscape in Australian Protestant Dissent.[76]

The first chapter examines the origins of Protestant Dissent grounded in the English landscape. The long backstory of relations with the state plays into colonial experience, as does Dissent's orientation toward personal and social improvement in the light of the Word. The various denominations within Australian Protestant Dissent did not begin with a clean slate but brought their stories with them.

The second landscape is one of skepticism and belief experienced in the Holy Land, then published, and then performed for audiences in lantern slide shows around Australia. While England's political and religious landscape gave birth to Dissent, the lands of the Bible captured Dissent's imagination, and, in the age of steamships, many individuals made the pilgrimage to experience the place for themselves. The Churches of Christ's primitivist outlook relied especially on the tangibility of the church of the New Testament and the practical recoverability of the past. The travel literature produced was written for audiences to *stay at home* and read. The chapter explores the nature of travel in biblical space and time, and how the writers reconciled their own enduring missional dislocation and came to terms with life on Australian soil.

The third landscape is that of urban transformation during the depression of the 1890s and the years that followed. Publicity and performance was central to The Salvation Army's work of transformation in city slums as it generated donations and recruited willing workers. Like Joseph Hocking's old preacher and his "howlin' wilderness," Salvationists assumed that Christians ultimately do not belong to this world. Unlike the preacher of "howlin' wilderness," they developed schemes and manifestos of improvement for the time being. Traces of the Army's Social Salvation scheme are visible in newsprint, stage performance programs, and the remnants of turn-of-the-century film extravaganzas. They reveal a denomination with loyalties to Empire, to Australia, and to another time and place, another landscape of belief.

During the Great War, many poets wrote of battlefields and trenches, but a number of Congregational poets wrote of home under the Southern Cross. This landscape of here and elsewhere provides the fourth vista to Australian Protestant Dissent. Poetry has long been accepted as a form of Christian literature for devotional purposes, and the use of landscape in religious poems typically owes much to the Romantic tradition. However, influenced by a tradition of religious liberty and of self-consciously Australian poetry and bush ballads, three Congregational poets constructed and adapted popular visions of what it is to be Australian. In this way they wrote an Australian spirituality.

The fifth landscape to be explored is that of the mission field portrayed in twentieth-century adventure fiction for adults and children. Fiction writing blossomed among Methodists in the early twentieth century as a wholesome entertainment and a means of popularizing support for mission and church planting that drew on long-established evangelical uses of imagination. Novelists created literary worlds in which readers could imagine themselves riding through Queensland or sailing the islands of Papua. Discipleship was portrayed as an exciting, romantic life where God was close at hand in the surrounding landscape. The social gospel and the sacred landscape were closely entwined.

The landscape of Australian flora was explored in close-up by natural history artists from the Religious Society of Friends. The Quakers had a long tradition of depicting the detail that evidenced the divine in the landscape and this led to writings on beauty, art, and the natural world. Appreciation of the beauty of the landscape intersected with moral consciousness about First Nations spirituality and displacement, and these issues play a significant part in Quaker attempts to write a spiritual vision of belonging in the Australian landscape in the mid-twentieth century.

The terrain of this study is as varied as the landscapes of Australia and the Holy Land. Almost all of the literature is previously unexplored, or has been read without an awareness of how it reflects religious identity in relationship to landscape. This is a significant oversight, a gap in understanding. When Dissenters wrote of "Plains, rivers, bays, mounts, city, village, and headland," they sought imaginative belonging, a highway in the desert, and God in the landscape.[77]

2

Landscape of Dissent: Dissent's British Origins and Colonial Australian Experience

Exile in the wilderness was not new to Protestant Dissent when it arrived in Australia. Dissent, as the name suggests, had a long and complex history of separation, exile, and belonging. The term emerged in the 1630s to refer to those who dissented from the Church of England in matters of worship. Some separated from its communion, disagreeing not only over worship but with the very idea of a state church. But the state insisted that the church and nation were one: the church would unite the land. In 1662 it forced the issue with the Act of Uniformity. Lines of division hardened, and punishment for separation ensued. The collective identity of Dissent, or Nonconformity, sharpened through suffering under these new laws. Many would not assent to the Act of Uniformity's mandate to use the *Book of Common Prayer* in worship, nor would the clergy consent to being (re-)ordained by a bishop.[1] More than one thousand ministers, including one-third of ministers in London, were ejected from the Church of England, doubling the number of Puritan clergy forced to leave their Church of England ministries in just a few years.[2] Dissenters published in response to being "ejected and silenced."[3] The publishing history of Dissent has long linked memory and the rhetoric of patient suffering under oppression.[4]

A number of further Acts, known collectively as the Clarendon Code, effectively exiled Dissenters, sending them out of the villages and into the countryside. The Conventicle Act of 1664 forbade unauthorized meetings (or conventicles of more than five people who were not of the same household) whether they were held in houses, outbuildings, or fields.[5] A year later, the Five Mile Act forbade Nonconformist ministers from residing within five miles of a parish from which they had been ejected. They continued to meet secretly with their congregations on hillsides, in rural outbuildings, and at kitchen tables in the homes of the faithful and brave.[6] According to John Bunyan, those who would persecute Dissenters had to "climb trees, and range the woods a days ... to find out the meeters."[7] Many Dissenters found solace and the sacred in the fields and the fells.[8] Beneath the traditional civil and religious division of parish, an alternative religious geography grew.

Ministers banned from the towns took to preaching in the fields or the rubble of their torn-down meetinghouses, hoping the landscape would provide refuge from civil authority and the Established Church. They risked imprisonment and crippling fines for freedom of belief. Quakers were especially known for their uncompromising stance and, with their reputation for radical theology and its potential for social disruption, they bore the worst persecution under the Acts with up to fifteen thousand gaoled between 1660 and 1668.[9] Congregationalists, Presbyterians, and Baptists suffered too; the implementation of the penalties under the Acts varied according to local factors.

Exiled from public life, the independence-seeking Baptists built chapels in disguise: the Baptist church in Monksthorpe was designed to look like a barn set in the Lincolnshire fields.[10] The little stone chapel at Sunnybank, founded in 1678 by "messengers [evangelists] and elders from the church of Christ in Derwentwaterside," was positioned away from Lancaster's villages and towns.[11] Its baptistery was a pond cut into the hillside, accessed by wooden steps and built to facilitate full immersion consistent with a literal interpretation of New Testament baptismal practice. At Hawkshead Hill a single-room Baptist chapel was discretely positioned between two whitewashed attached houses. William Wordsworth explained its unusual location in his 1809 "The Scenery of the Lakes": "The building is mean and from the outside has so little to distinguish it as a place of worship that one might think that it had been constructed in an intolerant age for the purpose of avoiding notice."[12] Indeed it had.

A generation later, the "intolerant age" was somewhat mitigated by the 1689 Act of Toleration, which removed penalties for Dissenting churches and provided toleration within limits for Trinitarian Protestant Dissenters (deliberately excluding Unitarians and Catholics).[13] Ministers were required to pledge oaths of supremacy and allegiance, and ascribe to thirty-six of the Thirty-Nine Articles of the Church of England. Ministers could preach in public as long as their meeting places were registered by the state. The registration of sacred place brought Dissent back within the reaches of the state. Many limitations on civic life remained: Dissenters were excluded from town corporations, and teaching remained a banned activity for another ninety years. Further Acts followed and, by the early 1700s, Dissenting churches were effectively exiled at home, "limited within the four walls of a chapel or meeting house."[14] But, through publishing, the story of Dissent's limitation under the state spread beyond the walls of the chapels.

Works of literature and philosophy were influential in articulating the spirit of the times, and the idea of toleration grew in popularity. Writings such as John Milton's *Of True Religion* (1673), Andrew Marvell's *The Rehearsal Transpos'd* (1672-3), and John Locke's *Letter Concerning Toleration* (1689), as well as the writings of Congregationalist John Owen and the Quaker William Penn, all came out of this period.[15] While the Act of Toleration restricted Nonconformity to the local sphere, Locke's *Letter Concerning Toleration* described religion as "the inward and full persuasion of the mind." Faith was not only local and congregational but also an "inward" matter of individual conscience and piety.[16] Faith was within four walls and within the confines of the mind.

Later, in the eighteenth and nineteenth centuries, attempts to control what was taught within Dissenting denominations proved increasingly difficult. Despite efforts at internal conformity via preaching and scholarship, the people in the pews often believed otherwise.[17] Religious freedom became the principle that united Nonconformity. Liberty was prized in the churches and in the consciences of individuals. Other Enlightenment ideas were also deeply influential on the development of Dissent. Locke's notion of the human mind as a *tabula rasa*, a clean slate that could learn from experience, allowed for an optimism that the doctrine of original sin did not.[18] However, rather than set up a dichotomy between the strictures of doctrine and the freedom of the Enlightenment, some Dissenters incorporated Lockean thinking into their systematic theology.[19]

Methodists preached that one could merely decide for Jesus and change one's life. Churches of Christ, The Salvation Army, and the New Connexion of General Baptists likewise discounted theology around election in favor of Arminianism.[20] They assured their adherents that salvation was there for all, not just for the elect: a person could *choose* salvation. This had a distinct evangelical advantage.[21] There was no agonizing wait for a sign of salvation. Instead, a penitent sinner could learn the truth and be saved. According to stories, such assurances were carried in writing to Ohio and beyond by the founders of the Stone-Campbell movement (including Churches of Christ). Denominational histories repeatedly tell of their leaders traveling on horseback through frontier America with a bible in one saddlebag and the works of John Locke in another.[22] Although scholars increasingly question the nature and extent of the Lockean influence,[23] the persistence of the saddlebag story has (paradoxically) forged a legend around the influence of reason in the Stone-Campbell movement. Biblically informed reason was also essential to independent reformed congregations and General Baptists, along with much of nineteenth-century Dissent.

Denominations such as General Baptists, Methodists, and The Salvation Army embraced Evangelicalism. This spiritual movement saw personal conversion as a path to salvation, and thence to the improvement of society. Significantly, while Puritanism sought to *replace* society with the Kingdom of God on earth, Evangelicalism sought to *reform* society and this resulted in a proliferation of missionary works beyond chapel walls.[24] Prison reform, sexual morality, temperance, and education became key concerns in an agenda of improvement in this world, with consequences for the next.[25] With these objectives in mind, and their own liberty now assured, Nonconformists in late-nineteenth-century England welcomed state intervention in moral matters.[26] They welcomed it in the colonies too.

There were consequences for Evangelicalism's emphasis on turning from the errors of the past toward the truth received today in scripture. The narrative of a sinful past not only propelled believers on to personal and social reform but also reinforced the suspicion felt toward those churches that looked to tradition as evidence of apostolic inheritance: the Church of England, Catholicism, and Orthodoxy. It also made for uneasiness with history itself and demanded constant reinvention and renewal. Given the authority of scripture within Evangelicalism, there were consequences for its relationship with the biblical past too. Indeed, it required that the biblical past be not really past, but ever-present.[27] The Word alone was authoritative and must be lived in newness. For those who had eyes to see, the Word was manifest in the here and now: available to be read and relayed to others in speech and in print.

Dissent under Southern Skies

Protestant Dissent brought with it to colonial Australia the ideals of religious toleration, an ethos of personal and social improvement, and the priority and newness of the Word. Its history of strained relations with the state lingered even as Dissenters, following the British experience after the repeal of the last effects of the Clarendon Code, became increasingly involved in the public affairs of the colonies and, later, the nation. However, there were significant local differences that led to a much-expanded role for Dissent in Australia. Colonial governments did not enshrine the Church of England as the state church with the attendant disadvantages to Roman Catholicism and Dissenters.[28] Rather, aware that the population of convicts, military, and free settlers was significantly diverse, Governor Bourke maintained that "it will be impossible to establish a dominant and endowed church without much hostility, and a great improbability of its becoming permanent."[29] The state's decision not to establish the Church of England in the colonies and, instead, to subsidize the churches in general, triggered a very different set of religious debates under southern skies.

Governor of New South Wales from 1831 to 1837, Richard Bourke was no supporter of ecclesiastical privilege and its effects. His personal sympathies, witnessed in personal connection and daily prayer meetings, were with Evangelical Anglicanism and its impulse for Christian social reform,[30] and he had supported the lifting of the Test and Corporations Acts in England in 1828 and the Catholic Emancipation Act of 1829, officially permitting Dissenters and Catholics to participate in civil government.[31] He believed that inequity between the churches would lead to religious rows, and that the association of church with government would not play out well in the very different climate of colonial New South Wales.[32] Nevertheless, he saw that religion had significant social and moral benefits for the penal colony and the individual, and promoted it accordingly. In 1836, with the "advancement of the Christian religion and the promotion of good morals [through] Public Worship" in mind, Bourke introduced "an Act to Promote the Building of Churches and Chapels and to Provide for the Maintenance of Ministers of Religion in New South Wales," popularly known as the Church Act.[33] It offered government subsidies not only to Anglicans but also to Presbyterians and Catholics. Provisions were later extended to Baptist and Wesleyan churches and, in the 1850s, colonial parliaments debated grants to Jewish synagogues.[34]

In accepting government subsidies under the Church Act, Dissenting (and Catholic) churches were effectively enlisted alongside the Church of England in the state's agenda to provide a kind of moral guardianship for the colonies.[35] They established numerous societies to promote personal moral reform and used church-related activities to improve social cohesion, and many Protestant Dissenters stood for public office.[36] In South Australia, where the Dissenting churches were especially strong, voters and parliamentarians took an interest in the politics of the colony as an extension of the work of faith.[37] There were a host of moral concerns brought to the colonial legislatures of the nineteenth century including the age of consent, prostitution, gambling, restrictions on the sale of alcohol, and keeping the Sabbath.[38] Sabbatarian laws differed between jurisdictions but local councillors across the landscape used their positions to exert moral influence, even locking children's swings on Sundays.[39]

While Dissenters welcomed the opportunity to influence society, the state aid offered under the Church Act proved contentious. The Act supplied stipends for ministers where one hundred people or more declared their intention to attend the church, and the government agreed to help in the funding of any Christian building by providing funds equal to public donations where the value was between £300 and £1000.[40] Small Dissenting churches built on a more modest scale and could not raise the funds. Others would not build their walls with the money of unbelievers. The long history of separatist Dissent and the Puritan disdain for the things of this world figured in this new place.

In the colony of South Australia, state aid was short-lived owing to the strong presence of Dissenting churches and their support of voluntaryism, preferring that the churches remain free from financial obligation to the state.[41] The response to government aid to religion in South Australia was summed up in 1850 by the colony's medical officer in his guide for potential emigrants. Dr. Duncan described the situation: "The Churches of England and Scotland, and the Wesleyan body, have accepted the Government aid; but the Roman Catholics, the Independents, and Baptists have declined it; with this essential difference, that the Roman Catholics object only to the details, while the Independents and Baptists disapprove of the principles of the bill."[42] State aid to churches in South Australia ceased shortly after.[43] Churches would have to be funded by their members in South Australia's "Paradise of Dissent."[44]

Elsewhere, the Dissenting churches' inability or unwillingness to accept state aid led to the perception that government assistance, originally intended to encourage religious equality, was in fact an agent of injustice.[45] Dissenters railed long and loud against state aid to churches and church schools, and the provisions of the 1836 Church Act were gradually unwound. This led to the establishment of state-funded secular education. It was, in effect, equality in absence.[46]

Dissent's opposition to government aid can be read in the titles of their publications: *Objections to the Policy of Perpetuating State Aid to Religion in Tasmania* (1867) by the Reverend George Clarke, Methodist preacher in Hobart, Tasmania; *Reasons for Not Accepting Pecuniary Aid from the State for the Support of Religion* (1869) by the Reverend J. Johnston, Congregational Minister in Fremantle, Western Australia; and, addressed to "Friends of the Lord Jesus, and Lovers of Civil Liberty" (as surely the two were indistinguishable), *The Melbourne Medley: Political, Moral, Religious and Anti-State Aid Advocate* (1858) by Robert Service, lay preacher with the small Disciples (later, Churches of Christ) congregation in Melbourne, Victoria.[47] Expressions of opinion, on both sides of the argument, were also printed in colonial newspapers. Further evidence of Dissents' early relationship with the state may be found in petitions and parliamentary debates; such was their earnest engagement with the topic. Without a common liturgy, Dissent united in its use of the printed word to engage with colonial politics and society.

At the Inauguration of the Commonwealth of Australia a grand procession provided a kind of civic liturgy in which the various churches' understandings of their constitutional rights and civic allegiances were self-consciously acted out for the audience of state and citizenry that lined the procession route. At the dawn of a new nation, amid the patriotic optimism and momentum for unity in many aspects of Australian life that Federation inspired, the churches of Protestant Dissent actively sought participation with the state. They wanted a Christian nation, even as they were alert to the corrupting power of politics.[48] Anglicans, Catholics, and Dissenters alike were caught up in the fervor of Federation. Many churches supported the mention of God in the Constitution and participated in official Federation celebrations. The Seventh-day Adventists, harboring concerns about the enforcement of Sunday as Sabbath, were alone in opposing the naming of God in the Constitution. Only the smaller and more fiercely independent churches did not plan to participate in the procession: Adventists (who numbered 0.09 percent of the population), Brethren (0.23 percent), and Quakers (0.02 percent).[49]

On Tuesday January 1, 1901, there was a long procession to Centennial Park, Sydney, where the *Commonwealth of Australia Constitution Act* was proclaimed, officials sworn in, and Australia became a nation. The route through Sydney was made grand with temporary stone-look arches and the proclamation took place in an ornate pavilion of plaster of Paris. It was a theater set for a drama. The procession attempted to represent a diverse federated Australia and so it included tradesmen, miners, mounted police, military and fire brigades, unions, religious leaders, the judiciary, friendly societies including Rechabites and Druids, state premiers, and floats representing other recently federated nations. Last and most importantly, as they were arranged in reverse order of precedence, was Governor-General Lord Hopetoun who would sign the Act on behalf of Queen Victoria. The New South Wales premier's office explained pragmatically that the governor-general had to be last so that the crowds would stay in their places along the streets and not disperse as less distinguished groups processed. The entire procession was an interesting exercise in egalitarianism; so many ordinary people were included, and yet ranked (for practical purposes) in ascending order.[50] The omissions were profound—neither First Nations people from Australia nor women workers were represented although, of course, many were employed in industries such as agriculture, textiles, and domestic service. The ranking brought into public view the churches' relationship to the state and to each other.

The religious leaders were to process in two separate groups: the Anglican primate was last (and therefore "first") and the leader of the Catholic Church in Australia just in front of him (ranked second, in effect), but both of them were toward the back of the procession near the governor-general. All other religious leaders were grouped together further toward the front, effectively forming a second tier. The churches read this symbolism in the light of the new constitution that enshrined religious liberty and prohibited the establishment of a state church and attendant privileges. The day before the inauguration, leaders from three churches, representing the religious faith of nearly 50 percent of the population, withdrew from the procession.

Catholic Cardinal Patrick Moran (representing 23 percent of Australians) refused to process in a less important position than the Anglican Archbishop Smith (representing 39 percent), because Cardinals outrank Archbishops.[51] The third- and fourth-largest churches also withdrew. After the meeting of a committee, Methodists (representing

13 percent) cited the cause of religious liberty and equality.[52] Presbyterians (representing 11 percent) cited equality, but not liberty, harboring resentment about the preferential treatment of the state Church of England over the state Church of Scotland.[53] Australia simply did not have a highway wide enough to represent the equality of the churches.

On the morning of the procession the heavens opened and rain poured down on the plaster of Paris. By half-past ten, the skies had cleared and the grand procession set off on time. The carriage of the Anglican primate was toward the end of the procession as planned. Some way toward the front were the leaders of those churches that were small enough to be simply grateful they were included, each representing between 0.6 and 2.4 percent of the population.[54] In one carriage were a Lutheran pastor and two evangelists from the Churches of Christ: the smallest Christian group present, but one that was growing fast and hoping to share the stage with the larger churches. In another carriage there were three rabbis.[55] In another were the Baptists who had complained in the press about the order of precedence and declared their support of the "absolutely *free and equal* condition of things," but participated all the same.[56]

Just ahead, in another carriage, were several Congregationalists, including the Reverend Nicholas Cocks, minister at Pitt Street Congregational Church.[57] The Congregationalists had revised the old script about separation of church and state, and they now advocated an integration of sacred and secular in the new nation under the cross that hung over southern skies.[58] Congregationalism's later story suggests that their involvement in preparations for Federation cemented their denominational identity as small and urban but with an intellectual influence that spanned a continent. They were in the procession because Federation figured in their vision of an Australian Christianity.

Then, in the front carriage was a denomination that had long appreciated the value of a noisy parade through the streets. The Salvation Army's marches had previously seen members arrested under public nuisance laws or attacked by the citizenry, and they thought themselves persecuted for their beliefs. The year before Federation they had even made a film about early Christian martyrs with whom they clearly identified. But now, in the first (or "last") of the religious leaders' carriages was Commandant (and film director) Herbert Booth with three Salvation Army officers.[59] Over twenty years in the colonies, Salvationists had built strong relationships with governments for the funding of welfare (which they also funded through ticket sales to their films), and they had every reason to be optimistic about their role in the new nation. Without question they would be present in the procession.

The Salvation Army had another role in the inauguration parade. At the request of the New South Wales government, the Salvationists' Limelight Department filmed the inauguration of the Commonwealth. This was the first time a nation's beginning had been filmed, and the footage was screened around the world. They used fixed cameras at five points near the podium and along the procession route. In one scene the religious leaders' carriages pass under a temporary arch, but it is difficult to identify individuals. The passengers look ahead or to one another. The footage is grainy and they all wear dark hats. But Salvationist leader Herbert Booth takes his hat off and looks toward the viewer. He would have known where the cameras were.[60] The relationship between the churches was performed and enacted at the birth of the nation. The new story of

Dissent in twentieth-century Australia reflected a nationalism that the people of earlier centuries could not have imagined.

In the decades before and after Federation, Protestant Dissenters also produced large quantities of literature that creatively reflected their relationships to the nation and its landscape. Travel literature was eagerly devoured by church members who made a pilgrimage of the heart through the Holy Land. Publicity and performance were integral to the Salvation Army's telling of their story through pageant, film, and periodical. Then, during the Great War, poetry became a valued means of bridging the chasm between loved ones half a world away, and between the self and the divine. Adventure novels popularly expressed spirituality and often conflicted relationships with God's creation in a land that was both wilderness and haven. As appreciation of the Australian landscape grew, essays on beauty gave theological foundation to generations of artists of the natural world and dared to contemplate a spirituality that drew (controversially) on First Nations Kaurna and Arrernte stories. The chapters that follow explore the terrain of Australian Protestant Dissent's literature of landscape.

3

Landscape of Skepticism and Belief: Churches of Christ Travel Literature from the Holy Land to Australia, 1889–96

Aaron Maston's letters from the Holy Land were a testament to observable fact, the kind of fact on which faith could be built. Like many believer baptists, he visited the Jordan: "I don't want these letters to take a doctrinal turn, but just one word in the interests of simple truth. I have heard it stated over and over again that the current of the Jordan was too strong for immersing in … but … there are plenty of places to baptise along the Jordan without going near the current at all."[1] His tour group had a swim to prove the point, then "lunched in the shade." With his readers' appreciation of realism in mind, Maston added, "About 10,000 small black gnats, a good collection of mosquitoes, and a few flies lunched, or tried to lunch at the same time, and from the way they went at it they had been fasting for many days." His letters were popular; readers enjoyed his chatty, factual style and might even have imagined traveling alongside. But when Maston mused on metaphysics his language was less direct and much less assured. He tried to convey a truth well known among religious primitivists who sought an authentic New Testament faith: the biblical past was not truly past, but ever-present, and the future depended on it:

> Nor is it of the past only that the name of Jordan tells, for in the more thoughtful hours of not a few they hear it whispering to them before, strange shadowy truths of that future, happier land that lies over the stream … Some speak of it as a *divine* river. This may be so; but with me it is divine only as all other rivers are divine.[2]

This was a Romantic age, and even evangelists who were attuned to the commonsense reading of scripture could not deny that the waters of the Holy Land held "strange shadowy truths." More than that, if the Jordan shared its holiness with "all other rivers," surely God would be found in the landscape of Palestine—and beyond.

Dissenters traveling to the Holy Land in the nineteenth century went seeking the sacred ground of a landscape central to their faith and the solid ground of religious certainty and authority.[3] They wrote as they walked. Despite disclaimers about not feeling "nearer the Son of God" or "any special blessing" in the physical landscape, accounts of travel to the Holy Land are interrupted again and again with the arresting thought that here the sacred may be glimpsed, here proof may be had, and here (rather than elsewhere) Jesus' reality may be more personally felt.[4] The often arduous physical journey was integral to writing the landscape of the Holy Land. But it was more than physical. Travelers to Palestine also described a journey of the faithful heart and pious imagination. In their writings, metaphorical journeys of faith and long-imagined biblical scenes comingle with Enlightenment rationalism and the Dissenters' mistrust of older religious traditions. In the landscape of Palestine, imagination mattered. The idealized, longed-for landscape of the Holy Land was discerned through the lenses of religious belief and skepticism.[5] Both lenses were integral to truly pious belief.

In describing the Holy Lands for readers at home in Australia, two writers from the Churches of Christ transcribed biblical imagination on to landscape. Palestine was a foreign land and travelers' expectations were rarely met, and so Aaron Maston and Albert Ludbrook traveled as much in their imaginations as they did by foot or pony, hoping to see Jesus in the landscape. They saw the hills and valleys of Palestine as holy because Jesus once walked there. Returning to ministry in Australia, in the unending pilgrimage of the heart, they walked with Jesus on Australian roads, traveling not to Emmaus or Bethany but to Nunawading and Wollongong.

Traveling with Ludbrook and Maston

Ludbrook and Maston each traveled to the Holy Land in the period 1889–96 and sent letters home for publication in Australian Churches of Christ journals. The two evangelists went on to travel around Australia, with lantern shows depicting the Holy Land and lectures exhorting audiences to find Jesus in their midst, in the here and now. Their appearances were advertised in city newspapers and intended to draw crowds well beyond the small world of Australian Churches of Christ (part of the wider Stone-Campbell movement and Restorationist movement, which also includes Disciples of Christ), which was less than sixteen thousand strong.[6]

Albert Milton Ludbrook (1863–1948) was born in London and migrated to Australia in 1890 as a young preacher. He came highly recommended: "Bro. Albert M. Ludbrook is a young man of great promise … Australian churches will do well to keep their eye upon him."[7] Although Churches of Christ do not recognize saints, in the nineteenth century they did have a strong tradition of naming children after pillars of Dissent. Albert's younger brother Frederick Milner Ludbrook was perhaps named after Thomas Hughes Milner, a prominent Scottish Churches of Christ publisher and essayist.[8] Another brother, Ernest Campbell, was named for Thomas and Alexander Campbell, founders of Churches of Christ. Albert's sister Jessie Dorcas found her names in scripture. In the light of such faithful naming, it is reasonable to assume that Albert Milton might refer to the English Puritan poet John Milton.[9] We cannot be certain, but it is an engagingly poetic possibility for an evangelist traveling in search of "Paradise Lost."

After moving to the colonies, Albert spent much of his life moving between churches as a congregational minister, supplementing his ministry with a long, intermittent tour as a "traveler and lecturer," in which he presented lantern show talks and expressed his "specially novel" views and "amusing personal reminiscences."[10] Following his success with Jerusalem, Ludbrook expanded to talks about Egypt,[11] South Africa,[12] and the Roman catacombs.[13] Combining his love of words and travel, he left the ministry during the Great War to become librarian at the Royal Geographical Society in Adelaide.[14] Ludbrook's Holy Land narrative, "Notes of Travel," was published in installments in the Churches of Christ journal, *Australasian Christian Standard*, in the latter half of 1896. Travel both characterized and changed the course of his life.

Aaron Burr Maston (1853–1907) was born in Crooked Run, Ohio, but the family was poor and moved house repeatedly during his childhood.[15] His favorite childhood book, "over which he loved to pore during the evenings," was *The Pilgrim's Progress*.[16] Its introductory verse set Maston's course for a journey both metaphorical and literal:

This book will make a traveller of thee,
If by its counsel thou wilt ruled be;
It will direct thee to the Holy Land,
If thou wilt its directions understand.[17]

Like Ludbrook, Maston was named auspiciously: Aaron Burr Sr. was a Presbyterian minister and son-in-law of Jonathan Edwards of Great Awakening fame; Aaron Burr Jr. was the controversial third US vice president, who was acquitted of treason but never lived down having earlier killed Alexander Hamilton in a duel. Maston turned to the Disciples of Christ at 15, becoming an evangelist only a few years later. He gained a Bachelor of Arts from the unremarkable Northern Indiana Normal School, a fact that he did not advertise as it set him apart from both his poorly educated congregations and his better-trained colleagues. In 1879 he left his church in Hebron, Indiana, for New Zealand where he toured extensively as an itinerant preacher. He sailed to Hobart, Tasmania, in 1884 where the small Churches of Christ congregation had been served by fellow American, Oliver Anderson Carr. From 1885 Maston lived in Melbourne, serving in three congregations, between travels to London via Palestine and America seeking treatment for an ultimately fatal cancer in his eye. He was rarely in one place for more than a few years, and the names of his daughters reflected both his travel and his feeling for his adopted country: Hobia Tasma (Hobart, Tasmania) and Melba Victoria (Melbourne, Victoria).

Maston's first narrative of travel was published in the Churches of Christ journal, *Christian Pioneer* (July–October 1889), as "Letters of Travel," though it was romantically retitled along the way as "A Horseback Ride through Palestine." Perhaps he imagined himself another Robert Louis Stevenson whose *Travels with a Donkey in the Cevennes* begins "we are all travellers in what John Bunyan calls the wilderness of this world."[18] The letters contain much eyewitness information about the history and geography of the place, along with unguarded remarks and revelations of his discomfort. Maston's journey to Palestine, partly funded by his local congregation, aided his high profile and evangelical credibility. Soon after his return in 1890 he was elected President of the

Victorian Conference of Churches of Christ and, during that term, went on to establish the Austral Printing and Publishing Company by church member subscription. The publishing company, and the publications he produced, became Maston's chief legacy to the church. In the years after his death, he was remembered for his travel writings, "fragrant with his quaint humour, and fresh and breezy with his own views of things."[19] Perhaps this was because Maston reworked the 1889 "Letters of Travel/A Horseback Ride through Palestine" and published a long *second* series. Based on the same journey, this second account appeared with illustrations in the *Australasian Christian Standard* (March 1891–October 1892), under the evocative title "Walks about Palestine." This later version of Maston's trip was more literary, self-conscious, and ambitious. It adopted an elevated style and included a selection of images: plates by various artists (including Gustave Dore) bought from the publisher of Farrar's *Life of Christ*.[20] Maston's single trip and double contribution to travel writing—in the *Christian Pioneer* (1889), then substantially rewritten for the *Australasian Christian Standard* (1891-2)—provides a valuable opportunity to observe the crafting and construction of landscape.

Holy Land Travel Writing in Nineteenth-Century Dissent

The old spiritual discipline of pilgrimage was relatively new to Protestantism. Catholic and Orthodox pilgrimage to Palestine was witnessed to by a well-established route of shrines and sacred sites. However, the Reformation rejected pilgrimage as a work leading to salvation. While many Protestants insisted on literal readings of scripture, for centuries they undertook only metaphorical pilgrimage. Modeling the metaphorical pilgrimage of the protagonist Christian in *The Pilgrim's Progress* by gaoled Dissenter, John Bunyan, the inner life of the believer came to be described in the language of religious journey. It was not until the late eighteenth and early nineteenth centuries that Protestants came to view the Holy Land as both a religious metaphor *and* a viable geographical destination, belonging not just to Orthodox and Catholic worshippers but also to them.[21]

Rising middle-class wealth and improved transport, including the opening of the Suez Canal in 1869, meant that a great many Protestants could experience the Holy Land for themselves. They set out to rediscover the physical reality of the Holy Land and prove the facts of scripture. Sorting the myth from observable reality became a modernist religious obsession undertaken by amateur and professional alike, many of whom were armed with an archaeologist's spade and trowel. In this way, new archaeological science and biblical geography found their way into objective, provable Protestantism and onto the itineraries of package tours. Travelers followed in the footsteps of clergyman geographers and archaeologists such as William Thomson, Edward Robinson, Arthur Stanley, and Frederic Farrar, whose journeys offered them the opportunity to verify the facts of the Bible by matching text with landscape. A number of guide books were already in circulation by the time the Australian Churches of Christ travelers went to Palestine: Thomson, Farrar, and Stanley, among others. Stone-Campbell movement writers including James T. Barclay and John W. McGarvey had also produced fact-laden guides to the land. Some of these texts were almost encyclopedic in scope, as if it were possible for travelers to know all there was to be known. Certainly the Australian writers were aware of such books, even quoting them as authorities in their published letters.

Yet, in any journey seeking the objective and real, suspicion lurks close to the surface. While some travelers wrote of profound religious experiences—clergyman William Prime's emotional and rhetorical account is perhaps best known—others reported overwhelming disappointment.[22] The "wreck of a country" and its people did not match the travelers' pious longings.[23] There was conflict and uncertainty over archaeological sites. The near two millennia seemed to have brought only poverty and superstition to the land of the Bible. Writers such as Mark Twain and Herman Melville used their journeys to shape narratives of disbelief, parody, and suspicion. On the continuum of skepticism and belief, the traveler was counselled to expect the worst: "No country will more quickly dissipate romantic expectations than Palestine—particularly Jerusalem. To some the disappointment is heart sickening."[24]

Journeying Outside Time

It was into this landscape of clashing hope and experience that Ludbrook and Maston journeyed in the 1880s and 1890s. As members of a Restorationist denomination, Churches of Christ, they brought an interesting extra dimension. Restorationism and the particular eschatological vision of Churches of Christ led the denomination to conceive of itself as ultimately beyond the ordinary realm of time.[25] Its writers traveled across the land, not as an historically layered landscape, but as though they might access Jesus through the very ground beneath them. This apparent ahistoricism was rooted in the denomination's firm belief that it could read the book of Acts and transpose the first church's practice into modern times, unmediated and uncorrupted by church tradition, doctrinal development, and sociopolitical circumstance. As if to silence doubters, their position was inscribed on the walls of their church buildings: "The Church of Christ Founded at Jerusalem AD 33, Organized in Sweetwater AD 1882"[26] and "Church of Christ Founded AD 33, Established in Wangaratta—1927."[27]

This earnest collapsing of time was reflected in Churches of Christ's practices. Following the New Testament they observed the "breaking of bread" as the central weekly ritual, were led by elders and evangelists rather than priests, and argued that adult believers' "baptism by immersion" was a tautology as any baptism without immersion was not truly baptism. They approached the land of Palestine as they approached the Bible, for land and book were closely related. Just as Churches of Christ believed that New Testament practice might be transposed directly and unaffected by time, so they tended to imagine the land of the Bible as timeless. In this context the modernization of Palestine (from the second to the nineteenth centuries) was especially hard for Maston and Ludbrook to reconcile with the landscape of their biblical imagination. One or other would have to be forsaken.

Expectation of Christ's Second Coming also contributed to the Churches of Christ's (and Disciples') timeless relationship with the New Testament and Palestine. James T. Barclay (1807–1874), medical missionary to Palestine and amateur archaeologist, advocated for the conversion of Jews and their repatriation to the Holy Land in preparation for the end times.[28] A founder of the Stone-Campbell movement, Alexander Campbell (1788–1866) believed that his church was uniquely positioned to hasten Christ's return, for, when other churches followed their example in discarding practices and doctrines encrusted with tradition and instead found unity in the original primitive simplicity of New Testament times and practices, the Second Coming would be ushered in.[29] In the context of America's historic nationalism, the Disciples of Christ's approach might be seen as "a form of American exceptionalism … stepping squarely outside time and history."[30] But the position was not unique to the American branch of the movement. It had its basis in Ulster Presbyterianism, and its effect was found wherever American Disciples preachers and publications exercised influence.[31] In the British colonies the influence of British Churches of Christ was stronger, but American preachers and their ideas had a presence in late-nineteenth-century Australia.

The Holy Land in Australia, America, and Britain

In the period 1850–1917 hundreds of travel narratives were published in the English-speaking world, a great many of them dealing with the spiritual experience of visiting the Holy Land.[32] Aside from books, tales of travel appeared as serialized stories in newspapers and were presented in limelight lectures by ministers and laity of many denominations around the world and in Australia.[33] Within the four walls of the Wagga Wagga Wesleyan Church, the Reverend Dr. Sellors took the audience "in an easy manner out of Wagga down the Murrumbidgee and round the voyage to the Holy Land."[34] When the Reverend W. C. Bunning lectured on his Holy Land travels at the Baptist Church in Castlemaine, Victoria, he displayed "many curios he collected" and four women (locals, presumably) "arrayed in native costume."[35] Others focused on biblical archaeology and geography.[36]

Tales of travel appeared in the United States of America too, but there the American mythic connection with the Holy Land meant that they spoke to national identity. The connection had been established by New England's Puritans two centuries earlier. John Cotton (1584–1652) imagined that they might dwell in "True Antiquity" in Massachusetts Bay.[37] His grandson, Cotton Mather (1663–1728), described the recent American past in biblical terms as though time was collapsible. His approach to history writing was something akin to exegesis, in which events in the American story were interpreted typologically, the characters in the American narrative fulfilling roles previously played by Adam and Moses, among others.[38] Many generations later, the prophetic identification of the United States of America as the New Jerusalem (Revelation 20–21) meant that nineteenth-century Holy Land travel literature by US authors contributed to the construction of American national identity.[39] The American fondness for biblical place names, along with the hundreds of Holy Land travel narratives and touring shows, were considered yet further evidence that America's national identity is intimately connected with that of the Holy Land.[40] Travel narratives, while always about strange lands and people, are nevertheless mostly about home.

Australia also had many Holy Land publications and touring shows, and there is a Jerusalem—mountain, bay, or suburb—in four of the six Australian states. There is a Beulah, Jericho, and Pool of Siloam in three states, and the town of Promised Land may be found near Hobart in Tasmania. Most astonishingly, the geographic features of the remote Walls of Jerusalem National Park in Tasmania's central plateau are named after over a dozen biblical sites. However, unlike the Mormons' Mount Zion National Park in Utah, the Tasmanian park was not named by a religious sect searching for their new Zion, but by a nineteenth-century surveyor who noted a physical resemblance to Jerusalem's Western Wall, and some twentieth-century recreational walkers who carried on the theme.[41] Despite its biblical place names, Australia has not confidently identified with Canaan. Unlike America, it has had no covenant with God, no echo of Exodus. There are two reasons. First, because the colonies of New South Wales (which included areas later known as Victoria and Queensland) and Van Diemen's Land (later Tasmania) were initially established as British penal colonies, the earliest narratives were more often of a journey into bondage. Second, separation between church and state, which was fiercely maintained and frequently iterated in Dissent's denominational journals, meant that religious roots were not to be confused with those of the nation. Holy Land travel narratives written for the Australian readership cannot be interpreted in terms of the nation's identity or its role in the popularly expected millennium of Christ.

If travel writing is always partly about home, in Australian travel writing it was a home in the absence of a coherent religious nationalism. The idea of a national home was frequently uncertain too, as Australia was then not a nation but separate colonies belonging to the British Empire. Most readers were recent arrivals and their birthplace was elsewhere: England, Ireland, Scotland, the United States. Colonial soil was essentially not a place of comfort and belonging but one of distance. This fueled the Dissenters' belief in a true home as the heavenly life hereafter. For evangelists, this sense of earthly homelessness was compounded by the itinerant nature of their calling: "the Son of Man has no place to lay his head" (Lk. 9:58, NIV).

Into the Terrain by Train, Horse, and Foot

Itinerancy, half a world away and on the tight schedule of a package tour, required reliable transport. Protestant travel accounts are divided between giving account of the process of travel—by ship, train, horse, and foot—and the inner journey. For travel writers, modes of transport could affect both the vision of the landscape and authority with readers. Aaron Maston was especially aware of this, naming and renaming his travel writings, from "Horse-Back" to "Walks." But Maston was not actually walking. As the earlier title reveals, he had a horse provided as part of a package tour. While a Catholic pilgrim might have taken on the penitential bodily experience of walking in order to share in the sufferings of Christ, the Protestant traveler momentarily put aside biblical literalism and rejected the burden of walking as a "work," electing instead the "grace" of transport by horse.

Albert Ludbrook, more irreverent and less artful than Maston, reported that two biblical modes of transport were available on his tour: "Some of us rode on donkeys, others preferred Shank's pony."[42] He was much more coy about arriving in Jerusalem by steam train: "Rising ground prevents one from seeing Jerusalem from the railroad,— and fortunately so, for it would seem somewhat incongruous and very unromantic to behold the Holy City for the first time from so modern and prosaic a view-point as a railway train."[43] How would readers enter into that "incongruous" experience and travel with him in Jesus' footsteps? The writers recognized that they were undertaking the journey on behalf of their readers. Walking in the footsteps of Jesus was best achieved with pious commitment and transport modes consistent with the time-collapsing view of a church that sought to travel not just to Palestine but to the New Testament.

Comparisons with Australian Birds and Flowers

The Australian authors Ludbrook and Maston wrote with their readers (rather than national destiny) in mind. They brought with them to the Holy Land a mixture of scientifically minded skepticism and heartfelt belief, hoping to see a pure and timeless biblical landscape made real. The objective observation of the natural landscape was essential. Alongside description of biblical sites, Ludbrook and Maston noted details such as birds, flowers, grasses, trees, and rivers. Interest in the natural sciences had grown considerably since the Enlightenment, epitomized in the phenomenon of the nineteenth-century clergyman naturalist, geographer, or archaeologist,[44] and this thinking was integrated in Churches of Christ's newly developing theology. An appreciation of science sat comfortably alongside a reasoned, commonsense approach to scripture. Alexander Campbell had encouraged Christians to apply inductive reasoning to the facts of the Bible in the same way they might approach scientific subjects. Campbell's *Christian System* begins, "One God, one system of nature, one universe,"[45] and continues in the second chapter, "*Sense* is his guide in nature, *faith* in religion, *reason* in both."[46] The Churches of Christ authors reflect this in their observation of birds and flowers along the journey.

Maston was at pains to compare the relative merits of the flora and fauna in Palestine for the Australian readership. He wrote, "I have seen prettier and larger wild flowers in New South Wales, but I never before saw such a variety of these little messengers."[47] God's "messengers," a term often denoting evangelists, could be seen everywhere and the performance of studied comparison mattered in the establishment of Maston's authority. Not merely of interest to those readers who had also seen flowers in New South Wales, Maston proved himself to be a reliable observer, a man with a keen eye and a wide interest in the world around him. Ludbrook, too, remarked on the "wonderful profusion of wildflowers!"[48] For both Ludbrook and Maston, the natural world was the place for encounter with the sacred, and its study was valuable.

Ludbrook assumed an unlikely local knowledge of birdlife when he noted "the dulcet notes of the cuckoo, and this as early as the beginning of March."[49] Alongside the Jordan River, Maston also listened to the birds:

I was especially interested in the birds, as we had seen none to speak of during our travels in Palestine … The Australasian birds, you know, have beautiful plumage, but they can't sing a bit more than I can, and that's not saying much for the birds of the "Great Southland." The most musical bird I heard in that country is the Laughing Jackass, which for power and range of voice can't be excelled I am sure, but the music might not suit all tastes.[50]

The mistaken idea that Australia was a land of "songless bright birds" was established in the popular imagination by the poet Adam Lindsay Gordon in 1870, the year of his suicide.[51] Maston called on Gordon's unhappy accepted wisdom without attuning to the poet's songless despair. Instead, Maston's style is chatty, jocular, and plain-speaking; he was, after all, careful not to portray himself as more educated than his congregation. His content is apparently objective and analytical; there are pros and cons to birds, and his allegiance is not to Australian or Palestinian birds but to objectivity itself. Yet, ultimately, birds and flowers have a limited interest for Maston and they are almost absent from his reworked 1891 account. There they serve only as poetic superlatives: "the most enchanting music to which I had ever listened."[52] They set the scene for the real business of theological reflection. Maston believed his use of the natural world was following after Jesus' example:

> Jesus of Nazareth … was one of nature's true noblemen. He practically spent His life in the fields and on the mountains [sic] side, and when He spoke to men of the stirring truths of immortality, He drew from the great storehouse of nature's wonders, and hence is universally acknowledged the world's great teacher, not only for what He taught, but the way He taught it.[53]

Maston believed that there was something profound and elemental about Jesus' teaching via nature, an opinion he may have absorbed through reading William Thomson: "Christ was a lover of landscape."[54] While the young Ludbrook exclaimed at the scenery, Maston self-consciously modeled himself on his Savior. He observed nature as a teacher and speaker of truth.

The Near-Sacred Land and the Baptists' River

The grandeur of the natural landscape was similarly edifying, though caution in expression was advisable. For Maston, Palestine was "this divine wonderland" replete with vistas of incomparable spiritual beauty.[55] Sunsets led to moments of reverie by the Sea of Galilee and, while asserting that he was "not a worshipper of sacred places,"[56] Maston found himself suggesting that the land was itself sacred:

> The sun was just going down over the western hills, leaving me in the cool, soft shade, but giving the lake the appearance of a sea of gold, and painting the eastern hills with what seemed to me an almost divine glory. And was it not divine? That

sea, those hills and quiet valleys between, have they not been consecrated by the presence of the Son of God."[57]

He was drawn into Romanticism's representation of the land as monumental—nobler than any human monument—where the inhabitants appeared as small, incidental figures in the landscape of God's grandeur.[58] In Maston's reworked 1891 account, the description of the Galilee sunset was accompanied by an image, borrowed from Farrar, depicting tiny people beside a glorious sea.[59]

However, the second account of Maston's journey is more circumspect about the consecration of the land. It reprints the story of sunset at Galilee but ends instead with "almost divine glory!"[60] In the same way, his later account consistently describes the landscape as merely "almost sacred."[61] Romanticism had found its limit in the commonsense world of Churches of Christ.

William Thomson's *The Land and the Book* (1859) also claimed that Palestine was inscribed with an almost sacred quality, as though it might be studied in parallel with the Bible.[62] Sacred geography became a well-established subject of study for Protestant ministers in the nineteenth century, and textbooks proliferated. The Australian Churches of Christ, at their night school in Melbourne, 1904, used Zollars's *Bible Geography*, published within the Stone-Campbell movement in the United States.[63] At Bethany College in West Virginia, Alexander Campbell had lectured at Bethany College on sacred geography and history with special emphasis on the Jordan River. He unequivocally rejected anything approaching idolatry or nature worship.[64] Topography was a text in support of the Bible, and, in Churches of Christ, it was text that persuaded and brought people to faith. In Maston's experience, the land was a text to be read, made "almost sacred" through the "presence of the Son of God."[65]

The Jordan River, as a secondary text of faith, held a special place in denominational identity. It was the site of John's baptism of Jesus and the place in which the practice of baptism, central to Churches of Christ, began. The American Churches of Christ evangelist John William McGarvey (1829–1911) preached on "The River Jordan" and Maston reprinted his sermon for an Australian audience. McGarvey iterated the Churches of Christ position that the Jordan was *the* place for believer baptists to meet Jesus:

> If you would have Jesus your Redeemer by your side when you come to the last hour, you must have him by your side on the journey. How did he go? He first went down to that literal Jordan, and there, as we have seen, he was baptized by John, though he had no sins to wash away. Follow Him there.[66]

Having traveled to the Jordan, its pebbles and grains of sand made worthy mementoes. They were closer to Jesus, in the minds of Dissenters, than the relics and shrines celebrated in the Catholic and Orthodox traditions. The sale of relics and keepsakes flourished in the towns where tourists traveled: Maston reported having to fight off the street traders.[67] As a reader of *Pilgrim's Progress*, he knew the dangers of Catholicism's souvenirs: at Vanity Fair "the ware of Rome and her merchandise is greatly promoted."[68] Maston, like so many skeptical Dissenters, preferred his souvenirs collected by his own hand in the waters of the Jordan River: "We spent some time ... gathering some pebbles and sand as mementoes."[69] In the United States such natural mementoes found a ready market on the Holy Land talk-circuit: there was more faith in the natural world than in works of human manufacture.[70]

When Maston came to write the second edition of his travels in the *Australasian Christian Standard* in 1891–2, he included a selection of plates by various artists first published in Farrar's *Life of Christ*. He did not reprint any of Farrar's images of towns and buildings, but instead preferred the landscape images: hills and trees and one titled "Flowers and Grasses from Palestine," which Maston used to accompany his account of Jesus' death near Jerusalem.[71] Was it Victorian funeral practices that prompted Maston to associate flowers with death? Did he hope the flowers would prompt thought of the temporal nature of this life? Or did the continuity of biblical flowers in the landscape represent a living link between past and present? Dried flowers were often sold as mementoes of the Holy Land. The locals read them as a symbol of nationalism,[72] but Protestant tourists saw a "natural" souvenir.

"God Made the Country, though Man Made the Town"

Ludbrook and Maston both valued the natural landscape associated with Jesus' ministry because it seemed to them to be unchanged, allowing them to step back through time. On the road between Jerusalem and Jericho, Ludbrook exclaimed, "Yes, God made the country, though man made the town. Jerusalem is indeed greatly altered since the time of Christ, but the country in its general features is the same."[73]

In contrast to the pebbles of the Jordan River, the built environment of the Church of the Nativity was a conflicted holy site in the minds of Dissenters. Package tours were becoming established by 1889 and the reputed place of Jesus' birth was part of the itinerary for most travelers, though, in deference to the religious leanings of Protestants, routes had been adapted to avoid many other shrines.[74] On visiting Jesus' birth place, beneath the Church of the Nativity, Maston wrote, "It looks from the outside like some great half-ruined fortress, and from within like a gloomy prison ... I place but little stress on their traditions, but as I stood in this place, I could but think that if this was not *the* place, it was near it."[75] Clearly he wished to feel the significance of the site, yet, in the phrase "their traditions," drew a line between Churches of Christ's life in the New Testament and Catholic and Orthodox expressions of faith that occupied tradition's "gloomy prison."

For nineteenth-century Dissenters, tradition was a word with only negative connotations. Maston made the point repeatedly: "I do not place much confidence in this traditional business"[76] and "Tradition has been busy about Bethlehem, but of these things I care but little."[77] The writings of Ludbrook and Maston consistently contrast all things natural, real, and biblical with the human innovations of urbanized shrines. In Churches of Christ's foundation, innovations in ritual and tradition were identified as a barrier to Christian unity that must be discarded in favor of pure and unmediated observance of New Testament practice. Little wonder these travelers also preferred the rural landscape, viewed via direct, unmediated vision, rather than the urban shrines whose authenticity was so much harder for an amateur to discern and whose truth appeared to be clouded by layers of tradition and seeming error.

Nineteenth-century Protestants tended to locate the moment of the church's corruption with the conversion of Emperor Constantine in 312, and the church's subsequent alignment with the state. According to primitivist Christians, the rot set in much earlier. Maston explained to Churches of Christ readers that the period immediately after the writing of the New Testament epistles was "the fountain from which has flowed all the great rivers of corruption which have polluted, and laid in ruins the Church of God."[78] For primitivists, all change beyond the New Testament was death. Despite idealized imaginings, time had not stood still in the Holy Land. Authenticity within the churches of Palestine was going to be hard to find.

The preference for the natural landscape was not only a bias toward nature but also an objection to liturgical and creedal Christian tradition, to the church's alliance with the state, and to development beyond the practices of the New Testament book of Acts and the Epistles. Buildings themselves were not viewed as an obstacle to relationship with God. Indeed, in Australia, new church buildings in the towns and countryside were regularly celebrated as signs of the progress of the Kingdom of God.[79] Progress toward the coming reign of Christ was indisputably good. Modernity was wished upon Arabs.[80] But the landscape of the Bible was different. It was set apart in the hearts and minds of religious visitors. There, progress signified corruption of the eternal landscape of biblical truth.

"Nobody of any Sense Believes It"

In searching for the landscape of biblical truth, travelers to the Holy Land were caught between Dissent's native skepticism of tradition and its urge to prove the truth of the Word of God by correlating bible stories with specific places. The writers were forced to address popular assertions of authenticity around all manner of structures, mountains, and even flora. Ludbrook found himself scoffing at the claims about olive trees: "On the further side, near the Bethlehem road, is a solitary blasted tree on which, it is said, Judas hanged himself. It may be a hundred years old!"[81] In the same way, when visiting the house of Simon the Tanner, he asserted, "Nobody of any sense believes it to be the identical abode referred to in Acts 10." Although Ludbrook's account depends heavily on that of Arthur Penrhyn Stanley, Dean of Westminster, he was quick to defer to common sense: "but Dean Stanley thought it the identical site."[82] For the irreverent young Dissenter, Anglicans were less trustworthy than his own empirical reasoning.

Another Australian Churches of Christ traveler, known only as "An Australian Abroad," traveled through the Suez Canal in 1890. On the way they passed a place reputed to be where the Israelites crossed the Red Sea. They reflected with uncertainty, "From the passing view which we could get, it looked a likely place, fulfilling the conditions of the history, and we saw no other place that seemed to fulfil them."[83] If the topography was a text, it was harder to read than expected. The writer realized their inability to make a considered judgment in a complex argument, and resorted to bald biblical assertion: "We are not disposed to enter into the controversy as to the place. The fact remains whether here or elsewhere."[84] Tourist guides were unreliable and tradition was tainted, but at least the Bible could be assumed to be wholly true.

Indeed, with conflicting opinions from the literature, local guides, and, most especially, new archaeological works, devout travelers such as Ludbrook turned to the Bible as their ultimate geographic authority. Ludbrook dismissed the sign-posted location of the tomb of Absalom "because as a matter of fact he met with his unique and tragic death near Mahanaim beyond Jordan."[85] Likewise, Ludbrook approached the new science of archaeology with circumspection lest it throw doubt on biblical truth: the Pool of Siloam "is several hundred yards outside the city, which fact seemed to discredit Nehemiah's narrative (Neh. 3:15); but recent excavations of the Palestine Exploration Fund have proved that the ancient wall of Jerusalem included the pool within the city limits."[86] Skepticism and empiricism were applied to archaeology, but not the Bible.

Archaeology in Palestine had started as a means to prove the Bible's truth, and religious amateurs including Robinson and Barclay were enthusiastic drivers. By the late nineteenth century, however, archaeology had thrown much in doubt. Certainly by the mid-twentieth century archaeology had "turned on its own source—the biblically inspired religious imagination."[87] Or, to put it another way, the Bible at first interpreted the archaeological evidence. But when archaeology began to interpret the Bible, many evangelical Christians responded as they had to the scholarship of Higher Criticism: they retreated to the irrefutable evidences of sacred geography, defiant literalism, and assertions of the evangelical heart. It is clear that in the last decade of the nineteenth century Australian Dissent felt compelled to choose between biblical and archaeological evidence. They chose the Word.

A Land as Familiar as the Bible

Maston and Ludbrook, like many before them, were caught between the expectations of the biblical imagination and their perceptions as wary and vulnerable travelers in a foreign land.[88] They had not necessarily expected the land to be foreign. Rather, they had considered it theirs. Both Maston and Ludbrook read the Bible extensively while in Palestine, and their travel narratives read the landscape through a biblical lens. Ludbrook heard the local musicians of Joppa and was reminded "forcibly of the apostolic allusion to 'sounding brass and tinkling cymbal.'"[89] The local fruit called to mind Prov. 25:11 and Song 2:5.[90] Maston read the entire New Testament while in Palestine, including while traveling on horseback: "Owing to the roughness of the way I had to travel very slowly, and so was enabled to take my New Testament from my pocket and read a number of the incidents in the life of Jesus which occurred about this sea."[91] He reminded his readers that this was not mere tourism but a journey mediated by scripture.

The biblical imagination's mediation of Protestant travel was a near-universal phenomenon. Pilgrims arrived in the Holy Land with a sense that they had been there before, that this was the land of their childhood faith.[92] When Maston and Ludbrook first traveled to Palestine they came with a sense that they remembered this land, that its contours were already familiar, that its rivers and fields were part of their Christian self and identity.[93] Nostalgia for a land of childhood memory frequently vied with avowed empiricism, and a great many travelers to the Holy Land felt stirred to recall childhood, mother, and home.[94]

At first sight of the Holy Land, Ludbrook rapturously declared it "the country of all countries, the most full of sweet and sacred associations."[95] Although, defying expectation, Egypt appeared to him remarkably wet and hilly:

> I had always thought of it as a rainless country; but during the first few days of my stay the weather was very showery, at times raining quite heavily. However, it never rains, I think, in *Upper* Egypt. Then also I had an impression that this country was as flat as the proverbial pancake. But this is not the case.[96]

He had to reconcile his lack of recognition of a land he thought he knew. In the same way, Maston struggled with the sight of Bethlehem that he had imagined since childhood: "Like all the towns of Palestine Bethlehem looks best from a distance."[97] Considering the dark disappointment of the Church of the Nativity, perhaps Bethlehem was most advantageously viewed from the log cabin in Crooked Run, Ohio.

By the late nineteenth century, disappointment and dissonance between biblical imagination and traveler experience were common. Disappointment at the sight of modern-day Jerusalem was so well established that Ludbrook found himself responding to the tacit assumption: "My first impressions of Jerusalem were most decidedly *not* disappointing."[98] Maston, however, was disappointed and frustrated with the people and the vegetation: the Bedouins were the "dirtiest, hardest looking specimens of humanity I have ever dropped across" and the land was "overgrown with the rankest vegetation I have ever seen outside of the tropics."[99] When crafting his second account, the Holy Land is made to conform to imagination and hope. Galilee is nothing but glorious, and the genre's expected reflections on childhood imaginings are provided for the reading public: "From earliest childhood I had thought of 'Sweet Galilee,' and hundreds of times had pictured to myself what it must be like but all this was more a dream than a reality; but now here it was actually spread before my eyes."[100] In the light of the two different accounts of Galilee, the distinction between "dream" and "reality" is highly arguable. Pious belief overrode skepticism. Literary expectation was fulfilled.

Maston owes a heavy literary debt to Anglican clergyman Frederic William Farrar, author of the best-selling *Life of Christ* (1874) and later Dean of Canterbury. Clearly impressed by the style and orientation of Farrar's work, Maston's second account emulates his mix of information, theological reflection, and romantic vision, and reprints plates from Farrar's book. Maston also quoted Farrar and, without acknowledgement, freely paraphrased and borrowed at will.[101] In turn, Farrar is occasionally indebted to William Wordsworth—or perhaps they merely share a vision of landscape and "smiling sea."[102] Maston was likely unaware of the ready comparison between the borrowed "deep seclusion" of Joseph's carpentry shop and that of Wordsworth's description of a cottage above Tintern Abbey because, as a rule, Maston was careful to borrow only that part of Farrar's writing untainted by ecclesiasticism.[103] He also added biblical references where Farrar (and Wordsworth) did not: Farrar (and Wordsworth) wrote of "crystal water/s," but Maston added Rev. 4:6, "sea of glass, like unto crystal."[104] With the clear vision of Protestant Dissent, Maston used "crystal waters" again in his final instalment: "We have sailed with Him over the crystal waters of Galilee."[105]

With encouragement to mission in mind, Maston reminded readers of their role as "fishers of men," and, adding authenticity and authority, provided real-life experience of Galilee fishermen. He revealed that the Galilean fishermen requested the tourists stop disturbing the peace of Galilee and cease "frightening the fish into deep water."[106] Living people often got in the way of Maston's vision. His disregard for the inhabitants of Palestine, typified by descriptions of Bedouins and fishermen, reflects an imaginative ownership of the biblical landscape to the exclusion of living people. For many travelers, the land was so strongly identified with Christian faith, they could not conceive of it belonging in any sense to the people who lived there.[107] Yet the local people are present in the narratives by Ludbrook and Maston (1889). Dragomen and guides are the often-mistrusted negotiators of the route. There are biblical figures too: lepers, fishermen, women, and children working in the fields and towns. But unlike the figures in Farrar's etchings, these people would not conform to the biblical vision. They did not step through the land as if it was made "almost sacred" by the "presence of the Son of God," but treated it as their ordinary place of work and dwelling.[108] It frustrated travelers. Their accounts complain regularly about the customs of the people and the unpleasant nature of interactions, and the writers seem not to see the irony in expressing annoyance at the Palestinian people while professing a faith centered on God's incarnation in a man from Nazareth.

Walking in the Footsteps of Jesus

In Maston's cultivated account of 1891–2 most of these figures recede into the landscape as the journey comes to focus on the traveler and reader. Indeed, the interruptions come from an imagined group of biblical people rather than a nineteenth-century tour group. This second account imagines a "mob" of first-century locals at Gethsemane that threatens to interrupt the readers' spiritual experience: "We can not [sic] tarry longer amidst these sacred scenes, because, if we did, our deep emotions might be disturbed by the howling mob."[109] Maston used the literary moment to urge readers to return again to Gethsemane on a journey of the heart: "Shall I not venture to express the same for all the *Standard* readers, and say that *we* may go more frequently into the deep and quiet shadows of Gethsemane, and watch and weep with Jesus there."[110] No longer the skeptical tourist but the trustworthy guide, Maston openly sought to "take the reader" with him "to walk with Jesus" in a journey of belief.[111]

Evangelist travel-writers took their readers to see the fields of flowers Jesus saw, to wade in the Jordan, walk beside Galilee's "crystal waters," and weep with Jesus at Gethsemane. Descriptions, like Ludbrook's, enabled readers to join in gazing "upon these very hills, where the sheep are browsing and the goats are leaping from rock to rock,"[112] and in stopping by the "Watering-Place, where is the only spring of water between Jerusalem and Jericho; so Jesus and His company must oft have quenched their thirst here as we did."[113] The experiences they described appealed to the romantic imagination of readers as pure, natural, and uncorrupted by developments in religion since "A.D. 33."[114] They formed the solid ground of the readers' journey of the heart.

A Land Twice Imagined

Even as the writers asserted the priority of the real travel that lent them authority, they revealed the act of religious imagination that was fundamental to the experience of the Holy Land: "To walk in thought around the city is an inspiration, while to be there in reality is a revelation, as every one of its hills and valleys speak in the most eloquent terms of the world's highest hopes and desires."[115] The physical landscape needed a religious imagination to hear it speak and translate it to the reader: "As I walked along amidst my almost sacred surroundings, it did not require much of an effort to imagine myself in the company of the weary Christ."[116] The reader was implicitly invited to join the writer in the easy imagination of Christ, for a pious journey of imagination was required whether in Palestine or Australia. Yet, Maston persisted in the rhetoric of reality: "To the extent that I shall succeed in making Jesus more of a reality, to that extent will I have gained the object in view in writing these articles."[117] What kind of reality was this? In Maston's carefully reworked account, the facts of the place recede. Little mention of local life and geography is made. They are not needed for "the great lessons which the places and incidents connected with them teach to every day Christian life."[118] It is enough that the writer-guide once walked (or rode) across the land. After that, all is biblically inspired imagination.

In a world in which Holy Land publications and traveling shows were good business,[119] both the Australian authors saw an evangelistic edge in joining the talk-circuit. In traveling to Palestine they gained little more information than they would have had they read Farrar and Stanley from cover to cover, which perhaps they did. Yet, in a land where imagination and reality overlapped, they had walked with Jesus. It was this authority, this experience, that they needed. Both Ludbrook and Maston used the fact of their having been to Palestine to distinguish themselves as entrepreneurs of the gospel. They developed their writings into "popular lantern entertainments,"[120] delivering a mixture of fact and gospel and "Sixty Beautiful Views" for the price of sixpence admission (children half price).[121] Ludbrook toured South Australia, Victoria, New South Wales, and Queensland. Using "splendid views thrown on the screen," he lectured on "various incidents connected with the life of Christ."[122] Maston traveled widely too, exhibiting images and providing "chatty description," speaking "of the places he saw with so much confidence."[123]

Other Holy Land shows were undoubtedly more spectacular but the different intent is revealing. The Cyclorama of Jerusalem, commercially exhibited in Melbourne and Sydney, required a purpose-built round building and layers of painted images on a canvas fifty feet high and four hundred feet long to create a 360-degree experience of the sublime and pathetic.¹²⁴ Despite the professed moral and educational motivations of Cycloramas, they cost tens of thousands of pounds to build and needed ticket sales to recoup costs.¹²⁵ The accompanying booklet emphasized the history of the city and the experience of viewing the Cyclorama but asserted merely enduring "interest" in the "death on Calvary of Christ Jesus."¹²⁶ The call to conversion was powerfully absent. Even on a weeknight in a draughty church hall, the evangelists would not have missed an opportunity to call listeners to walk with Jesus to the Jordan, to Calvary, and to Emmaus.

"Were Not Our Hearts Burning within Us?"

Maston's 1891 account included selected etchings from Farrar's *Life of Christ*, complete with illustration titles. But Maston relabels one of Farrar's illustrations: an image of a solitary figure walking toward a town nestled in the hills. Farrar calls it "Emmaus," that place where the disciples recognized Jesus, asking, "Were not our hearts burning within us while he talked with us on the road …?" (Lk. 24:32).¹²⁷ The location of Emmaus is and was historically disputed so its geography is debatable. However, Maston reprints the same illustration and labels it "Bethany." Perhaps his readers would not know the difference between one Palestinian town and another. Perhaps geography was less important than evangelical imagination. When Maston labels the road to Emmaus as "Bethany," the home of Jesus' friends Lazarus, Mary and Martha, he writes at length on the virtues of women's work in the home.¹²⁸ How could a home be confused with an encounter on the road with the risen Lord?

If every travel narrative ultimately speaks of home, these Australian preachers found their home on the road: traveling with Jesus, calling to conversion, hearts burning within. For them, unlike American writers of travel guides, home was not reflected in the exceptionalism of a national identity bound up with the destiny of the Holy Land. Nor was it in the building of a great denomination. Neither was it in heaven, for the landscape of the real Holy Land firmly situated the Christian life on this "almost sacred" earth.¹²⁹ Instead, the travel writings of these Australian Protestant Dissenters reflect a home found forever on the road: in itinerant ministry and church halls from Hobart to Toowoomba.

For Ludbrook and Maston, the journey to the Holy Land recurred again and again in each lantern lecture. It was an endlessly repeatable journey: a journey outside time.¹³⁰ On a weeknight far from Palestine, the audience traveled with Jesus through "almost sacred surroundings" and for the price of only sixpence.¹³¹ Ludbrook and Maston were no longer intrepid tourists, but trusted guides. What may have initially looked like curiosity ended in evangelism: anticipation of the audiences' reception was never far from the writers' minds.¹³²

The Holy Land held an immense attraction as a landscape at the heart of faith. For empirically minded nineteenth-century Dissent it was a proof of the real life of Jesus and the tangible truth of primitivist Christianity. Physical landscape and objective facts mattered, fulfilling the imprimatur of a reasoned Enlightenment faith. Skepticism, companion to a reasoned faith, was applied to every shrine and tourist destination, and ultimately to the work of archaeology, which might have been seen as a partner in the cause had it not conflicted with the Bible.

The rhetoric of reality reigned, and it did matter that Maston and Ludbrook really went to Palestine. Yet the Holy Land was, more than anything, a place of imagination shaped by the stories of childhood and a hermeneutic of heartfelt metaphor. The internal landscape of pious memory and hope dominated nineteenth-century Dissent's response to Palestine. The real came to signify not the society found there, with their ancient shrines and modern railway, but the truth of Christ in the heart of the reader. Primitivist evangelists chose to see beyond the immediate and present, to a timeless land of imagination. Bringing their audiences with them, they encountered the real Jesus on a journey of belief, and a life on an Australian road made "almost sacred" through the "presence of the Son of God."[133]

4

Landscape of Urban Transformation: Salvation Army Publicity and Performance in the Parish of the Streets, 1890–1909

Cornelie Booth took the ticket-holders at her limelight show on a virtual "tour through the haunts of despair, poverty and vice" of Melbourne.[1] According to The Salvation Army's own publicity, "the hearts of the vast audience were thrilled." Booth was an accomplished speaker whose tours of the slums on the big screen drew in both the converted and the curious. Throughout the late 1890s, her illuminated talks, staged at the Melbourne Town Hall and regional meeting places, walked a line between entertainment and religious service:

> Mrs Booth portrayed the black recesses of Darkest Melbourne and, if anything, still darker Sydney ... The brilliancy and size of the life-model pictures enabled the audience to follow the speaker from slum to brothel, from opium den to prison, and from the haunts of deplorable squalor to the abode of gilded vice.[2]

But these were not real-life views of a city's sorry inhabitants. The photographs were "life-model pictures"—tableaux staged for the purpose of publicity. The impoverished, the repentant, the pitiful, and their earnest Christian rescuers were roles played by Salvation Army officers in costume. This was theater.

Performance and publicity went hand in hand in the work of The Salvation Army. The membership was small and its resources limited. To effect spiritual and moral transformation of the poorest members of society, funds were first needed to transform their life circumstances. Places of reform needed to be built and training for work provided: faith would come with enterprise. Engaging the public's attention and its generous donations, Salvationists modeled the transformation of the world by transforming themselves on stage. Exchanging the costume of military uniform for that of drunkard or prostitute, they acted out moments of self-awareness. Sin was realized, lives were changed. While the scenes were staged and artificial, they asked that viewers undergo real transformation; that they change in heart and deed. At the dawn of a new nation, The Salvation Army's use of publicity and performance was essential to its mission in the Australian civic landscape.

Salvationists in Australia were part of an international movement under the direction of General William Booth and their publicity and performance was both typical of the movement and utterly extraordinary. Their local Commandant was Booth's "talented" but "restless" fifth child Herbert who was keen to make a name for himself and the movement, and not unhappy to be half a world away from his father and brothers.[3] He undertook a number of new and attention-grabbing initiatives in a movement already known for its rejection of staid church ways. Building on the spectacle of marching bands, street preaching, and magic lantern lectures, Herbert added the conducting of annual general meetings in song, the deployment of bicycles, and the very latest in performance technology, the cinematograph.

Portraying Transformation with Booth, Booth, and Perry

Herbert Henry Booth (1862–1926) was born in England and given charge of the Officers' Training Home at a young age before being made Commandant of Army operations in Britain in 1888.[4] He was a publicist extraordinaire, a natural performer—William would later warn his son against "worldly swagger"—with skills in music and oratory and a great feeling for what would appeal to audiences.[5] It was these skills that saw him stage a "grand demonstration" at London's Crystal Palace in 1890 using his compositions that, like many Salvation Army songs and much of nineteenth-century Evangelicalism, look forward to heaven.[6] A capable administrator, family tensions saw him request overseas transfer and he headed Salvation Army operations in Canada from 1892 and in Australia from August 1896. When he arrived at The Salvation Army Headquarters in Victoria, the colony had spent years in severe economic depression brought on by the end of a speculative land boom and the collapse of financial and banking sectors. Infrastructure projects and building had stalled, and unemployment ran at between 17 and 30 percent.[7] Years of drought, from the mid-1890s to 1902, compounded problems for Victoria. In contrast to the prevailing economic and climatic conditions, and despite the fact that tensions within the Booth family prompted Herbert to leave The Salvation Army shortly after, he publicly recalled his time in charge as "five conquering years."[8] Ever the publicist, Herbert knew that it was how the story was told that mattered.

During his time in Australia, Herbert had two creative partners: his wife Cornelie and the cinematographer Joseph Perry. Cornelie Booth, née Schoch (1864–1920), was a Dutch Salvationist and an immensely competent individual who spoke a number of languages, ministered to women in the Melbourne slums, sang solos, and delivered public lectures at large venues. She cowrote two hymnbooks with Herbert and coproduced major public events with him, confidently taking the stage when he was unable to perform.[9] Despite her nationality and their residence in Australia, her English husband patriotically referred to her as "Our Boadicea."[10]

Joseph Perry (1863–1943) was born in England and spent his adolescence in New Zealand where he joined The Salvation Army in 1883. He came to Australia as an officer in 1885 and served in a number of cities before taking up management of the Ballarat Prison-gate ministry on the Victorian goldfields. In 1891, while on compassionate leave after the death of his first wife, Perry was asked to assist Commissioner Coombs to produce a lantern-slide presentation about William Booth's *In Darkest England*. He toured Australasia with a limelight projector and a collection of three hundred slides.[11] Further officers were assigned to work with Perry, forming the Limelight Department in June 1892 and operating as the Biorama Company in the 1900s. In 1896, only a year after the arrival of cinema in Australia, Perry began filming documentary footage of the Army's work. A studio was established at the Melbourne Headquarters in Bourke Street, where both film and still photography could be developed and edited. Short films of biblical stories followed.[12] Perry's potential was encouraged within the Army and, when combined with Herbert Booth's creative drive, the projects grew in ambition and scope.[13] After the Booths' departure, Perry carried on as cinematographer for a number of productions until 1909 when new Commissioner to Australia, James Hay, made the decision to close the Limelight Department in favor of more serious evangelical methods.[14] Perry left The Salvation Army in the serious pursuit of cinematography.[15]

While the work of Perry and the Booths was widely recognized, many significant Salvation Army contributions to writing the Australian landscape were not attributed; especially the illustrations, advertisements, and articles in The Salvation Army's local periodical the *War Cry*. There is currently little known about either the writers or the colonial editors, but there is a degree of consistency in content and style.[16] It was evident that the *War Cry* was based on the English edition and represented a strong centralized authority.

Parish of the Streets

The Salvation Army thrived in urban centers within late colonial Australia, and it claimed the streets of the cities and towns as its great open-air parish.[17] Marching bands, street preaching, public testimony and prayer, and even the uniforms of the officers were part of the spectacle of the work of salvation.[18] In this way the Army distinguished itself from other churches, hoping that its performance of the joyful excitement of salvation would appeal to the poor and working classes. They pointed to an alternative life in the struggles of earthly existence and a sign of the glory to come. Salvationist exuberance represented a life of light and bliss without the aid of alcohol and opium that so often led to moral dissolution, unemployment, and homelessness on city streets. In this fallen world, the urban landscape was concentrated with dangers to the soul. It was the same the world over, for just as the gospel was universal, so was sin. Unlike other Protestant Dissenters who prided themselves on their knowledge of natural history and local terrains, geography made little difference to The Salvation Army. Catherine Booth (1829–1890), Salvation Army cofounder with her husband William (1829–1912), described the true state of the world as one nearing the end-times: "The World is dying—souls are being damned at an awful rate. Men are running to destruction. Torrents of iniquity are rolling down our streets and through our world."[19] The parish of the streets was awash with signs of sin, and it was this landscape that compelled the Army to action.

The Salvation Army's war on sin often drew negative responses, especially in the 1880s and 1890s. Street preachers and marching bands were regularly pelted with rotten vegetables and stones. Locals actively opposed the Salvationists' work, not least because of their marches past gambling dens and public houses, calling the paying customers to repent. Bylaws regarding noise and nuisance were introduced and Salvationists were prosecuted. Newspaper reports provided details of the events. From his headquarters in England, William Booth remained unperturbed and counseled his members that all publicity was good.[20] In his sermon titled "Jeremiah; Or Putting Down the Salvationists" (*c.* 1889), William reminded his troops that those who suffered publicly were the victors in any exchange: "Cruelty creates pity, and pity leads to enquiry, and enquiry leads to salvation. Publicity means success."[21] Public suffering, both of Salvationists and of people in the "haunts of despair," would lead to salvation. Catherine Booth drew on apostolic precedent in her exhortation to endure future suffering for Christ's sake: "Though you should be tied to a stake, as were the martyrs of old, and surrounded by laughing and taunting fiends and their howling followers—that will be a dignity which shall be crowned in heaven with everlasting glory."[22] The Salvation Army's motto of "Blood and Fire" suggested not only the blood of Jesus but also that of the martyrs. Their religious fervor was fueled by their perception of themselves as victimized in their righteousness.[23] This persecutory turn of mind set the scene for an especially melodramatic representation of the Christian conversion narrative in the Australian landscape.

Publicity and Performance in Late-Nineteenth-Century Dissent

Most Australian churches in the Dissenting tradition shared approaches to publicity. Denominational periodicals informed members of activities and facilitated connection between congregations. They contained expression of denominational identity in articles on theology, ecclesiology, and ethics. But, serving a subscriber base of church members, they did not need, and rarely used, enticing pictures. The Congregationalists' *Victorian Independent* featured neat columns of text and subdued headers for its relatively literate readership. The Churches of Christ, which shared the Salvationists' less educated demographic, ran so-called common-sense argument and statistics, along with the occasional portrait. Breaking ranks with the rest of Protestant Dissent, The Salvation Army used illustrations extensively in its periodical, gave it the colorful title *War Cry*, and sold it on the streets.

In July 1883, a month after the Victorian edition of the *War Cry* commenced publication (and only three years after The Salvation Army had begun its work in Australia) they claimed to have sold 9,630 copies in a week.[24] The Salvation Army's six corps in Victoria had been established for less than a year, so passers-by must have purchased most of the copies. They were sold at one penny each. Unlike other denominational periodicals that advertised opinion and a calendar of meetings and bazaars, early issues of the *War Cry* are full of melodramatic testimony. Covers often feature rescue scenes, potent metaphors of burning buildings and shipwrecks. Inside, there are entertaining and inspiring tales of missionary success from North Melbourne and Ballarat and, further afield, London and New York. Accounts of street preaching are rich with metaphor and read like reports of an army's battle: "after firing some shots, we marched off ... making Our Voices Ring Through the Streets."[25] Through the selling of the *War Cry*, the voice of The Salvation Army was transported yet further than their drums and exhortations would carry—into the citizens' homes and workplaces.

The Salvation Army also adopted the morally instructive performances known as "services of song" that were so popular in other churches' Sunday School anniversaries and special worship services.[26] The pattern of readings and songs in costume owed much to oratorio, but so committed was The Salvation Army to the "service of song" they laid claim to it as their own particular invention.[27] Alert to new evangelical strategies for engagement with the public, Salvationists also adopted the limelight lecture, popular among other denominations. Limelight produced a bright light through the heating of calcium oxide with an oxyhydrogen flame and this allowed the old technology of the magic lantern slide to be projected on a large screen.[28] A crowd could share the experience of the "magic" and, centuries after the Reformation in which the Word reigned and chapels were whitewashed of imagery, Dissent again welcomed visual drama and performance.

With the addition of the cinematograph in the late 1890s, Salvationists made screen entertainments their own. In 1897 The Salvation Army purchased a newly invented Lumiere Cinematograph that could produce moving pictures of ninety seconds duration and project them with the aid of a carbon-arc light.[29] The Salvation Army's film screenings were uniquely early among the Australian churches, and its filmmaking was at the leading edge of Australian cinematography. The public thronged to their events. The Army established a special Limelight Department in 1892, and from 1898 they readily mixed the technologies of cinematograph and magic lantern, public lecture and "services of song" to produce original multimedia performances.[30] The movement's ventures in publicity were relentlessly forward-looking and innovative. Their performances crossed social and religious boundaries, and called people off the street to share in the visual spectacle and the vision.

The Salvation Army in the Field of Publicity and Performance

The Salvation Army's approach to publicity and performance was fundamental to their identity, and, despite similarities with other evangelicals, especially eighteenth-century Methodists, the scale and audacity of their efforts set them apart.[31] Publicity around ministry to the urban poor drew the attention of other Nonconformist churches, which quickly came to appreciate the Army's expertise, even requesting that they provide tours of the slums.[32] When David Ewers, editor of the Churches of Christ periodical *Christian Pioneer*, accompanied Salvationist Major James Barker on his nightly rounds in Lonsdale and Bourke Streets in 1889, he noted the authority with which Barker walked the slums. Ewers wondered why the government had not intervened to stop gambling and prostitution, and enforce sanitation. Nevertheless, rather than encourage political lobbying or establish new denominational welfare work, Ewers exhorted Churches of Christ readers to donate to The Salvation Army.[33] Evangelicals shared the Army's conversionist agenda, if not their publicity-seeking ways, and even sectarian groups recognized the Army's ministry in the streets.[34] They saw the Word in action.

Some churches continued to disapprove of Salvationist strategies, especially the use of street language and music-hall pageantry to "win" the streets. Other denominations regarded spectacle as a cause of notoriety rather than evidence of holiness; Dissent had long considered plain speech and modest deportment to be signifiers of piety.[35] Through Christian adherence, the colonial governments and churches desired a respectable civil society that could leave behind its convict origins. But the Salvation Army was an exception to the theology of middle-class piety, and historians have missed the Army's distinct and resolute refusal to equate wealthy respectability with salvation.[36] In contrast, contemporary newspaper reports most certainly did not overlook the discordant "nuisance" of the Army.[37] They wished that Salvationists would turn to "the ways of common sense and decency."[38] But Salvationists the world over mocked the idea that religion should provide a veneer of civility.[39] They preferred arrest for disturbing the peace and, subverting expectations about religious people, courted often violent local opposition.[40] Salvation Army officers elected prison over the payment of fines and, exchanging their uniforms for prison garb, were photographed.[41] Lists of injuries appeared in the *War Cry*: head wounds from projectiles, bruises from fights with larrikins, and the deaths of male and female officers from injuries received. These lists attested to the Salvationists' commitment to destabilize social norms, to minister in the streets (as almost all prosecutions were associated with "open-air" ministry), and, most especially, to their own identity as the persecuted faithful.[42] In this way, the Army situated itself in a long literary tradition of Christian martyrdom from the stoning of Stephen in Acts 7, to Eusebius's *History of the Martyrs of Palestine* (*c.* 315), John Foxe's *Acts and Monuments* (better known as *Foxe's Book of Martyrs*, first published in 1563), and Edmund Calamy's *Account of the Ministers and Others Ejected and Silenced* (1660–2).

Claims of persecution often provoked incredulity. The *South Australian Register* could not fathom the Salvationists' unreasonable refusal to observe the town of Kapunda's bylaws, even though the laws were instituted specifically to restrict their activities: "We do not see, therefore, that those who have been prosecuted can claim to *pose* as martyrs."[43] Posing melodramatically was seen as a large part of the problem, along with the fact that Salvationists constantly sought publicity which served to "gratify their love of notoriety."[44] The *Protestant Standard* defended its mockery of Salvationist lyrics saying that, if Salvation Army literature was of such a low standard, they "must expect to be criticised."[45] In 1882 the Reverend John Jefferies twice visited a Salvation Army service in Darwin. It was, he said, a "circus meeting." He observed the scripture verses on banners around the hall and the large cautionary notices beneath them warning people that police may arrest "any person interrupting the service or using profane language." Despite this, he complained, "all the noise and rampage, of which there was much, came from the platform and the band."[46] He suggested that decent (middle-class) behavior might have avoided persecution. However, the Army's distinctive style resonated with the largely working-class membership and implicitly criticized the ineffectiveness of the churches represented by ministers such as Jefferies.[47]

Unlike the public events of other Dissenting churches, those held at Salvationist meeting houses were specifically directed toward a working-class audience, forming part of the work that became known as Social Salvation. For instance, in the church notices in the local Brighton (Vic.) newspaper for September 22, 1900, was the news that the Baptists would hold a lecture titled "Mission Work in India" and the Congregational Church would host a "united Sunday School gathering," but The Salvation Army had invited the "South Australian Champion Rabbit Skinner ... to conduct special meetings and ... give his life story."[48] The fact that the "Champion Rabbit Skinner" would appear "in special costume" only added to the apparent social and cultural difference between the churches and The Salvation Army whose military costume already set them apart.

Military, Imperial, Social Transformation

The military metaphor provided much opportunity for the movement to differentiate itself from more staid churches and, with an element of theatre, create a distinct public identity. The Salvation Army began in 1865 as the East London Christian Mission, adopting its distinctive military name in 1878.[49] For William Booth, the military metaphor opened up a rhetorical world: congregations were known as corps and members were given military rank and costume. Uniforms designed for the women officers, or Hallelujah Lasses, provided them with a new way of being in public that was modest and yet attracted attention and that enabled them to speak with the authority of rank.[50] Military-style brass bands carried the sound of the Army in the open air, so that it could be heard throughout The Salvation Army's great parish of the streets.[51]

The military metaphor also fitted well with William Booth's imperial tendencies, and he dispensed with the organization's democratic structures, a legacy of its Methodist origins. The move to an autocratic structure coincided with a period of organizational expansion across England, the Empire, and America: from 72 congregations in 1879, the movement swelled to 1,749 British and 743 international congregations by 1886.[52] The growth in Australia was rapid too, numbering 31,100 members after the first two decades and claiming 0.82 percent of the Australian population in the 1901 census.[53]

Imperialism, capitalism, and revivalism came together in General William Booth.[54] He was concerned not only with the numerical growth of the movement in England but also with colonizing new lands. He suggested that the Salvationists might found "another Empire ... Why not?"[55] Booth pointed out that "in South Africa, Canada, Western Australia and elsewhere, there are millions of acres of useful land to be obtained almost for the asking."[56] In the book, *In Darkest England and the Way Out* (1890), Booth proposed that The Salvation Army could "secure a tract of land in one of these countries, prepare it for settlement, establish in it authority, govern it by equitable laws, assist it in times of necessity, settling it gradually with a prepared people, and so create a home for these destitute multitudes."[57] He explained that although his plans "ought to be taken up and carried out by the Government itself," The Salvation Army would have to step in because "there is no very near probability of Government undertaking it."[58] What sounds like audacity was actually the accepted practice in the colony of Victoria where The Salvation Army's first relief missions had begun seven years earlier in 1883. The Victorian government, more so than other colonial governments or the British government, relied on churches and benevolent organizations for the provision of welfare and it subsidized their work.[59] This colonial experience established an approach to relief provision that suited The Salvation Army with its hierarchical structures and ability to implement strategies unilaterally.

Before similar Salvationist institutions in London or New York, the Prison-gate home for men needing temporary accommodation on release from Melbourne's gaol was initiated by James Barker in December 1883, with the support and example of evangelical Anglican, Dr. John Singleton.[60] It was quickly followed that same month by a home for fallen women in Launceston, Tasmania, and in January 1884 by the Women's Prison-gate home in Carlton, Victoria.[61] A home and farm for delinquent youth, who were assigned to the Army's care by the colonial government, was opened in Heidelberg, north of Melbourne, in 1891. Again, this was the first Salvation Army institution of its type in the world, and a model for the organization internationally.[62] In Victoria where it all began, the work was appreciated by the colonial government which provided funding and the use of buildings at low rent.[63] In the last years of the nineteenth century, The Salvation Army, which had previously been known for its nuisance noise, became a great asset to the state. Public opinion shifted in favor of the organization and its pragmatic helpfulness. Public donation aided the growth of The Salvation Army to become, a century later, the largest of the faith-based charitable organizations in Australia.[64] The public put aside thoughts of The Salvation Army's confronting images of "Blood and Fire" and, along with government, supported practical Social Salvation in the cities.

On the inside cover of William Booth's *In Darkest England and the Way Out*, a visual aid to outreach was provided in the form of a folding colored lithographic map.[65] Amid a sea of human misery is the lighthouse of salvation: a popular nineteenth-century trope. Wretched individuals reach to be saved by Salvation Army officers on the shore. Beyond them is productive employment, first in the "city colony" with its Salvation Army enterprises, training schemes, and refuges. Then, stretching into the middle ground, there is the idyllic patchwork of the "Farm Colony" with its "five acres and a cow" (an acre more than Chartists had hoped for in the 1840s).[66] Above that, in the heavens, is "The Colony across the Sea": not a celestial destination, but a green land of work and redemption. At the peak of the arch that stretches over Booth's map of salvation are the words "Work for All." Unlike the schematic charts of premillennialist preachers, there is not just one path along which an individual must progress to be saved.⁶⁷ In Booth's architecture of social salvation there are many curving paths, each leading away from moral ruin and waste and into industrious productivity and economy of the saving of souls.⁶⁸

Despite the green landscape, this is not so much a vision of Arcadia⁶⁹ as an admittedly imperfect and pragmatic approach to the saving of souls in this time of sin.⁷⁰ William Booth confessed that he aspired to return the urban poor "not to the Garden of Eden, but to the ordinary conditions of life as they exist in healthy small community," for it is there that children "can grow up with a chance of saving both body and soul."⁷¹ Accordingly, the book has no Arcadian shepherds or sheep, except "the Lamb, the bleeding Lamb" of God.⁷² So, too, there are few agricultural terms but hundreds of references to labor, poverty, employment, and work. Salvationists saw no path back to Eden, no recovery of an uncorrupted pastoral age, but only a fallen world that was fast on the road to damnation. This vision applied not only to *In Darkest England* but also to every place on earth. It applied in Australia, and it required a life on the road where the "Son of Man has no place to lay His head" (Lk. 9:58). Following on from this passage, Catherine Booth preached that people everywhere were "going to everlasting death" and exhorted Christians to "put your hand to the plough."⁷³ The reference is to Lk. 9:62: "No one who puts a hand to the plough and looks back is fit for service in the Kingdom of God." Christian conversion demanded turning from the error-ridden past toward a holy future in which "work for all" created the necessary preconditions for salvation of all. The universal scope and saving ambition of William Booth's vision is forward-looking. Salvationists were not headed back to Eden.

When it came to practicalities, movement of people to other lands under the scheme proved difficult, not least because of the people who already lived there. Between 1891 and 1908, Booth, with the support of Cecil Rhodes, unsuccessfully attempted to gain funding from the British South Africa Company and the British government for a migration scheme and colony in southern Africa that would have housed and trained Britain's unemployed and their families, its reformed drunks and criminals.⁷⁴ Canada was likewise unreceptive.⁷⁵ Western Australia, having shaken off convict transportation as recently as 1868, was especially disinclined to accept Britain's unemployed and criminal classes regardless of promised moral reform. After several rounds of negotiations with the Western Australian government and a loss of heart on William's part, the 20,017-acre Collie Estate in the southwest did not become a colony but instead a Salvation Army children's home and farm.⁷⁶

Into the Terrain: Forward in the Darkness

When Commandant Herbert Booth arrived in Australia, he laid out his own forward-looking "Move-On Manifesto" in a sixteen-page edition of the *War Cry* for November 21, 1896. On the cover of this special edition, ranks of soldiers rally in the darkness. The scene is framed so that the viewer is alongside the soldiers, sharing their perspective, ready to be swept up into their cause. White light reflects on the soldier's hats and swords and, mounted on a white horse, Herbert calls them to charge "Forward" up the hill to the fortress of "immorality," "idolatry," "gambling," and "drink."⁷⁷ The landscape is precipitous and the flora buffeted by winds, while a valley that might accommodate five-acre lots shines beyond. The metaphorical fight between darkness and light carried on, and an English castle could represent Australian sin just as easily as English sin. Herbert's scheme was based on his father's, but this was an Australasian manifesto. It was addressed to the regular troops of The Salvation Army, destined to be read by the public who purchased the *War Cry* from street sellers, and its publication was reported by city newspapers across the country.[78]

Herbert had flair for organization and publicity, highly useful skills in a practical denomination in which theology was undertaken by those further up the chain of command. He arranged for a public launch that filled the Independent Church (Congregational) in Collins Street, Melbourne. The *War Cry* proudly reported on the success of this publicity event, noting the observations of the Congregational minister Dr. Llewelyn Bevan that "his church was too small for us now. We had to go to the Town Hall or the Exhibition, but he fully expected we should soon want the cricket ground."[79] In Booth's manifesto launch, Bevan witnessed the scope of Salvation Army ambition, and his approval bolstered publicity.

In the broader writings of The Salvation Army, darkness hung over the people of Britain and her colonies in a rhetoric that had its origins in scripture: "people loved darkness instead of light because their deeds were evil" (Jn 3:19). The rhetoric of darkness was popular in colonial texts too. In the 1880s, the journalist and adventurer Henry Morton Stanley had returned from "Darkest Africa" with reports of evil and exploitation. General William Booth's manifesto, *In Darkest England and the Way Out*, argued that evil was not some exotic threat, for "Darkest Africa" has its "parallel at our own doors": there are "within a stone's throw of our cathedrals and palaces similar horrors to those which Stanley has found existing in the great Equatorial forest."[80] The same applied in Australia because, as Booth insisted, it was "absurd to speak of the Colonies as if they were a foreign land. They are simply pieces of Britain distributed about the world, enabling the Britisher to have access to the richest parts of the earth." The General's colonialist economics acknowledged distance, but terrain played no part and colonial Australians were "the same people" as those back in England.[81] Mainstream slum journalism, more concerned with shock value than soteriology, also relied on the rhetoric of light modern civilization and dark primitive slums.[82] In an article headlined "Slumtown, Its Curious Inhabitants, Dark Alleys Visited," there is a description of a laneway in the vicinity of Little Lonsdale: "It is a long lane that has no turning … At the end is the great shadow of shadows, the portals of death."[83] Darkness, with its long prehistory, was powerful. It required a powerful force to drive it back: an Army, a manifesto, and artillery of pageantry, pathos, and literary tropes.

In Herbert Booth's "Move-On Manifesto," there is no mention of "Darkest Africa" or "Darkest England," despite the castle on the cover and the heavy reliance on General Booth's book. No longer in the old world, Herbert wrote for an optimistic readership in anticipation of a new federated nation. He began with headlines in a variety of bold fonts, "Hallelujah! Advance Australasia! A Bold and Daring Declaration."[84] There was a "Splendid Array of Projects," some of which were deemed too ambitious and hastily forgotten after the pageantry of their announcement.[85] Social welfare institutions were already strong in Victorian Salvationism, and they became a priority for Herbert who saw a significant number through to operation. His manifesto listed those planned for specific Australian and New Zealand towns: food and shelter depots for Newcastle, Adelaide, Bendigo, Melbourne, Sydney, Brisbane, and Christchurch; and rescue homes (new or enlarged) for Hobart, Bathurst, Perth, Townsville, Ballarat, Newcastle, Melbourne, Sydney, Christchurch, and Dunedin.[86] New accommodation would provide many more beds for the poor. But the detail of costs and fundraising was beyond the scope of the manifesto. This was publicity, and all about covering the territory.

Traveling the Far Reaches of Empire

Herbert Booth's proposed programs were those of the Army's proto-empire, delivered with only a little local adaptation, a tweak for circumstance or argot. The "Great Circle Scheme," intended to evangelize the countryside, resembled Methodist circuit ministries in Canada and Australia. Selling the idea afresh to "Australasia's Troops" in 1896, Herbert explained how the Army "must also reach the inhabitants of the village, the hamlet," and, supplementing these English terms with some Australian places, "the gold-digger's camp and the cattle-drover's hut."[87] He gave the example of how a "Circle Corps" might have charge of "five villages, namely—Potter's Bar, Potter's Bank, Smithfield, Bisley, and Norton's Green."[88] These English place names exposed his British assumptions. But below the paragraph there is a diagram, a "Plan for an Australian Circle Corps" drawn in an unknown hand. Perhaps it is Herbert's. The western Victorian town of Kaniva (where a corps was already established) is identified as the "centre," and the roads to Lillimur, Bunyip, Cove, and Lawloit (misspelled "Lowloit") are marked. This small drawing mapped Herbert's scheme, trans-Atlantic in origin, onto the Australian landscape.

Australia was not a "foreign land" in the Salvationist imagination, but Herbert recognized that it was not entirely like Britain either. He thanked heaven that "we are no longer in a land, the rural districts of which are ruled exclusively by the Squire. We are citizens of a free country."[89] Herbert was grateful that in Australian towns "the braid of the Captain commands as much respect as the surplice of the Parson," school buildings could be rented for meetings, and governments supported the Salvationists' welfare work.[90] This was a great wide land of evangelical opportunity. Not even distance would pose a problem in Herbert's scheme. Travel within a "Circle Corps" would be facilitated by the willing supply of farmers' horses, borrowed for weekend use. His officers could then cover "ten, fifteen, or even twenty miles." Never mind that it was nearly thirty miles from Lillimur to Lawloit. Herbert was determined to move forward with practical solutions to the problems of the Australian landscape.

Lack of transport had, to date, hampered The Salvation Army's progress in rural areas and on the cities' edges. Transgressing the boundary of sacred and secular, Herbert proposed using bicycles. They were, he admitted, "a powerful instrument in the service of the Devil" but, if used strictly for the purposes of mission, the "Wheel for Jesus" could be a great asset.[91] This new land demanded that The Salvation Army deal pragmatically with the old-world prohibitions: "Think what a Company of red-hot Salvationists, who could be concentrated [via bicycle] upon any given point ten or twelve miles from a City, could accomplish."[92] Herbert Booth thought of the landscape as something that must be crossed. For red-hot modern missionaries, Australia's ancient soil was a place of transit and transition.

Through the Lens

Adjutant Joseph Perry traversed the Australian continent a number of times with his "Triple Lantern Oxy-ether Limelight."[93] He presented his "Limelight Entertainment" in cities and in country towns where, in some cases, such technology had never been seen before. It was a ministry of evangelism and goodwill that generated positive publicity for the Army and funds for its projects. It also provided wholesome entertainment, a novel alternative to gambling dens and public houses. The local press regularly reported large crowds that Salvationists hoped put a dint in the profits of the towns' pubs. Over the course of several evenings in each country town, Perry presented a range of melodramas, scenic views, and biblical narratives that he augmented with dramatic sound and lighting effects. In the early 1890s, most of these magic lantern shows were presented using commercially produced slide sets: English melodrama and biblical scenes from French lantern-slide manufacturers were readily available.[94] These were purchased with a text for recitation, which Perry performed along with his wife Julia. One of the most popular was "Jane Conquest, or How She Rang the Bell."[95] It was a story of a woman with an ailing baby who sees a boat burning and goes to the church to raise the alarm so that the crew can be rescued. The tropes were recognized by Christians everywhere, but scenes of self-denial and rescue from drowning spoke to Salvationists with their colored lithographs. Hundreds of miles inland, in southwestern New South Wales, the sacred truth of rescue off the British coast was immediate and present, and Perry's lighting and sound effects were "almost too real."[96] In decoding the story through a Salvationist lens, viewers became insiders. Conversions were anticipated.

Scenes tell stories of the people's relationship to the landscape. While there are no transcripts of Perry's commentary, his choice of landscape slides and the reporting of their reception by audiences are revealing. The thirty slides of "A trip to Coolgardie and back," depicting the newly opened Western Australian goldfields, were "appreciated" and "possessed a fascinating interest."[97] More enthusiastically, the many English-born residents of Hay in southwestern New South Wales were "delighted" with scenes of London: "It would be impossible, in cold print, to give any idea of the effect the various pictures had upon an intensely interested audience, and applause was plentiful."[98] Scenes of the motherland elicited heartfelt response. In 1896 the Australian landscape spoke of progress and possibility, but not yet of home.

Australian patriotism was on the rise as momentum toward Federation grew, and Perry filmed as he traveled. He photographed The Salvation Army corps in towns around Australia and displayed them in his lantern shows.[99] At Goulburn in New South Wales he showed scenes of Queensland, Tasmania, and New Zealand.[100] He indulged the melodramatic interests of audiences with his own images of disaster: the Footscray powder factory fire in Melbourne, and the erupting Waimangu geyser in New Zealand.[101] Notoriety, novelty, and the exotic otherness of Aboriginal people were thrown together in slides depicting the Western Australian house of murderer Frederick Deeming, palm trees, and "native prisoners chained to the wheelbarrows."[102] Such images drew a crowd, and Perry took the opportunity to show them slides of The Salvation Army in Australia. Working towards the vision of *In Darkest England*, he displayed scenes of the Farm Colony at Pakenham in Victoria and various institutions for rescue and reform.[103] The Army fulfilled its call to cover the territory of Australia through Perry's photography.

As the Salvationists crossed the landscape, they used publicity to advantage. Cornelie and Herbert Booth traveled to all the colonies on a tour promoting the "Move-On Manifesto" during 1896–7, and the *War Cry* carried pictures of their reception in major cities and suburbs. The drawings make the venues appear as great cavernous auditoriums, filled with the faithful who are focused toward the Booths on the distant stage. Casual readers of the *War Cry* are drawn in as they too view the scene from within the crowd: participants in the spectacle.[104] After the Booths arrived in Sydney, the cover of the *War Cry* was dedicated to the success of the publicity campaign, which saw the event of their arrival reported in the daily press. Aspiring to showmanship, the lead article boasted that the colorful parade "made as effective an advertisement as even the great Barnum himself could have desired."[105]

Publicity attracted opposition too and, despite William Booth's insistence that all publicity is good, Herbert found himself in conflict with the established players on the stage of Australian religious life. While reporting on the Booths' tour events, the local press also ran articles on the furor over Herbert's plans for the Pacific. The Salvation Army's mooted expansion into Fiji, Papua, and the East Indies was outlined over three pages in the "Move-On Manifesto." The scheme included a hand drawn "War Map of our New Missionary Operations," though the details appear to be derived from popular nature and travel guides. The extensive references to "luxuriant lands that besprinkle the Southern Seas," inventories of flora and fauna, and the listing of seemingly exotic island peoples alongside population statistics (as an indicator of potential converts) read like so much nineteenth-century travel literature. Booth's plans were loosely draped over lands that were almost completely unknown to their would-be missioners.[106] Nevertheless, other denominations and mission agencies, already feeling the loss of membership to The Salvation Army on Australian soil, were outraged over the new "War" and quickly on the defense of their Pacific missions. In an interview in Brisbane's *Telegraph*, Herbert deflected Wesleyan and Anglican concerns while conceding that the Army would in fact focus its efforts on the East Indies, especially Java where there was already a Salvationist presence.[107] In the end, Java remained the only outpost.[108] Herbert would have enough challenge implementing the manifesto in the Army's home territory, the city streets.

Players in the Drama of the Streets

"We are in touch with slums. They are our speciality! … We know 'how the poor live' and also 'how they die.' We know because we are there."[109] Following the pattern set in England and North America, The Salvation Army's first Australian corps had formed in urban areas and they remained numerically stronger in cities. In Victoria's July 7, 1883, issue of the *War Cry*, the corps are listed as Melbourne, Little Bourke

Street, Collingwood, Prahran, Hotham (North Melbourne), and Ballarat. All were urban areas with substantial areas of poverty. The July 14 issue ran news from the 1st New York corps that, in the fight against the devil, called itself "The Invincibles."[110] By July 21, 1883, the Melbourne corps had adopted fighting names too. Hotham was the "Death and Glory Band," Prahran was "Daniel's Band" who "hold the gospel banner high; / on to vict'ry grand; / Satan and his host defy, / and shout for Daniel's band."[111] With reference to the Heavenly King, the Ballarat corps became "The King's Own" and the IV Melbourne corps based in Little Bourke Street was, like New York, "The Invincibles."[112] The adoption of a name could signal a new public persona and a new resolve. It also signaled allegiance. Colonial Anglican and Catholic churches were named for saints from other lands in the hope that the sacred associations of these names and places might be transferred to what seemed to be a spiritually vacant landscape. Salvationists named their corps for the universal landscape of battle.

In the rhetoric of The Salvation Army, the landscape of the city was a backdrop to the theater of good and evil, with The Salvation Army officers as the heroic protagonists. The language is revealing. In 1883 the *War Cry* reported that the soldiers of Emerald Hill undertook "a march into the enemy's territory."[113] In Moonta, South Australia, preaching was described in similarly theatrical and military terms: "Mrs Gibbs opened fire inside," while "Sister Ross … started to shoot in the open air," and at Hotham a "prisoner was taken."[114] In Little Bourke Street, Melbourne, it was reported that "the old devil has got some mighty forts here but by God's help we mean to pull them down and rescue the perishing inmates."[115] Their rhetoric was distinctive. Other denominations preaching in the streets did not employ the language of "mighty forts" and "the enemy's territory." In contrast, Methodist missioner W. G. Taylor described a Sydney street corner where he regularly preached as "Consecrated!," "a hallowed corner," "a sacred spot," and "a garden of the Lord."[116] Unlike other denominations, The Salvation Army understood the city as a place of sin, and the streets and laneways constituted a stage on which the drama of the war with the devil was enacted.

Mapping the Territory's Dangers

Toward the turn of the century, the military rhetoric became more subdued and talk of enemies tended to focus less on sinners and more on social evils. The political agitation of temperance campaigning accompanied the Army's rescue work with abused women and neglected children. In 1901 a temperance map of Melbourne was "specially drawn for the War Cry."[117] The "Map Showing the Liquor Shops of Melbourne City" followed the precedent set by London's 1886 map of public houses[118] but marked out Melbourne's streets and pinpointed the "Public-Houses, Wine Shops and Merchants, Licensed Grocers, Betting Clubs [and Salvation] Army Institutions."[119] The map provides a graphic demarcation between the many places of evil and the few places of good. While London's map is distinguished only by the red dots of public houses, the "Map Showing the Liquor Shops of Melbourne City" shows the central Melbourne grid bordered with chains, kegs, and bottles. A skull and crossbones hover above the map's legend. This was not only information, but drama.

The Salvation Army's temperance map closely resembles the sparsely styled "Hutchinson's Exhibition Pocket Map of Melbourne," which was produced for the Melbourne Exhibition in 1880 and highlights the General Post Office, Eastern Market, Victoria Market, and "Old Cemetery," Flagstaff Gardens, hospital and gaol, government offices, and parliament house.[120] This was, in turn, based on a map of "Melbourne and Its Suburbs," published in 1855 by the office of the colony's surveyor general, which shows properties, banks, schools, churches, markets, and other places of interest.[121] But unlike Kearney's detailed map and Hutchinson's tourist map, The Salvation Army's map is highly selective in its choice of landmarks.

The city's coat of arms with its motto of progress, *Vires Acquirit Eundo* (we gather strength as we go), is prominent in the top left corner as a starting point for readers and followers of an army. However, only sinister civic institutions are shown: the police courts and gaol, the hospital and the cemetery (while Queen Victoria Market, which shared the site, is unmarked). For those seeking direction, the compass rose rests in the cemetery grounds, loaded with moral imperative. The map demonstrated that Salvationists knew the city landscape well and that they viewed it through a distinctive lens. In contrast, the 1903 conference program of the theologically conservative Churches of Christ featured

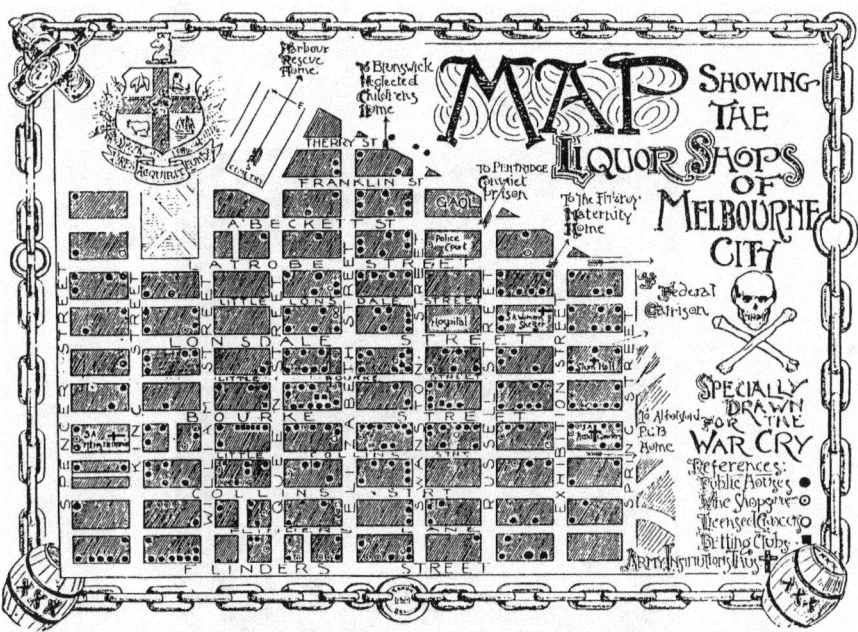

Figure 4. *Map Showing the Liquor Shops of Melbourne City*, August 3, 1901, *The War Cry*.
Source: The Salvation Army Australia Museum, Melbourne.

photographs of Melbourne's major public institutions as if the church and city were one.[122] Most often the didactic religious imagery of this period served to socialize Christians to a life of quiet moral citizenry.[123] But Salvationist images readied their readers for the "great battle for souls" in streets where menace lay just around the corner.[124] The earthly landscape, Australian or otherwise, was largely enemy territory.

Signposts and "Social Salvation"

The extant lantern slides from Cornelie Booth's "Social Salvation" depict a dire urban landscape too. There are no bucolic scenes, and domesticity is most often portrayed in decay and anguish. In a slide labeled "Your Mother Still prays for You, Jack," Salvation Army officers, nurses, and a gravedigger with shovel in hand stand around a coffin. The painted canvas backdrop features a high wall and, beyond that, outlines of cypress against a dark sky. This landscape is not about particular Australian locales but universal mortal drama. In the slide "Sowing the Wind," subtitled "10. Gave a shame-faced recognition," a band of Salvationists (including Herbert Booth himself) stand with tambourine, flag, and drum at the end of a dead-end road. They are flanked by towering brick factory walls, hand-colored in tan brown to match the stone paving. A man in a brown suit departs the dead-end road. He is a part of this brown industrial scene, embodying its moral load.[125] The Salvationists' dark blue uniforms and red ribbons contrast with their surroundings.

Figure 5. *Sowing the Wind, 10. Gave a shame-faced recognition.*
Source: Glass lantern slide, *c.* 1898, The Salvation Army Australia Museum, Melbourne.

Scenes such as this were hailed for their reality, but their constructed nature is clear. Canvas backdrops and Melbourne's bluestone paving in tan brown were not real. They were pictures made to tell a contemporary story: a story without local geographic distinction, a universal story that could be told anywhere the Salvationists traveled. The lantern-slide scenes were part of the show in which reality was a selling point. With "the aid of camera and limelight" and the new technology of film sequences, such images were constructed in response to what Salvationists described as "the popular cry ... 'Let us see something that will burn through our eyes, thrill our being, and help us to comprehend the reality of what you say.'"[126] Truth required the signposts of a carefully composed photograph.

Salvation was embodied and therefore gendered. These extant lantern slides depict scenes that correspond to Salvationist patterns of men's testimony: "narrow escapes from death" and recognition of the sinfulness of their violence, abuse, and wasteful neglect that resulted from drinking and gambling.[127] Women's testimony more often spoke of conversion as an answer to unfulfilled longing: a completion of the self in God.[128] Salvationist narratives portrayed women's religious fulfillment as a substitute for hopes dashed in the broken domesticity of abusive men and unmarried motherhood, and a prompt to escape such situations. In the pages of the *War Cry*, few women reported on their own shame and rescue from prostitution, but third-person tales abound. Rescue stories were used to promote the "Social Salvation" lecture in a semi-regular column titled "The Social Cinematographe."[129] Characterized by a sense of urgency and drama, the stories are located in the landscape only by mention of Salvation Army institutions, as if they are the only reliable signposts: "G____ was a bright, noble-looking girl, yet her bright sky was darkened by the same cloud which has overshadowed so many lives ... She came to our Launceston Home."[130] Herbert and Cornelie Booth made clear to readers that such women were not wicked, but victims whose sad circumstances might be changed.

"The Social Cinematographe" and Slum Journalism

The stories in "The Social Cinematographe" form a narrative background to the life-model images of rescued women used in the limelight and film event, "Social Salvation." Publicity for Herbert and Cornelie's "Powerful, Thrilling and Pathetic Lecture" appeared in the *War Cry* and lantern slides from the lecture were reproduced in its pages. The cover of the May 7, 1898, issue of the *War Cry* depicts a crowd of "Hallelujah Lasses" standing among the prostitutes, children, and Chinese who were out at night "In Melbourne Slums."[131] Virtuous women were otherwise unheard of in such streets after dark. Even journalists typically traveled the streets of the slums at night with police guard, if not for protection, at least for rhetorical purposes in the reporting of darkness and danger.[132] The Salvationist women are likewise situated rhetorically: outside Beecham's timber yard and joinery factory. At the corner of Spencer Street and Bourke Street, it was a "dangerous locality" recognizable to Melbourne readers.[133]

More often, Salvationist scenery was universal, like their mission to convert. The cover of the June 18, 1898, issue of the *War Cry* depicts a woman's rescue. The walls are stained and the room unfurnished. A timber box serves as a bedside table, while the young woman sleeps disheveled and vulnerable under a crumpled blanket on the floor. This fallen woman's lowly status forms the picture's low horizontal axis. Dominating the scene, the neatly uniformed Cornelie Booth stands upright in the doorway, her head inclined and finger pointing. Mrs Booth's presence creates a "benevolent moment" in which the reader might identify with the rescuer and join her in benevolent sympathy for the fallen.[134] As the manifesto stated, transformative change would come with "a place of refuge whereunto they may safely resort and find board and lodging without having to risk their very souls as the price."[135]

Reports of the evils of Melbourne's slums, especially those of Little Bourke Street, appeared intermittently in Melbourne's press. Slum journalism almost always assumed that "slum-dwellers inhabited a separate moral universe," where prostitution, gambling, and addiction were rife.[136] Reporters confided to their readers, "The worst of the hovels and loathsome dens exist in the very heart of the city, and one may walk round the block almost without knowing of the nearness of the evil."[137] The residents, especially the Chinese, were portrayed as subhuman, and calls to rid Melbourne of slums followed. But here Salvationists differed. While they were resolutely melodramatic in their representation of human suffering and regularly detailed the wounds and infestations of abused women for readers, they did not depict the slum-dwellers as other than human or as necessarily deserving of their fate.[138] Challenging popular sentiment, Herbert Booth claimed that the pregnant women in the refuge were from decent families, as were the fathers of the unborn children. They were not mere lower-class domestic servants as the public might imagine and, in any case, poverty was not a sin.[139] Others, according to the *War Cry*, were victims of abuse; it was holy and right to seek out such victims for God's sake, and without the reporter's police guard. As the temperance map demonstrated, all the people of earth were fallen. Only salvation offered light.

Limelight and Transformation in Bricks and Mortar

The "Social Salvation" limelight lecture publicized the rescue work of The Salvation Army. It was reported with interest and approval in newspapers across the continent as the lecture was presented in cities and towns. Importantly, the lectures aided fundraising to further the refuge-building program. At Prahran Town Hall in June 1898 over £40 were received in donations and ticket sales.[140] At South Melbourne Town Hall they raised £23, and at Malvern Congregational Church £25, equating to perhaps 460 and 500 in attendance.[141] Cornelie Booth's lecture, "Life in the Slums of our Great Cities," delivered on a rainy winter's night, resulted in over £80.[142] The metrics mattered in the Booths' salvation economy. Ticket sales were counted, as were beds, meals, and souls.

The "Great Social Salvation Carnival" held at Melbourne's Exhibition Building in August 1898 was intended to further publicize the social work of the Army and raise funds for its expansion. Herbert had successfully produced gala events in London, managing multiple live acts, music, and lighting. With over 180 performers in acts

Figure 6. *At Noonday and Midnight in Gaol, Slum and Opium Den.*
Source: *War Cry*, June 18, 1898. The Salvation Army Australia Museum, Melbourne.

scheduled to the minute at one of the biggest venues in Melbourne, he was in his element. While other denominations held public annual meetings where reports were tabled for discussion and motions debated, The Salvation Army performed their annual reports in song and in costume—and they charged admission too, at one shilling a ticket.[143] These were not the Army's well-known songs about salvation and heavenly reward. They were very much about the practicalities of earthly existence. To The Salvation Army tune "He's the Lily of the Valley," they sang,

> In eighteen ninety-seven
> Sixty thousand beds supplied!
> Tis a triumph which we joyfully relate:
> And workmen, hunger-driven,
> The gnawing wolf defied,
> For ninety thousand meals we sold at cheapest rate.
>
> Come patronise the shelter!
> The Workman's Metropole!
> An institution always up to date;
> If out of cash, no matter,
> For here, without a dole,
> You can earn your bed and breakfast "while you wait."[144]

The men at the Workingmen's Metropole chopped wood and worked to pay for their lodgings and meals. Scheduled on the "Great Social Salvation Carnival" program for 8:30 p.m. was a film illustrating the Army's aid to the industrious poor: a "kinematographe view of a dead-beat earning his dinner."[145] Further Carnivals staged in 1899 and 1900 reiterated that a moral life was to be found in productivity.[146]

Herbert Booth explained his approach to aid and enterprise on a lecture tour around Australia. Outlining the Army's strategy to an audience in Brisbane, Herbert was reported as saying, "To give a man food without also giving him work is only to make his stomach a medium for demoralising his character."[147] The touring "Social Salvation" lecture included footage of "the wood yard where men earn their meals by chopping and sawing wood."[148] It is almost certainly the same film that was remembered in *The Victory* as "Wood-chopping at the Metropole" (perhaps also shown with "Richard earning his breakfast in the morning") and as "a dead-beat earning his dinner." Local reporters and crowds received the film with great enthusiasm.[149] Herbert was careful to be seen to insist that the cinematograph must "assist the Salvation and Social Work" if it was to be part of the "Salvation Army's armoury."[150] The innovative technology had enormous potential for publicity and there was no room for idle entertainments, just as there was no room for idle lodgers. In The Salvation Army's urban landscape of transformation, change came about through industry, works were measured, and—"always up to date"—modernity was key to expansion.

Church buildings altered the landscape of Australia. The Salvation Army's citadels and meeting halls were modest, but their program of social institution building was on a scale disproportionate to their membership. The 1890s depression aided the acquisition of property. Herbert told audiences in New South Wales that the Melbourne

Metropole was built for £8000 on land worth £1000, totaling £9000 in value, and astutely purchased by the Army for only £2000. Even with £1000 in "fittings and repairs," they had made an excellent capital investment.[151] No donation would be wasted in the Army's program of institution building through the Federation depression.

Later in the evening of the "Great Social Salvation Carnival" of 1898 the limelight lantern provided "fascinating views of our most recent institutions for the young." Salvation Army reform for adolescents included moral instruction and basic education but was focused on training for employment in domestic work, factories, and farming. This was celebrated in a performance by the girls of the Industrial Home in a song "with effects":

> Good evening, friends! We all reside at Heidelberg Girls' Home,
> Where we from sin are taught to flee and to the Saviour come ...
> And we are taught to useful be, as time is flying past—
> To sweep and dust, to wash and iron—not slow, but very fast.[152]

Verses about reading and arithmetic, knitting and gardening follow. Children were often used in pageantry and publicity by churches and charitable agencies, coopted to represent the future of a busy young nation.[153] A performance by the boys of the reformatory in Bayswater (now The Basin, Vic.) declared, "If you want dairying seen at its best, / Come to 'The Eden' by special request."[154] In reality, the boys themselves did not request to enter The Eden but were sent there by the government as wards of the state. The institution's name was likewise incongruent with Salvationist theology, but Herbert Booth was more of an entrepreneur than a theologian. The Eden was not a paradise and the nickname was forgotten in favor of the title Bayswater Boys' Home, reflecting the loss of innocence that came with a history of institutional abuse.[155]

"What Is Needed Is a System"

Booth had visited The Eden earlier in the year, and productivity and modern systems of farming featured heavily in the resulting publicity. In April 1898 the *War Cry* illustrated The Salvation Army's new social institution on acreage at Bayswater via sketches of the various buildings and facilities intended to provide wayward boys with farming skills. "The Dormitory—Interior" shows the two neat lines of beds for the boys in a long room. Below is a sketch of "The Piggeries" with two neat rows of stalls, and, on the next page, "The Cow Sheds and Dairy" repeats the theme with two rows of cows lined up for milking in a "scientific looking" purpose-built cow shed and dairy.[156] Modern efficiencies were applied to all. The latest technology was in use: "22,000 gallons of water can be pumped in a few hours," part of "an almost perfect system of irrigation." This was a model farm committed to productivity and the elimination of waste.[157] The headline read "H. H. Booth, Farmer, Bayswater," and the farm was claimed as the magnificent result of Herbert's "Manifesto." The *War Cry* reported that the "Commandant of The Salvation Army is justifiably proud."[158]

In his "Move-On Manifesto" Herbert had argued that "what is needed is a system … [a man from the city] is trained to become a son of the soil; a system which, having thus released him from the City Maelstrom, plants him out upon the rich and generous lands."[159] Herbert owed a good deal to his father's Farm Colony scheme from *In Darkest England* and to the widespread late-Victorian view that time spent in the country air or, better, a rural life was healthy and perhaps even redemptive.[160] By 1898, the Army in Victoria had some experience in training for agriculture, having established a farm colony at Pakenham in 1892. There the "colonists" (named according to William Booth's Farm Colony scheme, rather than Herbert's poetic "son of the soil") were trained in agricultural skills and heard lectures on horticultural science by botanist Christopher Mudd, FLS, FRGS, who had recently come to faith through the preaching of Herbert's brother, Ballington Booth.[161] Mudd also had a poetic appreciation of the natural world, though the publicity around the farm colonies suggests that neither Pakenham's "colonists" nor Bayswater's "son of the soil" had time for contemplation of the rural idyll. Unlike the first Eden, this was a place of hard labor. It was not a return to nature or an ideal society borne of late-nineteenth-century utopianism.[162] It did not address the political and economic causes of social problems. Rather, the farming program within Booth's "Social Salvation" attempted to provide practical training for employment at a distance from dense human populations where sin was rife.[163]

Visiting Bayswater in 1898, Herbert conducted a tour for the benefit of Salvation Army officers who had come to Melbourne from around Australia for the Army's Inter-colonial Congress. He also invited members of the press. As a measure of the resulting publicity's success, comment from an article in the *Age* was reprinted in the *War Cry*: "A great number of improvements have been effected since the Army came into possession" of the farm.[164] The reporter noted that the enterprise was "built upon the most modern lines" and listed several statistics, no doubt supplied by the Army. But the article was not reprinted in full. Editor Brigadier Etherington omitted the mocking conclusion to the article in the *Age*: "One [boy] told me yesterday that he would like to spend his life in gaol, for then he would have a good long rest."[165] This was systematic reform in which idleness was sin and productivity a precursor to salvation. Paradise and rest, in Salvationist eschatology, was for the life to come.

"Soldiers of the Cross" in a Landscape Transformed

Heavenly reward for martyrs was assured, as Joseph Perry and Herbert Booth reminded audiences of "Soldiers of the Cross." Like "Social Salvation," "Soldiers of the Cross" consisted of lantern slides, music and singing, short film sequences and narration by Herbert and Cornelie Booth, but it was longer, grander, and, innovatively, one continuous narrative.[166] Opening at the Melbourne Town Hall in 1900 and touring for over a year, "Soldiers of the Cross" was the story of Christ and the persecution of early Christians. After years of arrests for open-air evangelizing, persecution had become part of The Salvation Army's own narrative. This film event situated the Army's story in the long literary tradition of Christian martyrdom.

Herbert Booth, who played the part of a martyr alongside his duties as director and narrator, had personally felt the sting of criticism for his work. Salvationists had attacked him over the constant attention he received in the *War Cry*, his propensity to fraternize with the ruling class, and his pursuit of social salvation infrastructure at the apparent expense of spiritual matters.[167] He responded saying, "I know no difference between spiritual and secular in the Army."[168] "Soldiers of the Cross" represented a return to spiritual themes. It also blurred the boundary of spiritual and secular in the work of The Salvation Army and the landscape of Australia.

"Soldiers of the Cross" required that both people and landscape be costumed and transformed. Local officers acted in the lantern-slide tableaux and film, and, just as they had put on uniforms to become Salvation Army officers, they donned Roman robes to become early Christian martyrs. The local Victorian landscape was transformed into that of the early church. The tennis court at the Murrumbeena Girls' Home became the hills outside Rome and the landscape of the Holy Land. Canvases were painted with Mediterranean scenery and suspended from the tennis court fence—stone city walls and flat-roofed houses, rocks and steep hills unlike anything in Melbourne's southeastern sand belt. The secular landscape of social reform at Murrumbeena was overlaid with the sacred inscribed on canvas flats. Other scenes used the borrowed landscape of local grass and trees, adding a canvas Roman wall beside which the persecuted huddled and prayed. The Limelight Department's Life Model Studio in the roof space at The Salvation Army Headquarters in Bourke Street, Melbourne, was transformed into all manner of dwellings from the biblical past. Behind the city building, early church martyrs were burned at the stake, the landscape converted with the unrolling of a painted backdrop.

Another canvas was unrolled for the projection of the fifteen films and two hundred lantern slides at screenings across Australia and New Zealand.[169] Sometimes film was projected directly on to the side of city buildings. Crowds gasped at the graphic portrayal of the martyrs' deaths and reporters penned their approval of the authenticity of the scenes.[170] Decades of Holy Land tourism pictures, Sunday School geography lessons and illustrated bibles acquainted a broad audience with the landscape of Christian origins. Many of the backdrops appear familiar, possibly based on earlier representations of the biblical world. Sometimes the lineage is clear: a lantern slide of Jean-Leon Gerome's "The Christian Martyrs' Last Prayer" (1883) was included in the presentation and another scene featured Salvation Army actors against a canvas backdrop painted to resemble Gerome's Colosseum. One representation authorized another. The Australian landscape was a dressed set, a theatre readied for the work of conversion.

Performing Transformation

The stage is inherently a place of transformation. Herbert and Cornelie Booth, Joseph Perry and the *War Cry* understood the power of dramatic narrative to change lives and to recast an audience's vision, even if that meant making the landscape universal rather than peculiarly Australian. Their approach was theatrical: melodramatic stories and images in the *War Cry*, parades and news reports, limelight presentations that were

Figure 7. *Cross Series, Christians in Valley, 38b. The Arrest by the Soldiers.*
Source: Glass lantern slide, *c.* 1900, The Salvation Army Australia Museum, Melbourne.

"almost too real," and film and stage productions that rivaled secular shows. When Melbourne's satirical newspaper, *Punch*, mockingly observed that "The Salvation Army furnishes the adherents with both church and theatre," it did not realize the praise it offered.[171] Indeed, The Salvation Army happily claimed that it had "come nearer to solving that much-discussed problem—the union of the church and the *stage*—than any other body of people."[172] On stage, in the streets, and in the press, The Salvation Army invited the public into its transformative vision through pageantry and contagious exuberance.[173]

Publicity was an essential work of The Salvation Army in the period leading up to 1901 and its glorious participation in the procession at the Inauguration of the Commonwealth. The Army appeared well established in urban Australia after only two decades, and its visible contribution to state welfare made it seem promisingly close to the heart of the new nation. This further aided the Army's few members in the raising of funds and the conversion of wasted lives to productivity. The Salvation Army's practical ministry served a transformative purpose, and this purpose colored its vision of any landscape, including Australia's. Change was needed everywhere in this fallen world. Earthly existence was a transit, a place of many curving paths which might (or might not) lead on to Glory. Salvationists, with their model farms, metropoles, and reformatories, altered the landscape with little concern for the particularities of place. Through their performances and publications, they treated the parish of the streets as a stage on which the drama of salvation was played out. The Australian landscape itself was altered only a little but, through a Salvationist lens, it was seen as a stage set for the transformation of lives and identities. In the end, earthly geography made little difference. The Army unrolled its manifesto across the landscape like it unrolled a canvas backdrop from a tennis court fence.

5

Landscape of Here and Elsewhere: Congregational Poetry at Home in War and Peace, 1914–30

In the dark years of the Great War, poetry offered those left at home here in this sunny land a means to speak of bleak tragedy elsewhere. Australians traveled half a world away to join the fight. Mothers waited, keeping vigil. The sons they had called in from play had been called away to war.

> Mother, such a long way back
> Before I left the mountain track,
> I knew you set the candle high and opened wide the door,
> And when the last bend came in sight
> I knew I'd see the watching light.[1]

Despite Australia's geographic distance from Europe's catastrophe, poetry gave voice to the memory of faraway sons. Men and women sent their poems to be published in newspapers, church journals, and booklets.[2] They hoped to give comfort to the bereaved and expression to the experience of those left at home, far from the action and yet intimately involved in its grief and consequence. In the face of the Great War's enormity and significance, these poets struggled with the limits of language.[3] Their verse was often earnestly mediocre and reliant on Romanticism's clichés of honor and heroism.[4] Many poems peddle a mixture of patriotism and politically compliant pastoral concern; they are a far cry from the bold stance of earlier Dissenters unaligned with the concerns of the state. Yet such seemingly ordinary poems reveal much about this corner of Dissent's developing relationship with the Australian landscape. Not only do they demonstrate an increasing identification with nationalism and the self-conscious cultivation of the bush myth, but they also locate sanctity and redemptive sacrifice under the "wattle bloom."[5]

Beatrice Bevan, Margery Ruth Betts, and Nicholas Cocks were Congregationalists who wrote prolifically for a church readership and the wider public during the First World War and the peace that followed. As their poetry demonstrates, Congregationalism exemplified the changing relationship between parts of Protestant Dissent and the state. The poems are the work of patriots who were closely connected with a Congregational leadership that no longer maintained a traditional separation from government.⁶ Australian Congregationalism aspired to be a part of the nation's Establishment. Accordingly, Congregational poets penned a landscape of faith using the language of Australian nationalism. Christianity in early-twentieth-century Australia has been described as "an alien culture that had not taken root in the native soil."⁷ Yet analysis of Congregational poetry reveals that the poets believed they were actively grafting Australian identity on to faith, and disseminating a spirituality for a new nation.

The poetry by the two Congregational women is interesting both for gender and denomination. Women had long used poetry as a socially acceptable means of religious expression, attempting to touch the numinous in language that is beyond everyday prose. It is not always theologically orthodox. Even when their poems were printed in denominational journals alongside sermons and editorials, they focused on spiritual experience rather than confessional concerns. Theologically they trod in "no-man's land" and went unnoticed. The research of church historians too has tended to rely on men's sermons, official statements, and documents that track the fault lines of dispute.⁸ The faith and humanity of these prolifically published poets is barely on the edge of the church's historical consciousness.

Remembering Bevan, Betts, and Cocks

Among the most prolific of the period's Congregational poets was Beatrice Bevan (1876–1945). She was one of eleven children, including a number of high-achieving sisters, born to the civic-minded Rachel Lennox and William Mountford Kinsey Vale.⁹ A budding poet, Beatrice joined the poetry circle run by Louisa Bevan, wife of the Reverend Dr. Llewelyn Bevan. She married their son, the Reverend Willett Bevan, in Hong Kong in 1901 and traveled with him to Medhurst College in Shanghai where he served under the auspices of the London Missionary Society for a number of years. After their only child, Medhurst Llewelyn Willett Bevan, was diagnosed with tuberculosis they returned to pastoral ministry in South Australia.¹⁰ It was in Kilkenny (from 1913) and then Gawler (from 1919), a prosperous country town with a cultural self-assurance, that Beatrice wrote her many wartime poems. She was even called "Gawler's Laureate"¹¹ and became a champion of patriotic poets: Caroline Carleton, author of the patriotic "Song of Australia,"¹² and Adam Lindsay Gordon, whose work Marcus Clarke described as the "beginnings of a national school of Australian poetry."¹³ Beatrice Bevan's short drama entitled "Adam Lindsay Gordon" was published in 1938 after she retired to Black Rock in Victoria, not far from the coastal scrub where Gordon shot himself, though a world away from Poets' Corner, Westminster Abbey, where he remains the only Australian. Bevan's self-consciously Australian poems were published in the newspapers of Adelaide and Gawler, but reprinted across the country. She also had a number of poems published in Congregational journals and produced small collections of verse that were received as "joyous songs of open spaces."¹⁴

Margery Ruth Betts (c. 1891–1981?), known as Ruth to her family, was aged 23 and living with her widowed mother in the eastern suburbs of Melbourne at the outbreak of war. Her religious poems appeared in Congregational journals and her secular poems in the mainline Australian press. Like Beatrice Bevan, male relatives in ministry greatly assisted her recognition within the Congregational churches: her father, the Reverend Robert Arthur Betts, ministered at the Kew Congregational Church, Victoria, from 1896 to 1912 and as Principal of the Congregational College of Victoria until his death in 1913, and both grandfathers, Robert Wye Betts (1825–1886) and Thomas Edward Noyes (c. 1830–c. 1883), had been Congregational ministers in England.[15] Betts did not marry and, after the Great War, returned to England, which she had left as an infant. Like Beatrice Bevan, she was a Congregationalist who took up her place in the city's cultural life, gaining a wide readership beyond the church. Her poems appeared in English newspapers, anthologies of Australian and English war verse, and in her *Remembering and Other Verses*, which was reviewed as "far above" the many "little rhymesters of the suburbs [who] are turning out war-verses by the bushel."[16] Her poems were excerpted beneath chapter headings in Mary Grant Bruce's popular Australian wartime adventure novel, *Jim and Wally* (1916), and "Remembering" was set for memorization by school children in the Victorian Education Department's *School Paper for Grade VII and VIII* (1918). But Betts herself is forgotten. Despite once seeming-renown, details of the life of Betts are poorly documented and there are no known photographs.

The Reverend Nicholas John Cocks (1867–1925), who once rode in the procession to Centennial Park at the Inauguration of the Commonwealth of Australia, was a minister with a high profile in the Congregational Union of Australasia. He served at Kogarah, then at North Sydney, before moving, in 1907, to Sydney's central Pitt Street Congregational Church. He served as chair of the Congregational Union of New South Wales in 1899–1900 and, again, in 1917–18, and lectured at Congregationalism's Camden College.[17] During the war years he hosted intercessory prayer sessions at the Pitt Street church and published five poems in a booklet titled *Songs of the Dardanelles*.[18] A lengthier pocket-sized book of wartime poems, *The Betty Songs*, was published in 1919.[19] It featured several illustrations by Olive Crane (1895–1936), a young artist who had come to attention at Sydney University with her drawings on women's emancipation and who later worked as a freelance illustrator and watercolorist.[20] After a brief illness, Cocks died in 1925 and his widow Elizabeth (née Proctor) published a final anthology, *Australian Songs and Other Poems*.[21] Despite writing many hymns and three books titled "songs," Elizabeth Cocks asserted, "My husband was not a verse-maker—he was a poet."[22] Denominational historians agreed. According to John Garrett and L. W. Farr, Cocks was "a man with the sensitive temperament of the poet." He was also highly intelligent and at university he had been a "gold medallist in Philosophy ... placed ahead of the classical scholar and poet, Christopher Brennan." Congregationalists would not be outdone by Catholics like Brennan. Besides, they added with denominational pride, Cocks's poetry was also reminiscent of "the American Congregationalist Emily Dickinson."[23] Others note that his poetry illustrated a "love of Australian landscape," that he had a "mystical awareness," that his intellect and insight spoke to "intelligent seekers" beyond his local church and yet also to "ordinary men and women."[24] His poems were not anthologized in larger collections and quickly lost currency. But clearly, his memory as a poet of theological significance was championed within the Congregational churches.

The works of the three poets rarely appear in anthologies of wartime literature. In the years following the war, amateur poets who had been on the battlefield were treated as authoritative and the voices of women, no matter their experience, were forgotten.[25] The memorialization of war in poetry anthologies mirrored trends in public ceremony: by the 1930s men were welcomed at commemorative services and women increasingly shut out.[26] Ruth Betts and Beatrice Bevan together had over ninety poems published in the daily press and denominational journals, but the volume of their output is not represented in Australian compilations.[27] Betts wrote more than once of the silencing of women. In her poem, "The Red Brother," she implores the wind to carry "A song that a mother sang to the child at her breast," now a soldier killed in war, and to take it to the Kaiser's palace and "beat at the windows and trouble the gateways with crying, / And speak at the fast-closed doors the word of the Lord."[28] Her volume, *Remembering*, is dedicated "To their mothers." In "The Reckoning" she hopes that there will be a day when women are heard: "Ah! You could not hear it then, the bugles blew so loud. / Martial splendour hath a voice more strong than women's pain."[29] Her poems have been waiting a long time. The Reverend Nicholas Cocks is also significantly underrepresented in anthologies, suggesting that the bias toward men did not extend to clergy. Later literary editors preferred a secular liturgy.

Poetry in First World War Dissent

Poetry has long been used to touch the numinous in language that is beyond everyday prose. Spiritual experiences of landscape, belonging, and distance were often expressed in verse, and so too the immense drama of war, too raw to speak of in ordinary ways. Writing from home, Bevan, Betts and Cocks rarely described the battlefield but instead authored and re-authored the landscape of home in the light of events elsewhere. War prompted a need to find expression for the experience of staying home while family members went to fight abroad. Throughout the Commonwealth, much poetry was penned.[30] Many of the poems published in church journals were by ministers and women who could not enlist to fight and so were compelled to reconcile what it meant to remain at home away from the action, to wait and endure rather than join the fray, to be here and not elsewhere.[31] For those at home, who could not express their patriotism through enlistment, poetry became an expression of nationhood and contributed to the legend of Anzac.[32] Landscape and nature have often been coopted to reconcile war's brutality with nobler ideals, but the wartime poetry of Australian Protestant Dissent contributes uniquely to the imaginative creation of Australian landscape and spirituality.

War prompted poetry from many denominations. The poems of the Reverend Laurence Rentoul, Professor of Theology at the Presbyterian Theological Hall, Ormond College, Victoria, featured in local publications and anthologies, as did those of Catholic poet Father Maurice J. O'Reilly, Anglican Dorothy Frances McCrae, and Methodist

Leon Gellert. Poetry reflected conflicted responses, within and between denominations, to war. Methodists submitted patriotic poems to the regular column, "War News and Notes," in the *Spectator and Methodist Chronicle*.[33] But the same church periodical also reported on the poems of American pacifist and women's rights advocate, Miss Angela Morgan.[34] Regrettably, denominations that were more united in their pacifist stance published little poetry in the period: the Religious Society of Friends favored debate over lyricism in the morally tense atmosphere that greeted minority views.[35] At the other end of the spectrum, Congregational poets were prolific and almost all their poems were "on song" with the war effort.[36] This large body of patriotic, pastoral, and pastorally concerned work provides ample scope through which to examine issues of landscape, spirituality, and identity. A number of other factors add interest to the study of Congregational poetry: there are male and female poets; the denomination's theology reflected mainstream Christianity while allowing for religious liberty; and, for a small denomination, historical claims suggest that Congregationalism exerted a disproportionate influence on wider Australian society.[37]

Congregationalism and the Field of Wartime Poetry

Congregationalism traces its origins to the English Reformation when it took a stand on the scriptural authenticity of church government and, seeking a pure form of Christianity untainted by association with the state, separated from the Established Church. Congregationalists insisted on the autonomy of the worshipping congregation and their right to adopt the theocratic patterns of governance and authority witnessed in the New Testament.[38] Such a radical approach to independence and authority had ongoing consequences for their relationship with the state. From the sixteenth century, Congregationalism maintained that Christians should not be compelled to belong to the church but should come freely in faith. Likewise, it held that congregations should not be compelled by the laws of the state but should exist as autonomous communities of faith beholden only to God. In Australia these ecclesiological stances manifested themselves in strong-minded individuals and weak organizational structures, and an adherence to the Voluntary Principle by which churches typically refused to accept state funds and, as a corollary, state involvement in the affairs of the church.[39]

Congregationalism's traditional distance from the state is not the end of the story. After generations of avoiding the gaze of the British government, its people stepped into the sunlight in Australia, taking an increasingly prominent role in civic affairs. Individual Congregationalists involved themselves personally in the affairs of state, standing for election to government and serving in public and cultural roles in large numbers.[40] While the service of such individuals often arose out of social conscience, it was not usually characterized by an identifiably Congregational viewpoint and therefore perhaps not driven by denominational concerns. Rather, Congregationalism's reportedly disproportionate service to the nation was likely due to the fact that the denomination's relatively small membership was unusually well educated, professional, and wealthy when compared with other Nonconformist groups and with larger denominations that had a broader demographic encompassing society's working classes, the poor, and the illiterate.[41] Congregationalism's intellectualism, the lack of centralized organization, and refusal of state sponsorship have also been used to account for its poor traction in rural Australia.[42] Until joining Methodism and Presbyterianism in forming the Uniting Church in 1977, Congregationalism found its place in the Australian cities, and its ministers in major city churches assumed the right to speak with government on matters of morality and faith.

In the early 1910s, as hopes for peace faded, Congregationalists expressed their disappointment and resolve. Some years earlier the influential Reverend Dr. James Jefferis of Adelaide had preached that Britain and Germany should not be enemies. His sermon was reprinted in Adelaide newspapers and reportedly conveyed to Kaiser Wilhelm II by a delegation of British clergy.[43] Jefferis was known in Australia as one of the fathers of Federation, but his influence did not extend to European powers. War was declared and, with resignation and pragmatism, Congregational leaders including Jefferis advised their young men to enlist. The Reverend Dr. Llewelyn Bevan, the "Patriarch of the Churches" (and formerly of the Independent Church (Congregational) in Melbourne) also arranged for a letter to be sent. Bevan maintained a high public profile as President of Adelaide's Peace Society, and while newspapers reported on public campaigns for the internment of Germans living in Australia, he persuaded the South Australian Council of Churches to send a letter to the German churches expressing sympathy with their people and gratitude for the great German Christians of the past.[44] Both Bevan and Jefferis had hoped communication might bring understanding: words mattered in Congregationalism and earnest debate led the church through disagreement and into purposeful action. Bevan and Jefferis had a history of independent-minded disagreement with one another over church matters, but in 1915 they reluctantly agreed on support for the war.[45]

For a denomination made up of autonomous congregations and independent minds, the Congregational churches were remarkably united in their support for Australia's war effort.[46] There were only a few alternative voices among the Congregational clergy. The Reverend Albert Rivett was a well-known pacifist (with Quaker influences in childhood) whose clashes with church officials led to his resignation from Whitefield Congregational Church in Sydney in 1915. The pacifist views of the Reverend E. Hope Hume led to his being forced to leave the ministry of the Deepdene Congregational Church in Melbourne in 1916.[47] In a denomination where clerical employment depended on agreement with the dominant voices in the congregation, their minority views cost them their pastorates. In contrast, the Reverend E. W. Weymouth, minister at the Wollongong and Mount Drummond Congregational Churches, retained his position throughout the war while actively supporting military efforts via his service on the Wollongong Recruiting Committee.[48] The triumvirate of God, King, and Empire was nigh impossible to disentangle in many Protestant churches at the time. Little wonder historians identify the period during and shortly after the First World War as the "high point of Christian patriotism."[49] Or, more damningly, that the major churches were more concerned with status and relationship to power than with the message they preached and were consequently "content to echo the general platitudes" about war, God, and Empire.[50] Despite their broad support for the war and the official statements of the churches, the Congregational poets were a little more thoughtful and varied than this.[51]

While the freedom of individuals and the autonomy of worshipping communities were guarded within Congregationalism, cooperative denominational bodies were formed in the 1800s for the purpose of mission.[52] These colonial and, later, state Congregational Unions followed the pattern set by other denominational church bodies in making public statements on behalf of the denomination. Accordingly, Congregational Unions around the nation made statements of allegiance to Britain's war effort. In 1915 the Congregational Union of South Australia declared that "we believe in the righteousness of the cause for which the Empire stands in the devastating war now raging, we undertake to do all in our power to support the King and his advisors, civil and military, in the prosecution of the war."[53] In 1916, as the issue of military conscription became increasingly heated, the Congregational Unions' various responses reflected the denomination's ecclesiological identity.

Voluntaryism and Conscription

Across Australia the major Protestant denominations were largely united in their support for conscription.[54] Congregationalism, seeing itself as small but influential, was also broadly in support. However, in South Australia, where members of the Peace Society were prominent in the Congregational Union and Protestant Dissent flourished, the question of which way to vote in the conscription referendum was officially left to individual conscience.[55] At the same time, the annual conference expressed its collective "esteem and admiration for the men who have voluntarily responded to the call."[56] The church was not alone in experiencing societal pressures to affirm the sacrificial service of soldiers and promote further enlistment. The prominent Congregationalist and South Australian parliamentarian Thomas Hyland Smeaton publicly campaigned for the "yes" vote.[57] In Victoria the Congregationalists supported conscription through public announcement and church publications, advising against conscience after centuries of insisting upon it.

With the authority of denominational publication behind the war effort, pacifists such as Rivett and Hume resorted to self-publishing.[58] In the denominational journals pacifist opinion was printed only for the purpose of ridicule. The Melbourne Meeting of the Religious Society of Friends (Quakers) wrote to the Congregational journal, *Victorian Independent*, to argue against conscription. The editor responded to the letter, at some length, on behalf of Congregationalism in Victoria. He retorted that the Quakers' argument was "silly" and that "the Friends and all others of similar views ought to be profoundly thankful to God that the British Army and Navy guarantees them their conscience, and prevents them being shot for the privilege of having one."[59] God and the military were aligned in Victoria's official publication of the Congregational churches. Unsurprisingly, therefore, between 1914 and 1918 almost every poem published in the *Victorian Independent* was about the war and broadly supportive of it. The poetry consistently conveyed patriotic feeling, resignation, and sympathy for the grieving.

Congregational poetry was rarely provocative but, instead, sentimental, personal, domestic, and pastoral in both the caring and idyllic senses of the word. During the Great War it encouraged the acceptance of tragedy and sympathized with the bereaved. A few poems railed at the Kaiser but not the enemy soldiers. Some poems (all authored by men) remained abstract in their expression of faith. The majority tapped into Romanticism's reservoir of feeling and expression, finding the imagery of nature and landscape most consoling, encouraging and inspiring. Just occasionally, Congregational poetry made theological leaps that revealed the tension between God and nation.

Into the Terrain: Staying Home and Writing

When Beatrice Bevan wrote "O Christ who died on Calvary, / Our cross is marked Gallipoli," she brought two images and two places into proximity, accommodating an imaginative leap that orthodox theology could not make.[60] Congregationalists knew that salvation was achieved through Christ, not through the deeds of an Empire's military. They knew that the world was redeemed once and for all at Calvary, not on the battlefield day after bloody day. But the impulse to sacralize matters of life and death was overwhelming, and poetry's creative, heterodox pliability allowed all these things to be implied. Sometimes these things were preached from the pulpit too.

Responding to pastoral concerns and patriotism, ministers often likened fallen soldiers to crusaders in a holy war.[61] These men were fighting for God, King, and Empire, a threefold cause that could not be disentangled. Despite Dissent's suspicion of saints, their poets went further, likening soldiers to Christ.[62] Betts mingles the words of Jesus with the sacrificial death of soldiers in her 1915 poem "The Sacrament":

> "This is my blood I give for all the world," He said,
> And, "This thing do in memory of Me."
> And, lo! The sands are crimson with the blood they shed,
> And crimson is the sea.[63]

Similarly, she depicted Christ as a soldier, spiritually present in "Communion on the Battlefield":

> Just in a flash it came, just in a word,
> Before I knelt to take the bread and wine,
> For, Soldier-Christ, it was as though I heard
> For the first time those old, strange words of Thine,
> ...
> "Take and lift up thy cross and follow Me."[64]

At this Lord's Table the words of institution, "this is my body which is broken for you" (1 Cor. 11:23, KJV), are replaced with a call to arms. A fresh sacrifice is demanded because "the world was blind, and would not heed, / So men must write it yet again in blood." As the debate over conscription grew, Betts presented a voluntarist denomination with a choice between Christ-like sacrifice and condemnation as "a coward who hears and will not go" (after Ezek. 12:2).[65] Patriotism and fear distorted the Word. But Congregationalists were not alone in this.

During the Great War many writers and commentators brought Scripture and current events into meaningful proximity, reinforcing the popular association between Christ and the fallen. Among troops and the wider public the biblical phrase "Greater love hath no man than this" (Jn 15:13, KJV) mixed readily with a hazy Pelagianism, in which the good works of sacrifice were substituted for salvation by faith,[66] and the ideal of mateship replaced the loving God. These non-doctrinal adaptations appealed to those who had sympathy for Christianity's moral principles and little tolerance for the institution.[67] In the public square God-shaped language was draped over political events in an attempt to reshape brutality under a cloak of eternity. But cloaking war in the language of divinity diminished the churches' moral authority and distorted soteriology for political purposes. A kind of civic religion developed around Armistice and Anzac Days from the 1920s.

Australian popular culture adopted a theology of redemption that justified, even demanded, death in war.[68] It should have been anathema to scripturally minded Congregationalists, but it infiltrated sermons by chaplains and ministers as a pastoral response to grief.[69] That soldiers fought for God underpinned the assumption that war was redemptive. Through sacrificial death and the shedding of innocent blood, a sinful society might be cleansed and reformed in Godly ways.[70] This belief was widespread among the churches, evidenced in sermons by Anglican, Catholic, and Dissenting ministers.[71] The soldier and Congregational poet Alan J. Kerr articulated this hope in a poem written *en route* to Europe: "Humanity will rise from out the mire / To better, finer things; and thus will come / The glorious kingdom of the Lord our God."[72] Likewise, Beatrice Bevan acknowledges that "though we crawl / And drag through wastes of misery, / The path of anguish leads to Thee."[73] Her "Lord God of Empires" (a once-unthinkable title from a poet of Protestant Dissent) reminds readers that "to reach the rose we grasp the thorn."[74] In Congregational poetry a society stained with original sin forms part of the urban backdrop. Nicholas Cocks asked the nation if it would "bend to the hoarding of gain / And the slumber of impotent pride, / Or leap for the battle." However, the poem promises fulfillment rather than cleansing for the "land of the dawn and the star."[75]

In her 1916 poem, "We Would Not Have Thee," Betts suggested Melburnians preferred comfort and distraction to matters of life and death: "For us the common trivial things suffice."[76] She wrote here of city dwellers and located sin in city streets; the righteousness of rural roads was not in question. Her speaker addressed Jesus, "come not down our Melbourne streets, we pray, / Oh, lonely Man, who calleth men to die." The poem damns hedonism and cowardice, and suggests that those who reject heroic death in war also reject Jesus. However, it does not suggest that the city might be cleansed through war, but that individuals might be brought into right relationship with God. Strongly evangelical, Betts's poem is more concerned with personal morality and redemption rather than with civic duty to fight for Empire. She reiterates this individual focus in "The First Night" when a mother speaks to her dead son saying, "And you were cleansed and healed."[77] It is not the city but the individual young man who is redeemed. Salvation is personal. In "A Mean Street,"

Betts has a dead soldier return to wander "unseen" along his street and to watch with "eyes that blest":

> You stretched your hand to touch them, neighbour, friend,
> Your hand that was redeemed and cleansed and shriven,
> Then went your way. And at the mean street's end
> You found the gates of Heaven.[78]

The soldier is made Christlike in death. Poverty's proximity to holiness sees heaven at the end of the street. Yet the street remains "mean": blest in its unchanging poverty. The Congregational poets shared a belief in original sin and a moral theology of empire but, in their patriotic hope for a new nation and evangelical hope for individuals, did not dwell on the theme of war's purging of society's sin.

Theological ideas brought holy justification to the Empire's war and encouraged enlistment, but the internal logic of atonement theory did not sit comfortably with the evidence of a society at war. Atonement, as Anselm noted in the eleventh century, relies upon the innocence of the sacrifice, but that proved a problem in the early days of the war when Australian soldiers were neither suffering nor innocent but instead taking "their leisure in Cairo."[79] Then, later, as news of so many dead reached Australia, there was a distinct lack of evidence for the redemption of society in spite of all the sacrifice.[80] Cocks noted this too, musing that Australia's potential as a Christian nation remained unfulfilled:

> And when war muttered his colossal fears
> It made the thunder of the march of kings.
>
> But though we have such mingled music won
> From these great chords, as yet we do not know
> The fullness of their slumbering beauty—tense
> With power, that only waits what shall be done
> By our own faith and love to overflow
> The wide-worn earth with new magnificence.[81]

For the Reverend Cocks, it was faith, not war, which would make Australia truly Christian and fulfilled. The idea that redemption might be bought in war missed the point that in the cross of Christ redemption is accomplished for all time.

Just as soldiers were depicted as Christlike, the landscape of war was described through a religious lens. Australian Congregational poets rarely described the battlefield landscape, but, when they did, they described a landscape made sacred. The Reverend Nicholas Cocks described Gallipoli and France in just a few poems, penned in his pastorate in Sydney, and was understandably vague on the details of a landscape that he did not know. Geographical accuracy was not his objective; rather, his allusions to imagined scenery were entirely religious and patriotic in intent. He claimed Gallipoli as sacred Australian territory: "They've put our name in gold on rocks, in scarlet on the sea," and "Through surf and scrub like fire we wound, / And made that hillface holy ground."[82] Such ideas resonate with secular commemorations: Australia put its name on the rocks of the Gallipoli peninsula, and in 1985 Turkey officially recognized the place as Anzac Cove/Anzak Koyu.

Beatrice Bevan described a sacred scene in her poem about Germany's execution of Edith Cavell in Belgium 1915. Cavell was an English nurse who had been running a medical clinic and training center for nurses in Brussels when war broke out, but was arrested by German-occupying forces. She confessed to having aided the escape from German territory of Allied prisoners of war and Belgian and French citizens. Convicted of treason, Cavell was sentenced to death by firing squad in October 1915. Her death sparked outrage, inspired poets, and was used by Britain's bureau of war propaganda to great effect.[83] Imperial forces used the idea of avenging Cavell's death as an incentive to enlist. The Australian government used it as incentive to invest in Peace Bonds. Memorials were built across the Empire, and her Christian confession, combined with controversy around her execution, saw her feted as a martyr.[84] In effect, both her body and her name were "occupied" by Allied forces and their propaganda.[85] When Beatrice Bevan wrote about Cavell, she did not situate her death in the landscape of war but poetically relocated Cavell's martyrdom to Golgotha.[86]

> On Golgotha their guns they set—
> Fit set for such as they,
> Whose awful deeds are meet to rank
> With theirs whom Christ did slay—
>   Edith Cavell!
>
> Where our dear Lord in anguish hung
> They raised their battle cry;
> And in a garden fair and sweet
> They led you forth to die—
>   Edith Cavell!
>
> ...
>
> Like Him, you served, were slain like Him,
> By those for whom you bled—
>   Edith Cavell![87]

Belgium's shooting range was overlaid with the sacred geography of Golgotha as Bevan places Cavell's death in the redemption narrative, embodying the Christological center of the Anzac legend. The poem is punctuated with her name—"Edith Cavell!"—in the manner of a responsive reading in which the people of the church speak a sacred refrain. While enlistment propaganda rallied for the avenging of Cavell's execution, Bevan's orientation to feminine suffering found that a woman could represent divine sacrifice.[88] For women poets of Protestant Dissent, the landscape of war could mix powerfully with the landmarks of faith.

Familiar Lands and Foreign War

The European landscape was transformed in war, no longer the inspiration for poems about pleasant vistas.[89] But Romantic poetry encompassed the tragic as well as the idyllic, and soldier poets on the battlefield described a geography of horror and loss far from home.[90] Australians serving overseas sometimes saw the ruined landscape of military campaigns through the lens of a barren homeland: the outback, beachhead, and dry creek bed.[91] Influenced by the poetry of "Banjo" Paterson, some thought of home, open space, and sunshine.[92] Others recalled the landscape of home as they lay dying, just as poet Dorothea Mackellar had patriotically promised she would do when she penned "My Country."[93] The topography of Anzac intersected with the Australian bush legend. The experience of another place could prove a man's belonging.

English war poetry also focused on the landscape of home. Many poems, such as Rupert Brooke's "The Soldier," rested on the assumption that young men left England to die abroad because of their love for England's landscape.[94] These poems attempt to connect one landscape with another; to find continuity between war and home, and meaning in chaos. The poetry of the British Commonwealth takes a different view: less focused on love for English landscape and more concerned with their own nations' identities and the churches' desire to identify as a Christian nation in alignment with Britain.[95] Reacting to this rhetoric of green fields, Cocks dared to suggest that Australians had earned a piece of England in fighting and dying for it: "We dare to tread your flowers, / For part of that red sprinkling / Is ours, England, ours."[96] Such sentiment echoed his poetic annexation of Gallipoli, but the "scarlet on the sea" of Gallipoli is explicitly identified as "blood" in England: "The green fields of England / Are dewy now with blood."[97] Cocks hesitated to write in detail about the terrain of European battlefields, but England and Australia's "common blood" and the "red sprinkling" that was Australian troops' baptism in blood purchased a piece of England's green fields. Olive Crane's accompanying illustration features an Australian soldier standing in a field of flowers. The soldier is "at ease," but it is an uncomfortable composition. The soldier appears out of place: the futility of bloody claims for a piece of England is etched in black and white. When Cocks wrote his poem, "England," his words were those of the disenfranchised living on the edge of the Empire, concerned that their contribution was unnoticed by the powers that be. Loyalty, powerlessness, and disenfranchisement concerned the Congregational poets.

Across the Commonwealth, descriptions of home provided comfort to readers on the battlefield and encouragement to enlist.[98] In a poem titled "O, Sydney!" Nicholas Cocks described the city's picturesque landscape, implying that it was the duty of men to leave such beauty and ease:

O, Sydney of the waterways,
O, Sydney of the surf.

Can you go where Honour leads
On the deathly way?
Can you do the burning deeds
England asks to-day?[99]

The poem is accompanied by Olive Crane's illustration of a uniformed soldier reclining on a rocky outcrop overlooking Sydney Harbour. Leaning forward next to him is his fiancée, Betty. Her tense posture belies the "chartered ease" of which Cocks writes in his poem. Enlistment's impact on women was noted by the illustrator if not by the poet.

Landscape of Here and Elsewhere 77

Figure 8. Olive Crane, *O, Sydney!*
Source: Illustration in Nicholas Cocks, *The Betty Songs* (Sydney, 1919).

With more rollicking patriotism Cocks issued a roll call of rural New South Wales towns in "The Riding of the King's Men": "They're coming from Condoblin, from Wagga and from Ryde, / From Milparinka and from Bourke and many a town beside."[100] The city minister drew heavily on the bush myth that celebrated the special kind of fighting man only found in the country. Such sentiment was powerful but it denied the fact that Australia's population was largely urban and most men who enlisted (and most Congregationalists) were from the cities.[101] Olive Crane's illustration features only heads and shoulders of five men in hats and coats against an abstract background.

There is no suggestion of place, but only of unified movement. All her illustrations offer tacit commentary.

In "The Crowning," Margery Ruth Betts describes the young nation of Australia as a Queen wreathed in flowers, beautiful and innocent: "faith with careless joy and hope serene, / And baby faith where weeping had no place." But "under distant alien skies" a crown of thorns has been wreathed to place "above your glorious eyes, / Your eyes grown old in woman's faith and tears."[102] In just a few months, a foreign war has transformed Australia, aging her with women's grief and crowning her with the thorns of Christ's humility and sorrow. Here it is not Australia's soldiers that are Christlike but the nation, and its women, in mourning.

Both Betts and Bevan are attuned to the suffering of women. In their poetry, parochial landscape description is a common concern, as if attention to the minutiae of house and garden might bring meaning and perspective to international struggle.[103] They depict women waiting at home or absorbed in the detail of daily life. Betts, in "The Day You Went," describes a mother who did not, could not, watch her son's march to war but retreated to her garden where she "saw instead the sunlight on the flower, / The jewel-winged insects dance and pause."[104] The knowing move to focus on a tiny scale did not hide the enormity of war but contrasted its ugliness and a mother's overwhelming grief with the divinity of nature.

An Australian Landscape of Memory and Imagination

The Congregationalists' religious descriptions of the landscape of war and elsewhere drew on a long tradition of seeking the sacred in the landscape. Bevan described communion in the Australian bush in a poem published the day before Australian troops landed on the Gallipoli peninsula: a bush track was "an aisle to an altar fair / Where the bread and wine are spread!"[105] Bevan was careful to articulate that the spiritual feeling experienced in the bush derived from the rituals of organized religion, not paganism. However, by the early twentieth century there had developed a widespread desire to find the sublime and the sacred in the Australian landscape that went beyond adherence to particular forms of religion. Such was the desire to see the sublime that some writers invested the land with a sacredness of their own devising, inventing places with divine associations.[106] Others appropriated and adapted First Nations mythology in an effort to add authentic location and ancient time to the imagined landscapes of their fiction.[107]

First Nations peoples are profoundly absent from the poems of Congregational writers in the period from 1914 to the 1920s. Instead, English-born Betts imagined a landscape peopled with fairies, "little folk," and goblins.[108] Adelaide-based Congregationalist Thomas Hyland Smeaton wrote of fairies too, "spirits of the glen," and enchanted forests.[109] These poets expressed great sentiment over the beauties of nature and its patriotic associations but invested it with European memory rather than personal observation. Even as scientific and wildlife societies sprang up, the absence of detail in Congregational poetry about the bush and the paddock suggests unfamiliarity with the landscape beyond the cities' edges.[110] Their view out of the window was essentially British. They added gum trees and wattle for a patriotic Australian readership but largely described a landscape of memory and invention. Perhaps the same could be said for many writers of the Australian bush myth.

Congregationalism was concentrated in major cities. It made faltering inroads into rural areas, and its enduring country churches tended to be situated in larger towns.[111] When Congregational poets wrote about the bush, they described a landscape they did not inhabit. They borrowed the language of the bush to lend an identifiably Australian tone to urban lives. The bush grounded their poetry in Australia and appealed to a patriotic readership whose sons and husbands were overseas. Bevan, who had lived overseas herself and who promoted Australian causes such as Caroline Carleton's "Song of Australia," self-consciously adopted the language of the Australian countryside to lend patriotism and pathos to her poetry. In "Under the Hedge" (1915), a poem about a swagman in rural Australia, Bevan uses the language of the bush:

Time to light my fire,
Make my "billy tea,"
After supper smoking,
This the life for me.
Heaven shall my roof be,
Stars shall be my light,

Wrapped within my "bluey"
'Neath the hedge to-night.[112]

Her repeated use of quotation marks undercuts the authenticity and familiarity of the scene she describes. Certainly she is uneasy in her imagined landscape. But adoption of landscape and its language is the point. In all likelihood she would have read the poem aloud in cultivated tone among the ladies' social circle in her local Congregational church. She may well have read it at a literary society too. Swagmen and jackaroos sleeping under cover of (English) hedgerows were not her intended readers. Bevan articulated a romanticized Australian identity for those with a desire to belong in their landscape of adoption.

Differentiating Australia from Britain was an important task in the literary creation of Australia and cultivation of allegiance to a new nation. Nicholas Cocks questioned in exasperation why Australia so resembled Britain: "A century and more, and we are still / As Anglo-British as when first we came."[113] But much of the landscape of his poems is indistinct: the "cloud and cliff, the noontide glow" could be anywhere.[114] He also wrote poems for the cities in which he had lived, Adelaide and Sydney, and poems about bushfire and drought and Australian birds.[115] Yellow robins are mentioned several times, along with "an English lark," nightingales, and so many generic singing birds.[116] A few poems self-consciously tap into themes of the Australian dead center. The landscape of "Dawn and Death" was "clay like blood long-dried," and, with the exception of a city poet, "only the men who know" the "blinding heat" and "gaunt-eyed sheep" could understand "The Music of the Rain."[117] In "The Mother" the lie of the land is written in the "torn" body of a ewe as she bravely resists "three wedge-tailed eagles screaming to and fro / Above a fallen lamb."[118] Such imagery echoed the balladeers of outback despair, but it did so in imagery redolent of the Lamb of God, of self-sacrifice, and redemption. Perhaps too, the "fallen lamb" may have resonated with a generation of Australian mothers of fallen soldiers.

Australia's landscape poets borrowed from one another, compounding the association of words with sentiment. When Nicholas Cocks wrote "The March of the Anzac Men," he described the place of the soldiers' belonging as "wide and sunburnt spaces."[119] The sunburnt phrase evokes Dorothea MacKellar's poem, published as "Core of My Heart" in England in 1908 and as "My Country" in Australia in 1911.[120] Before MacKellar, Grace Jennings Carmichael's "Evening on the Plains" (1892) described a similarly burnt land.[121] By the time Cocks came to write "The March of the Anzac Men," the "sunburnt" landscape carried a wealth of patriotic association. He needed no further geographic description: a "sunburnt" space was sufficient evocation.

Writing a Garden of Poesy and Pathos

In his patriotic *Australian Songs*, Cocks lamented the exclusive cultivation of European flora in Australian gardens. It was, he implied, an indication of cultural dependency: "the old-world flowers here in our gardens flame."[122] However, apart from a mention of wattle in a poem about Adelaide, his writing overwhelmingly features "old-world flowers" such as roses and lilies.[123] He seems to have had the intention to cultivate an Australian poesy, but lacked the vocabulary. Perhaps he was not a gardener or a bushwalker with eyes attuned to the poetic potential of Australian wildflowers. Congregational poets wrote about daffodils, primroses, and forget-me-nots, bringing to mind the vocabulary of English springtime and all its accrued meaning. Inevitably, their poetic expression was shaped by their floral lexicon.

In the English literary tradition, flowers have long been used to symbolize female beauty, fruitfulness, decay, the bodies of women and children, and, in the scriptural tradition, transience.[124] In poetry of the First World War they represent men's bodies too—wildflowers for transience, and red Flanders poppies for blood, their black centers for the eyes of the dead.[125] Flowers clothed mortality and molded memory in more bearable images. Bevan composed in a softer palette, avoiding red blooms such as Flanders poppies and fleshy, thorny roses. In the poems of both Bevan and Betts, the bloody duty of soldiers was often overwritten with the innocence and purity of tender flowers in cool colors: snowflakes, primroses, daffodils, violets, and forget-me-nots.[126] They composed a bloodless, sexless memory even as they called to mind the inevitability of decay and death. Life's transience has long been represented by flowers: in the words of the psalmist, "The life of mortals is like grass, they flourish like a flower of the field; the wind blows over it and it is gone, and its place remembers it no more" (Ps. 103:15–16, NIV). But the annihilation of self and memory is not the aim of war poetry. Remembering scripture, the poets clung to the memory of loss as if to life itself: in Betts's words, "All else we dare, except forgetfulness."[127]

In the poems of Bevan and Betts, the garden is a place of memory and retreat, a bittersweet landscape where soldier sons once played in innocence and safety. In

Betts's poem "The Route March" (1916), a mother cannot bear to hear the blackbird "a-singing in her garden there, / Pouring, it seems, your very heart away."[128] She watches the soldiers march, maintaining her public stoicism. But such stoicism is undone in the privacy and safety of the garden with its "blossoming tree." Emotions are laid bare in her Eden with its Tree of Life. Her son, who has blossomed into manhood, once played there in safety. In his absence the garden is no longer a play space but a sacred place: "memory has a hallowed place."

> But now she must not hear that song you sing
> About the sweet blue eggs, the mate's warm breast,
> About the innocent glad things of spring,
> About the folded bud, the dear, safe nest.[129]

The bodies of Australian soldiers killed in the Great War were not repatriated and families lacked a physical focus for their grief. This eventually led to the establishment of public war memorials.[130] Yet as the women's poetry reveals, in the absence of a grave to visit and tend, a childhood garden could become a place of private memorial and grief.[131]

Images of "the blossoming tree" recur in Betts's poetry. An injured soldier experiences a moment of hush before death in which he "heard once more / A blackbird sing" and was transported to his mother's garden to "hear beneath the blossoming tree, / The lure and passion of his mating-call."[132] The promise of new life inhabits death's threshold, calling to mind the tradition in which the Tree of Life and the "tree" of Calvary occupy one sacred place. Even upon crossing through the veil, Spring "shall bring you news of me / In every dew drop and blossoming tree."[133] Often the abundance and joyful abandon of the natural world was contrasted with the man-made catastrophe of the Great War. An article by Philip Gibbs, English journalist and war correspondent, was reprinted widely in the Australian press in April 1918: "Everywhere daisies are powdering the fields. The contrasts of this beauty with the horrors of war is [sic] almost overpowering."[134] His words prompted Betts to write "Earth to the Spring." While Gibbs had seen daisies transforming the English landscape, Betts had been reminded of English cemeteries where daisies dot the graves. She wrote of a floral path to heaven so that the dead could "travel remembering / Not only the blood and the pain and the dirt, / But my innocent daisies."[135] Earthly beauty could cover up ugliness in remembering. The fallen could recapture childhood innocence with a daisy-chain to heaven.[136]

With life's transience in mind, flowers frequently represent memory in popular culture. South Australia held a "Violet Memory Day" in August of each year to commemorate their losses in the Great War. "Violet Memory Day" involved church services, public events, and bunches of violets that were sold by the Cheer-Up Society to raise funds for returned servicemen. In community-minded support Bevan wrote several poems that were published to coincide with the special day: "The Purple Call" (August 1916), "A Bouquet" (July 1921), "A Crown of Violets" (July 1922), and "Violet Memory Day" (August 1933). In 1917 she contributed to an anthology titled *Violet Verses* a poem titled "The Sphinx," which imagines Mary the mother of Jesus and Australian soldiers in

Egypt.[137] Bevan understood the power of symbolism and used it to call to mind women's grief. By the 1930s the memory of the losses suffered by individual women was suppressed in the public commemoration of the Great War.[138] Without explicitly mentioning women or their exclusion from commemoration events, in "Violet Memory Day" (1933) Bevan questions what it is we remember when we "gather, with reverent fingers, / The violets, dewy wet?" Her quiet commentary on the memorial ritual of picking violets asserted that women's losses remained vivid, albeit in private.

A Heart of Wattle Blossom

Informed by a liturgical and civic calendar, Bevan also wrote poems for other annual events: Christmas, Easter, New Year's Day, and Wattle Day.[139] In the nineteenth century, as support for Federation grew, a number of patriotic groups had formed around the promotion of wattle as a floral emblem for a new nation. However, they soon disbanded and it was not until September 1, 1910, that an annual Wattle Day began to be observed formally in Adelaide, Melbourne, and Sydney.[140] Enthusiasm for wattle as a national emblem gained momentum in the early days of the Great War. Some were wary of the growth of nationalism and its potential to divide. When the Reverend Dr. Llewelyn Bevan was invited to speak to the Wattle Day League in Adelaide in 1912, he chose as his topic "Wattle Blossom: Its Symbolical Significance" and took the opportunity to counter some of wattle's more divisive associations. Noting that the wattle flower is a "gathering" of blooms, Bevan welcomed immigration from foreign lands and advocated living together in service "for each other's good."[141] Llewelyn Bevan sought to use the patriotic wattle to redefine patriotism. Like her father-in-law, Beatrice Bevan used wattle selectively and with theological intent.

Bevan wrote two poems for Wattle Day in 1915. In "Wattle Blossom and Southern Cross," she sought to redefine patriotism in gentle terms:

> You see the symbol of this nation's heart.
> As glows this golden blossom, so her heart
> Shall glow with kindliness and sympathy:
> And, as the scent which rises now to us,
> So shall her honour be, strong, clean, and sweet.[142]

A day later, in a poem titled "Wattle Blossom," she invoked the wattle's therapeutic power:

> Sweet, tender memories awake,
> When springtime brings again
> The fragrance and the golden bloom—
> My heart forgets its pain.[143]

In 1915, it was a heavy heart and mourners dared hope only for fleeting consolation.

Wattle's wartime association with healing was greatly aided by the fundraising activities of the Red Cross and hospital auxiliaries. Women and girls sold sprigs of wattle each spring.[144] It was so popular and such supplies of wattle were required that country residents and Wattle Day organizers pleaded that wattle trees not be irreparably damaged in the cause of collecting blooms.[145] Fortunately for tree lovers (and allergy sufferers), the "wattle-button" also grew in popularity. With its "printed spray of golden wattle looking well on the dark-brown ground of the brooch button," these badges were sold for a shilling each.[146] After the war and extensive fundraising by the Wattle Day League and Red Cross, a wattle tree was ceremoniously planted by Matron Hancock at the opening of the Orthopaedic Wing at the Keswick Military Hospital in South Australia. Bevan's poetry tapped into wattle's cultural associations with healing, and the life hereafter.

Wattle was not more popular than cypress in Australian cemeteries at the time, but the idea of a grave beneath the wattle spoke of Australian belonging. Less than a year before his death in 1870, the poet and horseman Adam Lindsay Gordon famously wrote of a stockman's dying wish to sleep beneath the wattle in death.[147] The image was echoed in a popular wartime verse that was quoted in countless death notices for soldiers who died in foreign lands: "Only the grave of a hero, only a mound of earth; / Far from the land of wattle, and the spot that marked his birth."[148] When Bevan wrote "No golden of that wattle bloom / Sheds light above that far-off tomb" she drew on popular depictions of grief, made patriotic through unbridgeable distance. Confronted with the death of loved ones in Europe, Australians expressed a growing feeling that Australia was home and that Australian soil was the true place of sacred rest. In one of Bevan's last poems, "A Tribute to the ANZACS: The Deathless Army," wattle is a symbol of noble and patriotic death: "The golden wattle marks the men who 'crossed'."[149] Bevan implies that these men live on in glory, set apart with wattle bloom.

Wattle had a long association with life everlasting. In the story of Moses the burning acacia bush was not consumed by fire, but lived on.[150] Freemasonry, which was popularly attended by Protestant men in the early twentieth century, picked up on this and other myths around acacia. It was an important symbol in their private system of knowledge and ritual, and one that did not directly conflict with Christian theology. For the masons, a sprig of acacia represented immortality, and they regularly placed acacia in the graves of their members.[151] Bevan made knowing use of these traditions in her poetry: her late father had been a freemason and her husband Willett became chaplain to the Masonic Lodge in Gawler.[152] Immortality and identity (and Christianity and Freemasonry) came together in the wattle.

In 1919, wattle, the symbol of this nation's broken heart, was incorporated into the design for a badge that the Federal government intended to issue to widows and mothers of fallen soldiers. In gold thread on black silk, "sprays of wattle-bloom, the words 'for Australia,' and the rays" (the military crest's reminder of the sunburnt country) combined the secular and sacred to represent a nation in mourning.[153] Meanwhile, British garden designer Gertrude Jekyll incorporated the symbolic planting of indigenous plants from Australia and other Commonwealth countries to supplement the roses and perennials in the Imperial War Cemeteries in Europe.[154] The idea of wattles planted by war graves had immense popular appeal in Australia.[155] Government schools encouraged the planting of native species too. The Victorian

Education Department's 1917 catalog advertised seven different varieties of wattle among the thirty native plants available to schools,[156] along with a quite remarkable listing of dahlias and chrysanthemums. The catalog advised schools to retain the natural features of the landscape: "creeks, fern gullies, striking groups of rocks," and original trees.[157] The beauties of the Australian landscape were to be appreciated and supplemented with plantings of acacia. Tangible, fragrant reminders of the immortal dead might bloom in every school yard.

Writing under the Southern Cross

The golden wattle signified patriotic belonging and a particularly Australian grief experienced far from Europe's battlefields. With distance and loss ever present, poets turned also to the imagery of the Southern Cross. From Gallipoli, the Congregational soldier-poet Alan J. Kerr called on "ye who live / Beneath the splendour of the Southern Cross / In peace."[158] He depicted Australia as a distant but blessed place, a landscape lit in darkness by the light of the cross. Similarly positive, Nicholas Cocks wrote of living "under the banner of our cross-crowned sky" in these "prophetic lands."[159] Beatrice Bevan described the constellation as a burden and a signifier of the nation's destiny to suffer. She lamented that the "sunny land of Southern Cross / Has learned by bitter, bitter loss," and that "the Cross upon this land" symbolized how "by pain, by agony, shall she be tried."[160] The feminine pronoun was commonly used for the nation and for the Empire's female personification, Britannia, but in Bevan's writing it also speaks of female suffering. Unlike the golden wattle, the Southern Cross did not always glow with patriotism in Congregational poetry.[161]

While the stars in constellation could be made to speak of loss and moral burden, in the poetry of Margery Ruth Betts stars more often signified distance and eternal life. In "Gallipoli" she described the youth who have stepped "over the edge of the world / And past the stars."[162] In "Faith" she observed that "the far stars that look on Calvary / Look also on Gallipoli."[163] Betts describes the chasm between living and dead in "His Wounded Wait": "the way from here to there is strange and very far, / Beyond the outposts of the dawn, beyond the furthest star."[164]

Poetic allusions to landscape and sky in the Great War are almost always about distance and the longed-for return of Australians to the landscape of their belonging. In "The Betty Songs" by Nicholas Cocks a sequence of poems narrates a soldiers' journey to war and then home to his fiancée Betty. In "Coming, Betty" the speaker lies crippled in a military hospital, but a letter from Betty has him look toward "lilac hill and tender sky. / To where within a month I'll be … / Across an ever-lessening sea."[165] Sea and sky and outlying hills, those frequent markers of Australian landscape poetry, are each suggestive of the skylines of Dorothea MacKellar's poetry.[166] Here they denote the distance to be traveled just in order to see such a view.

Cocks's extended ode, "Is It Peace," described the postwar Australian landscape as a liminal space. Despite winning the war, "great dark things endure." It is a country where the sun "shall climb slowly to a heavenly noon; / And men are summoned to a holier war," a war on hopelessness.[167] His poetry had pastoral intent, addressing the damage suffered by returned soldiers. The emotional arc of "The Betty Songs" (1920) sees the bounding rhyme and optimism of "The Call" and "O, Sydney!" give way to sonnets and contemplations of the "tawny and tremulous" on eternity's threshold.[168] The Australian landscape, once a place of clear moral demand, was imaginatively reconstructed by a war that took place elsewhere.

While Cocks was concerned with the mental health of returned servicemen, Betts and Bevan were overwhelmingly concerned with women's experience. They too described a liminal space. It was a mystical meeting place between this life and the next in which sons were reconciled with their grieving mothers and husbands with their waiting wives. Bevan, the "laureate of Gawler," wrote, "Are you coming back to Gawler, to the hill-encircled town, / Where you dreamed and worked and lived in olden days?"[169] Anticipating the town's skeptical response to the minister's wife, she went on:

> "They will never come again," you say!
> But listen to the Bells!
> "Lo, I am with you always," One has said.
> And your hero may be at your side, unseen …
>   "Not dead!"

Alluding to Christ's promise to be spiritually present, she suggested that those killed in war might occupy a place between the living and the dead that allowed them to return somehow to the place of their belonging. She envisaged mystical reunion on Australian shores.

The eternal is summoned in parochial scenes as Bevan asks which roads the soldiers might take and what landmarks they might pass on their return.

> Will you take the Bentley Road …
> Will you stand upon the crest there, looking over Gawler South,
> Where the gardened houses cluster down below?
> And the Lyndoch Road? You miss those trees.[170]

The poem was written for the unveiling of the Gawler Memorial, a place designed to hold the memory of the town's fallen. In naming and describing each place where the fallen might pass on their mystical return, Bevan associates the particular landscape of the town and countryside with the memory of its sons. She called to mind particular stories of the men and their families who lived in particular places and had particular haunts. In this way she invested the local Australian landscape with sacred memory.

In the poetry of Betts, the distance between the dead and the bereaved was imaginatively bridged in the act of calling. It is a word rich with religious association: Jesus calls his disciples, congregations call their ministers, the country calls young men to war. In Betts's poems, mothers call to their sons, and sons to their mothers. In "The Recall" (1915) a dead soldier requests that he be summoned from his place of rest. The soldier says he may be found "in Heaven or Hell, / Or sleeping in my shroud," and asks to be called back to the familiar landscape of the Australian countryside:

> Call me up the valley road,
> And call me up the hill;
> Though I'm a million miles away,
> Your voice shall find me still.[171]

It is the act of calling, with all its military and religious connotations, that brings the distant dead back to the living in an Australian landscape. Sons are called, not only to war or religious vocation, but also to home and their mothers. In "The Ghost" (1919) Betts writes,

> Call to him, oh!
> Call to him,
> Beside the bend he knew.
> Beneath the fairy wattle-tree,
> And there I shall be for you.[172]

Written for a secular audience, "The Ghost" might be seen to have spiritualist leanings. Spiritualism surged in popularity after the Great War, building on a late-nineteenth-century interest in the supernatural and fed by grief and uncertainty and the desire to reconnect with loved ones.[173] The movement certainly had currency within Australian society.[174] However, the Australian landscape Betts described was not inhabited only by ghosts but by the magical folkloric creatures of a European childhood. The Australian landscape was invested with European mythology "beneath the fairy wattle-tree." In "Called" (1916), a third poem about calling, Betts presented a dialogue in which a mother speaks with her son who is at once a child and a man, present and absent. As the mother calls her son in from play, he hears the call to serve his country. She sees her son "coming up the valley road, with twilight closing in, / … Hasten, you, and cross the threshold, 'ere the goblin-hours begin."[175] The Australia that Betts described was overlaid with European folklore and the innocence and relative safety of childhood it evoked. It was a place of imagination in which mothers and young wives waited out the war years on the threshold and called their boys home.

Betts knew her audience and wrote accordingly. She imagined the path to heaven in her poems for the *Victorian Independent*, conjured ghosts and fairies for the *Australasian*, and, for the British Press, wrote of "English primroses in an English lane!"[176] Like many women poets who wrote about the Great War, she focused on places that spoke of home. It was not always her home, in the leafy Melbourne suburb of Kew. When she described "The mountains that I love; / The gum trees dark against the sky"[177] she called to mind a rural Australia that was more myth than reality to her and her overwhelmingly-urban Congregational readers.[178] Betts wrote of an idealized Australian elsewhere that called back its sons, not to well-to-do Kew but to some imagined place of belonging along the "valley road."

Landscape of Here and Elsewhere

The bridging of distance in space and time preoccupied the Congregational poets. Soldiers returned victorious and broken, looking to Australia's "tender sky" even as they pondered eternity's "stiller galaxies of stars."[179] In domestic gardens and childhood haunts, memory made "a hallowed place" for women's waiting. Sons killed in action were mystically encountered by their mothers who met them traveling on the road in scenes reminiscent of Jesus' resurrection appearance to the disciples on the road to Emmaus (Lk. 24:15). In rhyming couplets ordinary young soldiers were transformed, like Christ, into immortals destined to return home. In words infused with religious imagination, Congregational poets called Australia's sons home to a landscape made more sacred by their presence.

The view of the landscape changed in the writing of it. Dissent's religious identity had long been tied up with elsewhere—with biblical landscape, mission, and afterlife. Now, cast in relief by the shadow of the Great War, Australian Protestant Dissent found that their identity was tied to Australian soil, wattle, and sky. As if seen from afar, the poets described those features that loomed largest in the young nation's identity. Congregationalists came to align their spiritual identity not only with the topography but also with the popular bush mythology of a young nation. Beyond mere jingoism, they wrote with spiritual purpose. The Australian Congregational poets overlaid the Southern Cross and golden wattle with Christian meaning, and found their calling in the writing of a new nation's spirituality of place. It was a place where they felt that they belonged.

6

Landscape of Adventure: Methodist Novels and Imagination on the Mission Fields, 1910–48

Methodist fiction portrayed the mission fields as a place of adventure and romance. Wilderness was enlivening. Missioners were men of courage and purpose, of Word and daring deed. In *The Sweet Heart of the Bush*, the missioner Gordon Stirling threw his whole self into his work. He preached from the prophet's commission in Isa. 6:1-8, addressing a people who looked but did not see and listened but did not hear (Isa. 6: 9-10). Then, while quoting Milton on the virtues contained in "lowly sheds," he fed his parishioners' pigs, chopped their wood, and knelt with them on their dirt floor to pray.[1] When bushfire engulfed the region, as it often does in self-consciously Australian fiction, Stirling was there to help: "He galloped away, regardless of danger, amid fire above him, fire below him and fire around him. Trees were crashing and fire showering about him from those burning overhead."[2] Women missionaries found their calling in adventure too. Far from the dull predictability of suburbia, they led exemplary lives where drama and significance mingled in a landscape that sang to them. In *The Locked Door*, the sea itself invited Margaret Lynde, calling like the voice of God, to find a home in the stirring landscape of mission: "And the wash of the waves sang: 'Coming home …'"[3] Mission is always about gospel in context and the context is very present in these novels, not merely as scenic background, but as an integral player in the drama and humanity of the story. The landscape is at once wild and human, completely other and truly home. In many stories the landscape's transformative power sees the missioner grow into God's purpose through engagement with the forest and the sea. More than mere advertisements for the work of Home Missions, Methodist adventure novels intentionally cultivated a readership and sensitized them to the complex relationship between gospel, landscape, and faithful living.

George Sargant, Joseph Bowes, and Edna Roughley each had close personal ties to the work of Home Missions and, in their spare time, wrote novels for adults, youth, and children. Their adventure stories reveal how Methodists saw the landscape in the early to mid-twentieth century. The books were sold well beyond Methodist circles; their imaginative ownership of the land and relationship with First Nations peoples resonated with other readers too and witnessed to shifts in Australian Protestant Dissent. By midcentury, the "wash of the waves" sang not only to fictional young missionaries but to readers across the country. In a denomination that was attuned to visual imagination of sacred scriptural scenes, Methodist novels show how religious imagination was turned toward the Australian landscape as a source of revelation and divine encounter.

Imagining Mission with Sargant, Bowes, and Roughley

The setting of novels mattered in missionary fiction, and the setting of the author ensured the confidence of buyers and increased the sales potential of books. While many writers had occasional short stories published in church journals, publication in books was most often granted to ministers, missionaries, senior teachers in church schools, and editors of church periodicals. Publishers, both religious and secular, could be assured of a readership for such authors. A little of the life stories of Sargant, Bowes and Roughley will shed light on their writings and their standing as authors in the Australian Methodist community.

George Sargant (c. 1867–1945) was a long-serving Home Missioner in the Methodist Church in Victoria. He was born in Whroo and raised in Gaffney's Creek, Walhalla, and Bairnsdale, each locality a Victorian gold-mining town.[4] During the Great War he served as a chaplain at the Seymour army training barracks in central Victoria. A popular guest speaker, he gave addresses around Victoria and Tasmania "in the interest of Home Missions."[5] Sermon topics included "Life in a Military Camp," "Child life in city slums," and, echoing the story of Gordon Stirling, "The experiences of a bush missionary."[6] Newspaper reports focus on Sargant's humour, his belief in the ability of people to make good the mistakes of the past, and his determination to show that "the Gospel was ample to ameliorate the worst conditions of degradation."[7] These same priorities are also evident in his three novels published in 1915, 1920, and 1921.[8] They are best captured in the depiction of an ideal missioner (serving as a minister but not yet ordained) in his first novel, *The Sweet Heart of the Bush*. Sargant's adventure romance tells of a young Methodist who proves his calling as a missioner when he is sent to the backblocks of Victorian farms and remnant goldfields at the turn of the twentieth century. Like many a first novel, it may be partially autobiographical.[9]

Joseph Bowes (1852–1928) wrote nine boys' adventure novels in the 1910s and 1920s while serving as a Methodist minister in New South Wales, like his father had done, and in several churches around Queensland.[10] He served as the first Secretary of the Queensland Methodist Conference, Conference President in 1903, Secretary and Treasurer of the Home Mission Society, and Connexional Editor.[11] He was "one of the best known figures in the life of the Queensland Methodist Church," and this would have aided immensely the sale of his books.[12] More recently he has been remembered for his call to the church not to neglect their duty to First Nations peoples.[13] He used his influence in the church and "worked strenuously" to advocate for the needs of Indigenous People and, when a volume on the history of Methodist mission to each of the peoples of the Pacific was produced in 1914, it was Bowes who was commissioned to write "The Australian Aborigine."[14] His chapter castigated previous generations for their mistreatment of the rightful owners of the land and appealed to the contemporary science of anthropology in the hope of reducing the churchgoers' fear through education and appeal to a common humanity. He also disputed James Frazer's conclusions about primitive religion, claiming instead that First Nations peoples lived in a "spiritual universe" and observed a "sacramental idea of life" in which they "visualize the unseen."[15] As a Methodist, schooled in the visualization of scriptural scenes, Bowes might well have been sympathetic. His fictional depiction of First Nations people makes sense when read through the lens of this concern. Tellingly, most of his obituaries omit to mention his advocacy but instead note his more popularly palatable concern for Australia's fauna. Fear and shame dominated response to First Nations peoples in the early decades of the twentieth century, but a minister's interest in natural history was a sign of both refined sensibilities and down-to-earth approachability. He was described as an "observant natural historian" when he spoke on brolgas for the children of the Cairns Methodist Church,[16] and a "real horseman, the master of much bushlore and bushcraft, a great lover of nature … a real sport after young Australia's heart."[17] The description echoed the title of Bowes's first novel, *Pals: Young Australians in Sport and Adventure* (1910).[18] It is almost certainly semiautobiographical in its disjointed narration of events, setting in northern New South Wales, and depiction of the minister's son Joe as the central figure. Bowes's 1923 novel, *The Jackaroos*, portrays the moral drama of two boys, new to the landscape of central Queensland in the 1870s, alongside cattle rustlers, local Aboriginal people, and Native Police.[19]

Edna Roughley (1905–1989) was a Sydney-based writer of fiction who published widely in mainline newspapers, church journals, and books.[20] She attended the Bondi Methodist Church with her children where she was the General Superintendent of the Sunday School. She moved to Epping with her sister's family in the 1950s, taught scripture in the local secondary schools, and ran a church Bible Study.[21] Building on her success as a prolific writer of short stories and serialized novellas, Roughley was appointed children's page editor in the *Methodist*, the weekly publication of the Methodist Church in New South Wales; from 1938 to 1954 she wrote and edited the page known as "Followers of the Star," using the pseudonym Rosemary.[22] This ministry at the *Methodist* enabled her to publish numerous serialized stories for children, which led to a book for girls, *Ellice of Ainslie* (1947). Her other books included three novels for a religious readership, a book of devotions, lyrics for children's songs, and a 1944 drama titled *The Inland Road* that was commissioned by the New South Wales Methodist Home Missions Department. In Roughley's *The Locked Door* (1948) the young Margaret sets out for missionary adventure in the Australian-governed Territory of Papua,[23] and despite the ravages of tropical disease, climate, and war, she finds herself gradually drawn in to the landscape and its people.[24] Her serialized novel for children, "The Lost Road" (1942–3), is centered on 12-year-old Jon, the child of a single mother whose estranged husband's death has left them in financial straits. Roughley's husband had left her too, taking the eldest of their three children. She wrote often of fractured families. Despite his circumstances, young Jon is the hero of the story—a child from the city who does the work of God in the bush as he builds relationships, changing both the moral and physical landscapes.[25]

From the mid-1950s Edna Roughley edited "Our Women's Page" for the *Methodist*, and in 1962 she represented "all Australian church women" at the Second Conference of Asian Church Women, having been recommended for the position on account of her writing, teaching, and public speaking.[26] Women were not ordained in the Methodist Church in Australia until 1969, and so religious authority was negotiated by other means.[27] While Sargant and Bowes came to writing through ministry, Roughley's later ministries developed out of her authority as a religious writer. For each of the authors, public recognition of their wider ministries aided the persuasive power of their books.

Fiction Writing in Dissent, and the Sacred in Australian Literature

The novel developed as a literary form in the 1700s, just as Methodism was born, and it grew in popularity throughout the nineteenth century. At the same time, linotype improved efficiency and printing costs decreased, populations expanded and literacy became more widespread, and fiction began to be used in education.[28] New Methodist fiction was enjoyed among churchgoers, though many perceived novels as "worldly," "pernicious," and a distraction from the work of the gospel.[29] In New South Wales, immoral books presented an opportunity for evangelism: the *Methodist* reported that the church "would be untrue to its mission were it to cease its efforts to provide wholesome literature for the people … We need to counteract the immoral tendencies of bad books, by sending a stream of wholesome reading running like a river of God throughout the entire country."[30]

Interpretive practices may have played a part in resistance to fiction. In nineteenth-century Evangelicalism and Dissent, the Bible was privately read and individually interpreted in religiously prescribed ways; insistence on a common-sense interpretation and shared moral viewpoint unified believers.[31] But the interpretation of novels was less closely determined, and this allowed readers to sympathize widely and to identify with different moral viewpoints. Free interpretation inherently clashed with accepted practices in the reading of scripture and prompted Evangelical calls for discipline in the reading of fiction.[32] But within the safe space of Methodist Book Depots, book choices and interpretations were bounded. Reviews of books sold through the Depots aided interpretation with expositions on the "fine wholesomeness" and "chaste humour" of their morally sound recommendations.[33] Story-writing competitions hosted by Methodist periodicals reinforced expectations around interpretation.[34] The people wrote their own stories according to the religiously prescribed formula.

The negative portrayal of clergy and parishioners in early Australian literature may have given further cause to mistrust fiction as a medium. Australian bush parsons were widely depicted as grasping, inept, or sanctimonious.[35] "Banjo" Paterson declared in verse, "For parsons and preachers are all a mere joke."[36] Most significantly, religious faith and bush ministers were frequently presented as profoundly out of place.[37] If Jesus had walked in "England's green and pleasant land," he had left well alone "the wastes of the Never Never ... Where brown Summer and Death have mated."[38] According to the emerging national psyche, the old country's cool climate religion was of little practical use against the extremes of drought and flood in the merciless Australian landscape. As Federation grew near, cultural critics such as A. G. Stephens predicted the demise of religion along with Britain's dominion: the two were tied together despite the official absence of an Established Church.[39] Reflecting this growing secularism, mainstream literature was "rational in tone" and "modernist in style."[40] Methodist novels provided an alternative in which ministers were heroic and the landscape sang with the presence of God.

Despite the reservations of some, fiction by writers of Australian Protestant Dissent blossomed in the late nineteenth and early twentieth centuries. The novels of Baptist author Matilda Jane Evans (1827–1886), who also wrote as Maud Jeanne Franc, were popularly awarded as Sunday School prizes.[41] A number of novels for girls were written by Marjorie Buckingham (1913–2003), a "daughter of the manse" who, decades later, became a Churches of Christ minister.[42] At least two works of fiction were produced by T. H. Scambler, principal of the Churches of Christ's College of the Bible, each fictionalizing the common experiences of newly graduated ministers.[43] Among the Methodists, the Reverend George Warren Payne (1859–1952) had a number of semiautobiographical stories of bush ministries published in the late 1800s, which he wrote under the landscape-inspired name of Tom Bluegum.[44] The Reverend William Henry Fitchett (1841–1928), Australian Methodist educationalist and prolific author, composed four novels set on battlefields in Europe and South Africa.[45] The Reverend Thomas Clement Carne (1888–1974) and the Reverend Wallace Deane (1878–1952) set their stories on foreign mission fields.[46] Others, such as Margaret Holliday (c. 1866–1949), wrote just a few stories set in the bush while focusing on novels of manners or morality where landscape mattered less.[47] In 1905 the short stories of Tilly Aston (1873–1947) depicted a quaint and pious Methodism but, perhaps owing to the author's blindness, contained little detail of the physical landscape.[48] Across the Tasman, Rita Snowden (1907–1999), Auckland-based traveling Methodist missionary and "one of the best known people in New Zealand," wrote *Safety Last!: Stirring Tales of the Pacific* and more than fifty books of devotions.[49] Religious adventure novels and children's fiction were a significant phenomenon, and Methodists led the field.

Methodism and the Field of Adventure Fiction

When John Wesley founded Methodism in an era of colonial expansion and increasing literacy he established fertile ground for creative religious writing. The distinctive practices of field-preaching, itinerant ministry, and camp-meeting revivals contributed to the development of Methodist adventure fiction. Wesley adopted the practice of preaching in the open air after the example of the evangelist George Whitefield.[50] Both men found overwhelming success, reaching large numbers of people in far-flung places. Their practice was prized among Methodist preachers.[51] Many preachers kept journals and wrote on open-air preaching and their travels between preaching posts. These journals established a rhetoric around field and forest, garden and Gethsemane, highway and wilderness that informed a Methodist appreciation of the natural landscape as a sacred place for divine work.[52]

Itinerancy was perceived as a part of Methodist ministerial calling: walking in the footsteps of Jesus with "no place to lay His head" (Lk. 9:58, NIV). Ceaseless walking or riding a circuit of far-flung places with a Bible in the saddlebag represented absolute dedication to the Word.[53] Christlike travel and open-air preaching lent authenticity to ministry and, as European settlement expanded across the country, the circuit-rider came to symbolize the growth of Methodism in America.[54] Travel to the frontiers of new societies built adventure in to Methodist expectation; adventure writing followed easily from the real lives of such preachers. Then, as field-preaching and woodland revival meetings declined in prominence, fiction writing became a valuable means by which to reach the world. Like the preachers' journals and tales of pioneers, frontier adventure fiction rehearsed and reiterated the Methodist story for new generations.

Early Methodism was colored by the seeking of holiness that followed intense conversion experiences.[55] These were built on visual and emotional imagination: encounters with God, empathic identification with the suffering of Christ, and feeling for the suffering of others that drove missionary outreach.[56] The habit of mind that imagined the experiences of others was encouraged as part of a spiritual life and rewarded in the reading of fiction too. Before Methodist fiction became popular, Methodist revivalism already had a well-established tradition of scenic imagination as part of corporate worship. In sermons, camp-meeting testimonies, and songs, listeners were invited to picture themselves in a sacred scriptural scene. Imaginative participation in those scenes was encouraged and emotional response expected.[57] It was a liturgy with an emphasis on visual imagination, and it contributed to Methodism's perception of the scriptures as a "picture book of sacred scenes rather than a reference book of sacred facts and data" (as fundamentalism later came to interpret the Bible).[58] The same mind that imagined entering a biblical scene could also imagine the landscape of the Methodist mission field. The description of landscape was essentially a religious act.

With such a predisposition for the appreciation of nature, of adventure and of empathic identification with the experience of others, Methodism was especially well placed to develop its own literature of adventure in the landscape. In the late nineteenth and early twentieth centuries Methodist readers moved beyond the literary staples of Protestant Dissent such as *Pilgrim's Progress* and *Paradise Lost*. Eager to participate in an increasingly popular pastime, but concerned about morality, Methodists welcomed the writings of Methodist authors. The novels of Salome Hocking and her brothers, Cornish Methodist ministers, Joseph and Silas Hocking, spoke to their church and beyond.[59] Joseph Hocking's books—including the story with the old preacher and the "howlin' wilderness"—were serialized in Australian mainline newspapers and religious papers.[60] Edward Eggleston's *The Circuit-Rider* (1874) was likewise immensely popular in the United States.[61]

American Methodist Corra Harris wrote *The Circuit Rider's Wife* (1910) and *The Circuit Rider's Widow* (1916). Each of these novels found an international audience. Books about faith communities on the frontier especially appealed to Australian Methodists where sparse populations meant that circuit ministries were a practical necessity.[62] Influenced by Christian-capitalist dreams of colonial expansion, the story was always about making good in a new place—a wilderness, a Promised Land, an unknown landscape where discovery might lead to revelation.

In Methodist fiction the landscapes were more distinctive than the denominations.[63] These were landscapes set apart: places for readers to travel imaginatively, places they might not go in real life unless called by God. They were described with theological intent. In the Mennonite novels of Rudy Wiebe, the Canadian prairie is more than background. Its isolation and empty sky play into the story of a displaced and persecuted people.[64] Social gospel novels used landscape evocatively too, with the aim of changing the missionary landscape. James Adderley's *Stephen Remarx* (1893), Vida Scudder's *A Listener in Babel* (1903), Winston Churchill's *Inside of the Cup* (1913), and Charles Monroe Sheldon's *In His Steps* (1896) were particularly concerned with the potential of words to change the landscape of church and society and pursue the social gospel's agenda to bring about the Kingdom of God on earth.[65] Within the plots of these novels, characters write, read, and are transformed to take positive social action. Novelists hoped that readers might also be so moved: perhaps fiction might not only convey theological ideas and serve as a barometer of popular theology, but also change the expression of theology in the churches.[66] Imagination is potent and conservative commentators were concerned at the potential. Henry Gyles Turner's preface to Tilly Aston's *The Woolinappers or, Some Tales from the By-ways of Methodism* tacitly acknowledges the power of fiction to influence. He praises Aston's book for avoiding "theological discussions under the guise of fiction" in favor of the depiction of pious individual character that would, in turn, inspire "mild introspection" as readers "consider the applicability of some of the stories to ourselves, and how we should have acted under the given circumstances."[67] Methodist fiction was a creative effort to "sort out some of its problems," according to Turner.[68] Edna Roughley, Joseph Bowes, and George Sargant also encouraged "mild introspection" and varying degrees of Methodist reform, but through high adventure.

As a literary critic, Turner had opposed the type of adventure fiction popularized in *The Bulletin* that had "become practically typical Australian stories." Such stories, he believed, cast Australians as possessing a "smartness" born of mean, dishonest pragmatism in search of personal gain or escapades.[69] The development of a national literary identity was an ongoing project in the early years of the twentieth century, and most Methodist writers addressed themselves to the task, attempting to reform both Methodism and the Australian soul. The depiction of landscape is central here, not just to the Methodist imagination but also to situating and shaping Australian identity. The novels by Bowes, Roughley, and Sargant depict distinctly Australian landscapes with religious purpose. They are remote and sometimes wild places, away from cities and the security of the known. In the tradition of the pilgrim, each place requires the traveler to come to know and respect the demands of the landscape and its spiritual and moral force.

Into the Terrain: Owning the Landscape

As Margaret, heroine of Roughley's *The Locked Door* (1948), sailed to an island off the east coast of Papua, she asked a missionary to describe the place where she would be ministering: "'It's a strange place,' answered the woman tolerantly, as one upholding and loving the land's strangeness. 'You will resist its spell—fight it—deny it; but you will never escape it. Papua has a way of making you its own.'"[70] The land itself is powerful; a player in the story of Margaret's pilgrimage. And, as the missionary foretells, Margaret returns to the islands of Papua as if they, and not the suburbs of Sydney, were the place of her belonging. She is called to ministry there by God and by the land itself, for the two were almost indistinguishable. Margaret was restless when she returned to Sydney on furlough, and the island of "Manulei called, and she felt the subtle and importunate pull of the tropics."[71] Returning again to nursing in Sydney, Margaret felt that her life in the city "held no excitement." She longed for the adventure of missionary life, then "the voice of Papua whispered, the call of home grew louder."[72] Home was on the mission field.

The call, and the invitation to adventure, is intended for faithful readers too; the novel functions to recruit volunteers to the cause. But the "call of home" is contentious. Roughley puts aside the tradition of following Christ with "no place to lay His head" in her attempt to portray a compelling connection between the faithful Christian and the landscape: when the missionary Margaret first travels to Papua she is full of doubt, but in her pilgrimage she finds the land is full of the spirit of God. More problematically, portraying Papua as "home" also overlooked the traditional sovereignty of the Papuans. The islands were their home, despite Australian territorial administration, Australian-led missions, and Australian trading and mining exploration. In the mid-twentieth century when Roughley wrote her book, Papua had been under Australian administration for decades and, as a 1949 book review in the *Methodist* noted, Australia's recent wartime deployments in Papua meant that "tens of thousands of Australians [had] been there and know the country, or parts of it, very well." Readers of the *Methodist*, and sponsors of Methodist missions throughout the Pacific, were reminded that it was "a familiar setting" as there was "nothing remote about Papua today."[73] Australian mining exploration and trade in Papua was condemned in *The Locked Door* for its exploitation of both the land and the local women.[74] Methodist novelists often included First Nations peoples in their stories, not just because the inhabitants were commonly identified as inseparable from particular landscapes, but because they were concerned with their treatment by colonizers.[75] Roughley portrays a moral chasm between the missionaries and the miners and traders but omits to reflect critically on the negative colonial impacts of missionaries at "home" in Papua.

Many nonfiction accounts of Methodist mission described First Nations peoples and their customs with educative purpose but infused the colonial gaze with pity and paternalism and prompted self-gratifying acts of charity toward a disempowered people.[76] However, there is little description of Papuan people in *The Locked Door*. They are present as actors in the story but, with the aid of the silhouetted figures on the dust jacket, it was assumed that readers would know how Papuans looked.[77]

Roughley more often described the physical appearances of the missionaries, perhaps encouraging her white-Anglo readers to identify with them. But she did describe the Papuans' responses to the missionaries' appearances—"terrified of her pale skin, she fled to the bush"—and this served to illustrate racial, cultural, and, implicitly, cognitive differences.[78] Roughley portrayed the missionaries' relationship with the Papuan people as culturally sensitive, though with diminished expectation for spiritual transformation.[79] Colonial condescension is ever apparent, and, with such low expectations of the local people, it is hard to imagine how Roughley's missionaries imagined the Papuans might truly become Methodist, with the Holiness tradition's high hope of Christian perfection or entire sanctification. Given the great spiritual divide between saved and unsaved, pale-skinned and Papuan, the joys and travails of the Papuan landscape became the common ground between the missionaries and those to whom they ministered.

In Bowes's *The Jackaroos* (1923), the landscape and the relationship between its original inhabitants and cattle graziers feature prominently, but the mission field is the readership. No religious activity is described, though Bowes's moral and spiritual vision is pervasive. In his role as a Methodist leader Bowes advocated for Aboriginal mission and understanding, accusing the Methodist Church in Queensland of "inexcusable neglect" having "not cast a pitying eye nor stretched a helping hand towards the poor Australian."[80] Likewise, as an author with a major international publisher, Bowes used *The Jackaroos* to portray Mandandanji people from the Maranoa River area in tribal settings, describing their habits with ethnographic concern and guiding reader responses.[81] Despite the distancing effect achieved by bringing difference to the forefront of discussion, a sometimes pitying stance, and confrontingly racist assumptions, Bowes intended his descriptions to bridge the "immeasurable gulf" and educate his young readers in the common humanity of all peoples.[82] Calling on the emotionally persuasive power of story, Bowes permitted readers to "feel a bit scared" in encounters between First Nations people and jackaroos because, like the protagonist Jim, their "experience of blacks [sic], so far, had been very meagre."[83] That a lack of "experience … so far" could be corrected by reading was a pious hope, but *The Jackaroos* provided sympathetic First Nations characters, condemnation of their mistreatment, and the equitable and reasoned example of Mr Huntley whom readers might emulate.

The Jackaroos reveals a great spiritual uneasiness about colonialism's effects on Australia's first inhabitants, echoing Bowes's earlier lament that "many hearts have been troubled."[84] In a narrative where formal religion is not present, the good Mr Huntley's voice elides into the author's, recognizing the landscape's "sanctuary" that First Nations people had known "through immemorial ages" and their dispossession "without any compensation, save for that most hypocritical dole, a blanket, at the yearly roll-up. In such a meagre fashion did the Government salve its conscience."[85] Bowes made explicit the spiritual compromise that colonial settlers had brought on themselves: having murdered First Nations people it was "wise to go armed."[86] Jesus' injunction in Mt. 5:38 had been forsaken and "White-pfeller [sic] must render an eye for an eye."[87] Dispossession and murder of First Nations people in their own land estranged Christians from God. While the prophetic Word is present, the church and its missions are conspicuously absent from *The Jackaroos*.

Modern literary scholars rightly recognize Bowes's writing as racist, paternalistic, and misogynistic (there are no women named in the book), though they miss his religious intent to promote the humanity of First Nations peoples to a readership accustomed to seeing them as villains in the pulp-fiction of frontier expansion.[88] *The Jackaroos* is a frontier tale, written for suburban boys but set near Roma, three hundred miles west of Brisbane, in more exciting times. The First Nations characters are on the side of good, but the ultimate heroes are white—the color of the intended readers. His heroes traveled across a landscape that was "big with promise to those who had eyes to see and hearts to adventure."[89] The evangelist can be heard in that last phrase, but the addition of a frontispiece by English illustrator Arch Webb (1866–1947) confirmed the publisher's sense that this was, first and foremost, a boys' own adventure. The land was "pre-eminently the land of the explorer and the pioneer."[90]

Ownership of the land was more nuanced and religious faith was more present in Bowes's earlier work. Bowes, like many Christians, relied on Acts 17:26 to preach a common humanity of all peoples. But the verse that insisted on "one blood" also justified colonial presence in the landscape: "And hath made of one blood all nations of men for to dwell on all the face of the earth, and hath determined the times before appointed, and the bounds of their habitation." In his novel, *Pals: Young Australians in Sport and Adventure* (1910), Bowes began with a biblical description of the local landscape in which the story is set: "The place where these boys lived, moved, and had their being was a district ... on one of the northern rivers in New South Wales."[91] The allusion is to Acts 17:28, just two verses on from the "one blood" and "bounds of their habitation" of Acts 17:26. According to Bowes, the Anglo, Irish, and First Nations boys belonged equally in this colonized and Christian land. They belonged with the authority of the Bible.

The boys adventured together through the bush and, Bowes made the point, it is the Aboriginal boy who topped the score in the English game of cricket.[92] As a minister, Bowes endeared himself to the people with his love of cricket and when he gave the role of cricketing hero to the boy he might well have intended it as a bridge for readers to grow in respect for First Nations people.[93] The fact that the boy was named "Yellow Billy" rather undermined Bowes's missionary endeavor. The character was almost certainly named after an Indigenous bushranger (highwayman or outlaw) nicknamed Yellow Billy who was active in northern New South Wales in the 1860s when Bowes was a boy.[94] Perhaps it mattered to Bowes that his Billy's designated color was not brown or black; unlike "Black Billy" who appeared as a "lazy young nigger" in Mary Grant Bruce's *A Little Bush Maid*, the first in her "classic" Billabong series for children published in 1910, the same year as *Pals*. And if the "regimes of truth about Aboriginal people" came to see "Black Billy" as a "venerable retainer" by the time the last of the Billabong books was published in 1942, so "Yellow Billy" might represent Bowes's challenge to those "regimes."[95] It is, nonetheless, color that identifies Billy and distinguishes him for readers who might otherwise forget that he is different from the other boys as Bowes labors to portray him as an equal among the "pals." Bowes's missionary message is often lost amid the demands of the adventure genre with its self-consciously Australian twist on frontier western narrative.[96]

Figure 9. Arch Webb, *From his elevation on the ridge he watched the round-up*.
Source: Frontispiece in Joseph Bowes, *The Jackaroos* (London, 1926 edition).

Eight miles inland from the Victorian coast, in the fictionalized mission fields of George Sargant's *The Sweet Heart of the Bush*, the church was present but First Nations people were not. Set in 1900, only the marks left on the eucalypts by tree-climbing and spear-making—a practice "beyond the skill of the white man"[97]—reminded the reader that "before the white man invaded these lands … black tribes [sic] traversed its shores and roamed through its bush in happy possession."[98] After Sargant's brief testament to First Nations peoples' dispossession and ingenuity, they remained powerfully absent from the fictional town of Black Creek.

Uncomplicated by further issues of race, Sargant's story rests on the ability of the young missioner from the city to get along in a landscape that belonged to country folk. The city-bush divide was a common theme in literature of the period, manifesting itself in representations of country dwellers as backward, simple, and naïve. Conversely, town dwellers were "wishy-washy, white-livered" and incompetent in the face of the special challenge of country life.[99] But the handsome and manly Gordon Stirling quickly overcame any stigma about being a town dweller new to the bush when he stopped to help drive bullocks through a narrow pass.[100] During pastoral visits to remote homes he readily joined in the life of the people by feeding the livestock, chopping wood, playing with the children, and, after these practical applications of the gospel, reading scripture and praying with the family.[101] The good reputation of the young minister spread through Black Creek. Sargant likely hoped that the good reputation of missioners everywhere might be promoted by such a heroic and practical portrayal. Similarly, Bowes portrayed the local minister in *Pals* as the voice of compassionate reason and exemplar of courage, among the last to give up on rescue missions through the floodwaters.[102] In *The Sweet Heart of the Bush*, Sargant presented a model for ministry that was entirely consistent with muscular Christianity's vision of spirituality. It also resonated with his belief that people may be lifted from degradation through a kind of practical Christianity, a living Word. He further attempted to mitigate perceptions of bush dwellers as backward by reminding readers of the essential nature of people everywhere and how those who live in the bush are afforded time to ponder the wisdom of the ages.[103] Like Bowes, Sargant educated his readers in a common humanity before God.

The "Dead Heart" and the "Sweet Heart"

While Sargant demonstrated that divisions could be overcome by a shared humanity and the social gospel, the land itself was a barrier between people. The heavily timbered landscape "dominates everything," and the towering eucalypts isolate neighbors from one another:

> It is forest everywhere. It lines up along the sides of the road; it clusters in upon the little farms and shuts them off from each other and from the outside world … and the smoke curled from the wooden chimneys of the bush homes, built of palings or slabs hewn from the forest timber, and looking so small and lonely.[104]

Grandeur was a perspective reserved for viewing from afar. From within, the size and scale of the forest functioned to place human life in perspective. But, in contrast to the common Australian narrative of the bush as a battleground for material survival, the bush landscape of Sargant's novel could also be a reflection of the divine. The grave of a young man is depicted as having God's protection through a natural-supernatural landscape: "wattles and mimosa have grown and arched over his grave like the roof of a cathedral to shelter it from the winter's storm and summer's heat."[105] In similar vein, "the deep blue night sky, with its star jewels, stretched like the roof of a great cathedral."[106] The Methodist tradition is alive here, with nature's open-air temple as a sacred place of religious experience.[107] It was a long way from the interpretive tradition in Australian literature that read depictions of the Australian bush in the nineteenth century as "harsh, raw, obdurate, cruel, barren and fickle" or in the twentieth century as "a wilderness, a void, a threat to be mastered."[108] Contemporary reviewers welcomed Sargant's approach saying, "The writer should be complimented on a title which is a welcome change from the stereotyped 'Dead Heart' or 'Howling Desert' type."[109] *The Sweet Heart of the Bush* was advertised as "very real,"[110] demonstrating an "intimate and friendly acquaintance with the bush."[111] In 1915 there was a market in Australia for naturalistic and supernatural narratives about the *beautiful* bush.

The landscape was a player in Roughley's *The Locked Door* too, and she drew a distinction between the landscape's defeat of the ungodly and its vocational call of missionaries. Both saved and unsaved were subject to dengue, malaria, blackwater fever, influenza, dysentery, pneumonia, and death in childbirth. The native Papuans lived with leprosy. A missionary's wife died of cancer and, on the Australian mainland, friends died of tuberculosis. Everyone suffered, and more so in Papua's climate. But their travails were fundamentally different from those of the avowedly godless. The Australian trader and rogue, Niven Trent, ridiculed the mission's work and exploited the land and people.[112] He stumbled into the mission requesting medical help for what he called his "damned" malaria, a term that spoke of his standing before God as much as it revealed him as an archetypal "ugly Australian."[113] More than that, he confessed himself to be "ill, body, mind, and soul, if I've a soul left! Shouldn't be here."[114] Observing Trent's expressions of ego and his lack of mastery over his own desires, the missionaries knowingly predicted that the land "would surely conquer" the trader.[115] He stayed on in Papua "because the land's got me!"[116] Trent was captured, not called, and this follows a thread in classic Australian literature in which the landscape is portrayed as consuming its victims, annihilating the identity of individuals and any hopes they might have for mastery.[117] The landscape was not only a barrier between the self and other but a threat to the self's very existence. In Roughley's fiction this held true for Niven Trent but not for the faithful, however "faint … [the] glimmer of the Light may have been."[118]

By way of contrast with Trent's consumption of and by the land, Margaret, as a missionary, perceived its calling. Similarly, in Roughley's novel for children, "The Lost Road," 12-year-old Jon believed he was called to work in the landscape, clearing the overgrown "Lost Road" as a means of reconciling relationships between neighboring farmers. Jon is the moral center in a novel in which the landscape must be changed, converted even, in order to connect people both physically and spiritually.[119] Despite an anxious heart, something he shares with Margaret in Papua, Jon's sense of mission sustains him in an unwelcome and unhappy place far from home.[120] In Methodist fiction the landscape participated alongside the saved in the work of the gospel. The annihilation common to classic Australian literature was reserved for the hedonistic, the superstitious, and those "who have eyes to see and do not see" (Ezek. 12:2).

A Moral and Reasonable Landscape

The landscape could also represent moral standing before God. In Sargant's *Sweet Heart of the Bush* a remote hard-drinking township is called to faith by the missioner Stirling, and the pub burns down and is replaced by a church.[121] The moral welfare of the people was altered through mission and this was made visible in the landscape. Missionary absence also affected the land. In the ups and downs of the more complex narrative of *The Locked Door*, Margaret is transferred to a mission island that, without the presence of the missionaries, had "fallen," like the fall in the Garden of Eden, "into decay."[122] The grasses and bushes are overgrown and the "forsaken island" is plagued with mosquitoes and spiders.[123] In this rank, malaria-prone environment the young missionary comes to share the Papuans' fear of spirits and finds herself "loathing her weakness but powerless to conquer it."[124] This is not panentheism; Roughley's landscape is not divine when it is not inhabited by God. Only transfer away from the "forsaken island" can settle Margaret's mind.

In Roughley's serialized novel for children, "The Lost Road," the unhappiness and degradation of the Leeson household is likewise visible in the disorder of its buildings, for happiness and order went together in the twentieth-century missionary worldview. The young protagonist, Jon, was sent to rural Queensland by his mother and made to stay with the Leesons and then with an uncle. Displacement of the main character in children's adventure fiction is a narrative device that casts light on the social and physical landscape into which the child is placed. It also reflected a common concern, with which The Salvation Army agreed, that children raised in cities lived an unnatural mechanized existence rendering them prone to degeneracy.[125] Jon, away from home and with his own life in unexpected disorder, is especially attuned to the ungodly disorder of others. He viewed the Leeson house as a "ramshackle affair" and "knew that in the morning he would find the ground neglected and the property run to waste."[126]

Jon's expectations about the landscape and the spirituality and morality of its people were fulfilled. Not only were the paddocks "a disgrace" but, in the next week's installment, readers also discovered the shameful physical abuse of the orphaned child Sunny who was in the Leeson's care.[127] Roughley allowed the naivety of Jon to speak for readers when he saw the weals on her back and observed, "It was like something from Dickens."[128] Roughley reminded readers that the suffering and abuse of children like the fictional Oliver Twist was a contemporary reality. In Roughley's novel, children rarely attend church and readers were awakened to the fact that the social gospel applied both in stories of Victorian England and in unchurched contemporary Queensland. Named for the bright light of the natural world, the orphan Sunny ran away from the Leesons (in the first of two "lost in the bush" scenarios in the novel). She never really belonged in the "pale light" of the Leeson home.[129] With Jon's help she finds a new and "well-kept" home in the care of a woman who sings "Rock of Ages."[130] In Edna Roughley's novels, care for the natural world goes hand in hand with faithful living.

Divine order in nature is a strong theme in Methodist fiction, and connection with the divine was often represented by connection with natural landscape. Order demanded the stripping away of superstition and mystery in favor of reason and authenticity. Methodism grew to maturity in the Enlightenment. Its concern with reason and order is visible not only in its rules of association and record-keeping[131] but also in the naturalist bent of its fiction. Roughley was careful to identify human carelessness as the cause of bushfire in "The Lost Road."[132] Bowes attributed the bushfire in *The Jackaroos* to evil cattle-duffers.[133] Sargant suggested that the bushfire in *The Sweet Heart of the Bush* was a product of the climate, and its ferocity dependent on the forest's fuel load. He also called it a "grim fiend."[134] The presence of bushfire in three of the five novels marks the texts as Australian: climatically distinct and rhetorically realist. God's providence was not to blame.

Realism extends to medical matters in Roughley's *The Locked Door* where disease was a fact of life, not an act of God or evil forces as the unsaved Papuans believed. Science and salvation went together in Roughley's fictionalized mission fields. In her 1930 short story, "The Crooked Tree," Roughley was even more explicitly opposed to irrational thinking when her heroine challenged superstition in life-threatening circumstances.[135] Malevolent myth had no place in her narrative either. On a windy night the young hero of "The Lost Road" asserts, "There aren't any ghosts."[136] Similarly, Sargant presented the landscape's dangers, such as dingoes, as acting out of their innate existential needs rather than as a representation of a malevolent force or punitive God.[137] These fictional landscapes used the rhetoric of civilization and science to distinguish reasonable Christianity from superstitious, dangerous animism or anarchy.

While not attributing natural disasters to God, Methodist narratives do describe these events as catalysts for spiritual renewal. In "The Lost Road" the child-hero Jon sheltered in a cave to escape a bushfire and "looked out into the vivid glare of the fire, his heart heavy and troubled." Then, "as he knelt, he felt they were not alone in the cave. He was so certain of the Presence beside him, and because he was certain his prayer became to him a heart to heart talk to a Friend."[138] God is there in the cave in the wilderness. Sargant's missioner Gordon Stirling and the Sunday School teacher Maggie are brought together in marriage after Stirling rescues her from drowning *and* she rescues him from fire. Suggesting self-consciousness about his deployment of such conventional dramatic devices, Sargant had a particularly plain-speaking character remark, "I wouldn't wonder if we get a weddin' out of this affair before long, as we often read of a weddin' follerin' a rescue."[139] Matters of the heart and conventions of genre led the plot. Providence, which was so conflicted in the light of reason, played little role.[140]

Providence is dealt with more directly in the 1936 historical novel by Methodist Phyllis Somerville (1904–1991), *Not Only in Stone*. It documents the long journey of Cornishwoman Polly Thomas against the transformation of the colonial South

Australian mining landscape and the "impenetrable scrub" of Moonta.[141] Although Somerville wrote out of her own Methodist heritage, her interest in Methodism was cultural rather than missionary and she promoted a vision of nationalist progress rather than the Kingdom of God.[142] The novel won a fiction-writing competition on the occasion of the centenary of the colony of South Australia, but even in the state later known as the "Paradise of Dissent," historical fiction had a nonreligious trajectory.[143] In *Not Only in Stone* reason becomes a means of overcoming the unhappy hand of Providence in the humanist-religious landscape. Plucky self-reliance proves more trusted than old-world faith. Somerville was not writing mission fiction to inspire a church readership, but telling a story of progress toward a secular landscape. The difference between Somerville and the authors connected with Methodist mission is striking.

In demonstrating material progress over time, Somerville's heroine reflects on the changes in the Cornish-Australian mining town of Wallaroo on South Australia's Yorke Peninsula. In the closing pages of the book Polly Thomas revisits the once-thriving town where she first made a home with her husband in Australia. Although Polly had been heavily involved in Methodist church life in Cornwall and then Wallaroo, taking up "her work in the church as if it had never been interrupted by change of scene," depictions of faith are absent in the end.[144] In seven pages of concluding scenic illustration there are descriptions of houses and mine buildings, but none of the many Cornish Methodist churches are mentioned.[145] Despite Polly's early religious activity and Somerville's historical interest in South Australian Cornish Methodist churches, they are omitted from the story in its most introspective moments.[146] Upon revisiting the grave of her husband and children Polly "hardly seems moved at all." It is not a sacred landscape but one of memory. Polly does not pray but pulls the weeds and asks for the herb symbolic of remembrance: "Where be the rosemary?"[147] Ultimately, religion is replaced by stoic practicality, and the meagre blessings of Providence are overcome through family, self-reliance, and, that vestige of Methodist faith, heart.

Landscape and Literature of the Heart

The faithful heart plays a large part in Methodist fiction and religious experience. In Roughley's *The Locked Door*, the protagonist Margaret's work began in the islands of Papua and her "heart lifted to a high resolve." "Heart" appears in the title of Sargant's *Sweet Heart of the Bush* and frequently throughout the text. While the "Sweet Heart" in the title may refer to the romance between Stirling and the Sunday School teacher, Maggie, there is also a sense that the "Heart" of the bush is the faithful heartfelt Methodism personified by the young missioner.

Among Methodist readers any literary reference to "heart" almost certainly recalled John Wesley's oft-quoted journal entry: when hearing Luther's description of "the change which God works in the heart through faith in Christ, I felt my heart strangely warmed."[148] Charles Wesley's hymns also recall the significance of the heart: in the lyrics "My chains fell off; my heart was free" and in the first lines of dozens of hymns.[149] But the rhetoric of the "heart" did not exist only in the words of the founders and preachers. It was a mainstay of Methodist testimony, spoken by every member.[150] Methodism asserted, in line with eighteenth-century empiricist philosophy, that personal change came about not through the power of the intellect but through experience.[151] The heart was vital to life-changing religious conversion and, thus, to Methodism.

The Methodist heart is represented as faithful and courageous in Gordon Stirling, George Sargant's model of mature masculinity. Reflecting gendered narratives of conversion, Edna Roughley's Margaret Lynde has "a divided heart" and struggles with her vulnerability and sense of calling throughout her decades of service.[152] Margaret struggles to accept the Synod's decision to separate her from her friends on the mission and send her to a deserted mission station. She envies the faithful acceptance shown by Sylvia whose "heart [was] wholly in her work and with the Papuans."[153] In Joseph Bowes's *Pals*, the boys' boat enters the flooded river and "the spirit of prayer was in each boy's heart" while God "sat above the floods."[154] The image recalls Genesis 1 and Psalm 29. As the boys travel through the floodwaters they hear a cry from a tree and see a human figure on a branch. One boy was sure that reaching her was impossible, but Yellow Billy says, "'s'pose your mother was over there?" He is the moral center, the still, small voice of God: "These few words of Billy, uttered in a quiet, even tone, went straight to the boy's heart."[155]

In "The Lost Road" a humble heart is required. As the young hero, Jon, picks his way through the smoldering landscape after the bushfire, he imagines himself a hero on his return when suddenly a "fair-sized bough" falls and hits him.[156] Nature admonishes the proud. Despite Roughley's strong leaning toward an enlightened and scientifically informed understanding of nature, she made it clear that the natural-supernatural did not abide haughty hearts. This apparent contradiction between reason and heart, natural and supernatural exemplifies a paradox that is inherent in Methodist spirituality and is a historic product of its development as a part of the Holiness movement in the Enlightenment.[157] In Australian Methodist fiction this paradox facilitates the landscape's involvement in the drama of faith.

Presence in the Australian Landscape

The landscape responds emotionally to Stirling's labors in *The Sweet Heart of the Bush*. When the missioner finds an infant drowned in the river, nature mourns with him:

> On the bank of the river was a row of fern trees with their fronds drooping to the water's edge, like drawn blinds in respect of the dead, and their giant pistils standing erect bowed their heads. On the other side of the river a kingfisher … paid its respects by sitting motionless … simultaneously the wind sighed and moaned in the trees.[158]

Stirling feels the "touching solemnity" of a landscape that grieves for the baby in the unnatural absence of a mother or father.[159] In Roughley's *The Locked Door* the Papuan landscape likewise responds to the burial of a Papuan convert after an outbreak of disease swept through the mission: "Waves came eagerly to the sand and sighed over the broken coral and the shells marking the line of the last tide. Palms whispered, and in whispers the tall grass answered."[160] The land both mourns and rejoices with the converted, whether they are missionary or local. When Margaret Lynde leaves the island of Minoa, where she had been stationed for a time, "the sky wept with the natives."[161] Margaret is later reunited with her colleague, Sylvia, and the land shimmers with good feeling as the two young women walk "past crotons with their many-hued leaves, past Mimosa trees laced like green mist against the sky, over tracks rough with embedded coral, along the sea-coast" where the water shone with the colors of honey, flowers, and jewels.[162] In the light of Methodism's heartfelt piety, the Pacific's picturesque tranquility coincides almost entirely with the emotions of the saved.

Writers of Methodist fiction sought to employ a language of immediacy and presence. This drew directly on Methodist spirituality in which transcendence was anticipated. There were precedents for this natural-supernaturalism in nineteenth-century Romantic literature too. Sargant's rich naturalist detail of Australian flora and fauna is closer to Tennyson (whom he quotes in *The Sweet Heart of the Bush*), in terms of theology and nature, than to classic Australian authors such as Henry Lawson or Marcus Clarke.[163] For all the nascent influence of Australian bush bards, it was the cool climate poetry of Milton, Cowper, and Tennyson that was most prized, bound in leather on the book shelves of ministers.[164]

Methodist fiction also came under the influence of other writers who sharpened the religious eye for Australian botany and birds. Methodist Home Missioner (and former Salvationist) Christopher Mudd, FLS, FRGS, preached and published about the Victorian and Tasmanian landscapes.[165] His post-nominal letters referred to his botanical expertise as a Fellow of the Linnean and Royal Geographical Societies, and his column, under the name "Peregrinator," in the *Spectator and Methodist Chronicle* used scientific knowledge of the Australian flora to write metaphorically about the Christian life. Nature had long provided missionaries with metaphors for conversion,[166] but Mudd's interest and spirituality seems to be grounded in the study of plants. His religious metaphors read as an afterthought and it is when he goes beyond metaphor that Romanticism and Methodist rhetoric are most apparent. On contemplating the buds of a tree Mudd writes, "That complicated, mysterious, perfect, living cohort of chemical compounds and differentiated tissues would be a life's study … For a time I was lost in this enlarging maze of miracles until a feeling of restfulness and mental satisfaction came over me."[167] Doctrine recedes in favor of mystery.[168] Intimate scientific study of nature could bring about cathartic religious experience, akin to that achieved by imagining one's self in sacred scriptural scenes. Like the traveling missionary heroes of Methodist fiction, Mudd found divine communion on a "walk with Nature through the Mallee."[169] It was close attention to the detail of the natural world around him that brought him into personal spiritual union with the divine: "I am in Jesus' Garden now."[170] It was a garden he shared with Methodist novelists.

Mission in Sacred Scenes

Fiction writing was a ministry for Roughley, Sargant, and Bowes. Their stories guided readers on journeys of moral or sacred encounter in strange lands. They enabled readers to picture themselves as the missionary hero who comes as a stranger and finds religious significance in the landscape—a landscape that did not, at first, belong to them. Each reader is like the pioneering circuit-rider, the open-air preacher of old, or the camp meeting participant who experiences God most vividly outside of the comforts of suburbia.[171] Methodist fiction in the first half of the twentieth century existed in a rich visual-poetic world that was informed by Methodist experience and Australian context. The natural and supernatural mingled in the imaginative spiritual exercises of revivals, the musings of botanists, and the autobiographies of circuit-riders. While each of these written forms invited the reader to enter into the religious experience, it was through novels that readers could most fully transcend the ordinary and imaginatively lose themselves in a journey *with God* through the landscape.

The novels of Roughley, Sargant, and Bowes are about being Australian and being Methodist. Unlike novels of religious heritage and modernist mindset, such as *Not Only in Stone*, fiction of the Methodist mission fields called readers out of their ordinary habitation into empathic engagement with the divine. Their writers hoped that through writing and reading, the transformative work of the gospel would be done. They asked readers, already practiced in visual imagination, to picture themselves in a sacred scene: not a biblical setting, nor the "Dead Heart" of Australian secularist prose, but the sacred scene of the mission fields. Writing and reading the landscape was a religious act. Finding divine presence on the mission fields and divine communion in nature, the Australian land was made sacred.[172] These novels declared Methodist belonging in Australia's mission fields because everywhere their missionary characters went, they went with God and the natural and supernatural spoke to the heart. The faithful read the Word in the landscape and experienced the wonder of "the footsteps of God in the glory of tropical skies."[173]

7

Landscape of Timeless Beauty: Quaker Essays on Beauty in Art and the Painting of Nature, 1922–63

As an appreciation of God in the landscape grew, Australian Protestant Dissent sought to illustrate that divine presence. Wildflowers were painted on teacups, kookaburras rendered in pokerwork, possums carved into furniture, and landscape artists everywhere sought to represent places that they knew to be beautiful—and sacred. For centuries, Nonconformist suspicion around the visual arts had meant that only biblical text adorned chapels and few Dissenters became artists of note. This new flourishing required a reimagining of what had been a restrained religious aesthetic. How could the painting of seashells be anything other than a distraction from the gospel? How could the decoration of walls and homewares be more than vanity? Artists put their brushes aside, and wrote. They explained the relationship between beauty and the sacred, and how it was that nature held the two together. Ernest Unwin mused, "In contemplating with a sympathetic insight the beauties of Nature, are we in touch with the art of God?"[1]

The study of nature became a holy pursuit, and its representation in art an expression of spiritual insight. In the Religious Society of Friends, a denomination without ordained clergy, teachers and artists became evangelists for the cause. Ernest Unwin advocated for the "cultivation of the sense of beauty" in the young, the planting of trees and flowers in schools, and the provision of outdoor seating so that students might sit and wonder.[2] The cultivation of gardens went hand in hand with the cultivation of a sense of beauty and the sacred. Mary Packer Harris considered the artistic observation of nature to be a balm for the soul, advocating for "the peace that painting and communions with nature brought."[3] Artistic appreciation of the beauty of nature, and of God in the landscape, was a way of holiness.

Seeing Beauty with Unwin and Harris

The Religious Society of Friends, or Quakers, were especially prominent in art and in writings on beauty. Among them, botanical and natural history illustrators are most noted, but there were also printmakers and craftswomen working in leather and tapestry, and (with reference to landscape's etymological origins in the painterly term *landskip*) painters of the Australian landscape. Many of these artists wrote no more words than the Latin names and descriptive notes of a field naturalist. Such simple expression is characteristic of Quakerism whose adherents were drawn to the natural sciences and an aesthetic founded in the observation of God's creation.[4] The articulation of that aesthetic fell to teachers and artists. In the landscape of twentieth-century Australia, two members of the Religious Society of Friends were especially able to articulate the Quaker vision of divinity in beauty. Ernest Ewart Unwin (1881–1944) was a teacher, biologist, and landscape artist who used watercolors to combine his interests in art and the natural world. Mary Packer Harris (1891–1978) was a teacher, gardener, and artist who worked in diverse media including watercolor and gouache, tapestry and woodblock print. The stories of their lives intersected with their art and writing, teaching and love of nature.

Unwin's book, *Religion and Biology*, explains evolution and argues that humans are of the animal world yet set apart in their connection to God through the natural world in which God works.[5] His final chapters are essays on beauty: "The Appeal of Beauty" and "The Kingdom of Man and the Kingdom of God." Published the year before his arrival in Australia, the book's reception and influence within Australian Protestant Dissent was undoubtedly aided by Unwin's powerful presence in the religious and educational landscapes. The book was advertised in the Tasmanian press and mentioned in association with Unwin's public speaking engagements.[6] It played a significant factor in building his reputation as an expert on biology and education.[7] *Religion and Biology* met with favorable reviews in the Australian newspapers of the 1920s: "a masterly exposition of the evolutionary concept," and "the story of animate nature is one long but not straight course of development … [of] essential, inherent spirituality. That story has never been better told than in this volume."[8] In 1932 he briefly returned to the theme of beauty and the sacred in a short essay "One Hundred Years" on the centenary of Quakerism in Australia.[9]

Unwin was born in Kent, England, the youngest child of Sophia Martin, a former servant, and Uriah Unwin, a bricklayer. He was educated at Quaker schools before becoming a biologist and teacher. He taught at the Friends' school in Ackworth, the University of Leeds, and the Friends' Bootham School in York. While science master at the Friends' school, Leighton Park, in Reading, he was approached by Edwin Ashby from South Australia to become the next principal of The Friends' School in Hobart.[10] Reportedly, "great things" were hoped of the new biologist principal as, according to a former Bootham student who had moved to Hobart, "Sports are taking too much of the time that might better be devoted to Natural History and other out-of-school pursuits."[11] Unwin served in this role from 1923, promoting both biology and Arts and Crafts, until his death in 1944 aged 63.

Ernest Unwin's presence consolidated the spiritually minded study of science and art, already valued among Tasmanian Quakers. He arrived with a long-standing interest in natural history writing and the Arts and Crafts movement.[12] Under his leadership, the syllabus expanded as part of his vision for education that extended beyond preparation for work alone and toward the nurture of souls. He set an example in the study of art—part of what they termed "training for leisure"—in his own painting and was noted within the Quaker community as an "outstanding" artist who had exhibited a number of times, including a "very extensive exhibition" of nearly a hundred paintings in 1929.[13] Unwin's photographic portrait shows him at his desk, in an office that was not austere and plain (in the purest Quaker tradition), but adorned with paintings.

Remembered as "kindly and sympathetic," the extent and breadth of Unwin's public service was extraordinary.[14] He was twice president of the Tasmanian Council of Churches, twice vice president of the Royal Society of Tasmania, a founding member of the Biological Club in Hobart, a Trustee of the Tasmanian Museum and Botanical Gardens, on the Tasmanian government's committee on educational extension, instrumental in establishing the Association of Headmasters and Headmistresses of the Independent Schools of Tasmania, president of Rotary and of the Free Kindergarten Association, and a member of the University Council and of the Council of the Art Society.[15] He is commemorated in the naming of Unwin Street, Weston, in the Australian Capital Territory. Running parallel, in Weston's suburban landscape of Australian artists, are streets named for Hans Heysen, Margaret Preston, and, a little further south along Streeton Drive, Arrernte artist Albert Namatjira.[16] Unwin's works are held in private collections and at the Tasmanian Museum and Art Gallery.

Mary Packer Harris was also born in Britain and resident in Australia. She worked in paint, printing, and textiles, and was a teacher of arts, crafts, and literature, and it was in this capacity that she wrote an illustrated hardcover book on the history and appreciation of art, titled *Art, the Torch of Life* (1946).[17] It was late in her career—she had been a teacher for thirty years and an artist for longer—and it was not Harris's first attempt to write on beauty.[18] This new effort was backed by her former colleague, then current Director of Education for South Australia, Dr. Charles Fenner, and was destined to be well read.[19] *Art, the Torch of Life* was intended as a school text providing specialized Australian content as art appreciation entered the mainstream secondary school curriculum.[20] It dwells often on the relationship between art, literature, the natural landscape, and spirituality. Harris's particular view on art is suggested in her title: art was the flame that animated life and, so, it was of God.[21]

Unlike other art primers, *Art, the Torch of Life* does not begin with classical civilizations or the so-called primitive art of Europe and America.[22] Instead it begins in Australia with the rock art of First Nations peoples. As reviewers noted, she omitted classical architecture (so favored by the Congregationalist and Baptist chapel builders) and proceeded quickly through medieval painting to chapter 13, "The Mystery of Rembrandt."[23] Harris was ever alert to mystery. Leaving European art with Rembrandt in the 1600s, Harris moved directly to nineteenth-century Australian landscape, dedicating entire chapters to paintings by each of Hans Heysen, and the Australian impressionists, Frederick McCubbin, Tom Roberts, Arthur Streeton, Emanuel Phillips Fox, and Sydney Long.[24] To Harris, always concerned with Inner Light, these painters of light and landscape appealed where modern art did not. She concluded where she had begun, with "The Development of Australian Art," and the suggestion (after Preston) that its distinctiveness and its future may lie in First Nations art. It was a most unusual survey of the history of art, having a distinct leaning toward Australian landscape and an emphasis on beauty as ethical and spiritual. The influence of the Arts and Crafts movement is very evident, prompting one reviewer of *Art, the Torch of Life* to write,

"Disciples of Ruskin are rare these days ... her whole approach to art is Ruskinian in its idealistic emphasis on ethical qualities. Even her style is exclamatory to suit!"[25]

Some of the oversights of the first book were addressed in a second volume published two years later: *The Cosmic Rhythm of Art and Literature* (1948).[26] It was welcomed by critics who warmly noted Harris as an established author.[27] This second text begins with an analysis of the poem "Testament of Beauty" by Robert Bridges (which was also the title of an exhibition organized by Harris in 1939). *The Cosmic Rhythm* then covers European painting from the late 1600s to the Impressionists, drawing connections with English literature. Contemporary European art was again omitted. The final chapters address stained glass, sculpture, terracotta, mosaic, and "Architectural Decoration." The focus is on Australian public art, leading one reviewer to comment that the book "will enable many of us to see with new eyes buildings in the capital cities which had been passed by without a thought."[28] The landscape looked different through the lens provided by Harris.

Born in Yorkshire, Mary Packer Harris was the daughter of Mary Elizabeth Packer, a former dealer in Berlin wools (for needlepoint) with a long Quaker heritage, and Clement Antrobus Harris, professor of music and organist at St Columba's Episcopal Church, Crieff, Scotland.[29] She studied at Edinburgh School of Art, before undertaking postgraduate work in woodblock printing.[30] During the Great War she was appointed as Art Mistress in Buckie, Banffshire, when the Art Master was killed in France.[31] The trauma of the Great War was a significant factor in her move from Anglicanism to the Quakers. Her elder brother Antrobus Harris, organist at St James Episcopal Church in Cupar, Fife, died in Armentieres, and her brother John Harris, a horticulturalist, was "broken in mind and spirit from Gallipoli."[32] Mary met with John in 1918, at the home of their uncle John Gilbert Baker, Quaker botanist and curator of the Kew Gardens Herbarium. It was there that her brother encouraged her to follow him to Australia.[33] Mary and her parents joined John in Adelaide in 1921.[34]

In South Australia, in connection with her mother's Quaker friends, Edwin Ashby, Professor Raymond Wilton, and Mrs. Annie Wilton, Mary Harris rediscovered her religious heritage and became a committed member of the Religious Society of Friends.[35] As with other Quaker women, the demands of Quaker principles and a sense of connection to a shared Quaker past imbued every part of Harris's life and work.[36] From 1922 Harris taught a range of crafts at the South Australian School of Arts and Crafts. In the summer of 1929–30 Harris visited Unwin at The Friends' School, Hobart, where they discussed their teaching curricula. She recalled, on finding that the subject "History of Art" was taught at The Friends' School, "the idea came to me that we should teach History of Art in our own School of Arts and Crafts in South Australia."[37] Quaker connections opened a new creative phase in Harris's life and work. On her return to South Australia the syllabus expanded accordingly and she taught both literature and the history and appreciation of art in the School of Arts and Crafts' newly formed Girls' Central Arts School. Her experiences here ideally placed her to write *Art, the Torch of Life* when, a decade later, an educational text was required for government schools in South Australia. Her book played an important early role in the state school curriculum.

Harris also taught at the independent nondenominational Wilderness School for girls and lectured on Sundays at the National Gallery of South Australia.[38] She exhibited with the Royal South Australian Society of Arts (1922–67) and held a number of other exhibitions. In the 1930s she edited the School of Arts and Crafts' annual, *The Forerunner*.[39] Harris directed her students in plays inspired by the lives of artists and the theme of peace, the first of which was staged in Adelaide's "Botanic Gardens, under the green depths of Morton [sic] Bay fig trees."[40] Students remembered her as a "motherly or maiden-aunt soul" or, alternately, an "avenging angel" who would not stand for artifice and self-interest: a stance consistent with Quaker "plaining."[41]

After Harris's death in 1978 the Walkerville Council declined the bequest of her home and garden, which she had called "Bundilla Sanctuary." The small and sufficient Quaker house was at odds with the dominant ethos of urban development and not deemed worthy of preservation. Next to her garden, the municipal park was renamed. The religious term "Sanctuary" was omitted, but the newly titled "Mary P. Harris 'Bundilla' Reserve" maintained cultural memory of Harris, even as it forgot her sense of sacred place.[42] Harris's works are held by the Art Gallery of South Australia, Ballarat Art Gallery, Walkerville Council, and in private collections.

The Religious Society of Friends in England and Australia

Twentieth-century Quaker writings on beauty represent an approach to landscape that is rooted in Protestant Dissent and particular to the denomination. The Religious Society of Friends was founded in 1646 by George Fox who became convinced that within each person the Inner Light of God could be found and nurtured. An insistence on continuing revelation put the Quakers at odds with a priestly Established Church, and their Dissenting views saw them suffer significant persecution in the 1600s. In nineteenth-century Australia the Quakers practiced a non-creedal, nonclerical faith: something they shared with other Nonconformists such as early Churches of Christ and Brethren. However, Quakers differed from much of Australian Protestant Dissent in that they did not celebrate sacraments, practice liturgical worship, or preach, instead preferring to pray in silence and express their theology in practical concern and advocacy.[43] Belief in continuing revelation and the cultivation of those virtues demonstrated by Jesus made for a faith characterized not by speaking the Word but by listening and acting. In contrast with the joyful noise of other Dissenters, silent listening played an important part in awakening Quakers to the spiritual presence in this seemingly silent land.

Along with other denominations, the Quakers in Britain and Australia were influenced by the rise of Evangelicalism.[44] However, by the turn of the twentieth century the impact of Evangelicalism on the Religious Society of Friends had waned and older ways were "reasserted."[45] While evangelical sectors of Dissent continued to focus on the interiority of the sinful heart, Quakers returned to looking to the interior divine: the light within. A more liberal theology came to the fore at this time also.[46] It was sometimes characterized by a Christology that held Jesus to be a prophet who, through his full relationship with God, became a revelation and an example for everyone who would seek intimacy with the divine.[47] Such a belief denied salvation through Jesus' sacrificial death on the cross and instead demanded studied personal transformation and ethical practice. Despite the changes, Australian Quakerism continued to appeal to its own tradition and this was aided by strong links with British Friends. The General Meeting for Australia remained officially a part of the London Yearly Meeting until 1964.[48] Mid-twentieth-century Australian Quakerism held onto much of old English Dissent.

The Religious Society of Friends have always been a small denomination in Australia.[49] Nevertheless, they produced a statistically significant number of recognized artists, all of whom found artistic inspiration in nature. Many combined their love of natural beauty with the collection of natural history specimens, as if divinity might be held and preserved. Quaker artist-gardeners exemplified the Quaker approach to the Australian landscape: in particular, Alison Ashby, Edwin Ashby, W. Lewis May, Alfred May, Elinor Robey, and Olive Pink. Several are remembered in the names of native Australian plants—for example, *Acacia ashbyae*—or the street names in suburban Banks, Kambah, and Downer in the nation's capital city Canberra. All grounded their art and spirituality in the Australian landscape. Such an appreciation carried with it a particular aesthetic. They were not drawn to the extroverted color and large flower heads of camellias and roses but to the myriad tiny wildflowers and subtle tones of the Australian bush. Together, these artists exhibited a generosity in their love of the Australian landscape that saw several bequeath their natural history collections or curated landscapes. Significantly, they did not gift their land and botany to the Religious Society of Friends, but instead quietly graced the wider Australian community with their faithful vision of landscape.

Cultivating an Aesthetic of Dissent

The Religious Society of Friends exemplified centuries-old concerns in Protestant Dissent over graven images and vain appearances, even eschewing colorful clothing and decoration within the home.[50] In the pursuit of a simplicity that would free the self from the concerns of the world—a self-forgetting humility—Quakers exercised an aesthetic of "moral restraint" and shunned the arts for centuries.[51] Instead, they adopted an ethos of "plaining," a preference for, or insistence on, simplicity in design, usefulness, and lack of vanity. In practice this meant that domestic objects were without ornamentation, homes without decoration, and all ostentation was spurned. Worship took place in meetinghouses that were likewise conspicuous in their simplicity and lack of ecclesiastical architecture and imagery.[52] Many adherents in the early twentieth century still wore clothes of Quaker gray, as had generations past. Not merely a de facto uniform and indicator of belonging, the adoption of Quaker gray was an ascetic practice that directed the gaze inward. It attempted to deflect the observers' focus to God who dwelled within the individual.[53] Despite this, in the eye of the public, it was Quaker gray rather than inner faith that characterized the Religious Society of Friends—a perception to which numerous references in the Australian press attest.[54]

Paradoxically, Quakers stood out for their cultivated artlessness, an aesthetic of "plaining" that bodily incorporated moral and spiritual dimensions.[55] In the light of such characteristically artless "plaining," how did the Quakers produce visual artists?

The experience of American and English Quakers provided precedents for artists working within Australian Quakerism. The American artist and Quaker preacher Edward Hicks (1780–1849) overcame his religious community's social prohibitions around the decorative arts with a series of paintings based on Isa. 11:6-9: "The wolf will live with the lamb, the leopard will lie down with the goat … and a little child will lead them … They will neither harm nor destroy on all my holy mountain."[56] For Quakers, these verses described a vision of the end times, of an eternal harmony between all creatures.[57] The more than sixty paintings of "The Peaceable Kingdom" by Hicks combined the powerful trio of nature, craftsmanship, and the Religious Society of Friends' earth-bound eschatological vision in which the "wolf will live with the lamb" (Isa. 11:6). As if to indicate the signs of the coming kingdom, Hicks included historical images of earthly peace in his portrayals of the Isaiah prophecy: for instance, William Penn's treaty with the Lenape People appears in one version.[58] Hicks's prophetic visualization of utopian landscape brought acceptance of art within the religious community—the "Peaceable Kingdom" kept the peace. Facing similar concerns in his faith community in England, Joseph Southall (1861–1944) conveyed his sacred vision through allegory.[59] Like Hicks, who began his working life as a craftsman coach painter before moving into decorative arts, Southall emphasized the useful craft involved in his art. He styled himself as an "artist-craftsman" whose paintings were a ministry that illustrated Quaker beliefs.[60] Southall's focus on craft, and in particular the demanding processes around tempera, lent his work the moral authority of honest labor in a religious community in which the value of decorative art was in question.[61] Nature, craft, and prophetic vision authorized the work of Quaker artists.

A number of other Dissenting denominations produced professional artists in Australia. Their tendency toward crafts and the realism of photography and nature studies reveal their shared prohibition of graven images. Winifred Scott Fletcher (1871–1962), wife of a Methodist minister and founding member of the Arts and Crafts Society in Queensland, was a woodcarver and metalworker specializing in pewter. Lillian Pitts (1872–1947), another Methodist, was a painter in oils. May Creeth (1854–1947) and her sister Helen Creeth (1859–1941), Congregationalists (and former Quakers), were china painters, pyrographers, and photographers. James Cunningham (1841–1903), a Baptist in colonial Sydney, was a woodcarver who specialized in ecclesiastical work in Baptist, Wesleyan, and Anglican churches. In 1911, Rex Hazelwood (1886–1968) turned from Baptist ministry to become a noted photographer whose works documented the late stages of the Great War and several government construction projects.[62] Despite the popularity of arts and crafts toward the end of the nineteenth century, and participation as amateurs and hobbyists, Nonconformists are underrepresented among recognized Australian artists. Commitment to Protestant Dissent appeared to be an impediment to life as an artist, except for the Quakers.

In the nineteenth century, arts and crafts became popular in mainstream education. The trend was also evident in Quaker schools as the Religious Society of Friends found the development to be compatible with their beliefs. It came at a time when the Quakers were increasingly open to broader social currents: the practice of shunning those members who married outside the faith declined, and aspects of Evangelicalism that were then sweeping through the Protestant denominations were adopted.[63] According to a study of American Quaker College syllabuses in the nineteenth century, it was the *useful* crafts such as sewing, embroidery, mapmaking, and mechanical drawing that were the first to be introduced into the curriculum.[64] Following the dictum of George Fox (1624–1691), founder of the Religious Society of Friends, that the young should be educated in matters "civil and useful," the inclusion of such studies was justified by an appeal to practicality. Courses in decorative arts followed, becoming widespread by the turn of the twentieth century.[65]

Civil and Useful, and Beautiful

In late-nineteenth-century Australia, numerous courses in crafts were offered by Mechanics' Institutes and Technical Schools.[66] This was followed, in the early 1900s, by the establishment of Arts and Crafts Societies in major Australian cities, a move influenced by the British Arts and Crafts movement.[67] Responding to currents in education and the Quaker call to usefulness, The Friends' School in Hobart, Tasmania, offered technical studies from the time of its foundation in 1887.[68] In the small circle of Tasmanian Quakers, former students returned to the school as teachers.[69] The studies expanded throughout the 1920s and were promoted as an important part of "training for leisure."[70] In 1938 The Friends' School's report to the Friends' General Meeting of Australia boasted that "the range of crafts is most extensive. It comprises watercolour sketching, carving, modelling and pottery; needlecraft, leather and metal work; woodwork, including individual work, as well as repair and other jobs for the community; the work is of high order."[71] The preference for crafts, and the inclusion of painting in watercolor as craft, is revealing. It speaks not only of the "civil and useful" but also of the persistent influence of the Arts and Crafts movement in Quakerism as it resonated with the Quaker aesthetic.

The Arts and Crafts movement began in Britain in the mid-nineteenth century and was led by critic John Ruskin and artist William Morris.[72] The movement shared much with Quaker values. Leading Arts and Crafts proponent William Morris (1834–1896) once studied for the Anglican priesthood and frequently undertook commissions for religious art and craft, but found his vocation in creating beauty in the home.[73] Morris was renowned for his advice, "Have nothing in your house that you do not know to be useful, or believe to be beautiful."[74] The similarity to Fox's "civil and useful" is immediately apparent, and more so on further examination of the principles of Arts and Crafts design.[75]

In an age of increasing mechanization, the Arts and Crafts movement advocated for a return to traditional handcrafts. The value of work was celebrated in making visible the craftwork of an object. Materials such as fabrics and timbers were also honored by the avoidance of fussiness or pretension or unnecessarily precious materials.[76] It was an aesthetic that recognized labor and shared humanity. Quakers appreciated the simplicity, truth, authenticity, and honest labor embodied in these principles. The cost of labor, however, put many useful and beautiful things out of reach of the masses. Likewise, Quaker meetinghouses were known to prioritize furnishings that were plain and restful for the spirit, even if expensive, rather than to furnish on a budget.[77] Delight in creating and in the beauty of creation held a special place in Quaker art and aesthetics. This coincided happily with the Arts and Crafts movement's fondness for imagery from the natural world.[78] The critic Ruskin (perhaps influenced by his evangelical background) located beauty not in "fancy-dress piety" but in the precise depiction of the botanical world.[79] With the Quakers' long interest in botany, this was an aesthetic they could embrace.

Observing Nature

A century before the rise of the Arts and Crafts movement, an avid interest in documenting the wonders of creation enabled many Quakers to find artistic expression in the form of botanical illustration. Indeed, the first Quaker known to visit Australian shores was the botanical illustrator and natural history draughtsman, Sydney Parkinson (1745–1771), who traveled aboard HMS *Endeavour* in the employ of Joseph Banks. Preceding a wave of Quaker immigration to the Australian colonies,[80] in 1831 the nurseryman James Backhouse (1794–1869) sailed to Van Diemen's Land on the barque *Science*, along with George Washington Walker (1800–1859), with the twin objectives of Quaker mission and the study of Australian flora.[81] They were capable artists: Backhouse in particular had a clear artistic skill and an eye trained in botanical observation.[82] Their observational science extended also to the study of First Nations peoples, noting their mistreatment, though Australian Quakers have since sought to distance themselves from the paternalism of such an approach.[83] In this way, two enduring concerns within Australian Quakerism—native botany and the rights of First Nations people—are present in the founding narratives of the Religious Society of Friends in Australia. Both concerns persisted into the twentieth century and produced a number of noted Australian anthropologists, botanists, and botanical illustrators.[84]

At The Friends' School in Hobart, botany and observational science were especially encouraged with the formation of a Natural History and Essay Society and the generosity of Friends in England who sent "valuable collections of geological and botanical specimens" to aid the students' education.[85] Early teachers and board members at the school maintained a particular interest in the subject and, in the 1920s, Principal Ernest Unwin drew on his Master of Science (in entomology) to introduce physiology and botany into the curriculum.[86] Collecting was encouraged, and in 1938 the school reported, "More than 60 flower collections were shown ... as well as others of insects and grasses."[87]

Australian Quakers rose to prominence in the promotion of indigenous plantings in gardens.[88] They were part of a long botanical tradition in the Religious Society of Friends in Britain and America.[89] Founder George Fox and influential leader William Penn both advocated the study of nature as part of a faithful life.[90] There were a number of reasons why so many Quakers were drawn to botany and other observational sciences. Scientific study, and fellowship in the Royal Society of London, was one of the few pastimes that enabled Quakers to participate in civil society "on equal terms" within the restrictions that applied to Nonconformists.[91] The Quaker community viewed the observational sciences as "innocent trades," free of ethical concerns, which delighted in God's creation.[92] After Darwin's *On the Origin of Species* (1859), botany proved a field in which the scientific skills of observation and classification could be exercised without significant consideration of theoretical science, and its theological consequences (which, under the influence of evangelicalism, were a concern).[93] Most importantly, botany afforded Quakers a spiritual aesthetic that was consistent with "plaining." Through the contemplation of beauty, botany led to the divine.[94] Appreciation of botanical beauty was sanctioned because flowers, however dazzling, and trees, however imposing, were the creation of the divine and not of human vanity.[95] Romanticism's emphasis on the natural was perhaps an encouraging factor, and botanical art was a popular pastime among educated women generally, but their influence follow Quakerism's first interest in botany.[96] Observational science and the "asceticism, truth and accuracy" of botanical illustration were thus inextricably related in what was an essentially religious aesthetic.[97]

Botanical illustration and writings were widely published within the Religious Society of Friends. Quakers excelled in the publication of botanical books and journals from the 1700s, and in the 1860s the denominational journals of the Religious Society of Friends in Britain ran regular columns on natural history.[98] Australian journals followed the British example, carrying articles on natural science in which plants, birds, and insects were described using scientific Latin names.[99] Their focus on unadorned science and simple observation is quite unlike nature columns in other Australian Nonconformist journals that tend to appropriate nature as a metaphor for human social and ethical matters.[100] Instead, the Religious Society of Friends' "Nature Notes" reads like a secular nature column of the period. But it is essentially Quaker. For the Religious Society of Friends, nature writing needed no human embellishment or analogy with human experience. Appreciation of nature was, in itself, a religious pursuit.

Into the Terrain with Pens and Brushes

Quaker artists found their inspiration in nature. They cultivated the soil, observed the fine detail of the natural world, and traveled the land in search of specimens for each one held within it evidence of the divine. Close and faithful focus on a single "blade of grass" led to questions of transcendence.[101] Ernest Unwin's study of insects led him to discussion of evolution and its purpose. He affirmed the work of Charles Darwin and subsequent evolutionists, finding that "there is no shred of doubt" that humans are part of "the scheme" along with the beasts.[102] He was not alone among scientists in finding that Darwinism could coexist with natural theology.[103] As a Quaker, Unwin had found divine inspiration in nature, and so his book sought to "see what help can be brought from the biological side towards the understanding of a problem which leads into the realms of philosophy and religion."[104] For Unwin, the biological and spiritual were intimately linked, and he found a host of philosophers and poets to attest that "the material evolution of the world becomes the incarnation and the expression of a spiritual meaning, a divine event."[105] God would be found in the beauty of biology.

For the scientist Unwin, nature held a divine key: "The beauty of the daffodil is something of a code through which something of a spiritual meaning comes."[106] Likewise, moving again from the specific to the universal, Unwin wrote that "the whole evolutionary story is a revealing, beauty is a revealing, for God's spirit is in all and around all, and the meaning can be read in some measure through each and all of these various codes."[107] His use of "some measure" and "something of" suggests both a scientist's studied, cautious findings and an inexpressibility when it came to spiritual matters. A sense of the ineffable characterized his conception of the divine.

Mary Packer Harris also looked for the ineffable, or the "mystic," as she called it, in the natural world. Writing some decades after Unwin, and for a secondary school readership, Harris affirmed that "God created the world in love, and in process of evolution man returns the adoration robes of love and imagination to his creator."[108] Unwin took a similar stance: "In contemplating with a sympathetic insight the beauties of Nature, are we in touch with the art of God?"[109] Both writers saw humanity as an essential part of Nature, and such a view engendered a great tenderness toward the created (and evolved) world.

Figs and Eucalypts in the Peaceable Kingdom

Harris dwelt on animals and birds in her artwork, portraying them in scenes of nurture and relationship. Her second textbook begins with the artist's own artwork on the theme. "Life is Sweet, Brother," a watercolor frontispiece to *The Cosmic Rhythm of Art and Literature* is captioned, "On a high farm at the Bluff, Encounter Bay, during the late war this boy, communing with his magpie, built a wattle-and-daub shelter for his pets by this fig tree."[110] Harris was a pacifist and the fig tree strongly suggests Mic. 4:3-4:

> Nation will not lift up sword against nation
> And never again will they train for war.
> Each of them will sit under his vine and under his fig tree,
> With no one to make afraid.

The painting's anti-war sentiment is clear, but, to Quakers familiar with the vine and fig tree on the mountain of the Lord's temple, it also spoke of eschatological hope in Mic. 4:1. Like the American Quaker Edward Hicks, Harris repeatedly drew scenes of the peaceable kingdom on the holy mountain. She perceived the landscape through the Word. The theme recurs at the beginning of her autobiography via a 1934 artwork that features the words of Isa. 11:8, "They shall not hurt nor destroy in all my holy mountain," surrounded by palm trees, birds, and possums (drawn with an awkwardness that suggested she was not entirely at home in this land).[111] In similar vein, her silk and wool embroidery fire screen "The Indian Upon God" (1929), which was based on Yeats's poem, captures a moment of peaceable coexistence among lotus, peacock, and roebuck.[112]

Beauty, art, harmony, and truth were inextricably linked for Harris. According to her former student and colleague Ivor Francis, "beauty was synonymous with 'truth,' and, although truth might be 'many-faceted,' it was always just the one truth." She understood good art to be that which was "inspiring, spiritual, uplifting and ennobling," and refused to focus only on visual aesthetics; there had to be meaning beyond the decorative.[113] Unwin too believed that beauty was linked "to the moral sense, the feeling of right and wrong."[114] Likewise, he advocated bringing "our decisions … before the threefold tribunal of goodness, truth and beauty."[115] He was writing at the intersection of natural science and spirituality, and was not critiqued for his aesthetics. Harris, who was teaching and writing on art, was sometimes seen as "a non-aesthetic and a humbug promulgating her own special psychic interpretation of style in the cause of religious political propaganda."[116] In contrast, Harris thought her work offered an integrated approach, and in the two school textbooks she uses religious language when delivering the highest praise.

Harris describes the landscape art of Hans Heysen as if he were a prophet. Drawing again on scripture, this time Isa. 2:4, she writes that his work "calls us to turn our swords into ploughshares and our spears into pruning hooks and knowledge of peace and beauty will be ours."[117] For Harris, beauty was inextricably linked with the Quaker vision of peace and, not for the last time, she willed an artist in to the spiritual fold.[118] Harris noted Heysen's advocacy on behalf of the Australian landscape and echoed Isa. 40:3 in saying that his "was the voice of one crying in the wilderness [about] the beauty of the gum tree."[119] In Harris's theology of beauty, gum trees were of God and they had their prophet in Heysen.

Harris appreciated Heysen as a landscape artist who did not specialize in grand vistas but in eucalypts and light that "makes us feel the side of things we cannot see."[120] Heysen's work sat well with her ideas about beauty in nature and art. Her two textbooks overlook artists of panoramic majesty and the painstaking realism of botanical illustration often favored by Quakers.[121] Instead, she reads artworks for the suggestion of spirit, for Inner Light, that key Quaker touchstone. In Heysen's painting of misshapen scrub and saplings, "Mystic Morn" (1904), Harris sees "the opalescent beauty of the wayward stems."[122] The painting had been well received and was awarded the National Art Gallery of New South Wales' Wynne Prize for the best painting of an Australian landscape, suggesting that Australians increasingly saw the beauty in such scenes of "scraggy" trees.[123] Harris, however, brought a theological vision to her interpretation when she wrote that the saplings are "possessed of an unruly grace."[124] Not only wayward elegance, Harris perceived divinity that would not be repressed.

Unwin, in his measured way, also insisted that humanity adjust its vision in order to perceive divine beauty. People are prejudiced, he said, against "earthworm and slug, and ignorance and fear may prevent us from recognizing beauty in insect and snake."[125] Better then, he suggested, we should use our "keener insight" to note the "reality of beauty."[126] Asserting that there is nothing ugly in nature, Unwin found a connection between the Quaker idea of "Inwardness" and a mechanistic examination of biological function and form. He located beauty in "usefulness of form," "adaptiveness," and in "the very substance of the organism ... [as] beauty is exhibited when a sense of harmony is awakened."[127] Through the lens of a microscope, the Quaker biologist could find the beautiful concord of the peaceable kingdom within a single organism.[128]

Earthly Revelation

A purely mechanistic approach to science and education disturbed Unwin, just as a "characteristic lack of mysticism" among Australians saw Harris write about art in a manner that verged on the evangelistic.[129] Unwin crusaded for a spiritual education that prepared children for life, not just for industry. Addressing businessmen at a Rotarians' meeting in 1930, he appealed to them saying, "Education should train one to enjoy all the beauty in the world, to follow after truth, to develop a tender and loving spirit."[130] His educational philosophy had its roots in his theory on beauty. Unwin argued that, through a religious vision of the "system of Nature," humanity

> calls upward to a better, more beautiful and more complete life. He knows himself as a moral agent, but he knows, too, that this moral nature has grown out of the ground of the Universe. He feels within himself the emotional thrills as he contemplates the beauty around him; but he is conscious at the same time that the beauty is inherent in the very substance of the Universe.[131]

Beauty was a source of divine revelation for both Harris and Unwin, and, for those who had eyes to see, it could be found in the ordinary things. As a teacher and biologist Unwin encouraged the study of nature because, "as our appreciation widens and deepens, we find stirrings in the spirits from the common things of life, and we learn Peter's lesson, that nothing is common or unclean" (Acts 10:14-15).[132] The examination of the natural world was a path to the spiritual inwardness that was so much a part of Quaker theology. In a tradition that did not celebrate baptism or Eucharist, Unwin noted that each pebble or feather "may call us with its note of beauty and become to us a sacrament."[133] Grace and revelation abounded.

Harris found beauty in the simple and ordinary too. In her analysis of the work of George Morland, eighteenth-century English painter of rural life, she focused on a broom made of hawthorn from the hedgerow in "The Minister's Garden":

> But this stable broom retains the rusticity of the hands that culled and bound its parts; hands of one whose soul was saturate, perhaps unconsciously, with the beauty of dale and hedgerow. For with the labourers in the field familiarity does not breed contempt. They, too, may lie in Abraham's bosom all the year, and worship at the temple's inner shrine, God being with them when they know it not.[134]

Harris's description reveals little about Morland and his painting but much about her own vision of an innate and effortless relationship with the divine through the virtues of craftsmanship and connection with the land. Her vision points to the influence of the Arts and Crafts movement, the Barbizon school of painting with its rustic scenes of peasant life, and spirituality rooted in "the good, wholesome, brown earth."[135]

Combining the Quaker idea of Inner Light with evolutionary theory, Unwin arrived at an earthy stance similar to that of Harris. He wrote, "God does indeed permeate all life as well as being the ground and substance from which the life draws its supplies for growth."[136] Unwin maintained that humans have evolved as a part of nature, and that if people are "conscious of the Spirit of God within," they will also "believe in the presence of the Spirit of God in all things."[137] In Unwin's thinking, evolutionary theory necessarily led Quakers towards panentheism. However, he pointed beyond the idea of God as the "Perfect Environment."[138] Instead, he argued, we are cocreators with the divine "Artist-Creator" in the "creation of his Spiritual Kingdom."[139] The moral and spiritual vision of Isaiah's peaceable kingdom was an ever-present undercurrent in Quaker relationships with the landscape.

Australian Place

While other Australian Quaker artists sought the divine in the detailed world of natural history illustration, both Unwin and Harris worked with a larger and more overtly theological canvas. Unwin painted scenes of rural idyll such as "Wheatfield on the Hill, Opossum Bay, Tas." and of geological interest such as the volcanic massif known as "The Nut" at Stanley on Tasmania's northwest coast and "Quamby Bluff" at the northern end of the Great Western Tiers mountain range in Tasmania's central north. He also captured in watercolor the long Quaker association with the Kelvedon estate at Swansea on Tasmania's east coast, where the Cotton family had lived since 1828.[140] These landscapes were chosen for both their attractiveness and the significance of the site. In painting the Cotton home, Unwin pointed to their belonging in the landscape. The apparent conventionality of the paintings also belies the theoretical understanding behind them, for paintings served to remind Unwin of the "beauties of Nature" and thus of "the Beauty of God, and this belief in the Beauty of God will surely help us to hold fast to the faith."[141]

Harris looked for an authentic Australian spirituality. She was not satisfied with the kitsch commercialism of souvenir Australiana: "Away with the cloven hoof of kookaburras and Sturt Pea, the anguish of stereotyped design, and let us pursue the elusive spirit."[142] Two years earlier Margaret Preston had declared her detestation of kitsch Australiana homewares, but on aesthetic rather than spiritual grounds. When it came to matters of Australian identity and art, Preston's secular thinking seemed to spur Harris to articulate the inner dimension. Rather than seeking an aesthetic patriotism in flora and fauna, Harris looked for God.

Harris also sought spiritual inspiration in literature, though initially not Australian literature. Throughout her writings she quotes the poetry of the *Oxford Book of English*

Figure 10. Ernest Ewart Unwin, *Quamby Bluff*, c. 1930s, Tasmania watercolor.
Source: The Friends' School Archive and Heritage Collection, North Hobart, Tasmania.

Mystical Verse (1917): for example, G. K. Chesterton's "The Holy of Holies," in which the poet finds God in "the heart / Of the smallest of the seeds."[143] In 1932 it did not matter to Harris that the poet was English and Catholic. It was mysticism that spoke to her. As she became more concerned with the place in which she lived, Harris looked for the mystical in the landscape around her. In her 1946 book, *Art, the Torch of Life*, Harris wrote that "Australians have been accused of a characteristic lack of mysticism," but that it may be witnessed in certain landscape paintings that spoke to "the borderland of the spirit."[144] Through the beauty of art, and its portrayal of a mystic landscape, connection with the sacred might be made.

Harris supplemented her early reliance on the *Oxford Book of English Mystical Verse* and English poet laureate Robert Bridges with the poems of Australians Rex Ingamells (1913–1955) and Mary Finnin (1906–1992) of the Jindyworobak literary movement. This group of poets, led by Ingamells, sought to integrate First Nations' culture and spirituality into Australian poetry, much as Preston did in art.[145] They were criticized for their naïve patriotism, Arcadian primitivism, and imitations of Aboriginality. Harris, a lifelong pacifist, did not care for patriotism, but an eschatological Arcadia was exactly what Quakers pursued in the restoration of Isaiah's harmonious vision. The Jindyworobak poetry sat well with Harris and aided her development of a theory of beauty that spoke to Australian art and to the Australian landscape.

In retirement, Harris painted the landscape around her home in Walkerville and the Torrens River/Karrawirra Parri many times, even mounting a solo exhibition, "Paintings of Old Walkerville," in 1963. While earlier exhibitions grouped paintings according to medium, at this stage in her career she arranged the works by terrain: "Trees," "Churches," "Old Homesteads," "Transmutation" (urban development), "Symbolic Pictures at 'Bundilla,'" and "Totemic Ground."[146] The categories speak of landscape and the sacred. Her explanations of the individual works frequently reference her disquiet at the changes to the Walkerville landscape, her ethical concerns, and the presence of the divine. For example, "Golgotha Uprooted" is described: "This tree was the first to fall on Nailsworth Terrace, when the beautiful site was given over to an eight-storey government building. Painted on a Good Friday, the fallen tree suggested an oblique crucifix."[147] Harris understood that the tree itself carried divine presence as well as echoes of the cross of Calvary. The act of painting on Good Friday reinforces the sense that art was a religious vocation rather than a labor for her. Painting was a vocation that demanded moral expression and a spirituality that knew the ancient story to be ever present.

Among the 1963 exhibition artworks with the theme "Totemic Ground" is a painting titled "Out of the Shadow." The accompanying notes mention the recollections of elderly Walkerville resident Mrs Barnard who described "how the aborigines [sic] placed their dead on these white gums."[148] Oral history about the death and absence of First Nations peoples had a powerful presence among colonial settlers, setting apart the holders of stories as the new inheritors of the land.[149] Even among those sympathetic to the movement for Aboriginal rights, such stories confirmed an historic absence. It was a space that had seemingly been vacated physically, morally, and spiritually, a space that might be filled by an artist, campaigner for justice, and mystic. Mrs Barnard's story about trees—ghost gums, no less—and local Kaurna peoples' death ritual made intuitive sense to Harris. She perceived a mystical connection between the death of Kaurna people, their displacement from the landscape, ecological degradation, and divine suffering on the cross. Harris hoped that this new Australian sacred story, rendered in modernist line and color, might fill the historic spiritual void.

Mystical trees permeated Harris's late works. These included her mid-1950s entry in the Blake Prize for Religious Art, "His Cross Is Every Tree,"[150] and "Urban Crucifix," in which the soft lines of tree and man contrast with the rigidity of cross and high-rise, and the soldiers' spears, presented as the finials of a cast iron fence, wait to pierce Christ's side. She revered the white trunked eucalypts at the river bend near "Bundilla" as an ancient funerary place[151] and understood the land to be sacred to a people who no longer inhabited it. In their apparent absence, she believed that since "the white man's coming, it has been sacred to artists, botanists, and youth."[152] In Harris's view, those who were uncorrupted by commercialism and artificiality naturally appreciated sacred places, even if they were newcomers to the land. It was an appropriation of sorts, and something she hinted at in *Art, the Torch of Life*.

The final chapter of Harris's first book mentions Margaret Preston (1875–1963) as an artist who was inspired by "the true spirit of Australian flora" and who understood the "source of creative energy" that was First Nations art.[153] Harris, too, hoped that "the symbolism of the Aborigines may prove a touchstone in this materialistic age."[154] They were both influenced by a movement in modern art that sought inspiration in primitivism.[155] Harris reprinted totemic images collected by Adelaide-based anthropologist Charles P. Mountford (1890–1976) in the book's endpapers and explained them, noting their relationship to "sacred totemic places," in her opening chapter. The designs were not merely decorative but were associated with "a certain magical element," and their "meaning has to be interpreted"—preferably, Harris observed, with the assistance of First Nations peoples from specific sacred lands.[156] Her understanding of totemic images as "magical" reflected her romanticism and her dependence on the religious interpretations of anthropologists who viewed the works and their makers as primitive, though she is careful to say that the art is also "unlike much primitive art" and that the artists were not primitive but merely "like primitive man"; the difference is almost imperceptible. Her use of the totemic images might be seen as totemic in itself. After all, they represented Harris's own "intimate and altogether special relation"[157] with the midcentury movement to promote First Nations art (and, sometimes, spirituality) "from which," she argued, "a characteristic Australian art should develop."[158]

In *The Cosmic Rhythm of Art and Literature*, Harris examined the "Aboriginal Theme in Ceiling Decoration" in two public buildings: the Children's Hospital in Adelaide and Winthrop Hall in Perth. Harris valued children's imaginations and so she applauded Dorrit Black's depiction of a First Nations' creation story for the ceiling for the Children's Hospital. George Benson's ceiling design in Winthrop Hall at the University of Western Australia was more problematic. Harris reported that Benson claimed to have used "every totemic and symbolic pattern" in the Spencer Collection of Indigenous Artefacts at Melbourne Museum, "without seeking to elucidate the meaning" of the symbols.[159] This last matter clearly concerned her. She framed her discussion of Benson's work around it. "Perhaps Mr Benson is wise not to endeavour to translate," she concluded charitably, explaining the variability of interpretation in different landscapes and implying the impossibility of finding meaning in Benson's jumble of imagery. Benson was hardly alone in his artistic approach. Author Eleanor Dark in *The Timeless Land* (1941) claimed that, in her depiction of the first inhabitants of Port Jackson, she "borrowed shamelessly from other tribes" and "enormously over-simplified" First Nations' religion lest it take up too much room in the novel.[160] For Harris, Benson's confused appropriation of First Nations art echoed the "cloven hoof" of secular souvenir Australiana. In her vision, beauty must be always moral, meaningful, and spiritually authentic.

A New and Timeless Vision

Reflecting her two textbooks, Mary Harris increasingly saw the landscape through the lens of contemporary First Nations art and story. She felt a connection with the land around her, especially with her sacred garden, "Bundilla Sanctuary."[161] Inevitably, she sought to bring her growing understanding of landscape into her painting. Still speaking in a Scottish brogue, she understood that her belonging to the land and its ancient symbolism was tenuous.[162] She took inspiration from Albert Namatjira (1902–1959) who had successfully adopted the "idiom which belongs to the white people."[163] Working in the European tradition and in her familiar palette of yellow, blue, and green, she changed her style in order to incorporate brushstroke and geometry suggestive of First Nations art, and the Western Arrernte Hermannsburg school to which Namatjira belonged, in particular.[164]

Seeking a new harmonization of First Nations and European cultures, Harris self-consciously adopted (and adapted) Namatjira's adopted idiom. Such circularity made a curious kind of intuitive sense in Harris's equally circular eschatological search for a future imbued with the ever-present past. Namatjira and the other artists of the Hermannsburg school had taken on "the European way of seeing," employing a palette and style reminiscent of nineteenth-century Holy Land scenes that had been printed on scripture memory verse cards.[165] In his paintings Namatjira represented, again and again, paradise lost. From the perspective of the mission station at Hermannsburg, it was a paradise that was at once both biblical and precolonial. His landscapes of Central Australia effectively mimicked Holy Land illustration that was, in turn, a Protestant artistic venture to recover the natural purity of the biblical landscape. Such Protestant artworks frequently omitted signs of modernity and contemporary people who did not belong in the narrative of the biblical past. Simultaneously, Namatjira depicted an Australian landscape untouched by European colonizers who were present in the land but, in his works, often unseen. Like the travelers to the Holy Land who resisted writing about the incongruent convenience of the modern steam train from Jaffa to ancient Jerusalem, Namatjira famously omitted the railway tracks that cut across the landscape at Heavitree Gap.[166] The depiction of paradise required a timeless imagination. With Preston encouraging artists to "be Aboriginal,"[167] Harris had no trouble in justifying the appropriation of First Nations approaches in her search for an Australian spirituality.

In her art, Harris increasingly strove to portray the land's mystical reality, transcending physical representation. Most Quaker artists sought accurate reproduction of nature's divine wonders. Harris was closer to Ernest Unwin's Ruskin-inspired thinking that believed art revealed an expression of the "stirring of the Divine Spirit … of the God who is all-beauty" via the "technique of an artist."[168] Mere representation was not enough. She reasoned that, in order to portray the beauty of the land, its mystical and authentic truth, she needed to (and was entitled to, even called to) convey the First Peoples' spirit of the land. It was something she believed she could feel as an artist and mystic: "I, an artist, so loved this place, I think the myths of the Aborigines became a part of my being."[169] Further inspiration came via a visit from Ngarrindjeri political activist Olga Fudge who warned against painting that was "too academic" and reportedly foretold that Harris would soon paint with the "true feeling of the Aborigines and their spirit world."[170]

After meeting with Olga Fudge, Harris produced four paintings based on Arrernte poems translated by the anthropologist T. G. H. Strehlow in *An Australian Viewpoint* (1950).[171] Strehlow's argument that "too few Australians really regard the land of their birth as their spiritual home" was one with which Harris readily agreed.[172] In 1956 these works were exhibited at Lady Symon Hall, University of Adelaide, alongside others "inspired by the Aboriginal motif."[173] These included bark paintings and several works by Eric Thake and Arrernte artists of the Hermannsburg school: Albert Namatjira, Otto Pareroultja, and Lindsay Imbarndarinja.[174] Strehlow himself opened the exhibition with an address, reported in the *Advertiser*, which commended Harris's "new vision" and noted that her paintings "remain European in execution, if not in concept."[175] Rita Dunstan, in Adelaide's *News*, reported that Harris's painting "The Timeless Time" was inspired by Olga Fudge "through her psychic sense," and that Harris had achieved this vision through observing the "rhythmic movements of a big gumtree."[176] In the 1940s, artist Margaret Preston and anthropologist Leonard Adams fostered the belief that "rhythm" was the "defining feature of Aboriginal art."[177] In the light of such thinking, Harris's painting of "rhythmic movements"—like the naming of her second book, *Cosmic Rhythm*—is an expression of her search for authenticity.[178]

Of Harris's four works in the 1956 exhibition, "The Timeless Time" was chosen to be purchased by the Religious Society of Friends and donated to the National Gallery of South Australia.[179] The title evokes Eleanor Dark's *The Timeless Land*, Preston's understanding of "Aboriginal peoples as a 'timeless' race," and the prevailing views in anthropology that all primitive people shared a timeless, storied past from which they would emerge as scientific thinkers.[180] From a historian's viewpoint, the concept of timelessness masks the complexity and dynamism of First Nations history.[181] However, Harris's timeless vision was not concerned with the past but with an eschatology of eternal presence, a past-present-future eternity of harmony, between all peoples, all creatures, all matter, and all spirit.[182]

"The Timeless Time" uses the same color palette as the earlier work, "Life is Sweet, Brother," which, likewise, addresses the text of Isaiah 11. But the color is flatter, sinuous

Figure 11. Mary P. Harris, "The Timeless Time," c. 1949, Adelaide, gouache on paper on board, 68.0 × 96.0 cm.

Source: Gift of the Society of Friends, 1956, Art Gallery of South Australia, Adelaide.

lines mark the earth, and the "rhythmic" white branches of a eucalypt dominate the composition. White tree trunks were so often a feature of the Hermannsburg school paintings, and the use of parallel lines and a less representational style suggests the influence of Otto Pareroultja.[183] The parallel lines may also reference Strehlow's translation of "Aranda couplets" in which he describes the patterns apparent in the outline of hills and valleys.[184] Harris's angular geometry suggests both totemic motifs and swathes of cut wheat drying in distant paddocks: a parallelism of First Nations and Christian spirituality.

In the same exhibition there appeared another of Harris's works that, in her autobiography, she refers to as "Rain Song," noting its inspiration by Strehlow's translations of an Arrernte (Aranda) Rain Song, "with its human figure and great boulder merged in one."[185] Harris recalled that Strehlow purchased the work, but descriptions of the work fit that of the Art Gallery of South Australia's 2012 acquisition, "Rain Ancestor of Kaporilja." This painting depicts Kantjia, described by Strehlow as the "mythical rain ancestor of Kaporilja" in "one of the Aranda Rain Songs."[186] The water of life runs over and through the immutable rain ancestor. Inviting further religious analogue, Strehlow reported that the Arrernte People believed this ancestor had killed and resurrected his son.[187] Such mystical connections were irresistible to Harris. In the foreground of the painting, further referencing the "Aranda Rain Song," is a wallaby depicted in the totemic style of Charles P. Mountford in the endpapers of *Art, the Torch of Life*.[188] Ever the evangelist, she imagined she was pioneering a harmonious and spiritual aesthetic. But Harris's blending of European landscape and Aboriginal-inspired design was not universally well received and she recalled that the exhibition was hurriedly dismantled without explanation. She was devastated and bewildered.[189]

Harris believed she was a champion of First Nations people and spirituality. She donated funds to Fudge's "Aboriginal Hostel," supported land rights campaigns, educated herself through the work of anthropologists, exhibited alongside Arrernte artists, mourned the ill-effects of colonization, and abhorred the commercialization of Aboriginal art motifs when divorced from their meaning.[190] She understood that place was deeply significant in First Nations art and life, and rarely borrowed motifs without reference to region, unlike Preston and Benson.[191] Finally, she believed that her use of Arrernte mythology, stylized motifs, and "rhythm" was not an appropriation but a sympathetic new harmonization of First Nations and European artistic representations of sacred land.[192] Critics disagreed, primed via their opposition to the pseudo-Aboriginal work of Preston and the pseudo-European work of the Hermannsburg movement.[193] They did not see a portrayal of mystic oneness, but something like the "false spiritualism of so-called 'white Aboriginals'" of which other artists were accused.[194] Harris was indignant when the critic at the *Advertiser* accused her of "muzzy mysticism" and, despite her two school texts, a "lack of knowledge of Aboriginal art."[195] White Australian critics and artists vied with one another, claiming superior knowledge of First Nations art; it was a quest for dominance that reflected their relationship to the First Nations peoples whom they sought, problematically, to protect and to promote both culturally and commercially. Harris imagined that her spiritual and artistic questing set her apart from the colonialist stance. She had spread the word, like a voice in the wilderness, about the aesthetic and spiritual value of First Nations art. She had sought a sacred connection with their land, and, despite awareness of colonialism's ongoing injustices, was confounded by the suggestion that her artwork could not express the oneness of all people. She turned her focus to the patronage of another artist who, like herself, felt that he had spiritual and artistic insight. William Ricketts, or "Brother Billy," as he liked to be known, considered himself an adopted brother of the Pitjantjatjara people of central Australia.

Art in the Peaceable Kingdom

In 1947, the year between the publishing of *Art, the Torch of Life* and *The Cosmic Rhythm of Art and Literature*, an exhibition of William Ricketts's clay sculptures of Pitjantjatjara people was held in Adelaide.[196] Harris took her students. She thought that Ricketts's work reminded her of the Dissenter artist, poet, and mystic William Blake. He denied such influences but, like Harris's art, his work reflected the Arts and Crafts movement and carried a (conflicted) concern for First Nations spirituality and landscape.[197] In the years to follow Harris became an ardent supporter of Ricketts and there grew between them, as she put it, "an everlasting friendship."[198] Eternity figured in their way of seeing.

Soon after Harris's house was built in Walkerville in 1952, she heard from Ricketts "in his Mount Dandenong Sanctuary," east of Melbourne, Victoria, with the news that he would give her "precious works to form a River Sanctuary on the banks of the Torrens at 'Bundilla.'"[199] She described with delight the clay sculpture "Billy and Tjikalyi" in which the "white man crouches and embraces the child Tjikalyi" with possum and lyrebirds in attendance.[200] In Ricketts's sculptures, Harris saw a vision of harmony like that in Isaiah: "The wolf will live with the lamb … and a little child will lead them." Others saw his work as kitsch midcentury Australiana (something Harris had previously railed against); or a discordant mix of Pitjantjatjara and Arrernte faces and the cool-climate fauna of the Dandenong Ranges assembled as "actors in his personal crusade"; or representations of Ricketts's sculpted self-identification as a "spiritually informed, and thus privileged, authority, a keeper or protector of the true spirituality that is embodied in the Aboriginal Other."[201] He certainly imagined he was some kind of savior.[202]

The lyrebird, as it featured in "Billy and Tjikalyi" at "Bundilla," was Ricketts's adopted totem. Harris explained this was a symbol of Ricketts's "gospel of love for all living things"—after all, the four Evangelists had their "symbolic creatures" too, equivalents to the "totem creatures of the bush": Mark's lion, Luke's ox, Matthew's angel (according to Harris) or winged man, and John's eagle with "visionary sight as far-reaching as the song of the lyre-bird."[203] Interpreters have struggled to make sense of Ricketts's syncretistic religious outlook, but Harris appreciated his feeling for the "oneness of all things with God."[204] Ever the teacher and evangelist, Harris would school Ricketts in the "holy mountain" of Quaker eschatology.

In the coming year Ricketts reportedly conceived plans for "a Holy Mountain as part of a great spectacle of life."[205] In 1954 he brought more sculptures to Harris's "Sanctuary,"

Figure 12. Mary P. Harris at Bundilla with "Billy and Tjikalyi" by William Ricketts.
Source: Photograph by Fred Whitney, 1974, courtesy of Charles Stevenson.

on his route north to Arrernte Country. She shared with him a copy of *Art, the Torch of Life* in preparation for the journey.[206] He shared with her his plans for "a Holy Mountain in the Centre" of Australia, "a monument which would force non-Aboriginal Australia to sit up and look at the destruction being wrought on *his* country and people."[207] In 1959 Ricketts exhibited further works on the lawn of St. Peters Cathedral, Adelaide, and camped behind in the grounds of the Quaker meetinghouse.[208] Before traveling north again, he wrote, "Dear Friends, I have spoken so often about my Holy Mountain; within the sanctuary of the Friends' Meeting House this beautiful conception of life itself has taken root still deeper. It is just as if I brought a beautiful wildflower and the people drank deep of the pure nectar ... With everlasting love, Billy."[209] Syncretistic and narcissistic, Ricketts adopted the language of Quaker eschatology as his own original, prophetic thought. Harris made exceptions for his behavior—it fitted her romantic vision of prophet-artists—and she continued to support his cause. But, as her two books on the appreciation of art and beauty demonstrate, her own pursuit of the peaceable kingdom demanded she credit every writer and artist who crossed her carefully curated pages. Her vision required a cloud of witnesses: Ruskin, Heysen, the Jindyworobak poets, and, too late to be included in her books, Ricketts. She recruited them all to the cause of truth and beauty, to carry the *Torch of Life*.

Beauty, as Unwin and Harris saw it, was about truth, ethics, and aesthetic feeling that connected with the divine spirit. They were strongly influenced by the writing of Ruskin and the work of the Arts and Crafts movement, years after other artists had moved on. Yet they also drew on a long Quaker heritage in which divinity was found within nature, in the light within all living things. Significantly, the Quaker aesthetic of "plaining" allowed for the representation of such beauty in natural history illustration. The beauty of natural history and art became a holy pursuit that, in the writings of Harris and Unwin, took on the zeal of the evangelist. Unwin undertook to change educational practice so that children were prepared not just for industry but for "all the beauty in the world." Harris espoused an eschatological vision of divine oneness: a union of God and humanity, of humanity and earthly creation, of First Nations and European peoples together in the peaceable kingdom. She found the mystical in the Australian landscape and, realizing the land's significance in First Nations spirituality, sought a new harmonization. In writing the modern Australian landscape, beauty was not beauty without peace and justice. In Harris's view, newcomers to the land must live in harmony with First Nations peoples, and "neither harm nor destroy on all my holy mountain."

8

God in the Landscape

Australian Protestant Dissenters crossed the landscape, witnessing divine revelation and interpreting it for readers through verse and prose infused with scriptural imagination. The Word was not past, but ever-present and manifest. It could be seen through the close observation of the natural world, in the people of faith, and in the walking of dusty roads. The poetic imagery of faith colored their views and its vocabulary spilled out over the pages they wrote. The writing of Dissenters was an expression of their experience in this land and beyond, couched in language brought from another time and place: from Isaiah, Micah, and Deuteronomy's "song of Moses," from Ezekiel and Luke, Tennyson and Bunyan, and, tentatively, from Strehlow's translations of Arrernte song. In crossing the landscape with these time-traveled words, Protestant Dissenters wrote a new place and a new identity for themselves in an ancient land.

Connection with nature and with place clearly mattered to the people. With time and imagination, the dichotomy of Deuteronomy's "howlin' wilderness" and Promised Land gave way to diverse stories as people experienced divine revelation in the land around them. These were not lone voices but well-known authors within the churches who wrote for established readerships. Among like-minded Nonconformists, the marketability of the works was bolstered by the writers' reputations as orthodox representatives of the faith, a fact worth noting in the light of their overwhelming absence from denominational historiography. The Word was prioritized in the Dissenting traditions, and the written word was not the preserve of the clergy but an irrepressible response among believers. Writing came out of experience and faith, and was penned with purpose. A number of the authors published their writings in mainline newspapers and books that were read by a broad cross-section of Australian society. For the authors it was a kind of evangelism: a vision of faithful living in the landscape.

These five interwoven studies each contribute to the exploration of how Australian Protestant Dissent found God in the landscape. Churches of Christ evangelists traveled to the Holy Land in the late 1800s and, finding that walking in Jesus' footsteps mattered more than the biblical proof of archaeology, continued their walking on Australian soil. In the few years either side of Federation, Salvationists transformed themselves by putting on uniforms and theater costumes, and changed the Australian landscape by the rolling out of a grand scheme for "Social Salvation" just as they rolled out the canvas screen on a film set for a drama of life and death. Congregational poets trod a line between their faith and the patriotism that was demanded in a time of war, finding sacred spaces in suburban gardens and otherworldly reunion by country roadsides. Early and midcentury Methodist novelists described the journey of faith through the genre of adventure, portraying a vision of the landscape as divinely inhabited. In the light of a long history of natural science, mid-twentieth-century Quakers wrote of encounter with the divine in the landscape via contemplations on beauty, art, and understandings of First Peoples.

It is tempting to suggest that this sequence points to a continuum of development over time and toward deeper engagement with landscape: from recognition of the Holy Land as the only timeless landscape to a dawning awareness of the sacred eschatological timelessness of Australian soil. But eschatology and ecclesiology play differently into each of the histories, as do biblical interpretation, Evangelicalism, and denominational identity. The studies attend to the particularities of belief, time, and place, and the research relies on the particularities of experience among diverse faith groups. There are limits to generalization. It is not possible to extrapolate from the writings of Congregationalists and expect to find similar expressions of identity in the landscape among Adventists. Churches of Christ authors may see the world differently from some of their nearest kin such as Baptists and Brethren. This speaks to the nature of Protestant Dissent and also to the close study of genre and authorship. Despite the variability in findings between one study and the next, there are a number of common threads to the Australian Protestant Dissent experience of landscape. Traveling across the landscape, traveling across time, and awareness of presence and absence in the landscape are abiding themes. These themes, long interwoven with Dissent's theology and heritage, are revealed through literary history.

Expansion, Progress, and the Past

Protestant Dissent arrived in the colonies with the residue of historical distance from the state, the consequence of adherence to religious liberty and scriptural authority above the dominion of earthly powers and the so-called error of tradition. Their belief in the separation of church and state was fundamental to their existence. Yet with new horizons in view, they were free to engage in colonial and Federation-period Australian politics and, over time, the relationship between most Dissenting churches and the state grew warmer, closer. Many denominations accepted government funding and engaged in political discourse. The Nonconformist ethos of personal and social improvement found a natural ally in the state's pursuit of progress. Finally, as the colonies moved to federate, so did the Dissenting churches. Unity was in the air. The divided strands of Methodism came together in 1902, just a year after Federation, and the congregationally autonomous Churches of Christ met together as an Inter-Colonial Conference in 1889 "under the influence of federalist sentiment" and established a "federal journal," the *Australian Christian*, in 1898.[1] The Salvation Army published a federal edition of *The War Cry* from 1897.[2] Australian Protestant Dissent shared in the Australian spirit of the age, the uniting spirit of Federation. Writers attempted to graft

Australian identity onto faith through wattle and gum trees, amid warnings about the spiritual danger of jingoism. By the time Salvationist Joseph Perry was commissioned to film the inauguration of the Commonwealth of Australia, some of the more remote corners of Protestant Dissent had found themselves in broad alliance with the new nation. Not wishing to deny the truth of the priority of religious liberty, Dissent merely found itself able to work with the state for a largely common purpose. Dislocation from Britain and a history of strained state relations gave way to a new age of progress and of worldly-wise patriotism.

Australian Protestant Dissent wrote its own histories in ways that reflected the patriotism and modernist progress of the new nation in the late nineteenth and early twentieth centuries. Statistics, charts, and lists of achievements punctuate the texts, providing proof of advancement and growth. Histories were often based on the primary evidence of reports written for church meetings and denominational periodicals that were eager to demonstrate success and to justify the continuation and expansion of church programs. This feeling spills from the letters and reports into the historical account. Narratives of migration and denominational development within Australia suggest that the frame of reference for Dissent's aspirations and identity was located inside territorial boundaries. In several denominational histories many places are named and, town by town across the landscape, the progress of each congregation is tracked.[3] Mirroring popular tales of continental expansion by heroic explorers who stretched the boundaries of civilization, religious biographies relayed the chronicles of pioneers who expanded the reach of the church. Denominational histories located church development within political and denominational borders, and it defended those borders through official church publications.

The period from late colonial times until after the two world wars was critical in the formation of church identity in relationship to state, and in the modernist move of churches toward alignment with values that eroded religious imagination. Histories produced by the churches of Australian Protestant Dissent in the late nineteenth to mid-twentieth centuries were about progress, heroism, identity, conflict, and the reasonableness of theological positions. In contrast, creative literary forms are far more variable and open to interpretation. Writing beyond the church walls, and often on their own initiative, some authors did not set out to maintain a theological position or represent the church. Others allowed imagery and narrative to come together in theological heterodoxy. Denominationally distinctive beliefs were not always preserved. Indeterminate meaning abounded. Yet these creative works about God in the landscape were widely read. The fact that the writing of landscape is largely absent from denominational histories is not a reflection on the significance of the landscape to the people but on the relationship between denominational identity and modernism's pursuit of progress.

History books relay, with enthusiasm and pride, the construction of places of worship. Dissent advanced across the continent by building chapels in the seeming cultural void of the Australian landscape. The chapels changed the landscape merely by their presence. Some were exported in material or design from England and some nodded to a purer classical past that predated Emperor Constantine's union of church and state. Others observed a domestic style and scale, reflecting the surrounding weatherboard dwellings.

Driving the building of these physical structures were the spiritual and emotional needs of a migrant people seeking the landmarks of faith in what seemed an empty land. But Dissenters had long known that God might be found beyond the chapel.[4] Indeed, religious buildings (such as Bethlehem's Church of the Nativity) sometimes figured as symbols of faith's containment, or even imprisonment, at the expense of a life lived after Jesus' radical example. In the creative literature of Protestant Dissent, few were called to stay and build. Most were called to travel further afield in discipleship.

Traveling across the Landscape

Travelers to the Holy Land such as Churches of Christ ministers Aaron Maston and Albert Ludbrook baulked at the institutionalization of faith in Palestine and sought instead to walk in Jesus' footsteps. Their writings reveal journeys of skepticism and belief. On their return to Australia they continued their pilgrimage and brought others on their walk of faith via traveling limelight shows. As evangelists, they were most truly home when on the road with Jesus. They believed themselves called to cross the landscape rather than to live a settled life on Australian soil. Methodist missionaries and preachers shared this perspective. George Sargant's *The Sweet Heart of the Bush* describes a circuit ministry in remote Victorian bushland where the missioner must travel in order to fulfill the calling that he shares with the prophet in Isaiah 6, and the minister in Joseph Bowes's *Pals* travels through rising floodwaters. Contrasted with the ease of a city pastorate, the missioner's continuing presence in the bush is a measure of both his faith and his humanity—and a counter to popular portrayals of religious men as unsuited to Australian conditions. It is also a call to readers to imagine the romance and adventure of riding through outback Queensland, the northern rivers region of New South Wales or the tall timber of Victoria with holy purpose. Following the Methodist example of circuit ministry, Herbert Booth's "Move-On Manifesto" responded to the many miles between rural settlements with plans for travel between towns on horse and bicycle. Itinerancy was integral to ministry in Protestant Dissent in the Australian landscape.

Journeys are likewise demanded of the faithful in Edna Roughley's *The Locked Door* and "The Lost Road." In both these works, God's "call" comes from afar and the story of faith is predicated on pilgrimage to Papua or the Queensland bush. When Congregational poets Marjorie Ruth Betts and Beatrice Bevan wrote of soldiers returning from war, their reunions took place on the road. They did not meet at the chapel or cemetery or in a Christian home. Instead, soldiers and women were reunited in the Australian outdoors. The reunions were often of a liminal nature—meetings between death and life. The Australian roadside landscape represented belonging better than the secure interiority of the parlor or chapel.

Boundaries between life and death, sacred and profane, were tightly drawn in The Salvation Army's vision of the urban streetscape. When the Army marched through the streets, bearing witness with brass and timbrel, it did so in enemy territory. Faith demanded that Salvationists walk the parish of the streets and laneways and, indeed, traverse the entire continent, as Booth's "Move-On Manifesto" outlined. Captain Joseph

Perry performed this act of faith a number of times, camera in hand. Unlike other denominations, the distinctive calling and vision of the Army meant that they saw the land as ungodly territory to be covered with holy purpose, and with the reformatory institutions that would create the circumstances needed for salvation.

Less evangelical and therefore less concerned with the overt emulation of Jesus, Quaker artists also traveled for religious purpose. They moved through the landscape in order to paint scenery and collect natural history specimens, before settling to garden in what Mary Packer Harris called "the good, wholesome, brown earth."[5] While denominational histories often recorded attendance statistics as a measure of the gospel's expansion, in each of these Dissenting stories attending church services was *not* the sign of a Christian life. Faithful belonging demanded pilgrimage. The migratory dislocation of Protestant Dissent was performed and performed again as an act of faith; following Jesus could not be done while standing still. In the Dissenting imagination, God came into view in the crossing of the Australian landscape.

Traveling across Time

Walking in the footsteps of Jesus was a timeless act of faith. Protestant Dissent was a movement that was seemingly tied up with the particularities of its past, and with the promise of the afterlife at the expense of the here and now. But the literature written by its people suggests that transcending time to live within a scriptural narrative was a constant preoccupation, even as the people crossed the landscape and established themselves within a particular place and time. This practice of living within story is an inheritance of Dissent's biblical imagination. The Word transcended time to walk in first-century Palestine. With such transcendence in mind, Protestant Dissenters walked through a landscape over which they laid page upon page of scriptural scenes.

Beyond church walls, the writings of Dissenters rested on a determination to read the landscape, to see and interpret the particular terrain in the light of faith. On horseback in the Holy Land, confronting a biblical geography first read in books, Maston and Ludbrook experienced a lack of recognition when the landscape and its people did not match their reading of the text. As religious primitivists, they assumed that the biblical past could be recovered. Yet archaeology disappointed, pouring doubt on the sufficiency of biblical literalism to sustain their journey. Such layers of disorientation required a new reading, a new writing, and a new crossing in another ancient land. Via biblical imagination, the landscape of the Holy Land enabled a renewed vision of the landscape of Australia.

When Booth produced *Soldiers of the Cross*, he transformed the Australian landscape into the Holy Land using canvas and limelight. Like Maston and Ludbrook's illuminated lectures, the text of the Holy Land was performed for the Army's evangelistic purposes. The story of one land was enacted in another, layering the Australian landscape with the myth and meaning contained within the holy terrain of Palestine. Against such a divine canvas, the ancient martyrs of the early church and the disciples of Jesus could walk here, now, in holiness. Methodist revivalists similarly encouraged believers to visualize biblical scenes and to imagine themselves as living within the text. Believers, and readers of adventure novels, were exhorted to engage their senses in experiencing seemingly remote moral and spiritual landscapes. Whether in Salvationist uniform, costumed to appear in tableaux, or in the plain garb of the traveling preacher or Methodist lay person, the story of discipleship could be performed in the Australian landscape as readily as in the landscape of the Holy Land. In the religious imagination of Protestant Dissent, one space crossed over another. Time collapsed.

Half a century on, in *The Timeless Time*, Harris depicted a past–present in the landscape of the Torrens River region. As a Quaker she did not reference a primitivist biblical past but the in-dwelling of the Spirit in the landscape akin to the Inner Light within each person of faith. Inspired by First Nations art and the modern European-influenced work of the Hermannsburg Mission artists, Harris sought to collapse time between the landscape's ancient past and its increasingly urbanized present in which environmental destruction signaled divine suffering. Moral consciousness of First Peoples' spirituality and displacement increasingly informed her thinking and her faith. Harris repeatedly painted images of the harmony of the Holy Mountain of Isaiah and wrote of other artists' works that shared her mystic vision of the land as divinely inhabited.

Presence and Absence in the Landscape

In her pursuit of divine harmony, Harris came to hold a story about absence. The mere fact that a recently migrated woman held a story of the ghost gums on the Torrens and the rain ancestor in the rock was, in itself, a symbol of First Nations absence from the landscape. Such absence is witnessed in Methodist fiction too. Sargant's protagonist, the missioner Stirling, sees evidence of "not a distant past" in the marks on an ironbark tree near the town of Black Creek. Much of the novel's events take place in a town named for the First People's absence, as if that absence forms the moral and spiritual backdrop to daily life in rural Australia. Joseph Bowes reminded the Queensland Methodist Conference of the dignified humanity of First Nations people and, in *The Jackaroos*, he spelled out the spiritual cost of their mistreatment and dispossession from their "sanctuary."[6] Southwestern Queensland was sacred land, but Europeans were estranged from such divinity. As a consequence of their mistreatment of First Nations peoples, Europeans could not live without moral compromise, and stolen land could not be experienced as holy land.[7] The conventions of adventure writing for boys did not demand Bowes make such claims, but the righteous anger of his Methodist faith did. In the Reverend Bowes's faithful Queensland adventure, First Nations peoples are present and the institutional church is absent.

On a wave of patriotic feeling furthered by a foreign war, the absence of European Australians came to be embodied in the Australian landscape too. In the wartime poetry of Betts and Bevan, the memory of soldier sons and husbands was made present in gardens and by well-worn roads. Self-consciously Australian, wattle and Southern Cross are layered with patriotism, grief, and faithful waiting. Women waited in "a hallowed place," the holders of stories of innocence beneath the Tree of Knowledge of Good and Evil since time immemorial. This was often imagined as the "blossoming tree," that is at once both the tree of Calvary and Eden's Tree of Life. It is the soldiers' absence from these ordinary sacred landscapes that most powerfully signifies their eternal belonging, and their spiritual presence.

Absence always alludes, with sure faith or, in Australian historian Manning Clark's famous phrase, "shy hope," to the possibility of presence.[8] With few exceptions, Protestant Dissent located God's divine presence in the Australian landscape, whether as an antidote to literature's "Dead Heart" or as its animating force. The beauty of the natural world was a significant source of revelation. For Quakers, with their long tradition of painting the detail of the natural world, God could be witnessed in a blade of grass. According to Ernest Unwin, close observation afforded an opportunity to see the divine through the creation: "Beauty is a revealing, for God's spirit is in all and around all, and the meaning can be read."[9] The inclination to seek God in the natural world was shared by many, and this sometimes stemmed from an aversion to seeking God in ecclesiasticism, a sentiment not exclusive to Quakers. Although the Churches of Christ denomination was hesitant to locate God in nature lest it lead to pantheism (and away from the Bible as the only source of revelation), it readily identified the natural world as a place of encounter with the sacred and of personal connection with Jesus. Across the centuries, a shared earthly existence could be held in a pebble from the River Jordan. Embracing the creative freedom of adventure fiction, Methodist novelists described a land that spoke for God, or described God's speaking in and through the natural landscape in a realist presentation of what the faithful knew to be the supernatural. In such religious thinking, science and mysticism are not polar opposites. There is some resonance here between Methodists and Quakers in their appreciation of science and reason that leaves room for mysticism. Scientific realism is an inheritance of denominations born in the Enlightenment and cannot be put aside. Rather, it is modernism and mysticism that cannot cohabit.

Modernist progress orders the narrative of Phyllis Somerville's historical novel *Not Only In Stone*. The characters move in a direct line from a life of hardship and faith to one of prosperity and secularism. But this is not religious fiction so much as an expression of mid-twentieth-century nationalism that prized economic progress and the industry of the family unit above all. This worldview saw religion as a mark of the primitive life from which society had evolved. For Somerville, heartfelt faith is domesticated, disarmed, and replaced by the sentimentalism of family loyalty. In effect, the story of progress provides a creation narrative for a colonialist nation, but it is one in which the sacred belongs in the primitive past.[10] In contrast, in the Dissenting imagination, the past is present along with the sacred.

Stories of God in the Landscape

We dwell within the stories we tell about ourselves. We shape narratives and narratives shape us, and so how history is told matters deeply. The imaginative bent of Australian Protestant Dissent has long been neglected in its modernist histories of progress and decline, and in its boundary-marking chronicles of doctrinal dispute. But there is so much more to tell. The addition of literary history provides richness, nuance, and inclusive heterodoxy to understandings of belief and practice. It speaks of hope and faithful imagination. It reminds us that many authors, both lay and ordained, found that a faithful life was one that engaged with the landscape as an integral part of the narrative.

In the Australian landscape, the familiar disembodied understanding of a transcendent, distant God did not satisfy, and was replaced by an awareness of sacred presence. This has profound implications for Protestant churches and their relationship with the landscape. In an age of ecological crisis, this long backstory of sacred presence in landscape might act as a reminder of a spiritual identity that is essentially earthly, and as a prompt to the protection of the natural environment as a locus of divine revelation. The literary tradition of Australian Protestant Dissent expects engagement with, not detachment from, the earth.

In the late nineteenth and early twentieth centuries, Dissent turned to the interpretive indeterminacy of creative literary forms in order to say what could not be said otherwise, but which clearly demanded expression. The authors witnessed the Word in the Australian landscape. They responded in kind, with words of religiously inspired imagination that wrote the landscape anew. They were concerned with issues of absence and presence, the limits of patriotism in writing an Australian spirituality, and walking here as the disciples did in the Holy Land, as if time-past could fold into time-present. With Protestant Dissent's heritage of religious liberty and reliance on the Word of God, language was the essential means of expressing faith. Even as individual believers acted out their faith by walking or painting or gardening or building reformatories, they wrote. They came into relationship with the landscape by crossing, imagining, and telling, by authoring their own affinity with the sacred here. In this way, Australian Protestant Dissent found God in the landscape.

Notes

Preface

1. *Handasyde, M'Millan and Co.'s Catalogue of Ornamental Trees, Shrubs, Fruit Trees, Herbaceous Plants, and Culinary Plants and Roots* (Melbourne: Walker, May, 1864).
2. Recent examples include Grace Karskens, *People of the River: Lost Worlds of Early Australia* (Sydney: Allen and Unwin, 2020); Tony Hughes-d'Aeth, *Like Nothing on This Earth: A Literary History of the Wheatbelt* (Crawley: University of Western Australia Publishing, 2017); Tim Winton, *Island Home: A Landscape Memoir* (Melbourne: Penguin Australia, 2015); and, Andrea Gaynor, ed., *George Seddon: Selected Writings* (Carlton: Latrobe University Press, 2019).
3. Cecil Frances Alexander, "All Things Bright and Beautiful," in *Hymns for Little Children* (London: J. Masters, 1848).
4. Presbyterianism in England is usually included in Nonconformist or Dissent studies, but in the Australian context Presbyterianism was largely represented by the established Church of Scotland or its offshoot the Free Church of Scotland, which was "free" from the Church of Scotland but rivalled its ecclesiastical parent in hoping to become a national church (an ambition not typically shared by Dissenters). Australian Presbyterian churches readily accepted government funds under the Church Act of 1836 and considered themselves to be a part of the Establishment. See Ian Breward, "Presbyterians," in *The Encyclopedia of Religion in Australia*, ed. James Jupp (Port Melbourne: Cambridge University Press, 2009), 524–6, 530–1; Keith Robbins, "Nonconformity and the State, ca. 1750–2012," in *T&T Clark Companion to Nonconformity*, ed. Robert Pope (London: Bloomsbury T&T Clark, 2013), 83.
5. Peter Read, *Haunted Earth* (Sydney: University of New South Wales Press, 2003), 21.
6. Nigel Yates, *Buildings, Faith, and Worship: The Liturgical Arrangement of Anglican Churches 1600–1900* (Oxford: Oxford University Press, 1993), 150–74.
7. Pamela J. Stewart and Andrew Strathern, "Introduction," in *Landscape, Memory and History: Anthropological Perspectives* (London: Pluto Press, 2005), 3.
8. E.g.: Stuart Piggin and Robert D. Linder, *The Fountain of Public Prosperity: Evangelical Christians in Australian History* (Melbourne: Monash University Press, 2018); Stuart Piggin and Robert D. Linder, *Attending to the National Soul: Evangelical Christians in Australian History, 1914–2014* (Melbourne: Monash University Press, 2019).
9. Manning Clark, *A Short History of Australia*, 6th ed. (New York: Mentor, 1969), 23.
10. Frank Bongiorno, "In This World and the Next: Political Modernity and Unorthodox Religion in Australia, 1880–1930," *ACH: The Journal of the History of Culture in Australia, Antipodean Modern* 25 (2006): 191. Bongiorno notes that Australian feminist history has sometimes overlooked religious influences on early suffragettes.
11. As research commenced the five denominations chosen had not been the subject of extensive recent study—with the exception of Glen O'Brien and Hilary M. Carey,

eds., *Methodism in Australia: A History* (Farnham: Ashgate, 2015)—whereas Baptists have a relatively extensive recent scholarly historiography in Australia. E.g.: Ken R. Manley, *From Woolloomooloo to Eternity: A History of Australian Baptists* (Milton Keynes: Paternoster, 2006); Marita Munro, *A Struggle for Identity and Direction: A History of Victorian Baptists, c.1960–2000* (Berlin: Peter Lang, forthcoming); Philip J. Hughes and Darren Cronshaw, *Baptists in Australia: A Church with a Heritage and a Future* (Nunawading, Vic.: Christian Research Association, 2013).
12. Russell E. Richey, *Denominationalism Illustrated and Explained* (Eugene, OR: Cascade, 2013), 198–222; Kerrie Handasyde, "Pioneering Leadership: Historical Myth-Making, Absence and Identity in the Churches of Christ in Victoria," *Journal of Religious History* 41, no. 2 (June 2017): 235–50.
13. Meredith Lake, *The Bible in Australia: A Cultural History* (Randwick, NSW: NewSouth, 2018), introduction.

1 Looking Out Across the Terrain

1. Christopher Mudd, *Whys and Ways of the Bush and Guide to Bush Plants, or In Nature's School* (Melbourne: Spectator, 1914), 59.
2. Ibid., 68. Cf. Ezek. 12:2.
3. Mudd, *Whys and Ways*, 71.
4. Ibid., 8.
5. Alexandra Walsham, *The Reformation of Landscape: Religion, Identity and Memory in Early Modern Britain and Ireland* (Oxford: Oxford University Press, 2011), 7.
6. "Interactive Warlpiri—English Dictionary: With English—Warlpiri Finderlist," 2nd ed., compiled by Stephen M. Swartz, and "Interactive Tiwi—English Dictionary—Tiwi finderlist," compiled by Jenny Lee, *AuSIL Interactive Dictionary Series* B-3 and A-4, ed. Charles E. Grimes and Maarten Lecompte (Darwin: Australian Society for Indigenous Languages, 2012–13), http://ausil.org/Dictionary/Warlpiri/aboutwarlpiri.htm and http://ausil.org/Dictionary/Tiwi/index-english/main.htm.
7. The terms "Dissent" and "Nonconformity," dating from the 1600s, refer to English Protestants who do not belong to the Church of England and, by extension, to their religious descendents throughout the British Empire. According to John H. Y. Briggs, "Dissent described those Christians who in conscience *dissented* from the teaching of the Established Church, while Nonconformity described those unwilling to *conform* to its discipline and practice, and, in particular, the totality of its liturgical demands." The seventeenth-century term "Separatists" and the nineteenth-century term "Free churches" also apply to Dissent or Nonconformity. See John H. Y. Briggs, "The Changing Shape of Nonconformity, 1662–2000," in *T&T Clark Companion to Nonconformity*, ed. Robert Pope (London: Bloomsbury, 2013), 5–7.
8. Meredith Lake, *The Bible in Australia: A Cultural History* (Randwick, NSW: NewSouth, 2018), chapter 3.
9. E.g.: "Western Drought—Country on the Georgina—Simply a Howling Wilderness," *Telegraph* (Brisbane), January 5, 1893; "Griffithston," *Kalgoorlie Miner*, October 12, 1896; Editorial, *Age*, December 3, 1897; "Our Darling Country—A Howling Wilderness," *Daily Telegraph* (Sydney), October 14, 1899. See also Katie Holmes

and Kylie Mirmohamadi, "Howling Wilderness and Promised Land: Imagining the Victorian Mallee, 1840–1914," *Australian Historical Studies* 46, no. 2 (2015): 191–213.
10. E.g.: "Our Inheritance in the North," *The Areas' Express* (Booyoolee, SA), October 10, 1890.
11. James Boyce, "Return to Eden: Van Diemen's Land and the Early British Settlement of Australia," *Environment and History* 14, no. 2 (May 2008): 292; Grace Karskens, *The People of the River: Lost Worlds of Early Australia* (Sydney: Allen and Unwin, 2020), 5.
12. Alan Atkinson, *The Europeans in Australia: Nation*, vol. 3 (Sydney: University of New South Wales Press, 2014), 371–4.
13. Christopher Mudd, *Tales and Trails of Austral Bush and Plain* (Melbourne: Spectator, 1912), 9–11.
14. Mudd, *Whys and Ways*, 67.
15. Joseph Hocking, "The Story of Andrew Fairfax," reprinted in *Adelaide Observer*, July 15, 1893, 38.
16. Paul Carter, *The Lie of the Land* (London: Faber and Faber, 1996), 6–8.
17. Timothy Gorringe, *A Theology of the Built Environment: Justice, Empowerment, Redemption* (Cambridge: Cambridge University Press, 2002), 36–8.
18. Keith Robbins, "Nonconformity and the State, ca. 1750–2012," in *T&T Clark Companion to Nonconformity*, ed. Robert Pope (London: Bloomsbury T&T Clark, 2013), 75.
19. This approach follows on from the work of several thinkers in the field of theology and the spatial turn, including Murray Rae, *Architecture and Theology: The Art of Place* (Waco, TX: Baylor University Press, 2017); Clyde Binfield, "Strangers and Dissenters: The Architectural Legacy of Twentieth-Century English Nonconformity," in *Protestant Nonconformity in the Twentieth Century*, ed. Alan Sell and Anthony Cross (Carlisle: Paternoster, 2003), 132–83; Philip Sheldrake, *Spaces for the Sacred: Place, Memory, and Identity* (London: SCM Press, 2001); John Inge, *A Christian Theology of Place* (Burlington, VT: Aldershot, 2003); Geoffrey Lilburne, *A Sense of Place: A Christian Theology of the Land* (Nashville: Abingdon Press, 1989); and Belden Lane, *Landscapes of the Sacred: Geography and Narrative in American Spirituality* (New York: Paulist Press, 1988); Gorringe, *Theology of the Built Environment*.
20. Thomas T. Reed, *Historic Churches of Australia* (South Melbourne: Macmillan, 1978), 131. In 1841 another prefabricated meetinghouse (no longer standing) was sent to Australind, the entrepreneurial but ill-fated settlement in Western Australia.
21. Moonta is derived from a Narungga word for "impenetrable scrub": "Area History," National Trust South Australia Moonta Branch. Available online: http://www.moontatourism.org.au/area-history (accessed August 28, 2017).
22. "New Wesleyan Chapel, Moonta Mines," *South Australian Weekly Chronicle*, August 19, 1865.
23. Arnold D. Hunt, *This Side of Heaven: A History of Methodism in South Australia* (Adelaide: Lutheran Publishing House, 1985), 21, 218. The United Methodist Free Churches, which were strong in Cornwall, had a low profile in South Australia, and many of those who had been members in the UK were absorbed into the Primitive Methodists and Bible Christians. Ibid., 119.
24. Ibid.
25. Anne O'Brien, "Religion," in *The Cambridge History of Australia: Indigenous and Colonial Australia*, vol. 1, ed. Alison Bashford and Stuart Macintyre

(Melbourne: Cambridge University Press, 2013), 424; Hunt, *This Side of Heaven*, 123–7.
26. "Moonta Mines," Organ Historical Trust of Australia. Available online: http://www.ohta.org.au/organs/organs/MoontaMines.html (accessed January 12, 2015). It is unclear which chapel in Truro was used as a model for the Moonta Mines Methodist church, but there are many similar Methodist buildings in Cornwall.
27. "Wesleyan Methodist Bazaar at Moonta Mines," *Wallaroo Times and Mining Journal*, August 23, 1869.
28. Hunt, *This Side of Heaven*, 117–27.
29. Ibid., 118.
30. "New Wesleyan Chapel, Moonta Mines."
31. "New Wesleyan Chapel, Moonta Mines," *Wallaroo Times and Mining Journal*, December 9, 1865.
32. Hunt, *This Side of Heaven*, 22. Different branches of Methodism (including Bible Christians, Wesleyan Methodists, and Primitive Methodists that united in 1902) had differing approaches to government aid such as land grants, stipends, and assistance in building chapels. But regional influences meant that state aid to religion was only available in the 1840s in the "Paradise of Dissent" that was South Australia. O'Brien, "Religion," 420; Ian Breward, "Methodist Reunion in Australasia," in *Methodism in Australia: A History*, ed. Glen O'Brien and Hilary M. Carey (Farnham: Ashgate, 2015), 119–31.
33. "New Wesleyan Chapel, Moonta Mines."
34. Clyde Binfield, "Nonconformist Architecture: A Representative Focus," in *T&T Clark Companion to Nonconformity*, ed. Robert Pope (London: Bloomsbury, 2013), 257.
35. Joan Kerr, "Churches—Our Australian Architectural Heritage," in *The Future of Our Historic Churches: Conflict and Reconciliation*, ed. John Henwood and Tom Hazell (Melbourne: National Trust of Australia (Vic.), 1988), 9.
36. The Johnsonville Uniting Church chapel formerly belonged to one of the three denominations that joined in 1977 to form the Uniting Church in Australia: Methodist Church of Australasia, Presbyterian Church of Australia, and Congregational Union of Australia.
37. Barbara Bolton, *Booth's Drum: The Salvation Army in Australia 1880–1980* (Sydney: Hodder and Stoughton, 1980), 21, 56–7.
38. "Hobart Churches, The Salvation Army," *Mercury*, June 12, 1905.
39. Ibid.
40. "Salvation Army Citadel in Russell Street, Bathurst," colorized photographic postcard, item no. 1986.0117.1704, National Museum of Australia (accessed March 19, 2015).
41. Graeme Chapman, *One Lord, One Faith, One Baptism: A History of Churches of Christ in Australia* (Melbourne: Vital Publications, 1980), 21–5, 41–2. Traditional Ownership is contentious in this region as it has been disrupted by colonization and the movement of Indigenous Peoples. Alternative claimants include the Kapurn (sometimes spelled Gubrun) and the Wangkathaa People who have a historic presence in the goldfields region following European settlement and close cultural ties to the Western Desert Cultural Bloc.
42. A. B. Maston, *Jubilee Pictorial History of Churches of Christ in Australasia* (Melbourne: Austral, 1903), 91.
43. Ibid., 92.

44. Ibid., 93; *Australian Christian*, January 13, 1898, 15. Rectangular windows, rather than Gothic arched windows, were significant not only for what they say about the congregation's financial fortunes but also for the ecclesiology they represented.
45. Ern West, *A History of the Christian Brethren Assemblies in Western Australia* (Western Australia: self-published, 1993).
46. This is the case in Open Brethren congregations, but not in the Exclusive Brethren whose sectarianism places them outside the scope of the thesis. Ken Newton, *A History of the Brethren in Australia* (Indooroopilly, Qld.: Aberdeen Desktop, 1999), 73–6.
47. Ibid., 9–11, 53–8; "Welcome to Christian Community Churches of Australia," Christian Community Churches of Australia. Available online: http://cccaust.org (accessed September 30, 2020).
48. Michael R. Watts, *The Dissenters: From the Reformation to the French Revolution*, vol. 1 (Oxford: Clarendon Press, 1978), 605.
49. William Y. Fullerton, *C. H. Spurgeon: A Biography* (London: Williams and Norgate, 1920), 137.
50. Miles Lewis, ed., *Victorian Churches* (Melbourne: National Trust, 1991), 46.
51. T. H. Pattison, "Congregationalism and Aesthetics," in *Religious Republics*, cited in Binfield, "Nonconformist Architecture," 73.
52. F. J. Jobson, *Chapel and School Architecture, as Appropriate to the Buildings of Nonconformists, particularly to Those of the Wesleyan Methodists* (London: Hamilton Adams, 1850), vii, 16, cited in Binfield, "Nonconformist Architecture," 270; Curtis W. Freeman, *Undomesticated Dissent: Democracy and the Public Virtue of Religious Nonconformity* (Waco: Baylor University Press, 2017), 141–2.
53. Pattison, "Congregationalism and Aesthetics," cited in Binfield, "Nonconformist Architecture," 73.
54. The building is described in a letter from the Director of the National Trust of Australia as "undoubtedly the best of its kind in Australia": Reed, *Historic Churches*, 25.
55. Patricia Curthoys, "Congregationalists," in *The Encyclopedia of Religion in Australia*, ed. James Jupp (Port Melbourne: Cambridge University Press, 2009), 299.
56. Ibid., 300.
57. J. Fowles, *Sydney in 1848* (Sydney: J. Fowles, 1848), 40.
58. Ibid., 39.
59. Congregational Church of South Australia, *Jubilee of Congregationalism in South Australia: Report of the Intercolonial Conference held in Adelaide, September, 1887* (Adelaide: Stow Congregational Church Manse Chambers, 1887), 92.
60. Cited in Ken R. Manley, *From Woolloomooloo to Eternity: A History of Australian Baptists* (Milton Keynes: Paternoster, 2006), 55. Original emphasis.
61. Ibid., 56.
62. Pattison, "Congregationalism and Aesthetics," cited in Binfield, "Nonconformist Architecture," 73.
63. "Sandgate Baptist Church," *Brisbane Courier*, September 5, 1887, 6.
64. "Queensland Baptist Churches 1849–1929 by Date of Commencement with Some Building Erection Dates," David Parker. Available online: http://www.dparker.net.au/churches1849-1929/index1.html (accessed September 30, 2020).
65. Donald Hansen, "The Adventist Press," in *Seventh-day Adventists in the South Pacific 1885–1985*, ed. Noel Clapham (Warburton, Vic.: Signs, 1985), 73.

66. The Australian branch of Seventh-day Adventism was deeply influenced by prophetess (and American ex-Methodist) Ellen White who stayed in Australia for eight years and whose son William was heavily involved in the establishment of the Sanitarium factory: Gary D. Krause, "The Growth of the Seventh-day Adventist Church in Sydney and Melbourne: 1885–1918," in *Seventh-day Adventists in the South Pacific*, ed. Noel Clapham (Warburton, Vic.: Signs, 1985), 122; in the same volume see also Herbert Clifford and Noel Clapham, "Hospitals and Healing," 78–9, and John B. Trim, "The Origin and Development of Adventist Health Work," 155–6, 160; James Jupp, "Seventh Day Adventists," in *The Encyclopedia of Religion in Australia*, ed. James Jupp (Port Melbourne: Cambridge University Press, 2009), 564.
67. Arthur N. Patrick, "Doctrine and Deed: Adventism's Encounter with its Society in Nineteenth-Century Australia," in *Adventist History in the South Pacific: 1885–1918*, ed. Arthur J. Ferch (Wahroonga, NSW: South Pacific Division of Seventh-day Adventists, 1986), 19–20; Jupp, "Seventh Day Adventists," 564.
68. "Sanitarium Factory Complex and Garden," Victorian Heritage Database. Available online: http://vhd.heritage.vic.gov.au/search/nattrust_result_detail/70262 (accessed September 30, 2020). The gardens surrounding the church's modern factory in Christchurch were reportedly "famous" and similar in style to the Warburton factory gardens according to Robert Parr, "Sanitarium Health Food Company," in *Seventh-day Adventists in the South Pacific*, ed. Noel Clapham (Warburton, Vic.: Signs, 1985), 103.
69. "Sanitarium Factory."
70. "Warburton Saved: 20 Houses and Mills Lost," *Argus*, January 14, 1939, 2. The extensive fires were the worst in Victorian history to date with seventy-one people killed, several towns near Warburton completely destroyed, and the loss of sixty-nine sawmills and millions of acres of bush. See Tom Griffiths, *Forests of Ash: An Environmental History* (Port Melbourne: Cambridge University Press, 2001), 129–34.
71. "Warburton Saved."
72. Hocking, "Andrew Fairfax," 38.
73. Chris Wakeling, "The Nonconformist Traditions: Chapels, Change and Continuity," in *The Victorian Church*, ed. Chris Brooks and Andrew Saint (Manchester: Manchester University Press, 1995), 83.
74. Carlo Ginzburg, "Microhistory: Two or Three Things That I Know About It," trans. John Tedeschi and Anne C. Tedeschi, *Critical Inquiry* 20, no. 1 (Autumn 1993): 27.
75. Tom Griffiths, *The Art of Time Travel: Historians and their Craft* (Carlton, Vic.: Black, 2016), 4.
76. Katie Holmes, *Between the Leaves: Stories of Australian Women, Writing and Gardens* (Crawley, WA: University of Western Australia, 2011), 13.
77. Mudd, *Whys and Ways*, 59.

2 Landscape of Dissent: Dissent's British Origins and Colonial Australian Experience

1. Michael R. Watts, *The Dissenters: From the Reformation to the French Revolution*, vol. 1 (Oxford: Clarendon Press, 1978), 218–19; John Coffey, *Persecution and Toleration in Protestant England 1558–1689* (Harlow: Pearson, 2000), 168.
2. Coffey, *Persecution and Toleration*, 168; Watts, *Dissenters*, vol. 1, 219.
3. E.g.: Edmund Calamy, "A Continuation of the Account of the Ministers, Lecturers, Masters and Fellows of Colleges and Schoolmasters who were ejected and silenced

after the Restoration in 1660," in *Calamy Revised: Being a Revision of Edmund Calamy's Account of the Ministers and Others Ejected and Silenced, 1660-62*, ed. Arnold Gwynne Matthews (Oxford: Clarendon Press, 1988); John Seed, *Dissenting Histories: Politics, History and Memory in Eighteenth-Century England* (Edinburgh: Edinburgh University Press, 2008), 16.
4. Seed, *Dissenting Histories*, 16-20.
5. Alexandra Walsham, *The Reformation of Landscape: Religion, Identity and Memory in Early Modern Britain and Ireland* (Oxford: Oxford University Press, 2011), 246-7; Watts, *Dissenters*, vol. 1, 225.
6. Watts, *Dissenters*, vol. 1, 225-7, 303-5.
7. John Bunyan, *The Life and Death of Mr Badman* (Glasgow: Robert and Thomas Duncan, 1772 [1680]), 111.
8. Walsham, *Reformation of Landscape*, 249-51.
9. Coffey, *Persecution and Toleration*, 171-2. In a later article, Coffey estimates imprisonments for the period 1660-8 at eleven thousand: John Coffey, "Church and State, 1550-1750: The Emergence of Dissent," in *T&T Clark Companion to Nonconformity*, ed. Robert Pope (London: Bloomsbury T&T Clark, 2013), 62. See also Watts, *Dissenters*, vol. 1, 227.
10. "Gunby Hall Estate: Monksthorpe Chapel," National Trust, UK. Available online: https://www.nationaltrust.org.uk/gunby-hall-estate-monksthorpe-chapel (accessed January 17, 2021).
11. William Farrer and J. Brownbill, eds., "Townships: Torver," in *A History of the County of Lancaster*, vol. 8 (London: Victoria County History, 1914), 363-5.
12. "Hawkshead Hill Baptist," UK and Ireland Genealogy. Available online: http://www.genuki.org.uk/big/eng/LAN/Hawkshead/HawksheadHillBaptist.shtml (accessed September 30, 2020).
13. John H. Y. Briggs, "The Changing Shape of Nonconformity, 1662-2000," in *T&T Clark Companion to Nonconformity*, ed. Robert Pope (London: Bloomsbury T&T Clark, 2013), 6. See also Deryck W. Lovegrove, *Established Church, Sectarian People: Itinerancy and the Transformation of English Dissent 1780-1830* (Cambridge: Cambridge University Press, 1988), 6.
14. Russell E. Richey, *Denominationalism Illustrated and Explained* (Eugene, OR: Cascade, 2013), 35.
15. Gary De Krey, "Dissenting Cases for Conscience, 1667-1672," *Historical Journal* 38 (1995): 53-83; Coffey, *Persecution and Toleration*, 171; Coffey, "Church and State," 63.
16. John Locke, "Letter Concerning Toleration," in Works 2: 235, cited in Richey, *Denominationalism Illustrated*, 47.
17. R. K. Webb, "The Limits of Religious Liberty: Theology and Criticism in Nineteenth-Century England," in *Freedom and Religion in the Nineteenth Century*, ed. Richard Helmstadter (Stanford, CA: Stanford University Press, 1997), 120-49.
18. John Gascoigne, *The Enlightenment and the Origins of European Australia* (Cambridge: Cambridge University Press, 2002), 19.
19. On the link between the doctrine of assurance and enlightenment thinking, see David W. Bebbington, *Evangelicalism in Modern Britain: History from the 1730s to 1980s* (London: Routledge, 1989), 50-4.
20. Richard Phillips, "Thomas Campbell: A Reappraisal Based on Backgrounds," *Restoration Quarterly* 49, no. 2 (2007): 87-8.
21. Bebbington, *Evangelicalism*, 27.

22. The saddlebag story has achieved mythic status in Disciples circles, as exhibited in the range of variants on the theme. E.g.: the contents of saddlebags belonging to Alexander Campbell are mentioned in Glaucia Vasconselos Wilkey, *Worship and Culture: Foreign Country or Homeland* (Grand Rapids, MI: Wm. B. Eerdmans, 2014), 215; the evangelist Walter Scott's saddlebags are explored in D. Duane Cummins, *The Disciples: A Struggle for Reformation* (St. Louis, MO: Chalice Press, 2008), 4.
23. E.g.: Phillips, "Thomas Campbell," 75–102; Hiram J. Lester, "An Irish Precursor for Thomas Campbell's Declaration and Address," *Encounter* 50, no. 3 (1989): 247–67.
24. Bebbington, *Evangelicalism*, 39, 41–2, 69–73.
25. Michael R. Watts, *The Dissenters: The Expansion of Evangelical Nonconformity 1791–1859*, vol. 2 (Oxford: Clarendon Press, 1995), 213–14, 639–43; W. R. Ward, *Religion and Society in England, 1790–1850* (London: B.T. Batsford, 1972), 13–15, 289–90; David Ceri Jones, "Evangelicalism," in *T&T Clark Companion to Nonconformity*, ed. Robert Pope (London: Bloomsbury T&T Clark, 2013), 593–6.
26. David W. Bebbington, *The Nonconformist Conscience: Chapel and Politics, 1870–1914* (London: Allen and Unwin, 1982), 60.
27. James Simpson, *Burning to Read: English Fundamentalism and its Reformation Opponents* (Cambridge, MA: Belknap Press, 2007), 184–5.
28. Significant favor and wealth had been planned (but implemented in only a limited way) for the Church of England under Henry Bathurst, England's Secretary of State for War and the Colonies, and so it is reasonable to say that in New South Wales the Church of England was treated as though it were the Established Church albeit without formalization of the role: J. S. Gregory, *Church and State: Changing Government Policies Toward Religion in Australia, with Particular Reference to Victoria Since Separation* (North Melbourne: Cassell Australia, 1973), 258–60; Michael Roe, *Quest for Authority in Eastern Australia 1835–1851* (Parkville: Melbourne University Press, 1965), 14; Naomi Turner, *Sinews of Sectarian Warfare?: State Aid in New South Wales 1836–1862* (Canberra: Australian National University Press, 1972), 19.
29. Cited in Turner, *Sinews of Sectarian Warfare?*, 8.
30. Stuart Piggin, "Power and Religion in a Modern State: Desecularisation in Australian History," *Journal of Religious History* 38, no. 2 (September 2014): 329.
31. Anne O'Brien, "Religion," in *The Cambridge History of Australia: Indigenous and Colonial Australia*, vol. 1, ed. Alison Bashford and Stuart Macintyre (Melbourne: Cambridge University Press, 2013), 420.
32. Turner, *Sinews of Sectarian Warfare?*, 9.
33. "No. 3 An Act to Promote the Building of Churches and Chapels," *New South Wales Government Gazette*, August 17, 1836, 609. The interpretation, within secularist Australian historiography, of the Church Act as a means of moral control without higher religious purpose has been challenged by a number of historians of religion; e.g., Piggin, "Power and Religion."
34. Turner, *Sinews of Sectarian Warfare?*, 1; "Legislative Assembly," *Sydney Morning Herald*, January 6, 1959, 4–5; "The Jewish Synagogue," *Argus* (Melbourne), February 10, 1859, 7.
35. Turner, *Sinews of Sectarian Warfare?*, 8–10, 17.
36. Winsome Roberts, "The Churches' Role in Constituting an Australian Citizenry," in *Spirit of Australia II: Religion in Citizenship and National Life*, ed. Brian Howe and Philip Hughes (Hindmarsh, SA: Australian Theological Forum Press), 62, 64–8; Ian Breward, *A History of the Churches in Australasia* (Oxford: Oxford University Press, 2001), 181, 198; Ian Breward, "Methodists," in *The Encyclopedia of Religion*

in Australia, ed. James Jupp (Port Melbourne: Cambridge University Press, 2009), 408; Watts, *Dissenters*, vol. 2, 652–6; Hilary M. Carey, *God's Empire: Religion and Colonialism in the British World, c. 1801–1908* (Cambridge: Cambridge University Press, 2011), 30.

37. Arnold D. Hunt, *This Side of Heaven: A History of Methodism in South Australia* (Adelaide: Lutheran Publishing House, 1985), 179–209; Roger C. Thompson, *Religion in Australia: A History* (Melbourne: Oxford University Press, 1994), 16.
38. Roe, *Quest for Authority*, 165–83 (Temperance), 184–206; Richard Ely, "Protestantism in Australian History: An Interpretative Sketch," *Lucas: An Evangelical History Review* 5 (March 1989): 15.
39. When children's swings were introduced to parks around the turn of the twentieth century, some were locked on Sundays by local authorities concerned with preserving the Sabbath. Momentum to make swings available on Sundays gathered in the 1920s and 1930s. E.g.: "Sins of the Swings," *Independent* (Footscray, Vic.), April 20, 1907, 3; "Swings on Sundays," *Ballarat Star* (Vic.), January 30, 1918, 1; "The Locked Paradise: Is It Wrong to Swing on Sunday?" *Daily Telegraph* (Sydney, NSW), April 16, 1923, 10; "The Sanctimonious Sabbath," *Southern Cross* (Adelaide, SA), November 17, 1933, 19; "Swings Locked on Sundays," *Examiner* (Launceston, Tas.), March 5, 1940, 6.
40. Gregory, *Church and State*, 18. It is not documented in the literature, but I wonder if the minimum amount of £300 was just too much for small independent congregations to raise so that the congregational ecclesiology of the smaller Nonconformists mitigated against their participation in the scheme regardless of principles.
41. Douglas Pike, *Paradise of Dissent: South Australia 1829–1857* (Melbourne: Melbourne University Press, 1967 [1957]), 249–279.
42. Handasyde Duncan M.D., *The Colony of South Australia* (London: T. and W. Boone, 1850), 63.
43. Pike, *Paradise of Dissent*, 421–41; O'Brien, "Religion," 420; Thompson, *Religion in Australia*, 15.
44. The term was coined by historian Douglas Pike (who had once trained for Churches of Christ ministry) for his 1957 history of South Australia, *Paradise of Dissent*.
45. Turner, *Sinews of Sectarian Warfare?*, 2.
46. Pike, *Paradise of Dissent*, 492.
47. The only extant text from *The Melbourne Medley* is a facsimile page from August 7, 1858, reproduced in A. B. Maston, *Jubilee Pictorial History of Churches of Christ in Australasia* (Melbourne: Austral, 1903), 170. Robert Service was known for public dispute, but his son James (a lapsed Presbyterian) became Victoria's Premier in the 1870s and defended the separation of church and state in schools as a remedy to "strife and dissension." Geoffrey Serle, "James Service," *Australian Dictionary of Biography*. Available online: http://adb.anu.edu.au/biography/service-james-4561 (accessed January 18, 2015).
48. Frank Engel, *Conflict and Unity 1788–1926* (Melbourne: Joint Board of Christian Education of Australia and New Zealand, 1984), 113, 124; Alan Atkinson, *The Europeans in Australia: Nation*, vol. 3 (Sydney: University of New South Wales Press, 2014), 290–8; Ian Breward, "Australasian Church Histories before 1914," in *Re-visioning Australian Colonial Christianity: New Essays in the Australian Christian Experience 1788–1900*, ed. Mark Hutchinson and Edmund Campion (Sydney: Centre for the Study of Australian Christianity, 1994); Thompson, *Religion in Australia*, 42–4.
49. Alex Mills, "One Nation Under God?: The Christian Contribution to Australian Federation," *Church Heritage* 12, no. 1 (March 2001): 7; Thompson, *Religion*

     in *Australia*, 43. These and following statistics are from the 1901 Australian census: Hilary M. Carey, *Believing in Australia: A Cultural History of Religions* (St Leonards, NSW: Allen and Unwin, 1996), 198.
50. Beverley Kingston, *Oxford History of Australia: Glad, Confident Morning, 1860–1900*, vol. 3 (Oxford: Oxford University Press, 1988), 310.
51. "Ecclesiastical Precedence: Memorandum from the Cardinal," *Daily Telegraph* (Sydney), January 12, 1901, 11. Instruction on precedence in the parade came from the Colonial Office and was defended on the basis that the number of religious adherents defined the order.
52. "Ecclesiastical Precedence," *Daily Telegraph*, January 19, 1901, 13.
53. "Ecclesiastical Precedence," *Daily Telegraph*, January 11, 1901, 4; and "Precedence: Cardinal or Primate," *Daily Telegraph*, January 9, 1901, 6.
54. "Commonwealth Day," *Sydney Mail and New South Wales Advertiser*, January 5, 1901.
55. Ibid.
56. "Ecclesiastical Precedence: Resolution of the Baptist Union," *Daily Telegraph*, January 10, 1901, 6. Emphasis added.
57. "Congregational—the Congregational Union, Represented by Rev. Dr. Fordyce (Chairman NSW), Rev. A. J. Griffiths, Rev. N. J. Cocks, and Rev. G. Campbell," *Daily Telegraph*, January 2, 1901, 14.
58. Atkinson, *Europeans in Australia: Nation*, vol. 3, 271–2. E.g. James Jefferis, "Religious Liberty in NSW" is all about state endowment and how Congregationalists were never tempted by such inducement but were committed to liberty: *South Australian Advertiser*, September 8, 1887, 5.
59. "Salvation Army: Commandant Booth, with Colonel Peart, Chief Sec., Brigadier Gilmour, General Secretary, and Brigadier Saunders, Architect and Builder to the Army in Australia, Its Oldest Officer," *Daily Telegraph*, January 2, 1901, 14.
60. "Inauguration of the Commonwealth," Australian Screen Online. Available online: https://aso.gov.au/titles/documentaries/inauguration-commonwealth/clip2/ (accessed April 13, 2017). In the footage two floats pass through the arch, representing the young federated nations of Italy and Canada whose success Australia sought to share. Herbert Booth is in the third carriage and the Congregationalists in the fourth.

3 Landscape of Skepticism and Belief: Churches of Christ Travel Literature from the Holy Land to Australia, 1889–96

1. A. B. Maston, "A Horse-Back Ride through Palestine: The Jordan (March 29, 1889)" serialized in *The Christian Pioneer*, October 24, 1889, 434.
2. Ibid. Original emphasis.
3. Selections from this chapter were first published as "Holy Land Tourism: A Horseback Ride from Public Theology to Private Faith," *Melbourne Historical Journal* 43, special issue: "Territories and Transitions" (2015): 61–71.
4. Maston, "A Horse-Back Ride through Palestine," *Christian Pioneer*, September 3, 1889, 379.
5. Stephanie S. Rogers, *Inventing the Holy Land: American Protestant Pilgrimage to Palestine, 1865–1941* (Lanham, MD: Lexington Books, 2011), 32.

6. Statistics are recorded for 1903: A. B. Maston, *Jubilee Pictorial History of Churches of Christ in Australasia* (Melbourne: Austral, 1903), preface.
7. "An Australian Abroad," *Australasian Christian Standard*, October 1, 1890, 276–7.
8. F. M. Ludbrook's auspicious name was treated with irreverence in Australia when he became a prominent early organizer of Australian overseas mission and, with the initials "F. M.," came to be known as "Foreign Missions Ludbrook."
9. To my knowledge, there were no men named Milton within Churches of Christ circles at the time. However, "Paradise Lost" had some currency in the movement, especially on themes of the fallen world.
10. "The Holy City," *Advertiser* (Adelaide), April 27, 1898.
11. "Advertising," *Gympie Times and Mary River Mining Gazette* (Queensland), September 1, 1900.
12. "Britons and Boers," *Queensland Times, Ipswich Herald and General Advertiser*, September 11, 1900.
13. Albert M. Ludbrook, *The Romance of the Roman Catacombs and Other Addresses* (Melbourne: Austral, 1936).
14. H. Cave, "A Pioneer Preacher," *Australian Christian*, June 29, 1948, 298.
15. G. P. Pittman, *Life of Maston* (Melbourne: Austral, 1909), 4.
16. Ibid.
17. John Bunyan, *The Pilgrim's Progress*, ed. Roger Sharrock (Harmondsworth: Penguin, 1965), 36–7.
18. Robert Louis Stevenson, *Travels with a Donkey in the Cevennes* (Boston: Roberts Bros., 1879), dedication.
19. Pittman, *Life of Maston*, 41.
20. Two images from Farrar's book are also used in the later installments of Ludbrook's "Notes of Travel," published five years after Maston's second account.
21. Neil Asher Silberman, *Digging for God and Country: Exploration, Archaeology, and the Secret Struggle for the Holy Land, 1799–1917* (New York: Knopf, 1982), 9.
22. Rogers, *Inventing the Holy Land*, 44–6. See also Brian Yothers, *The Romance of the Holy Land in American Travel Writing, 1790–1876* (Burlington, VT: Ashgate, 2007); Hilton Obenzinger, *American Palestine: Melville, Twain, and the Holy Land Mania* (Princeton, NJ: Princeton University Press, 1999).
23. William Thomson (1834) quoted in Simon Sebag-Montefiore, *Jerusalem: The Biography* (London: Phoenix, 2011), 329.
24. Herman Melville, *Journals*, ed. Howard C. Horsford with Lynn Horth (Evanston, IL: Northwestern University Press, 1989), 91 (January 1856–7).
25. John Davis, *Landscape of Belief: Encountering the Holy Land in Nineteenth-Century American Art and Culture* (Princeton, NJ: Princeton University Press, 1996), 146. The Churches of Christ's high level of evangelical engagement may be interpreted as being very much in this world and time, but it does tie inextricably with ultimate eschatological purpose and so may be interpreted as "in time" for "eternity." See also Richard T. Hughes and C. Leonard Allen, *Illusions of Innocence: Protestant Primitivism in America 1630–1875* (Chicago, IL: University of Chicago Press, 1988), 20–4, 102–8.
26. Richard T. Hughes, "Why Restorationists Don't Fit the Evangelical Mold; Why Churches of Christ Increasingly Do," in *Re-forming the Center: American Protestantism 1900 to the present*, ed. Douglas Jacobsen and William Vance Trollinger (Grand Rapids, MI: Wm. B. Eerdmans, 1998), 195.
27. Plaque at Wangaratta Church of Christ, Victoria, *c.* 1990. Photograph. Private collection.

28. Paul Blowers, "'Living in a Land of Prophets': James T. Barclay and an Early Disciples of Christ Mission to Jews in the Holy Land," *Church History* 62, no. 4 D (1993): 494–513; Jack P. Lewis, "James Turner Barclay: Explorer of Nineteenth-Century Jerusalem," *Biblical Archaeology* 51, no. 3 S (1988): 163–70; Victor McCracken, "The Restoration of Israel," *Restoration Quarterly* 47, no. 4 (2005): 207–20.
29. Hughes and Allen, *Illusions of Innocence*, 173.
30. Davis, *Landscape of Belief*, 146.
31. Ulster Presbyterianism was highly influential in this "American" movement. E.g.: Hiram J. Lester, "An Irish Precursor for Thomas Campbell's Declaration and Address," *Encounter* 50, no. 3 (Summer 1989): 247–67; James L. Gorman, "European Roots of Thomas Campbell's *Declaration and Address*: The Evangelical Society of Ulster," *Restoration Quarterly* 51, no. 3 (2009): 129–37.
32. Rogers, *Inventing the Holy Land*, 22.
33. E.g.: "Lecture" (delivered by Mr Arthur Field-Wolrige), *Methodist* (Sydney), December 9, 1893; "A Day in Bethlehem," *Watchman* (Sydney), December 23, 1905.
34. "Lecture on Palestine," *Wagga Wagga Advertiser*, January 29, 1891.
35. "Visit to the Holy Land," *Mount Alexander Mail*, July 21, 1892. The curious and quaint have been of recent interest in visual arts and culture studies: lantern shows, exhibitions, and several studies of Palestine Park at Lake Chautauqua, NY. See Lester Irwin Vogel, *To See a Promised Land: Americans and the Holy Land in the Nineteenth Century* (University Park: Pennsylvania University Press, 1993); Burke O. Long, *Imagining the Holy Land: Maps, Models and Fantasy Travels* (Bloomington: Indiana University Press, 2003).
36. E.g.: "Mount Tabor," *Methodist*, January 16, 1897; and "The Caves of Palestine," *Methodist*, July 25, 1896. For international examples, see also Rogers, *Inventing the Holy Land*; Sebag-Montefiore, *Jerusalem*; Karen Armstrong, *Jerusalem: One City, Three Faiths* (London: HarperCollins, 1996); Davis, *Landscape of Belief*; Silberman, *Digging for God and Country*.
37. Hughes and Allen, *Illusions of Innocence*, 32–7.
38. Obenzinger, *American Palestine*, 24.
39. Rogers, *Inventing the Holy Land*; Vogel, *To See a Promised Land*; Yothers, *Romance of the Holy Land*; Obenzinger, *American Palestine*.
40. Davis, *Landscape of Belief*, 5, 15; Yothers, *Romance of the Holy Land*, 3, 5. It is a recurring theme in Vogel, *To See a Promised Land*; Obenzinger, *American Palestine*.
41. T. Jetson, Email correspondence (March 11, 2014).
42. Albert Ludbrook, "Notes of Travel: Round about Jerusalem," *Australasian Christian Standard*, November 19, 1896, 314.
43. Albert Ludbrook, "Notes of Travel: First Impressions of the Holy City," *Australasian Christian Standard*, November 5, 1896, 300.
44. Sujit Sivasundaram, *Nature and the Godly Empire: Science and Evangelical Mission in the Pacific, 1795–1850* (Cambridge: Cambridge University Press, 2005); Lewis, "James Turner Barclay," 163–70.
45. Alexander Campbell, *The Christian System in Reference to the Union of Christians, and a Restoration of Primitive Christianity, as Plead in the Current Reformation*, 2nd ed. (Pittsburg, PA: Forrester & Campbell, 1839), Chapter 1: 1.
46. Ibid., Chapter 2: 1. Original emphases.
47. A. B. Maston, "A Horse-Back Ride through Palestine: Caesarea Philippi," *Christian Pioneer*, July 9, 1889, 314.

48. Albert Ludbrook, "Notes of Travel: Going Down from Jerusalem to Jericho," *Australasian Christian Standard*, December 17, 1896, 337.
49. Ibid., 37.
50. Maston, "A Horse-Back Ride through Palestine: The Jordan," 434.
51. Adam Lindsay Gordon, "A Dedication," *Bush Ballads and Galloping Rhymes* (Melbourne, 1870), 7. The despair of Gordon's "songless bright birds" was challenged by Andrew Barton "Banjo" Paterson in the optimistic years following Australia's federation, in "Song of the Future," *Rio Grande's Last Race and Other Verses* (Melbourne: Angus and Robertson, 1902). Paterson explicitly contrasted Gordon's songless birds with a landscape of "joyful sounds" in which "bell-birds ring" and the "wild thrush lifts a note of mirth." In 1914 the myth of songless birds was also refuted by botanist Christopher Mudd, *Whys and Ways of the Bush and Guide to Bush Plants, or In Nature's School* (Melbourne: Spectator, 1914), 15.
52. A. B. Maston, "Walks about Palestine: Caesarea Philippi," *Australasian Christian Standard*, March 1, 1891, 59.
53. A. B. Maston, "Walks about Palestine: No. VIII," *Australasian Christian Standard*, July 1, 1892, 197.
54. William Thomson, Preface to *The Land and the Book*, quoted in Davis, *Landscape of Belief*, 47.
55. A. B. Maston, "A Horse-Back Ride through Palestine: From Caesarea Philippi to Galilee," *Christian Pioneer*, July 16, 1889, 324; "Walks about Palestine: No. IV," *Australasian Christian Standard*, September 1, 1891, 226.
56. Maston, "A Horse-Back Ride through Palestine: Caesarea Philippi," 314.
57. Maston, "A Horse-Back Ride through Palestine: From Caesarea Philippi to Galilee," 324.
58. Long, *Imagining the Holy Land*, 16.
59. A. B. Maston, "Walks about Palestine: The Sea of Galilee," *Australasian Christian Standard*, May 1, 1891, 113.
60. Ibid., 114.
61. Maston, "Walks about Palestine: No. IV," 226.
62. Yothers, *Romance of the Holy Land*, 28.
63. E. V. Zollars, *Bible Geography: A Series of Lessons on the Old and New Testament Worlds* (Cincinnati: Standard, 1895).
64. Davis, *Landscape of Belief*, 137, 148. See also Michael W. Bollenbaugh, "Reason, Place of," in *The Encyclopedia of the Stone-Campbell Movement*, ed. Douglas A. Foster, Paul M. Blowers, Anthony L. Dunnavant, and D. Newell Williams (Grand Rapids, MI: Wm. B. Eerdmans, 2004), 627–8.
65. Maston, "Walks about Palestine: No. IV," 226; "A Horse-Back Ride through Palestine: From Caesarea Philippi to Galilee," 324.
66. J. W. McGarvey, "The River Jordan," in *The Gospel Preacher: A Book of Sermons by Various Writers*, ed. A. B. Maston (Melbourne: Austral, 1894), 105. McGarvey also traveled to the Holy Land and produced a book for American readers: *Lands of the Bible: A Geographical and Topographical Description of Palestine, with Letters of Travel in Egypt, Syria, Asia Minor and Greece* (Cincinnati: Standard, 1880). Maston does not refer to *Lands of the Bible* directly, but McGarvey was an important man in the relatively small denomination and it is possible that Maston had read it.
67. A. B. Maston, "A Horse-Back Ride through Palestine: Bethlehem," *Christian Pioneer*, September 3, 1889, 380.
68. Bunyan, *Pilgrim's Progress*, 125.

69. Maston, "A Horse-Back Ride through Palestine: The Jordan," 434.
70. Davis, *Landscape of Belief*, 50.
71. A. B. Maston, "Walks about Palestine: No. IX," *Australasian Christian Standard*, October 1892, 279. In Farrar the image is titled "Flowers and grasses of Palestine (*from nature*)," implying that the artist had been there and sketched from live specimens. Maston, having purchased the plates, could make no such claim. F. W. Farrar, *The Life of Christ* (London: Cassell, Petter and Galpin, 1884), 586.
72. Shahar Marnin-Distelfeld and Edna Gorney, "Why Draw Flowers? Botanical Art, Nationalism, and Women's Contribution to Israeli Culture," *Anthropology of the Middle East* 14, no. 1 (2019): 48.
73. Ludbrook's phrase "God made the country, though man made the town" was a popular one at the time, adapted from William Cowper's 1785 poem, "The Task, Book 1: The Sofa"; Ludbrook, "Notes of Travel: Going Down from Jerusalem to Jericho," 337.
74. Rogers, *Inventing the Holy Land*, 37.
75. Maston, "A Horse-Back Ride through Palestine: Bethlehem," 380. Original emphasis.
76. Maston, "A Horse-Back Ride through Palestine: Caesarea Philippi," 314.
77. Maston, "A Horse-Back Ride through Palestine: Bethlehem," 379.
78. A. B. Maston, "Conference Essay: The Church in the Light of History," *Australasian Christian Standard*, April 29, 1897, 117.
79. Maston, *Jubilee Pictorial History*. Almost every Churches of Christ chapel around Australia is photographed and an account of its building is recorded.
80. A. B. Maston, "Letters of Travel: Dignity and Dirt," *Christian Pioneer*, April 25, 1889.
81. Ludbrook, "Notes of Travel: Round about Jerusalem," 314.
82. Albert Ludbrook, "Notes of Travel: Joppa, the 'Beautiful'," *Australasian Christian Standard*, October 22, 1896, 290. Original emphasis.
83. "An Australian Abroad," *Australasian Christian Standard*, July 1, 1890, 197.
84. Ibid., 197.
85. Ludbrook, "Notes of Travel: Round about Jerusalem," 315.
86. Ibid.
87. W. Waite Willis, "The Archaeology of Palestine and the Archaeology of Faith: Between a Rock and a Hard Place," in *What Has Archaeology to Do with Faith?* ed. James H. Charlesworth and Walter P. Weaver (Philadelphia, PA: Trinity Press, 2002), 97.
88. Sebag-Montefiore, *Jerusalem*, 337.
89. Ludbrook, "Notes of Travel: Joppa, the 'Beautiful'," 299.
90. Ibid.
91. Maston, "Walks about Palestine: The Sea of Galilee," 114.
92. Yothers, *Romance of the Holy Land*, 1, 22; Sebag-Montefiore, *Jerusalem*, 354.
93. Armstrong, *Jerusalem: One City, Three Faiths*, 361.
94. Rogers, *Inventing the Holy Land*, 48–9.
95. Albert Ludbrook, "Notes of Travel: In Quarantine," *Australasian Christian Standard*, September 24, 1896, 266.
96. Albert Ludbrook, "Notes of Travel: Cairo the Magnificent," *Australasian Christian Standard*, July 30, 1896, 214. Original emphasis.
97. Maston, "A Horse-Back Ride through Palestine: Bethlehem," 379.
98. Ludbrook, "Notes of Travel: First Impressions of the Holy City," 301. Original emphasis.
99. Maston, "A Horse-Back Ride through Palestine: From Caesarea Philippi to Galilee," 313.

100. Maston, "Walks about Palestine: The Sea of Galilee," 112.
101. Compare "mounted him on his own beast" in Maston, "Walks about Palestine: No. VIII," 198, with the source passage in Farrar, *The Life of Christ*, 481. Likewise, compare "how delicious to Him must have been that hour" in Maston, "Walks about Palestine: No. IX," 278, with Farrar, *Life of Christ*, 584. Compare "beside those leaden waters" in A. B. Maston, "Walks about Palestine: No. VII," March 1, 1892, 65, with Farrar, *Life of Christ*, 133.
102. Farrar, *Life of Christ*, 203; Wordsworth, "Elegiac Stanzas," line 38 (1803/6), in *Norton Anthology of Poetry*, 3rd ed. (New York: W. W. Norton, 1983), 559.
103. Farrar, *Life of Christ*, 90; Maston, "Walks about Palestine: No. VII," 65; Wordsworth, "Lines: Composed a Few Miles above Tintern Abbey," line 7 (1798), in *Norton Anthology of Poetry*, 3rd ed. (New York: W. W. Norton, 1983), 523.
104. Farrar, Life of Christ, 732; Maston, "Walks about Palestine: The Sea of Galilee," 113; Wordsworth, "The Excursion. Book the Ninth: Discourse of the Wanderer, and an Evening Visit to the Lake," line 491 (1814), in *The Excursion: A Poem* (London: Edward Moxon, 1836), 315–43.
105. Maston, "Walks about Palestine: No. IX," 279.
106. Maston, "Walks about Palestine: The Sea of Galilee," 114.
107. Armstrong, *Jerusalem*, 361.
108. Maston, "Walks about Palestine: No. IV," 226; "A Horse-Back Ride through Palestine: From Caesarea Philippi to Galilee," 324.
109. Maston, "Walks about Palestine: No. V," 281.
110. Ibid. Original emphasis.
111. Maston, "Walks about Palestine: No. VII," 64.
112. Ludbrook, "Notes of Travel: Going Down from Jerusalem to Jericho," 337.
113. Ibid.
114. Hughes, "Why Restorationists?" 195; Plaque at Wangaratta Church of Christ, Victoria.
115. Maston, "Walks about Palestine: No. IX," 277.
116. Maston, "Walks about Palestine: No. IV," 226.
117. Maston, "Walks about Palestine: Caesarea Philippi," 59.
118. Ibid.
119. Rogers, *Inventing the Holy Land*, 22.
120. "Lantern Entertainments," *Queensland Times, Ipswich Herald and General Advertiser*, September 11, 1900, 1.
121. "Advertising," *The Independent* (Footscray), July 17, 1897, 2. There are no records as to how this money was used. Most Churches of Christ did not accept offering money from the unimmersed at this time, so it is unlikely that the admission fees went into general church funds. They may have gone to cover the costs of the hall and projector, or perhaps the evangelists derived some personal income. Equally there is no record of the source of the views. Neither writer mentions taking photographs so it is most likely that they purchased lantern slides to complement their narrative.
122. "Merewether, Lantern Lecture," *Newcastle Morning Herald and Miners' Advocate*, October 4, 1900, 10.
123. "Around the World," *Mercury* (Hobart), September 24, 1891, 2.
124. *Brief History of Jerusalem with Description of the Cyclorama, Victoria Parade, Melbourne* (Melbourne: Rae Bros., 1902), 36.

125. Mimi Colligan, *Canvas Documentaries: Panoramic Entertainments in Nineteenth-Century Australia and New Zealand* (Melbourne: Melbourne University Press, 2002), 163 and 176.
126. *Brief History of Jerusalem with Description of the Cyclorama*, 29.
127. Farrar, *Life of Christ*, 725.
128. Maston, "Walks about Palestine: No. IV," 226–7. At the height of suffrage campaigning, Maston drew criticism for this stance, later acknowledging he held unchanging and "rather old-fashioned views on women's work": "Walks about Palestine: No. IX," 278.
129. Maston, "Walks about Palestine: No. IV," 226.
130. Blake Leyerle, "Landscape as Cartography in Early Christian Pilgrimage Narratives," *Journal of the American Academy of Religion* 64, no. 1 (1996): 131.
131. Maston, "Walks about Palestine: No. IV," 226.
132. Davis, *Landscape of Belief*, 6.
133. Maston, "Walks about Palestine: No. IV," 226; "A Horse-Back Ride through Palestine: From Caesarea Philippi to Galilee," 324.

4 Landscape of Urban Transformation: Salvation Army Publicity and Performance in the Parish of the Streets, 1890–1909

1. "Life in the Slums of Our Great Cities," *War Cry*, June 24, 1899.
2. Ibid.
3. Barbara Bolton, *Booth's Drum: The Salvation Army in Australia 1880–1980* (Sydney: Hodder and Stoughton, 1980), 35.
4. Renate Howe, "Booth, Herbert Henry (1862–1926)," *Australian Dictionary of Biography*. Available online: http://adb.anu.edu.au/biography/booth-herbert-henry-5290 (accessed March 19, 2017).
5. Letter from General William Booth (September 16, 1902), quoted in Renate Howe, "'Five Conquering Years': The Leadership of Commandant and Mrs H. Booth of the Salvation Army in Victoria, 1896–1901," *Journal of Religious History* 6, no. 2 (December 1970): 190.
6. R. Howe, "Booth, Herbert Henry"; Herbert Booth and Cornelie Booth, *Songs of Peace and War* (England: Salvation Army, 1890).
7. Dingle cites 30 percent, while Swain (relying on P. G. McCarthy's "Wages in Australia 1891–1914," *Australian Economic History Review* 10, no. 1 (1970): 69) cites 17.6 percent. Tony Dingle, "Depressions," eMelbourne. Available online: http://www.emelbourne.net.au/biogs/EM00460b.htm (accessed April 5, 2017); Shurlee Swain, "The Poor People of Melbourne," in *The Outcasts of Melbourne*, ed. Graeme Davison, David Dunstan, and Chris McConville (Sydney: Allen and Unwin, 1985), 96. See also Graeme Davison, *The Rise and Fall of Marvellous Melbourne*, 2nd ed. (Carlton, Vic.: Melbourne University Press, 2004), 255–78.
8. Herbert Booth quoted in Bolton, *Booth's Drum*, 36. Herbert and Cornelie left their roles in Australian leadership, opting to run the Army's Collie Estate in Western Australia from 1901, then left the movement for independent evangelical ministry in the United States and England. Bolton, *Booth's Drum*, 65.

9. E.g., at South Melbourne Town Hall on October 1, 1900: "News in Brief," *Argus*, October 2, 1900. Booth and Booth, *Songs of Peace and War*; Cornelie Booth and Herbert Booth, *Heart Melodies* (Melbourne: Salvation Army, 1900).
10. H. Booth, "Move-On Manifesto," *War Cry* (Special Edition), November 21, 1896, 11.
11. "Science and Salvation," *The Victory: An Illustrated Record of Salvation Army Advances in All Nations*, Supplement—"Four Conquering Years 1896-1901" (September 1901), 440-3, reprinted in Ina Bertrand, ed., *Cinema in Australia: A Documentary History* (Kensington, NSW: University of New South Wales Press, 1989), 21-3.
12. Ina Bertrand, "Perry, Joseph Henry (1863-1943)," *Australian Dictionary of Biography*. Available online: http://adb.anu.edu.au/biography/perry-joseph-henry-8024/text13987 (accessed March 24, 2017).
13. Bolton, *Booth's Drum*, 63-5; "Science and Salvation," 22.
14. Bolton, *Booth's Drum*, 66.
15. Bertrand, "Perry, Joseph Henry."
16. R. Howe, "'Five Conquering Years,'" 188; Lindsay Cox, Territorial Archivist for The Salvation Army (Melbourne), notes that when looking for names of editors, "In Victoria, prior to 1896 I find mention of Captain Alfred Gaining. Post-1896 mentions Brigadier George Etherington" (email correspondence, March 22, 2017).
17. Bolton, *Booth's Drum*, 67.
18. Kerrie Handasyde, "Religious Dress and the Making of Women Preachers in Australia, 1880-1934," *Lilith: A Feminist History Journal* 26 (2020): 108-13.
19. Catherine Booth, "The Holy Ghost," *Papers on Aggressive Christianity* (London: The Salvation Army, 1891): 14.
20. Diane Winston, *Red-Hot and Righteous: The Urban Religion of The Salvation Army* (Cambridge, MA: Harvard University Press, 1999), 17.
21. William Booth, *Salvation Soldiery: A Series of Addresses on the Requirements of Jesus Christ's Service* (London: International Headquarters of The Salvation Army, c. 1889), no. 7, part 3.
22. Catherine Booth, "Aggressive Christianity," *Papers on Aggressive Christianity* (London: The Salvation Army, 1891): 16.
23. Blair Ussher, "The Salvation War," in *The Outcasts of Melbourne*, ed. Graeme Davison, David Dunstan, and Chris McConville (Sydney: Allen and Unwin, 1985), 139.
24. Bolton, *Booth's Drum*, 60; *War Cry* (Melbourne), July 7, 1883.
25. Report from Hotham Corps, *War Cry* (Melbourne), July 14, 1883.
26. Gypsum Street Baptist Church, *Barrier Miner* (Broken Hill, NSW), March 31, 1905; Ranelagh, Salvation Army Corps, *Huon Times* (Tas.), March 30, 1912. "The Shilling Sweepstake" may have been based on Hannah Harcourt Pickard's "A Shilling Sweepstake" (George Gibbons, 1902); *Weekly Advocate* (NSW), December 27, 1890, cited in Joan Mansfield, "Music: A Window on Australian Christian Life," in *Re-Visioning Australian Colonial Christianity: New Essays in the Australian Christian Experience 1788-1900*, ed. Mark Hutchinson and Edmund Campion (Sydney: Centre for the Study of Australian Christianity, 1994), 143-4.
27. Gordon Cox, *The Musical Salvationist: The World of Richard Slater (1854-1939), "Father of Salvation Army Music"* (Woodbridge, UK: Boydell Press, 2011), 61.
28. Robyn Karney, ed., *Cinema Year By Year* (London: Dorling Kindersley, 1996), 24.
29. Lindsay Cox, *The Salvation Army Soldiers of the Cross, 1900-2000: Centenary of the First Screening* (Melbourne: The Salvation Army Archives and Museum, 2000), 13.
30. Ibid., 2.

31. Misty G. Anderson, *Imagining Methodism in Eighteenth-Century Britain: Enthusiasm, Belief, and the Borders of the Self* (Baltimore: Johns Hopkins University Press, 2012), 130–7.
32. John H. Y. Briggs, "The Changing Shape of Nonconformity, 1662–2000," in *T&T Clark Companion to Nonconformity*, ed. Robert Pope (London: Bloomsbury T&T Clark, 2013), 16.
33. "The Dark Side of Melbourne," *Christian Pioneer*, May 28, 1889.
34. John Murphy, *A Decent Provision: Australian Welfare Policy, 1870–1949* (Burlington, VT: Ashgate, 2011), 42–8.
35. Diane Winston, "All the World's A Stage: The Performed Religion of The Salvation Army," in *Practicing Religion in the Age of the Media*, ed. Stewart M. Hoover and Lynn Schofield Clark (New York: Columbia University Press, 2002), 123; Anne O'Brien, *God's Willing Workers: Women and Religion in Australia* (Sydney: University of New South Wales Press, 2005), 24.
36. Winsome Roberts, "The Churches' Role in Constituting an Australian Citizenry," in *Spirit of Australia II: Religion in Citizenship and National Life*, ed. Brian Howe and Philip Hughes (Hindmarsh, SA: Australian Theological Forum Press, 2003), 66. Scholarship asserting that the working classes deserted Australian Protestantism is disputed by Renate Howe, *A Reappraisal of the Relationship between the Churches and the Working Classes, 1880–1910*, Uniting Church Historical Society Lecture, Synod of Victoria (October 1989), 1. The rise of denominations appealing to the working and lower-middle classes in the late nineteenth century (Churches of Christ, The Salvation Army, Brethren, Seventh-day Adventists) would also support the idea that the working classes did not desert Protestantism but instead moved within it.
37. E.g.: "The Salvation Army Nuisance," *Riverina Recorder* (NSW), August 24, 1892; "The Salvation Army at Kapunda," *South Australian Register*, January 21, 1885; "Salvation Army Nuisance Public Meeting," *Wagga Wagga Advertiser* (NSW), August 9, 1887. The term "nuisance" also appears in New Zealand newspapers: *Otago Daily Times*, January 6, 1883, and July 26, 1882, cited in Michael F. Hay, "'Onward Christian Soldiers': The Salvation Army in Milton 1884–1894," in *Building God's Own Country: Historical Essays on Religions in New Zealand*, ed. John Stenhouse and Jane Thomson (Dunedin: University of Otago Press, 2004), 114.
38. "The Salvation Army," *Kapunda Herald (SA)*, April 23, 1886.
39. Winston, *Red-Hot and Righteous*, 37.
40. Bolton, *Booth's Drum*, 13, 69–81; John Cleary, "Australia," in *Brass Bands of The Salvation Army: Their Mission and Music*, vol. 1, ed. Ronald W. Holz (Stotfold, UK: Streets, 2006), 277.
41. Handasyde, "Religious Dress and the Making of Women Preachers in Australia," 112–13.
42. *War Cry* (Sydney), n.d., cited in Bolton, *Booth's Drum*, 72; Bolton, *Booth's Drum*, 31; "The Salvation Army," *Kapunda Herald (SA)*, April 23, 1886.
43. "The Salvation Army Processions on Sunday," *South Australian Register*, January 9, 1885. Emphasis added.
44. Ibid.
45. "Salvation Army Hymns," *Protestant Standard* (Sydney), December 23, 1882.
46. "The Salvation Army," *Northern Territory Times and Gazette*, December 9, 1882.
47. Cleary, "Australia," 277–8; Anne O'Brien, "Religion," in *The Cambridge History of Australia: Indigenous and Colonial Australia*, vol. 1, ed. Alison Bashford and Stuart Macintyre (Melbourne: Cambridge University Press, 2013), 434; statistics

for Salvation Army membership according to profession in the UK are provided in G. Cox, *Musical Salvationist*, 109, and for Canada in Lynne Marks, "The 'Hallelujah Lasses': Working-Class Women in The Salvation Army in English Canada, 1882–92," in *Gender Conflicts: New Essays in Women's History*, ed. Franca Iacovetta and Mariana Valverde (Toronto: University of Toronto Press, 1992), 76; Pamela Walker, *Pulling the Devil's Kingdom Down: The Salvation Army in Victorian Britain* (London: University of California Press, 2001), 1.
48. "Church News," *Brighton Southern Cross* (Vic.), September 22, 1900.
49. Roger J. Green, *The Life and Ministry of William Booth, Founder of The Salvation Army* (Nashville: Abingdon Press, 2005), 30; Walker, *Pulling the Devil's Kingdom Down*, 1. Military metaphors were popular in Victorian England, as witnessed in the proliferation of Boys' Brigades and missionary organizations such as the Anglican Church Army. They carried connotations of obedience and self-sacrifice, and empire: see, G. Cox, *Musical Salvationist*, 15–16; Mervyn E. Collins, *Sounds of the Gospel: 125 Years of the Melbourne Staff Band* (Melbourne: The Salvation Army, Australian Southern Territory, 2015), 4.
50. For discussion of perceptions of women's ministry, see Shurlee Swain, *Constructing the Good Christian Woman* (Melbourne: Uniting Church Historical Society, 1993), 3–10; O'Brien, *God's Willing Workers*, 36–49, 100.
51. G. Cox, *Musical Salvationist*, 29; Collins, *Sounds of the Gospel*, 4; Dennis Taylor, *English Brass Bands and Their Music, 1860–1930* (Newcastle: Cambridge Scholars, 2011), 4; Bolton, *Booth's Drum*, 67.
52. Walker, *Pulling the Devil's Kingdom Down*, 42.
53. Bolton, *Booth's Drum*, 36; Hilary M. Carey, *Believing in Australia: A Cultural History of Religions* (St. Leonards, NSW: Allen and Unwin, 1996), 198–209. While the number of Australian Salvationists peaked in the 1980s, the movement had the greatest number of adherents as a percentage of the population in the early 1890s. In Victoria, at least, there had been a significant fall in numbers between 1891 and 1901, and Army members asked questions about the Australian leadership's focus on building welfare institutions at the expense of local corps. See R. Howe, "'Five Conquering Years,'" 188.
54. Norman Murdoch, *Origins of The Salvation Army* (Knoxville: University of Tennessee Press, 1994), 111.
55. William Booth, *In Darkest England, and the Way Out* (London: International Headquarters of The Salvation Army, 1890), 93.
56. Ibid., 93.
57. Ibid.
58. Ibid., 267.
59. Murphy, *A Decent Provision*, 5, 32–3, 47; Stephen Judd and Anne Robinson, "Christianity and the Social Services in Australia," in *Shaping the Good Society in Australia*, ed. Stuart Piggin (Macquarie Centre, NSW: Australian Christian Heritage National Forum, 2006), 111.
60. Green, *Life and Ministry of William Booth*, 167; Murdoch, *Origins*, 157. With the exception of Norman Murdoch in *The Origins of the Salvation Army* (1994) and Barbara Bolton in *Booth's Drum* (1980) who also acknowledges local Melbourne Salvationists, Dr. John Singleton and the Melbourne-based Prisoners' Aid Society (see note 108), few give credit to Barker for influencing Booth in this direction or make more than passing mention of the innovations in Melbourne. More often, Frank Smith and W. T. Stead who contributed to *In Darkest England*, and were later influential in The Salvation Army's implementation of the social gospel, are

given credit as the major influences on William Booth. E.g., Nancy J. Davis and Robert V. Robinson, *Claiming Society for God: Religious Movements and Social Welfare* (Bloomington: Indiana University Press, 2012), chapter 5, "The Salvation Army USA: Doing Good to Hasten the Second Coming"; Marks, "The 'Hallelujah Lasses,'" 95.

61. Bolton, *Booth's Drum*, 31, 109–12.
62. Ibid., 115–16.
63. Ibid., 110.
64. In 1995 The Salvation Army had an income of A$255.5 million, including A$149.8 million from government according to the report of the Australian Industry Commission in to "Charitable Organizations in Australia": Brian Howe and Renate Howe, "The Influence of Faith-Based Organisations on Australian Social Policy," *Australian Journal of Social Studies* 47, no. 3 (2012): 326; Carey, *Believing in Australia*, 209. Salvation Army membership constituted only 0.43 percent of the population.
65. "Work for All: Salvation Army Social Campaign," Lithographic print. London: International Headquarters of The Salvation Army, 1890. Object no. 706440, British Museum Collection Online. Available online: http://www.britishmuseum.org/research/collection_online/ (accessed April 3, 2017).
66. Alan Atkinson, *The Europeans in Australia: Democracy*, vol. 2 (Sydney: University of New South Wales Press, 2016), 421.
67. David Morgan, *Protestants and Pictures: Religion, Visual Culture, and the Age of American Mass Production* (New York: Oxford University Press, 1999), 133.
68. Ibid., 231.
69. "Arcadia" is a term used by historians to describe Booth's objectives under the influence of nineteenth-century rural utopianism. E.g., Esther Daniel, "'Solving an Empire Problem': The Salvation Army and British Juvenile Migration to Australia," *History of Education Review* 36, no. 1 (2007): 37; Esther Daniel, "Salvationists," in *The Encyclopedia of Religion in Australia*, ed. James Jupp (Port Melbourne: Cambridge University Press, 2009), 556; Davison, *Marvellous Melbourne*, 308. However, late-nineteenth-century Salvationist thinking dwelt very much in scriptural allusion and modernist pragmatism, and not in the legends of non-Christian classical Greece.
70. W. Booth, *Darkest England*, 270. Booth did not imagine that he was bringing about the Millennium via the Scheme, but that he was applying practical measures to increase the people's receptivity to salvation.
71. Ibid., 217, 255. Booth refers a few times to the Garden of Eden, but as a comparison with sinful cities and difficult mountainous farmland rather than as a place to be recreated: see 53, 127, 133, 217.
72. Ibid., section 4.
73. Catherine Booth, "The World's Need," *Papers on Aggressive Christianity* (London: The Salvation Army, 1891): 13–14.
74. Murdoch, *Origins*, 163; Norman Murdoch, *Christian Warfare in Rhodesia-Zimbabwe: The Salvation Army and African Liberation, 1891–1991* (London: Lutterworth Press, 2015), 38.
75. R. G. Moyles, "William Booth's Dream of an Alberta 'Oversea Colony,'" *Alberta History* (Summer 2016): 21–5.
76. R. Howe, "'Five Conquering Years,'" 181, 189, 192; Bolton, *Booth's Drum*, 117; "Salvation Army Settlement at Collie: Report by Inspector of Lands," *West Australian*, August 13, 1907.
77. *War Cry* (Melbourne), November 21, 1896.

78. E.g., "The Salvation Army," *Brisbane Courier*, November 23, 1896, 3; "The Salvation Army, Interesting Development, Plans for Housing the Criminal Outcast and Fallen Classes," *West Australian*, November 24, 1896, 3; "Local and General News," *Richmond River Herald and Northern Districts Advertiser* (NSW), November 27, 1896, 4.
79. "A Great Historic Scene, Launch of the 'Move-On Manifesto,'" *War Cry* (Melbourne), November 28, 1896, 3. The Independent Church is now St Michael's Uniting Church.
80. W. Booth, *Darkest England*, 12.
81. Ibid., 144.
82. Davison, *Marvellous Melbourne*, 289–90.
83. *Tasmanian News* (Hobart), January 2, 1907.
84. H. Booth, "Move-On Manifesto," 2.
85. R. Howe, "Five Conquering Years," 181.
86. H. Booth, "Move-On Manifesto," 2, 9, 11.
87. Ibid., 14.
88. Ibid., 1, 15.
89. Ibid., 15.
90. Ibid.
91. Ibid. Bicycles were already in use as early as 1893, as revealed in photographs held in the Salvation Army Heritage Centre.
92. Ibid.
93. "Limelight Entertainment," *Hay Standard* (NSW), October 28, 1896.
94. Lucerna: The Magic Lantern Web Resource lists the lantern slide sets in circulation in the late 1800s. Lucerna: The Magic Lantern Web Resource. Available online: http://lucerna.exeter.ac.uk/ (accessed January 17, 2021).
95. "Limelight Entertainment," *Bunbury Herald* (WA), October 20, 1894; "Evening Entertainments," *Daily Northern Argus* (Rockhampton, Qld.), September 10, 1895; "Limelight Entertainment," *Hay Standard* (NSW). There were multiple versions of lantern-slide sets of the biblical scenes and stories and "Jane Conquest" commercially available at the time, and it is not known which one Perry used. See Lucerna Magic Lantern Web Resource.
96. "Limelight Entertainment," *Hay Standard*.
97. Ibid.; "Salvation Army Limelight Exhibitions," *Warwick Argus* (Qld.), June 4, 1895. Perry traveled between Bunbury and Geraldton in Western Australia in 1894 ("Capt. Perry's Limelight," *Victorian Express* (Geraldton), October 5, 1894; and "Limelight Entertainment," *Southern Times* (Bunbury), October 18, 1894), and he often took his own photographs when traveling. However, I have found no evidence that he traveled inland to Coolgardie until 1897: "Salvation 'Army,'" *Daily News* (Perth), May 15, 1897. There was, however, a commercially available set of thirty lantern slides of Coolgardie with images dating from 1894 sold by English firm York and Sons: see Lucerna Magic Lantern Web Resource.
98. "Limelight Entertainment," *Hay Standard* (NSW).
99. "Salvation Army – Lime-light Entertainments," *Goulburn Herald (NSW)*, April 5, 1893.
100. "Salvation Army, Limelight Entertainment," *Goulburn Herald (NSW)*, October 21, 1896.
101. "Salvation Army," *Geelong Advertiser*, September 27, 1897; "Salvation Biorama," *Darling Downs Gazette* (Qld.), February 15, 1904.
102. "Local and General Items," *Maitland Daily Mercury* (NSW), November 5, 1895.

103. "Lantern Entertainment," *Windsor and Richmond Gazette* (NSW), January 28, 1893; "A Salvation Army Entertainment," *Geelong Advertiser*, August 7, 1894; "Adjutant Perry's Lantern Limelight Entertainments," *Northern Star* (Lismore), May 18, 1895.
104. E.g.: "The Commandant's Prahran Triumph" features interior and exterior sketches of the Prahran Town Hall in *War Cry*, November 28, 1896.
105. *War Cry*, December 5, 1896.
106. H. Booth, "Move-On Manifesto," 5–7.
107. "Salvation Army," *Telegraph* (Brisbane), December 2, 1896.
108. Howe, "'Five Conquering Years,'" 181.
109. H. Booth, "Move-On Manifesto," 11.
110. *War Cry*, July 14, 1883.
111. *War Cry*, July 21, 1883; Philip Bliss, "Dare to Be a Daniel" (1873). Available online: http://hymnary.org/text/standing_by_a_purpose_tree (accessed May 23, 2017).
112. *War Cry*, July 21 and August 11, 1883.
113. *War Cry*, July 28, 1883.
114. *War Cry*, July 14, 1883. Opening fire and shooting refer to street preaching, and the taking of a prisoner refers to conversion.
115. *War Cry*, July 28, 1883.
116. William George Taylor, *Pathfinders of the Great South Land* (London: Epworth Press, c.1925), 94–95.
117. "Map Showing the Liquor Shops of Melbourne," *War Cry*, August 3, 1901, 8.
118. "The Modern Plague of London," National Temperance Publication Depot (London: 1886), Museum of London. There were also allegorical maps produced as part of temperance campaigning, e.g., "Temperance Map" by C. Wiltberger (Pennsylvania, 1838), Library of Congress. Available online: https://www.loc.gov/item/2012592020/ (accessed April 9, 2017).
119. "Map Showing the Liquor Shops of Melbourne."
120. Edward Gilks (compiler), "Hutchinson's Exhibition Pocket Map of Melbourne" (Melbourne: J. Batten, 1880), State Library Victoria. Available online: http://handle.slv.vic.gov.au/10381/246568 (accessed April 13, 2017).
121. James Kearney (draughtsman), "Melbourne and Its Suburbs" (Melbourne: Andrew Clarke, Surveyor General, 1855), State Library Victoria. Available online: http://handle.slv.vic.gov.au/10381/89107 (accessed April 13, 2017).
122. *Souvenir Programme of the Jubilee Conference of Churches of Christ in Victoria* (Melbourne: Austral, 1903).
123. Morgan, *Protestants and Pictures*, 206.
124. *War Cry*, August 3, 1901, 16.
125. For the relationship between people and environment in literature of the period, see Joseph W. Childers, "Observation and Representation: Mr Chadwick Writes the Poor," *Victorian Studies* 37, no. 3 (Spring 1994): 411.
126. *War Cry*, June 18, 1898.
127. Walker, *Pulling the Devil's Kingdom Down*, 81–2.
128. Ibid., 82–3.
129. "The Social Cinematographe," *War Cry*, July 9, July 16, and July 30, 1898.
130. "The Social Cinematographe," *War Cry*, August 13, 1898.
131. "In Melbourne Slums," *War Cry*, May 7, 1898.
132. E.g., "Darkest Melbourne, Round the Slums," *Telegraph* (Brisbane), November 9, 1901; see also, Davison, *Marvellous Melbourne*, 289.

133. "Timber Yard Gutted," *Bendigo Advertiser*, November 25, 1912.
134. David Morgan, "'For Christ and the Republic': Protestant Illustration and the History of Literacy in Nineteenth-Century America," in *The Visual Culture of American Religions*, ed. David Morgan and Sally M. Promey (Berkeley: University of California Press, 2001), 57–8.
135. H. Booth, "Move-On Manifesto," 9.
136. Davison, *Marvellous Melbourne*, 289. For further discussion of slum journalism, see Graeme Davison, *City Dreamers: The Urban Imagination in Australia* (Sydney: NewSouth, 2016); Graeme Davison and David Dunstan, "'This Moral Pandemonium': Images of Low Life," in *The Outcasts of Melbourne*, ed. Graeme Davison, David Dunstan, and Chris McConville (Sydney: Allen and Unwin, 1985), 29–57. For similarities in Sydney, see Alan Mayne, *Representing the Slum: Popular Journalism in a Late Nineteenth-Century City* (Parkville: History Department, University of Melbourne, 1990), 84–115; and, in English literature, Childers, "Observation and Representation," 406.
137. "Darkest Melbourne, Round the Slums," *Telegraph* (Brisbane), November 9, 1901; Davison, *Marvellous Melbourne*, 289.
138. "One of the Lost," in "The Social Cinematographe," *War Cry*, July 16, 1898.
139. Shurlee Swain with Renate Howe, *Single Mothers and Their Children: Disposal, Punishment and Survival in Australia* (Cambridge: Cambridge University Press, 1995), 25.
140. *War Cry*, June 18, 1898. Wages were under pressure at this time and men working as butchers or carters might earn 25 shillings or 12 shillings and sixpence per week, respectively. At 20 shillings to a pound, £40 could be the equivalent of several months' wages: "Low Wages," *Argus*, September 2, 1898, 5.
141. *War Cry*, July 2, 1898.
142. *War Cry*, June 24, 1899.
143. "Amusements," *Argus*, July 16, 1898.
144. "Programme and Songs for the Great Social Salvation Carnival at the Exhibition Building, Melbourne on Monday August 1, 1898, under the conductorship of Commandant and Mrs Booth" (Melbourne: Salvation Army Press, 1898), 3.
145. Ibid., 7.
146. "Amusements," *Age*, July 29, 1899; "The Salvation Army Great Carnival to be held in the Exhibition Building, Programme, Tuesday April 3, 1900, under the Conductorship of Commandant and Mrs Booth" (Melbourne: Salvation Army Press, 1900), 9.
147. "Social Salvation," *Brisbane Courier*, October 12, 1899.
148. "The Salvation Army, Lecture by Commandant Booth, 'Social Salvation,'" *Morning Bulletin* (Rockhampton, Qld.), October 25, 1899.
149. "Social Salvation," *Geelong Advertiser*, September 21, 1899; "The Salvation Army, Lecture by Commandant Booth, 'Social Salvation,'" *Morning Bulletin* (Rockhampton, Qld.), October 25, 1899.
150. "Science and Salvation," 22.
151. "Salvation Army," *Goulburn Herald (NSW)*, September 28, 1898.
152. "Programme and Songs."
153. Simon Sleight, "'For the Sake of Effect': Youth on Display and the Politics of Performance," *History Australia* 6, no. 3 (2009): 14. E.g., W. F. James, *Souvenir of a Great Historical Event: The Union of the Methodist Churches of*

Australasia, consummated in Melbourne, February 25, 1902 (Melbourne: Spectator, 1902), 33.
154. "Programme and Songs," 8–11.
155. Jennifer Coate, Robert Fitzgerald, and Helen Milroy, "Report of Case Study No. 33, The Response of The Salvation Army (Southern Territory) to Allegations of Child Sexual Abuse at Children's Homes that it Operated," *Royal Commission into Institutional Responses to Child Sexual Abuse* (Commonwealth of Australia, July 2016), 67–72, 92–3.
156. *War Cry*, April 16, 1898, 1–2.
157. Model farms were developed in England in the nineteenth century. For example, Wrexham Road Farm in Cheshire (1870s), Leighton Estate in Powys, and Sturgeons Farm in Essex (mid-1800s).
158. *War Cry*, April 16, 1898, 1–2.
159. H. Booth, "Move-On Manifesto," 10. The term "son of the soil" was familiar to readers of popular Scottish novelist Margaret Oliphant who wrote a novel with that title in 1866. In postcolonial studies it has come to represent First Nations inhabitants, distinguishing them from migrant groups such as those which The Salvation Army served. See, e.g., Myron Weiner, *Sons of the Soil: Migration and Ethnic Conflict in India* (Princeton, NJ: Princeton University Press, 1978).
160. Davison, *City Dreamers*, 122–5.
161. Bolton, *Booth's Drum*, 126–7.
162. Alan Atkinson, *The Europeans in Australia: Nation*, vol. 3 (Sydney: University of New South Wales Press, 2014), 138–43; Davison, *Marvellous Melbourne*, 308; W. Booth, *Darkest England*, 266–7.
163. R. Howe, "'Five Conquering Years,'" 185.
164. "The Salvation Army, Excursion to the Bayswater Farm," *Age*, April 4, 1898, reprinted in *War Cry*, April 16, 1898.
165. Ibid.
166. L. Cox, "Salvation Army Soldiers of the Cross," 10.
167. R. Howe, "'Five Conquering Years,'" 187–90. Herbert Booth was also involved in disputes within the Booth family over organizational matters during this period. After leaving The Salvation Army Herbert toured extensively with "Soldiers of the Cross" while Cornelie raised their children in England. Bolton, *Booth's Drum*, 65.
168. *War Cry*, May 13, 1899, cited in R. Howe, "'Five Conquering Years,'" 188.
169. "Soldiers of the Cross," *Bendigo Independent*, August 20, 1901, 2.
170. "Soldiers of the Cross," *Register* (Adelaide), March 19, 1901; "The Salvation Army," *Bendigo Advertiser*, August 20, 1901; "A Salvation Army Lecture," *Sydney Morning Herald*, April 23, 1901; "News of the Day," *Age*, May 6, 1901; "Salvation Army," *Daily Telegraph* (Launceston, Tas.), January 16, 1901; "Soldiers of the Cross," *Telegraph* (Brisbane), April 9, 1901.
171. "Church and Organ," *Punch* (Melbourne), September 20, 1900.
172. *War Cry*, April 9, 1898. Emphasis added.
173. Winston, "All the World's A Stage," 129.

5 Landscape of Here and Elsewhere: Congregational Poetry at Home in War and Peace, 1914–30

1. Margery Ruth Betts, "Called," *Australasian*, August 19, 1916.
2. Sections of this chapter were first published as "Anzac Theology and the Women Poets under the Southern Cross," *Colloquium: The Australia and New Zealand Theological Review* 49, no. 1 (May 2017): 17–30.
3. Dorothy Goldman, ed., *Women and World War I: The Written Response* (London: Macmillan, 1993), 7; Janet Montefiore, "'Shining Pins and Wailing Shells': Women Poets and the Great War," in *Women and World War I: The Written Response*, ed. Dorothy Goldman (London: Macmillan, 1993), 54–6.
4. Samuel Hynes, *A War Imagined: The First World War and English Culture* (London: Bodley Head, 1990), 190.
5. Beatrice Bevan, "Via Crucis (For 25th April, 1916)," *Victorian Independent*, May 1, 1916.
6. Alan Atkinson, *The Europeans in Australia: Nation*, vol. 3 (Sydney: University of New South Wales Press, 2014), 271.
7. Michael McKernan, *Australian Churches at War: Attitudes and Activities of the Major Churches 1914–1918* (Sydney: Catholic Theological Faculty; Canberra: Australian War Memorial, 1980), 4.
8. Ibid.; John A. Moses, "Was There an Anzac Theology?," *Colloquium* 35, no. 1 (2003): 3–13.
9. Vale was a bookseller, barrister, supporter of women's education, member of the colonial Victorian parliament (serving as Attorney General and Minister of Justice), and trustee of Victoria's Public Library, National Gallery and Museum: "William Mountford Kinsey Vale," Collingwood Historical Society. Available online: http://collingwoodhs.org.au/view/collingwood-notables/entry/177/ (accessed July 19, 2017); One of Beatrice's sisters was an artist and another a doctor: "Mrs Bevan, Poetess," *News* (Adelaide), September 11, 1928. A further two sisters were involved in establishing a school: "William Mountford Kinsey Vale." As a measure of the family's talents, Beatrice's husband also had a sister who was a doctor, Dr. Sibyl Bevan. His brothers included a judge and a professor.
10. "Beatrice Bevan," Austlit: The Australian Literature Resource (online). Available online: http://www.austlit.edu.au (accessed February 9, 2016).
11. "Gawler's Laureate," *Bunyip* (Gawler, SA), January 7, 1921.
12. Atkinson, *Europeans in Australia: Nation*, 80.
13. Marcus Clarke, "Adam Lindsay Gordon," *Bird O'Freedom* (Sydney), September 16, 1893.
14. "Mrs Bevan, Poetess," *News* (Adelaide), September 11, 1928.
15. "Australian Authors," Graphic of Australia, November 23, 1917; Margery Ruth Betts, *Remembering and Other Verses* (Melbourne: Australasian Authors' Agency, 1917), held at State Library of Victoria; William Harnett Blanch, *Ye Parish of Camberwell: A Brief Account of the Parish of Camberwell; Its History and Antiquities* (London: Forgotten Books, 2013 [1875]), 230–1; "Memorial to Principal Betts A.T.S.," Victorian Independent, August 2, 1915.
16. "Some Charm of Song," *Sunday Times* (NSW), January 13, 1918.
17. "Commonwealth Day," *Sydney Mail and New South Wales Advertiser*, January 5, 1901; John Garrett, "Cocks, Nicholas John (1867–1925)," *Australian Dictionary*

of Biography. Available online: http://adb.anu.edu.au/biography/cocks-nicholas-john-5706/text9647adb (accessed February 3, 2016); Susan Emilsen, Ben Skerman, Patricia Curthoys, and William Emilsen, *Pride of Place: A History of the Pitt Street Congregational Church* (Beaconsfield: Melbourne Publishing Group, 2008), 166.

18. Nicholas John Cocks and D. H. Souter, *Songs of the Dardanelles* (Sydney: s.n., 1915). The poems are "Reprinted by permission from *The Scottish Australasian*, for the benefit of the Red Cross League" and include "The Graves of the Dardanelles" and "Do you hear the tramp of feet / Through your dreams and waking."
19. Nicholas John Cocks, *The Betty Songs* (Sydney: W. Geo. Smith, 1919).
20. Joseph Eisenberg and Joan Kerr, "Olive Crane," *Design and Art Australia Online*. Available online: https://www.daao.org.au/bio/olive-crane/biography/ (accessed March 30, 2016).
21. Garrett, "Cocks"; Geoffrey Lindsay Lockley, *Congregationalism in Australia*, 2nd ed., ed. Bruce Upham (Melbourne: Uniting Church Press, 2001), 159.
22. Elizabeth A. Cocks, foreword to *Australian Songs and Other Poems*, by Nicholas Cocks (Sydney: Bourne's Book Shop, 1925).
23. John Garrett and L. W. Farr, *Camden College: A Centenary History* (Sydney: Camden College, 1964), 22.
24. Emilsen et al., *Pride of Place*, 166; Garrett, "Cocks."
25. Michael Sharkey, "'But Who Considers Woman Day by Day?': Australian Women Poets and World War I," *Australian Literary Studies* 23, no. 1 (May 2007): 64–5.
26. Joy Damousi, *The Labour of Loss: Mourning, Memory and Wartime Bereavement in Australia* (Melbourne: Cambridge University Press, 1999), 35–8.
27. Two poems by Betts ("Remembering" and "The Fulfilment") appear in David Holloway, *Dark Somme Flowing: Australian Verse of the Great War, 1914–18* (Malvern: Robert Anderson and Associates, 1987).
28. Margery Ruth Betts, "The Red Brother," *Victorian Independent*, May 1, 1917; see also Betts, "The Kaiser's Boast," *Victorian Independent*, July 1, 1918.
29. Margery Ruth Betts, "The Reckoning," in *Remembering*, 21.
30. Similar increase in poetic response has been noted elsewhere. E.g., Gordon L. Heath, "Passion for Empire: War Poetry Published in the Canadian English Protestant Press during the South African War, 1899–1902," *Literature and Theology* 16, no. 2 (December 2002): 130–1.
31. Heath notes that, despite men's poems being heavily represented in war poetry anthologies, a third of poets in church journals were women: Ibid. The majority of poems published in the Congregational *Victorian Independent* from 1914 to 1918 were by women.
32. Marilyn Lake and Henry Reynolds, *What's Wrong with ANZAC? The Militarisation of Australian History* (Sydney: University of New South Wales Press, 2010); Honest History, http://honesthistory.net.au/ (accessed December 20, 2017).
33. E.g.: Alex Russell, "For the Lads of Our Church Who Have Fallen," *Spectator and Methodist Chronicle*, August 15, 1917.
34. *Spectator and Methodist Chronicle*, June 18, 1915.
35. This was also true around the Second World War when the Quaker journal published numerous articles by and about the Quaker Thomas H. Silcock's resistance to the war, but none of his poetry. His poems, some of which were written during his time as a prisoner of war in Thailand, were later published in a book of collected verse. See various articles in *Friend of Australia and New Zealand* (June 20,

1944) and *Australian Friend* (December 20, 1950); Thomas H. Silcock, *Tradeways* (Sydney: Currawong, 1971).

36. In the Melbourne-based congregation periodical, *Victorian Independent*, there are no poems opposing the war in the years 1915–20. There is an anti-war poem in 1934 by an ordained minister: R. Ambrose Roberts, "War," *Victorian Independent*, December 1, 1934.
37. E.g., Lockley, *Congregationalism in Australia*; Walter Phillips, *James Jefferis: Prophet of Federation* (Melbourne: Australian Scholarly, 1993); John Cameron, *In Stow's Footsteps: A Chronological History of the Congregational Churches in SA, 1837–1977* (Adelaide: South Australian Congregational History Project Committee, 1987). Patricia Curthoys notes that other historians also repeat this claim, but that "This assertion is worthy of further investigation": Curthoys, "Congregationalists," in *The Encyclopedia of Religion in Australia*, ed. James Jupp (Port Melbourne: Cambridge University Press, 2009), 304.
38. Lockley, *Congregationalism*, 11.
39. There were exceptions to the acceptance of State Aid: Ibid., 188.
40. Ibid., 128–9, 271–3, 267–70; Curthoys, "Congregationalists," 302.
41. Robert Humphreys and Rowland Ward, *Religious Bodies in Australia*, 3rd ed. (Wantirna, Vic.: New Melbourne Press, 1995), 115; Curthoys, "Congregationalists," 304; Atkinson, *Europeans in Australia: Nation*, 271. Census statistics from 1911 show there were 74,046 Congregationalists, constituting 1.6 percent of the Australian population: Hilary M. Carey, *Believing in Australia: A Cultural History of Religions* (St Leonards, NSW: Allen and Unwin, 1996), 199.
42. Lockley, *Congregationalism*, 147. Lockley's chapters on Congregationalism in each of the states suggest a broad national pattern involving the sometimes short-term establishment of numerous preaching stations and small congregations in rural towns in the various states, a concentration of congregations in city centers (capital and regional), and moderate to weak expansion on the cities' fringes where population growth was often strong.
43. Phillips, *James Jefferis*, 273–4.
44. "Dr. Bevan's Jubilee, The Public Recognition, 'The Patriarch of the Churches,'" *Daily Herald* (Adelaide), July 7, 1915; "Correspondence, Germans in Australia," *Register* (Adelaide), September 10, 1914.
45. Phillips, *James Jefferis*, 273–4.
46. Lockley, *Congregationalism*, 324.
47. Robert D. Linder, *The Long Tragedy: Australian Evangelical Christians and the Great War 1914–1918* (Adelaide: Openbook, 2000), 78, 97; C. B. Schedvin, "Rivett, Albert (1855–1934)," *Australian Dictionary of Biography*. Available online: (accessed February 10, 2016). See also McKernan, *Australian Churches at War*, 153. McKernan observes that Rivett worked in "isolation" but Linder notes that his efforts were "supported" by Congregationalists including the Reverend Dr. L. D. Bevan and a deacon at Richmond Congregational Church, Frank Tudor, who became federal parliamentary leader of the Labor party in 1916 and an anti-conscription advocate. Deepdene Congregational Church (est. 1909) was "planted" by the Kew Congregational Church and the first services were conducted by the Reverend R. A. Betts (d. 1913), father of Margery Ruth Betts. See Patricia O'Dwyer, ed., "Early Balwyn and Deepdene Churches," *A Compilation of Newsletter Articles*, Balwyn Historical Society (2010): 3–5.
48. Linder, *Long Tragedy*, 41.

49. Hilary M. Carey, "Religion and Society," in *Australia's Empire*, ed. Deryck Schreuder and Stuart Ward (Oxford: Oxford University Press, 2008), 206. See also Roger C. Thompson, *Religion in Australia: A History* (Melbourne: Oxford University Press, 1994), 57.
50. McKernan, *Australian Churches at War*, 3–4. McKernan focuses his study on Anglican, Catholic, Presbyterian, and Methodist responses to war, though these churches did not speak for all according to scholars of smaller denominations. E.g., Elisabeth Wilson, "'The Irregularity of Killing People': Tasmanian Brethren Responses to World War I," *Tasmanian Historical Studies* 14 (2009): 25–52.
51. This is evidenced not only in Congregational poetry but also in the published opinion of poets. E.g., Beatrice Bevan on enlistment and white feathers in "Enlistment," *Register* (Adelaide), May 18, 1915.
52. Lockley, *Congregationalism*, 255.
53. "Congregational Union," *Observer* (Adelaide), October 16, 1915.
54. McKernan, *Australian Churches at War*, 112. For the Victorian Congregational churches' declaration see *Age*, October 14, 1916. For a summary of Australian Anglican and Presbyterian, and Victorian Methodist, Baptist, and Congregational positions on conscription, see *Zeehan and Dundas Herald* (Tas.), October 27, 1916. The unity of the Protestant churches on this issue was also a product of the sectarian divide, as Catholic leaders such as Archbishop Daniel Mannix opposed conscription.
55. "Out of Order, Congregational Union Does Not Discuss Conscription," *Daily Herald* (Adelaide), October 20, 1916.
56. "Congregational Union," *Observer* (Adelaide), October 16, 1915.
57. B. K. Hyams, "Smeaton, Thomas Hyland (1857–1927)," *Australian Dictionary of Biography*. Available online: http://adb.anu.edu.au/biography/smeaton-thomas-hyland-8461/text14877 (accessed February 3, 2016).
58. Frederick Sinclaire, *Conscription and Christianity: Manifesto from Protestant Ministers* (Melbourne: Free Religious Fellowship, 1917). Rivett and Hume were among the nine signatories to the manifesto.
59. *Victorian Independent*, December 1, 1916. Although it is unlikely the editor of the *Victorian Independent* would have known of the practice, the British military court-martialed and sentenced to death thirty-four conscientious objectors while in the field in France, but commuted their sentences to "penal servitude"; Margaret Brooks, "Conscientious Objectors in their Own Words," Imperial War Museums. Available online: http://www.iwm.org.uk/history/conscientious-objectors-in-their-own-words (accessed February 10, 2016).
60. Beatrice Bevan, "Via Crucis (For 25th April, 1916)," *Victorian Independent*, May 1, 1916.
61. Moses, "Anzac Theology?" 11.
62. E.g.: Margery Ruth Betts, "Which Were Buried Together," *Victorian Independent*, October 2, 1916; Betts, "Silenced," in *Remembering*, 34; Beatrice Bevan, "Wattle Blossom and Southern Cross," *Register* (Adelaide), September 6, 1915.
63. Margery Ruth Betts, "The Sacrament," *Victorian Independent*, December 1, 1915. See also, "The First Australian Casualty List," in *Remembering*, 11.
64. Margery Ruth Betts, "Communion on the Battlefield," *Victorian Independent*, December 1, 1915.
65. Ibid.
66. Michael Snape, *God and the British Soldier: Religion and the British Army in the First and Second World Wars* (New York: Routledge, 2005), 24.

67. Ibid., 22.
68. Atkinson, *Europeans in Australia: Nation*, 409; Snape, *God and the British Soldier*, 24.
69. Moses, "Anzac Theology?" 13.
70. Nosheen Khan, *Women's Poetry of the First World War* (Lexington: University Press of Kentucky, 1988), 40–4; Joan Beaumont, *Broken Nation: Australians in the Great War* (Sydney: Allen and Unwin, 2013), 180; McKernan, *Australian Churches at War*, 110.
71. Moses, "Anzac Theology?" 10–12. See also the report on a sermon by Congregational minister in North Adelaide, the Reverend Alfred Gifford, "Congregational Church: The Moral Value of War," *Daily Herald* (Adelaide), January 4, 1915.
72. Alan J. Kerr, "At Sea," *Victorian Independent*, July 1915. While women poets were published with occasional mention of their ordained male relatives, Kerr's poem was accompanied with military authority—"24th Battalion, AIF. On board Euripides, June 1915." Only two poems by Kerr appear in the *Victorian Independent*, both written during military service. The second is titled "Adieu!" and was written in December 1915 and published in April 1916. Nominal roll lists an Alan James Kerr of 24th Battalion as Lieutenant, killed in action on July 27, 1916.
73. Beatrice Bevan, "Lord God of Empires" (first line in absence of title), *Register* (Adelaide), May 24, 1917.
74. Bevan, "Lord God of Empires."
75. Nicholas Cocks, "The Land and the Dream of It" (part 6), in *Australian Songs and Other Poems* (Sydney: Bourne's Book Shop, 1925), 69.
76. Margery Ruth Betts, "We Would Not Have Thee," *Victorian Independent*, June 1, 1916.
77. Margery Ruth Betts, "The First Night," *Victorian Independent*, December 1, 1917.
78. Margery Ruth Betts, "A Mean Street," in *Remembering*, 40–1.
79. McKernan, *Australian Churches at War*, 70.
80. Moses, "Anzac Theology?" 12; McKernan, *Australian Churches at War*, 88.
81. Cocks, "Australia—The Harp of the Name," in *Australian Songs*, 70.
82. Nicholas Cocks, "News of the Landing—Gallipoli," and "The Song of the Men Who Fell," in *Betty Songs*, 19, 21–2.
83. See, e.g., Robert Laurence Binyon, "Edith Cavell," in *The Cause: Poems of the War* (London: Elkin Matthews, 1917); William S. Murphy, *In Memoriam: Edith Cavell* (London: Stoneham, 1916); Eden Phillpotts, "Edith Cavell," reprinted in *Observer* (Adelaide), December 25, 1915, 51.
84. Beaumont, *Broken Nation*, 386, 98; Philip Jenkins, *The Great and Holy War: How World War I Changed Religion Forever* (Oxford: Lion, 2014), 105.
85. Jane Potter, *Boys in Khaki, Girls in Print: Women's Literary Responses to the Great War* (Oxford: Oxford University Press, 2008), 69.
86. The identification of sites of martyrdom with Golgotha or Calvary had a long tradition in Nonconformity. For example, in his poem "Jerusalem," William Blake asks of the gallows at Tyburn, "Is that Calvary and Golgotha?" See Curtis W. Freeman, *Undomesticated Dissent: Democracy and the Public Virtue of Religious Nonconformity* (Waco: Baylor University Press, 2017), 29.
87. Beatrice Bevan, "Edith Cavell," *Register*, October 22, 1915, 8.
88. See also Damousi, *The Labour of Loss*, 26–45; Jenkins, *Great and Holy War*, 102; See also Betts's celebration of Louis Bril who avenged Cavell's death by killing her informer and who was himself killed by firing squad: "Brussells Streets," *Victorian Independent*, February 1, 1919, 34.
89. Hynes, *War Imagined*, 196.
90. Winter, *Sites of Memory*, 2–5, 221.

91. Peter Hoffenberg, "Landscape, Memory and the Australian War Experience, 1915–1918," *Journal of Contemporary History* 36, no. 1 (January 2001): 116; C. E. W. Bean, "Letters from France," quoted in Hoffenberg, "Landscape, Memory," 119; Suzanne Welborn, *Lords of Death: A People, A Place, A Legend* (Fremantle: Fremantle Arts Centre Press, 1982), 78–80; Atkinson, *Europeans in Australia: Nation*, 409.
92. A. B. "Banjo" Paterson, "Clancy of the Overflow" (1889), in *My Country: Australian Poetry and Short Stories*, vol. 1, ed. Leonie Kramer (Sydney: Lansdowne Press, 1985), 269–70; Atkinson, *Europeans in Australia: Nation*, 409.
93. Dorothea MacKellar, "My Country" (1911), in *My Country: Australian Poetry and Short Stories*, vol. 1, ed. Leonie Kramer (Sydney: Lansdowne Press, 1985), 472–3.
94. Hynes, *War Imagined*, 31; Khan, *Women's Poetry*, 57–8.
95. Heath, "Passion for Empire," 129.
96. Nicholas Cocks, "England," in *Betty Songs*, 39–40.
97. Ibid.
98. Khan, *Women's Poetry*, 60.
99. Nicholas Cocks, "O, Sydney!" in *Betty Songs*, 25.
100. Nicholas Cocks, "The Riding of the King's Men," in *Betty Songs*, 11–12.
101. John Williams, "'Art, War and Agrarian Myths': Australian Reactions to Modernism 1913–1931," in *An Anzac Muster: War and Society in Australia and New Zealand 1914–1918 and 1939–1945*, ed. Judith Smart and Tony Wood (Clayton, Vic.: Monash Publications in History, 1992), 44.
102. Margery Ruth Betts, "The Crowning," *Australasian*, July 24, 1915.
103. Nicola Beauman, "'It Is not the Place of Women to Talk of Mud': Some Responses by British Women Novelists to World War I," in *Women and World War I: The Written Response*, ed. Dorothy Goldman (London: Macmillan, 1993), 132; Khan, *Women's Poetry*, 56.
104. Margery Ruth Betts, "The Day You Went," in *Remembering*, 35.
105. Beatrice Bevan, "Two Songs (Sorrow and Joy)," *Observer* (Adelaide), April 24, 1915.
106. Atkinson, *Europeans in Australia: Nation*, 353.
107. Frank Bongiorno, "Aboriginality and Historical Consciousness: Bernard O'Dowd and the Creation of an Australian National Imaginary," *Aboriginal History* 24 (2000): 40.
108. Betts, "Called," *Australasian*, August 19, 1916; "A Mean Street," in *Remembering*, 40–1.
109. Major Thomas Hyland Smeaton, "Hawthorne Dene," *Register* (Adelaide) June 3, 1922, and "Lessons of the Forest," *The Forest* (Adelaide: Vardon and Sons, 1920).
110. Atkinson, *Europeans in Australia: Nation*, 372–6.
111. Lockley, *Congregationalism*, 324.
112. Beatrice Bevan, "Under the Hedge," *Observer* (Adelaide), December 18, 1915.
113. Nicholas Cocks, "Anniversary Day," in *Australian Songs*, 95.
114. Nicholas Cocks, "Yet Is Their Strength," *Betty Songs*, 15.
115. Nicholas Cocks, "Adelaide," in *Australian Songs*, 92; Cocks, "O, Sydney!" in *Betty Songs*, 25.
116. E.g.: Cocks, "The Yellow Robin," "The Poison Trail," "Bird Music," "A Fragment," in *Australian Songs*, 95, 76, 82, 39.
117. Nicholas Cocks, "Dawn and Death" and "The Music of the Rain," in *Australian Songs*, 87, 78.
118. Nicholas Cocks, "The Mother," in *Australian Songs*, 86.
119. Nicholas Cocks, "March of the Anzac Men" (1915), reprinted in *Northern Star* (Lismore, NSW), June 9, 1926. Cocks refers to "sunburnt ground" and "our sunburnt

Autumn plains" in two other poems: "Dedication," in *Australian Songs*, 9; "England," in *Betty Songs*, 39–40.
120. MacKellar, "My Country."
121. Grace Jennings Carmichael, "Evening on the Plains," *Australasian*, January 23, 1892.
122. Cocks, "Anniversary Day," in *Australian Songs*, 95. His work here anticipates A. D. Hope's "second-hand Europeans" in the poem "Australia" (1939).
123. Cocks refers to roses more than a dozen times to represent women in his love poems: *Betty Songs*, 51, 78, 79, 81, 82, 85, and 88; *Australian Songs*, 10–11, 13, 27, 30, 48, and 59.
124. E.g.: Ps. 103:15-16; Job 14:2; Isa. 40:7; Jas 1:10-11; 1 Pet. 1:24.
125. E.g, Margery Ruth Betts, "The Ghost," *Australasian*, August 2, 1919; Betts, "The Red Brother"; Cocks, "England." See also, Montefiore, "Shining Pins," 63; Ann Elias, "War, Flowers, and Visual Culture: The First World Collection of the Australian War Memorial," *Journal of the Australian War Memorial* 40 (February 2007): 234–50.
126. E.g.: Margery Ruth Betts, "The Little Brother," *Australasian*, February 9, 1918.
127. Margery Ruth Betts, "Remembering," in *Remembering*, 9–10.
128. Margery Ruth Betts, "The Route March," *Victorian Independent*, August 1916; reprinted in *Remembering*, 42–3.
129. Ibid.
130. Ken Inglis, *Sacred Places: War Memorials in the Australian Landscape* (Carlton, Vic.: Miegunyah Press, 1998).
131. For broader discussion on the role of gardens in women's lives and writing, see Katie Holmes, *Between the Leaves: Stories of Australian Women, Writing and Gardens* (Crawley, WA: University of Western Australia, 2011).
132. Margery Ruth Betts, "The Homecoming," in *Remembering*, 45.
133. Margery Ruth Betts, "The Unforgotten," in *Remembering*, 16–17.
134. Philip Gibbs, "The Hazard of War," *West Australian*, April 15, 1918. Betts claims to have read it in the *Argus*, April 15, 1918, suggesting it may have been reprinted widely.
135. Margery Ruth Betts, "Earth to the Spring," *Victorian Independent*, June 1, 1918.
136. For the daisy's cultural associations, see also Jack Goody, *The Culture of Flowers* (Cambridge: Cambridge University Press, 1993), 292–3.
137. E. S. Abbott, ed., *Violet Verses* (Adelaide: E. S. Abbott, 1917).
138. Damousi, *Labour of Loss*, 35–8.
139. Selections from this discussion of wattle first appeared in Kerrie Handasyde, "Wattle: 'Symbol of This Nation's Heart'," *Australian Garden History* 29, no. 3 (January 2018): 12–14.
140. "Wattle Day," Wattle Day Association. Available online: http://www.wattleday.asn.au/about-wattle-day (accessed February 3, 2016).
141. "Wattle Blossom: Its Symbolical Significance," *Register* (Adelaide), October 8, 1912.
142. Bevan, "Wattle Blossom and Southern Cross."
143. Beatrice Bevan, "Wattle Blossom," *Register* (Adelaide), September 7, 1915.
144. "Wattle Day in Renmark: Red Cross Collections," *Murray Pioneer*, September 2, 1915; "A Successful Wattle Day," *Zeehan and Dundas Herald*, September 7, 1914.
145. "Wattle," *Weekly Times*, October 7, 1916; "Wattle Day," *Argus*, September 2, 1916.
146. "The Ladies' Page," *Advocate* (Melbourne), September 9, 1916.
147. Adam Lindsay Gordon, "The Sick Stock-Rider," *Colonial Monthly*, January 1870 (poem composed December 1869). Gordon was a great favorite of Bevan and she wrote a play about his life: Bevan, *Adam Lindsay Gordon* (Sydney: W. Bevan, 1938).

148. M. C., "Only a Name," *Independent* (Footscray), August 21, 1915.
149. Beatrice Bevan, "A Tribute to the ANZACS: The Deathless Army," *Bunyip* (Gawler, SA), April 21, 1933.
150. Richard Taylor, *How to Read a Church* (London: Rider, 2003), 231.
151. "The Green Sprig at Funerals," *Queensland Figaro*, September 4, 1913.
152. "William Mountford Kinsey Vale," Collingwood Historical Society; "Obituary—Rev. Willett Bevan," *Chronicle* (Adelaide), January 4, 1934.
153. "For Mothers and Wives," *Argus*, January 9, 1919.
154. Paul Gough, "'Planting' Memory: The Challenge of Remembering the Past on the Somme, Gallipoli and in Melbourne," *Garden History* 42, Suppl.1 (2014): 7.
155. "The Wattle and Australia Day," *Albury Banner and Wodonga Express*, September 10, 1915; "Wattle for Gallipoli," *Port Macquarie News*, December 25, 1915; "Pilgrimage to Gallipoli," *Cootamundra Herald* (NSW), October 13, 1925; Gough, "'Planting' Memory": 7.
156. Cyril E. Isaac, *Annotated Catalogue of Seeds and Plants Supplied to Members of the Victorian State School's Horticultural Society* (Oakleigh: Victorian State School's Horticultural Society, 1917).
157. Isaac, *Annotated Catalogue of Seeds*, 14.
158. Alan J. Kerr, "Adieu!" *Victorian Independent*, April 1916.
159. Nicholas Cocks, "Golden Chains," in *Australian Songs*, 74.
160. Bevan, "Via Crucis (For 25th April, 1916)"; Bevan, "Wattle Blossom and Southern Cross."
161. Cf. Henry Lawson's 1887 poem "Flag of the Southern Cross," which combines overt racism and patriotism in ways that have had enduring appeal to some white Australians.
162. Margery Ruth Betts, "Gallipoli," *Australasian*, December 25, 1915.
163. Margery Ruth Betts, "Faith," *Victorian Independent*, January 1, 1916.
164. Margery Ruth Betts, "His Wounded Wait" (first line in absence of title), *Lismore, Derrinallum and Cressy Advertiser* (Vic.), January 23, 1918.
165. Nicholas Cocks, "Coming, Betty," in *Betty Songs*, 65.
166. MacKellar, "My Country."
167. Nicholas Cocks, "Is It Peace," in *Betty Songs*, 69–74.
168. Nicholas Cocks, "A Sonnet," in *Betty Songs*, 88.
169. Beatrice Bevan, "Gawler Memorial," *Bunyip* (Gawler, SA), September 16, 1921.
170. Ibid.
171. Margery Ruth Betts, "The Recall," *Australasian*, August 14, 1915.
172. Betts, "The Ghost."
173. Winter, *Sites of Memory*, 54–77; Damousi, *Labour of Loss*, 131–3.
174. As an indication of Spiritualism's reach, see John Rickard, *A Family Romance: The Deakins at Home* (Carlton South: Melbourne University Press, 1996).
175. Betts, "Called."
176. Cited in Khan, *Women's Poetry*, 66. Khan naturally interprets Betts as if she were resident in England at the time, though she was living in Kew, Victoria.
177. Betts, "The Recall."
178. The cover of the *Victorian Independent* (December 1, 1915) lists the periodical's Honorary Agents, revealing that the churches that they served were located in twenty Melbourne suburbs and in two locations in the large central Victorian town of Bendigo.
179. Nicholas Cocks, "A Sonnet," in *Betty Songs*, 88.

6 Landscape of Adventure: Methodist Novels and Imagination on the Mission Fields, 1910–48

1. George Sargant, *The Sweet Heart of the Bush* (Melbourne: Lothian, 1915), 37–8, 42–4. Stirling quotes "Comus" (1634) by John Milton, poet of Protestant Dissent: "sooner found in lowly sheds, / With smoky rafters, than in tap'stry halls / And courts of princes."
2. Sargant, *Sweet Heart*, 267.
3. Edna Roughley, *The Locked Door* (Sydney: Australasian, 1948), 98.
4. "George Sargant," *Spectator and Methodist Chronicle*, January 7, 1916; "Obituary," *Argus*, September 7, 1945.
5. "Methodist Home Missions," *Horsham Times*, June 18, 1920.
6. "Methodist Home Missions," *Casterton News and the Merino and Sandford Record*, January 17, 1918; "Methodist Church," *McIvor Times and Rodney Advertiser* (Heathcote, Vic.), July 8, 1915.
7. "Methodist Church," *McIvor Times and Rodney Advertiser* (Heathcote, Vic.), July 8, 1915.
8. Sargant, *Sweet Heart*; *The Winding Track* (Melbourne: Lothian, 1920); and *My Inland Island* (Melbourne: Wyatt and Watts, 1921).
9. Sargant, *Sweet Heart*, 34. George Sargant and his fictional Gordon Stirling share initials and some physical attributes, as well as experience in bush mission and goldfields.
10. "Obituary," *Morning Bulletin* (Rockhampton), April 3, 1928; Eldred Dyer, "Joseph Bowes: A Minister Beloved," *Methodist*, April 7, 1928.
11. Dyer, "Joseph Bowes: A Minister Beloved."
12. "Obituary," *Warwick Daily News*, March 28, 1928.
13. David Andrew Roberts and Margaret Reeson, "Wesleyan Methodist Missions to Australia and the Pacific," in *Methodism in Australia: A History*, ed. Glen O'Brien and Hilary M. Carey (Farnham: Ashgate, 2015), 202.
14. "Rev. J. Bowes," *Week* (Brisbane), March 30, 1928, 26.
15. Joseph Bowes, "The Australian Aborigine," in *A Century in the Pacific*, ed. James Colwell (London: Charles H. Kelly, 1914), 153–73, esp. 165.
16. "Visit of Rev. Joseph Bowes," *Northern Herald* (Cairns), October 5, 1927.
17. Dyer, "Joseph Bowes." The reference is to Tennyson's 1847 poem, "The Princess."
18. Joseph Bowes, *Pals: Young Australians in Sport and Adventure* (London: James Glass, 1910).
19. Joseph Bowes, *The Jackaroos* (London: Oxford University Press, 1923).
20. E.g., Edna Roughley, "The Crooked Tree," *Queenslander*, December 4, 1930, 6; "Footsteps," *Australian Women's Weekly*, April 13, 1935, 53–61; "Laugh, Marienne," *Sydney Morning Herald*, June 29, 1937, 21; "Dream Mother," *Methodist*, July 16–October 15, 1938; *Ellice of Ainslie* (Sydney: Australasian, 1947).
21. Letter from the Reverend Norman Likiss to the New South Wales Women's Inter-Church Council, quoted in Donna Bryan, "First Ecumenical Assembly of Asian Church Women Held in Asia," Australian Church Women Inc. Available online: https://www.acw.org.au/post/first-ecumenical-assembly-of-asian-church-women-held-in-asia (accessed June 7, 2020); further information supplied by family members Caryn Kneale and Darren Hastings.
22. While men frequently added the honorific "Uncle" to their names when writing for children, women used first names as pseudonyms, losing their identity and being

represented as young girls. For example, the Reverend Andrew Pearce wrote for children as "Uncle Andrew" in his guide to mission life, *The Land of Sunburnt Babies* (Adelaide: United Aborigines Mission, 1946).
23. The Territory of Papua (formerly British New Guinea in the southeast of the island) officially came under Australian administration in 1905. The Territory of New Guinea (formerly German New Guinea in the northeast of the island and including several island groups) was placed under Australian administration by the League of Nations following the First World War. After the Second World War, the two territories were united under Australian administration as the Territory of Papua and New Guinea, and established independence from Australia as the Independent State of Papua New Guinea in 1975.
24. Roughley, *Locked Door*.
25. Edna Roughley, "The Lost Road," *Methodist*, June 6, 1942–April 3, 1943.
26. Letter from Rev. Likiss. For examples of Roughley's public-speaking experience: two Mothers' Day services of Bowral Methodist Church, *Southern Mail* (Bowral), May 7, 1943; Woonona Methodist Girls' Comrades, *South Coast Times and Wollongong Argus*, September 11, 1952; Methodist Ladies' Aid Anniversary, *Dungog Chronicle: Durham and Gloucester Advertiser*, June 12, 1954.
27. Kerrie Handasyde, "Mother, Preacher, Press: Women Ministers and the Negotiation of Authority, 1910–1933," in *Contemporary Feminist Theologies: Power, Authority, Love*, ed. Kerrie Handasyde, Cathryn McKinney, and Rebekah Pryor (Abingdon: Routledge, 2021).
28. Martin Wellings, "'Pulp Methodism' Revisited: The Literature and Significance of Silas and Joseph Hocking," in *The Church and Literature*, ed. Peter Clarke and Charlotte Methuen, Studies in Church History 48 (Woodbridge, Rochester, NY: Published for The Ecclesiastical History Society by The Boydell Press, 2012), 364; Robert Dixon, *Writing the Colonial Adventure: Race, Gender and Nation in Anglo-Australian Popular Fiction, 1875–1914* (Cambridge: Cambridge University Press, 1995), 31.
29. E.g.: "Base Publications, Methodist Protest," *Examiner* (Launceston), February 28, 1928; "Sex-Tainted Novels, Methodist Conference Concerned," *West Australian*, March 11, 1933; Helen Graham, "To Our Methodist Girls," *Methodist*, December 24, 1921. See also Matthew T. Herbst, "'The Pernicious Effects of Novel Reading': The Methodist Episcopal Campaign against American Fiction, 1865–1914," *Journal of Religion and Society* 9 (2007): 1–15; David W. Bebbington, "Methodism and Culture," in *The Oxford Handbook of Methodist Studies*, ed. William J Abraham and James E. Kirby (Oxford: Oxford University Press, 2009), 724.
30. "Methodist Literature," *Methodist*, May 16, 1896, 7.
31. Mark Knight and Emma Mason, *Nineteenth-Century Religion and Literature: An Introduction* (Oxford: Oxford University Press, 2006), 135.
32. Ibid. See also David Jasper, "The Study of Literature and Theology," in *The Oxford Handbook of English Literature and Theology*, ed. Andrew Hass, David Jasper and Elisabeth Jay (Oxford: Oxford University Press, 2007), 24.
33. "World of Books," *Methodist*, November 13, 1920 (on Lucy Maud Montgomery); "Bookland," *Methodist*, August 20, 1921 (on Zane Grey).
34. For example, stories on a theme were requested by the *Spectator and Methodist Chronicle*, February 28, 1915 (Easter), December 11, 1918 (Christmas), December 4, 1918 (Temperance); a Christmas story competition for junior writers was run by the *Methodist*, October 26, 1946, and an essay competition for all ages with the theme, "A Happy and Prosperous New Year," December 23, 1922.

35. Hilary M. Carey, "Bushmen and Bush Parsons: The Shaping of A Rural Myth," *Journal of Australian Colonial History* 14 (2011): 1–26.
36. A. B. 'Banjo' Paterson, ed., "My Religion," in *Old Bush Songs Composed and Sung in the Bushranging, Digging and Overlanding Days* (Melbourne: E. W. Cole, 1905). See also Victor J. Daley, "The Parson and the Prelate," in *The Penguin Book of Australian Ballads*, ed. Russel Ward (Ringwood, Vic.: Penguin, 1964), 217–19. While Methodist newspapers occasionally analyzed the reading of Australian poetry (e.g.: "Australian Verse," *Watchman*, June 21, 1902; "Australian Rhyme," *Methodist*, July 28, 1917), they omitted mention of these poems. This popular collection of ballads was compiled by Russel Ward who, as a historian, was known for his depiction of the Australian character as quintessentially egalitarian and, after rejecting the Methodist faith of his upbringing, positioned himself against institutionalized hierarchical religion.
37. For example: Anon., "Holy Dan," in *Australian Ballads*, 133–4; Henry Lawson, "The Shearers," in *Australian Ballads*, 140–1. See also Veronica Brady, *A Crucible of Prophets* (Sydney: Australian and New Zealand Studies in Theology and Religion, 1981), 7; Chris Wallace-Crabbe, *Melbourne or the Bush: Essays on Australian Literature and Society* (Sydney: Angus and Robertson, 1974), 10–11.
38. William Blake, "Milton," in *Seven Centuries of English Poetry*, ed. John Leonard (Melbourne: Oxford University Press, 1987), 266; Barcroft Boake, "Where the Dead Men Lie," in *Australian Ballads*, 111–13.
39. Graeme Davison, "Christianity and Australian Culture," in *Shaping the Good Society in Australia*, ed. Stuart Piggin (Macquarie Centre, NSW: Australia's Christian Heritage National Forum, 2006), 102–3.
40. Ibid., 104.
41. E.g., Maud Jeanne Franc, *Golden Gifts: An Australian Tale* (Kapunda, SA: Scandrett and Elliott, 1869); *Silken Cords and Iron Fetters* (London: Sampson Low, Son and Marston, 1870); *Minnie's Mission: An Australian Temperance Tale* (London: Sampson Low, Son and Marston, 1869).
42. E.g., Marjorie Buckingham, *In All These Things* (Melbourne: New Life, 1949 and London: Oliphants, 1953); *Broad Is the Way* (London: Oliphants, 1953); *Strait Is the Gate* (London: Oliphants, 1956).
43. T. H. Scambler, *Constant Stars* (Melbourne: Book Depot, 1946); "Big Enough for God," *Christian Standard* (Cincinnati), 1941.
44. E.g., Tom Bluegum (pseud. of G. Warren Payne), "The Middle Ridge Appointment," *Methodist*, July 22, 1899. These were later collated and printed as a book: G. Warren Payne, *From Bark Hut to Pulpit* (London: Epworth Press, 1924).
45. A. G. Thomson Zainu'ddin, "Fitchett, William Henry (1841–1928)," *Australian Dictionary of Biography*. Available online: http://adb.anu.edu.au/biography/fitchett-william-henry-6179 (accessed October 26, 2016); novels by W. H. Fitchett include *The Commander of the Hirondelle* (London: Smith, Elder, 1904) and *The Adventures of an Ensign* (Edinburgh: Blackwood, 1917), both published under the pseudonym Vedette.
46. E.g., Thomas Clement Carne, *Galilee by the Ganges* (Melbourne: Book Depot, 1944); Wallace Deane, *The Strange Adventures of a Whale's Tooth: A Missionary Story of Fiji for Young People and Others* (Sydney: Methodist Book Depot, 1919).
47. E.g., Margaret Holliday, "How Sundowner Ned Got on the Right Track," *Methodist*, December 21, 1907; and a series of fictional letters in *Australian Methodist Idylls* (Sydney: J. A. Packer, 1906); and novels where setting was not central, such as *The Day of Reckoning* (Sydney: Epworth Press, 1922).

48. Tilly Aston, *The Woolinappers or, Some Tales from the By-ways of Methodism* (Melbourne: Spectator, 1905); O. S. Green, "Aston, Matilda Ann (Tilly) (1873–1947)," *Australian Dictionary of Biography*. Available online: http://adb.anu.edu.au/biography/aston-matilda-ann-5078 (accessed August 6, 2015).
49. "Rita Snowden," *Upper Hutt Leader*, July 18, 1940.
50. John Wesley, "29 March 1739," in *The Journal of John Wesley*, ed. P. L. Parker (Chicago: Moody Press, 1951).
51. Russell E. Richey, *Methodism in the American Forest* (New York: Oxford University Press, 2015), 14–21.
52. Ibid., 7.
53. Russell E. Richey, *Early American Methodism* (Bloomington: Indiana University Press, 1991), 10.
54. Richey, *Methodism in the American Forest*, 31.
55. David Hempton, *Methodism: Empire of the Spirit* (New Haven, CT: Yale University Press, 2005), 65.
56. Ibid., 64; Phyllis Mack, *Heart Religion in the British Enlightenment: Gender and Emotion in Early Methodism* (Cambridge: Cambridge University Press, 2008), 81 and 262.
57. Steven D. Cooley, "Applying the Vagueness of Language: Poetic Strategies and Campmeeting Piety in the Mid-Nineteenth Century," *Church History* 63, no. 4 (December 1994): 579. See also Misty G. Anderson, *Imagining Methodism in Eighteenth-Century Britain: Enthusiasm, Belief, and the Borders of the Self* (Baltimore, MD: Johns Hopkins University Press, 2012), 9–10.
58. Cooley, "Vagueness of Language," 580.
59. Alan M. Kent, *Pulp Methodism: The Lives and Literature of Silas, Joseph and Salome Hocking, Three Cornish Novelists* (St Austell, Cornwall: Cornish Hillside Publications, 2002); Wellings, "'Pulp Methodism' Revisited," 362–73.
60. Hocking's *The Constant Enemy* was advertised in *Methodist* (Sydney), November 23, 1929. His novel, *The Dust of Life*, was serialized in *Spectator and Methodist Chronicle* (Melbourne), January 1918.
61. Bebbington, "Methodism and Culture," 724.
62. George Warren Payne, writing as Tom Bluegum, *The Backblock's Parson* (London: Charles H. Kelly, 1899); Eric G. Clancy, "Ecclesiastical Stock Riders: Wesleyan Methodist Ministers in Nineteenth-Century Rural New South Wales," *Church Heritage* 9, no. 3 (March 1996): 143–62.
63. Fictional depiction of charitable living rather than religious ritual, exemplified in the novels of the Hocking siblings, brought criticisms that Methodist fiction contributed to a loss of denominational distinctiveness. See Wellings, "'Pulp Methodism' Revisited," 369 and 372; Bebbington, "Methodism and Culture," 724; Roger Robins, "Vernacular American Landscape: Methodists, Camp Meetings, and Social Respectability," *Religion and American Culture* 4, no. 2 (Summer 1994): 165–91.
64. Vicky Schreiber Dill, "Land Relatedness in the Mennonite Novels of Rudy Wiebe," *The Mennonite Quarterly Review* 58 (1984): 50–69. See also the relationship between landscape and spirituality in the literature of Patrick White, Christina Stead, David Malouf and Thea Astley, discussed in Brady, *A Crucible of Prophets*, and *Caught in the Draught: On Contemporary Australian Culture and Society* (Sydney: Angus and Robertson, 1994); Elaine Lindsay, *Rewriting God: Spirituality in Contemporary Australian Women's Fiction* (Atlanta: Rodopi, 2000); Bill Ashcroft, Frances

Devlin-Glass, and Lyn McCredden, *Intimate Horizons: The Post-Colonial Sacred in Australian Literature* (Hindmarsh, SA: Australian Theological Forum Press, 2009).
65. Susan H. Lindley, "Women and the Social Gospel Novel," *Church History* 54 (March 1985): 56–73; William C. Graham, *Half Finished Heaven: The Social Gospel in American Literature* (Lanham, MD: University Press of America, 1995); Erin A. Smith, "'What Would Jesus Do?': The Social Gospel and the Literary Marketplace," *Book History* 10 (2007): 194; Lynne Hapgood, "The Reconceiving of Christianity: Secularisation, Realism and the Religious Novel: 1888–1900," *Literature and Theology* 10, no. 4 (December 1996): 334–5.
66. Jasper, "Literature and Theology," 24; Graham, *Half Finished Heaven*, 4–5; Clyde Binfield, "Breadth from Dissent: Ada Ellen Bayly ('Edna Lyall') and her Fiction," in *The Church and Literature (Studies in Church History Volume 48)*, ed. Peter Clarke and Charlotte Methuen, 349–61 (Rochester, NY: Published for The Ecclesiastical History Society by The Boydell Press, 2012), 349; Wellings, "'Pulp Methodism' Revisited," 373.
67. Henry Gyles Turner, preface to *The Woolinappers* (1905), iv.
68. Ibid., v.
69. Ibid., iv.
70. Roughley, *Locked Door*, 13–14. Roughley's drama is set on the islands off the east coast of Papua where real Methodist missions were located: e.g., Misima, Dobu, Normanby, Fergusson, and Goodenough. She renames the islands but not the mainland of Papua.
71. Ibid., 121.
72. Ibid., 180.
73. "Book Reviews," *Methodist*, June 18, 1949.
74. Roughley, *Locked Door*, 78–81, 88, 105–7, 207.
75. There is significant scholarship in the area of European portrayals of exotic lands and their Indigenous peoples, e.g.: Nicholas Thomas, *In Oceania: Visions, Artifacts, Histories* (Durham, NC: Duke University Press, 1997); and Doug Munro and Brij V. Lal, eds., *Texts and Contexts: Reflections in Pacific Islands Historiography* (Honolulu: University of Hawai'i Press, 2006).
76. E.g., Pearce, *Land of Sunburnt Babies*.
77. Roughley, *Locked Door*, 50.
78. Ibid., 100.
79. Ibid., 26–7, 48, 58–9, 108, 234.
80. Bowes, "Australian Aborigine," 172.
81. Bowes, *Jackaroos*, 70, 116, 244, 134–8, 127.
82. Bowes, "Australian Aborigine," 153.
83. Bowes, *Jackaroos*, 126.
84. Bowes, "Australian Aborigine," 172.
85. Bowes, *Jackaroos*, 116.
86. Ibid., 117.
87. Ibid., 70–2, 116–17, 136.
88. E.g.: Martin Crotty, "Frontier Fantasies: Boys' Adventure Stories and the Construction of Masculinity in Australia, 1870–1920," *Journal of Australian Colonial History* 3, no. 1 (April 2001): 55–76; Dixon, *Writing the Colonial Adventure*. Note also Christine Weir, "Deeply Interested in These Children Whom You Have Not Seen," *Journal of Pacific History* 48, no. 1 (2013): 44, which calls for a missionary reading of children's novels.
89. Bowes, *Jackaroos*, 18.
90. Ibid.
91. Bowes, *Pals*, chapter 1.

92. Ibid., chapter 4.
93. "Rev. J. Bowes," *Week*.
94. William White, the original Yellow Billy, was known as a rather nervous bushranger who often robbed for food. His memory was revived periodically in newspaper articles that sought to sensationalize the exotic. E.g.: "Old Bushranging Days—Yellow Billy—A Black Bandit—An Aboriginal Bushranger," *Mudgee Guardian and North-Western Representative* (NSW), December 13, 1900, 5.
95. Clare Bradshaw, *Reading Race: Aboriginality in Australian Children's Literature* (Melbourne: Melbourne University Press, 2001), 41–2.
96. Bowes, *Jackaroos*, 44–8. Bowes situates the story in Australia by using Australian terms, for example, "duffing" rather than "rustling."
97. Sargant, *Sweet Heart*, 17.
98. Ibid., 16.
99. Ibid., 28. E.g.: A. B. "Banjo" Paterson, "The Man from Ironbark" (1892), in *My Country: Australian Poetry and Short Stories*, vol. 1, ed. Leonie Kramer (Sydney: Lansdowne Press, 1985), 278–80; Edna Roughley, "Brindoonan," *Queenslander*, April 28, 1932; Carey, "Bushmen and Bush Parsons."
100. Sargant, *Sweet Heart*, 10–14.
101. Ibid., 45.
102. Bowes, *Pals*, chapters 5 and 10.
103. This approach was noted by the reviewer in *Register* (Adelaide), January 5, 1916. Compare Paterson's treatment of bush folk as pious but ignorant in "A Bush Christening" (1893), in *My Country: Australian Poetry and Short Stories*, vol. 1, ed. Leonie Kramer (Sydney: Lansdowne Press, 1985), 281–2.
104. Sargant, *Sweet Heart*, 14.
105. Ibid., 232. Graveside wattles allude also to Adam Lindsay Gordon's "The Sick Stock-Rider" (1870), as discussed in the previous chapter.
106. Sargant, *Sweet Heart*, 49.
107. See Hempton, *Methodism*, 131; Mack, *Heart Religion*.
108. Kay Schaffer, *Women and the Bush* (Sydney: Cambridge University Press, 1988), 61.
109. "Review of Books," *Observer* (Adelaide), January 8, 1916. Quoted as having appeared in *Adelaide Register*, January 5, 1915, in Sargant, *My Inland Island*, 333–5. The quoted date or newspaper title may be a misprint.
110. *Advertiser* (Adelaide), n.d., quoted in Sargant, *My Inland Island*, 333–5.
111. *Courier* (Ballarat) [*The Ballarat Courier*], December 18, 1915, quoted in Sargant, *My Inland Island*, 333–5.
112. Roughley, *Locked Door*, 78–81, 87–8.
113. The phenomenon was well known but the term came later: R. Scholes, "The Ugly Australian: The Wild Colonial Boors," *Bulletin* (Sydney, N.S.W), April 13, 1963.
114. Roughley, *Locked Door*, 79.
115. Ibid., 108.
116. Ibid., 106.
117. Schaffer, *Women and the Bush*, 56.
118. Roughley, *Locked Door*, 53.
119. Roughley, "Lost Road," August 22, 1942.
120. Ibid.
121. Sargant, *Sweet Heart*, 281.
122. Roughley, *Locked Door*, 71.
123. Ibid., 77.

124. Ibid., 75.
125. Graeme Davison, *City Dreamers: The Urban Imagination in Australia* (Sydney: NewSouth, 2016), 122–43.
126. Roughley, "Lost Road," June 20, 1942.
127. Roughley, "Lost Road," June 27, 1942, and July 4, 1942.
128. Roughley, "Lost Road," July 4, 1942. Further allusions to Dickens's *A Christmas Carol* are seen in the character Tim who is lame.
129. Roughley, "Lost Road," July 11, 1942, and June 13, 1942.
130. Roughley, "Lost Road," July 18, 1942.
131. Hempton, *Methodism: Empire of the Spirit*, 52.
132. Roughley, "Lost Road," November 21, 1942.
133. Bowes, *Jackaroos*, 193–5.
134. Sargant, *Sweet Heart*, 263–4, 266.
135. Roughley, "The Crooked Tree," *Queenslander*, December 4, 1930, 6.
136. Roughley, "Lost Road," August 22, 1942.
137. Sargant, *Sweet Heart*, 134–5.
138. Roughley, "Lost Road," December 5, 1942.
139. Sargant, *Sweet Heart*, 262.
140. For Methodism's conflicted approach to Providence, see Richey, *Methodism in the Forest*, 85.
141. Phyllis Somerville, *Not Only in Stone* (Sydney: Angus and Robertson, 1942). The work was first published in its entirety in *Advertiser* (Adelaide), September 1, 1936; however references throughout are to the 1942 book.
142. "Phyllis Somerville," Austlit: The Australian Literature Resource. Available online: http://www.austlit.edu.au/austlit/page/A36339 (accessed September 12, 2015).
143. "Centenary Novel and Play," *Advertiser* (Adelaide), June 5, 1934; Douglas Pike, *Paradise of Dissent: South Australia 1829–1857* (Melbourne: Melbourne University Press, 1967, first published 1957).
144. Somerville, *Not Only in Stone*, 60.
145. Ibid., 281–8.
146. Phyllis Somerville, "The Influence of Cornwall on South Australian Methodism," *Journal of the South Australian Methodist Historical Society* 4 (October 1972): 1–13.
147. Somerville, *Not Only in Stone*, 283.
148. John Wesley, "May 24, 1738," in *Journal of John Wesley*.
149. "Charles Wesley," hymnary.org. Available online: http://www.hymnary.org/person/Wesley_Charles?tab=texts (accessed September 13, 2015).
150. D. Bruce Hindmarsh, "'My Chains Fell Off: My Heart Was Free': Early Methodist Conversion Narrative in England," *Church History* 68, no. 4 (December 1999): 910–29.
151. Randy L. Maddox, "Holiness of Heart and Life: Lessons from North American Methodism," *Asbury Theological Journal* 51, no. 1 (1996): 152.
152. Roughley, *Locked Door*, 61.
153. Ibid.
154. Bowes, *Pals*, chapter 10.
155. Ibid.
156. Roughley, "Lost Road," December 12, 1942.
157. Hempton, *Methodism: Empire of the Spirit*, 54.
158. Sargant, *Sweet Heart*, 74.

159. Ibid.
160. Roughley, *Locked Door*, 57. The disease is not identified, so it is not possible to say if it was brought to the islands by the missionaries—but the possibility remains.
161. Ibid., 168.
162. Ibid., 94.
163. Sargant, *Sweet Heart*, 239. The missioner Stirling recites some lines from Tennyson's "In Memoriam," a poem concerned with faith and doubt, God and evolution. However, the never-doubting missioner intends the lines as a comfort to a grieving widow, suggesting that faith rather than doubt was the more common interpretation among early-twentieth-century Australian Methodist readers.
164. For the impact of Romanticism on Evangelicalism, see David W. Bebbington, "Evangelicalism and British Culture," in *Culture, Spirituality and the Brethren, Studies in Brethren History*, vol. 3 (Troon, Ayrshire: Brethren Archivists and Historians Network, 2014), 6–10.
165. E.g.: Christopher Mudd, *Whys and Ways of the Bush and Guide to Bush Plants, or In Nature's School* (Melbourne: Spectator, 1914).
166. Sujit Sivasundaram, *Nature and the Godly Empire: Science and Evangelical Mission in the Pacific, 1795–1850* (Cambridge: Cambridge University Press, 2005), 95.
167. Chris Mudd, "Peregrinations," *Spectator and Methodist Chronicle*, April 10, 1918.
168. Bebbington, "Evangelicalism and British Culture," 13.
169. Chris Mudd, "Peregrinations," *Spectator and Methodist Chronicle*, October 2, 1918.
170. Ibid.
171. For examples of and scholarship on these practices in Australia: "Open-air Preaching: A Paper Read before the Sydney Ministers' Meeting," *Methodist*, June 10, 1899; "A Religious Camp-Meeting at Queenscliff," *Camperdown Chronicle*, December 24, 1881; Glen O'Brien, "Australian Methodist Religious Experience," in *Methodism in Australia: A History*, ed. Glen O'Brien and Hilary M. Carey (Farnham: Ashgate, 2015), 170.
172. Comparison may be made here with the sacralizing of camp meeting spaces: Steven D. Cooley, "Manna and the Manual: Sacramental and Instrumental Constructions of the Victorian Methodist Camp Meeting during the Mid-Nineteenth Century," *Religion and American Culture: A Journal of Interpretation* 6, no. 2 (Summer 1996): 134.
173. Roughley, *Locked Door*, 14.

7 Landscape of Timeless Beauty: Quaker Essays on Beauty in Art and the Painting of Nature, 1922–63

1. Ernest E. Unwin, *Religion and Biology* (London: Swarthmore Press, 1922), 138.
2. Ernest E. Unwin, "The Spiritual Element in Education," *Laura Standard and Crystal Brook Courier* (SA), July 26, 1935, 4.
3. Mary Packer Harris, *In One Splendour Spun: Autobiography of a Quaker Artist* (Walkerville, SA: self-published, 1971), 32.
4. Geoffrey Cantor, "Aesthetics in Science, as Practised by Quakers in the Eighteenth and Nineteenth Centuries," *Quaker Studies* 4, no. 1 (1999): 7–8.
5. Unwin, *Religion and Biology*.

6. E.g.: *Mercury* (Hobart), March 2, 1925 and May 17, 1926; Unwin's speech to a Student Christian Movement event in Ballarat, "Students and Religion," *Advertiser* (Adelaide), January 30, 1925.
7. Unwin wrote articles on the topic of religion and biology for the Tasmanian press: e.g., "The Evolution Controversy," parts I and II, and "Evolution: The Purpose of the Theory," *Mercury*, November 28 and December 5 and 12, 1927. He participated in radio programs for schools on 7ZL Hobart, *Mercury*, October 11, 1939; and reports of Unwin's speeches often appeared in newspapers, e.g.: "Sex Education and Character," *Mercury*, August 17, 1944; "The Royal Society 'The Web of Life' Lecture by Mr Unwin," *Mercury*, July 12, 1927.
8. "Students and Religion," *Advertiser*, January 30, 1925; "Religion and Biology," *Sydney Morning Herald*, April 27, 1923. Two reviews which were largely positive also noted a lack of satisfaction with Unwin's explanation of the "existence struggle": "New Books," *Age*, January 6, 1923; "Religion and Biology," *Sydney Stock and Station Journal*, May 18, 1923.
9. Ernest E. Unwin, "One Hundred Years," in *The Centenary of Australian Quakerism: 1832–1932*, ed. Margaret L. Benson, Frederick Coleman, and Ernest E. Unwin (Hobart: General Meeting of Religious Society of Friends, Australia, 1933).
10. William N. Oats, "Unwin, Ernest Ewart (1881–1944)," *Australian Dictionary of Biography*. Available online: http://adb.anu.edu.au/biography/unwin-ernest-ewart-8899/text15633 (accessed July 11, 2016); "Obituary for Edwin Ashby," *Friend of Australia and New Zealand*, February 20, 1941.
11. Thomas Robson, Letter quoted in *Bootham Magazine* 11, no. 5 (December 1923).
12. Unwin delivered a paper titled "Richard Jefferies—Poet-Naturalist" in 1915 and "William Morris—Artist—Socialist" in 1916: "XII Book Club Minute Book," 2 (1915–31), *UK Red: The Experience of Reading in Britain*. Available online: http://www.open.ac.uk/Arts/reading/UK/record_details.php?id=27074 (accessed July 11, 2016).
13. "The Travelling Artist: Mr E. E. Unwin's Exhibition," *Mercury*, October 30, 1929; "Friends' School Report," *Friend of Australia and New Zealand*, March 20, 1938, 10; William Nicolle Oats, *The Friends' School, 1887–1961: The Seventy-Fifth Anniversary* (Hobart: The Friends' School, 1961), 42, 48; "History of the School," The Friends' School. Available online: https://www.friends.tas.edu.au/about-the-friends-school/history-of-the-school/ / (accessed January 18, 2021).
14. V. V. H., "Ernest Ewart Unwin," *Papers and Proceedings of the Royal Society of Tasmania* (Hobart: Royal Society of Tasmania, 1944).
15. Oats, "Unwin, Ernest Ewart"; V. V. H. "Ernest Ewart Unwin"; D. A. Ratkowsky, "A Little-known Scientific Club in Hobart, Tasmania—Its Early Years," *Papers and Proceedings of the Royal Society of Tasmania* 144 (2010): 37–42.
16. The road was gazetted in 1978 and named Unwin Place. In 2013 it was changed to Unwin Street. Environment, Planning and Sustainable Development Directorate—Planning, Australian Capital Territory Government. Available online: https://www.planning.act.gov.au/tools_resources/place_names/place-name-search (accessed January 18, 2021).
17. Mary Packer Harris, *Art, the Torch of Life* (Adelaide: Rigby, 1946); Ruth Tuck, "Harris, Mary Packer (1891–1978)," *Australian Dictionary of Biography*. Available online: http://adb.anu.edu.au/biography/harris-mary-packer-10438/text18507 (accessed July 11, 2016). Tuck, who was a colleague of Harris's in Adelaide, does not refer to Harris's autobiography.

18. Harris, *One Splendour*, 21. She had earlier begun a manuscript titled *Intellectual Beauty in Art*. The title was based on a poem by Shelley, but its emphasis on the intellectual points to Harris's interests prior to her joining the Religious Society of Friends.
19. Ibid., 33; Charles Fenner, foreword to Harris, *Art, the Torch of Life*.
20. "Paintings with a Story in Them," *Mail* (Adelaide), April 6, 1946; *Friend of Australia and New Zealand*, June 20, 1946.
21. The title possibly alludes to John Woolman's "flame of life ... kindled in all animal and sensitive creatures" (1772), quoted in *Quaker Faith and Practice: The Book of Christian Discipline of the Yearly Meeting of the Religious Society of Friends (Quakers) in Britain* (5th ed.): 25.05, https://qfp.quaker.org.uk/passage/25-05/.
22. E. H. Gombrich, *The Story of Art* (London: Phaidon, 1950).
23. "Primer of Art," *Argus*, December 28, 1946.
24. While Long moved away from the Heidelberg School, Harris identified him as a landscape artist in that tradition.
25. "Primer of Art," *Argus*, December 28, 1946.
26. Mary Packer Harris, *The Cosmic Rhythm of Art and Literature* (Adelaide: Frank Cork, 1948).
27. E.g.: "Streeton Show, Art and Literature," *Argus*, September 18, 1948; and "Cultural," *West Australian*, October 16, 1948.
28. "An Art Teacher's Testament to Beauty," *Mercury*, October 16, 1948.
29. Harris, *One Splendour*, 7, 25; Frederick W. Thornsby, ed., *Dictionary of Organs and Organists* (Bournemouth: H. Logan, 1912), 158.
30. Christopher Menz, "Mary Packer Harris," Design and Art Australia Online. Available online: https://www.daao.org.au/bio/mary-packer-harris/biography/ (accessed September 29, 2016).
31. Harris, *One Splendour*, 7.
32. Ibid., 8.
33. Ibid., 13–15.
34. Tuck, "Harris, Mary Packer."
35. Harris, *One Splendour*, 19–22, 25.
36. Sandra Stanley Holton, *Suffrage Days: Stories from the Women's Suffrage Movement* (London: Routledge, 1996), 166.
37. Harris, *One Splendour*, 33.
38. Tuck, "Harris, Mary Packer."
39. Menz, "Mary Packer Harris."
40. Harris, *One Splendour*, 33.
41. Ivor Francis, "A Personal Note on Mary," in *Mary Packer Harris 1891–1978*, ed. Rachel Biven (Walkerville, SA: Walkerville Town Council, 1986), 3.
42. Charles Stevenson, "Mary Harris (1891–1978)," Quaker Learning Australia. Available online: http://www.qlau.quakers.org.au/resources/quaker-biographies/mary-harris/ (accessed August 1, 2016).
43. E.g.: antislavery campaigning and the human treatment of prisoners, employees, and the mentally ill. Robert Humphreys and Rowland Ward, *Religious Bodies in Australia: A Comprehensive Guide*, 3rd ed. (Wantirna, Vic.: New Melbourne Press, 1995), 212. See also Charles Stevenson, *With Unhurried Pace: A Brief History of Quakers in Australia* (Toorak, Vic.: The Religious Society of Friends, 1973), 30; Roger S. Thompson, *Religion in Australia: A History* (Melbourne: Oxford University Press, 1994), 78. For examples of local Australian advocacy, see Edwin Ashby's letters to

the newspapers on compulsory military training, *Northern Miner* (Charters Towers, Qld.), December 2, 1910; and on conservation, *Register*, October 30, 1912.
44. Humphreys and Ward, *Religious Bodies in Australia*, 212–14; Geoffrey Cantor, "Quaker responses to Darwin," *Osiris* 16 (2001): 325–30; Stevenson, *With Unhurried Pace*, 13.
45. Stevenson, *With Unhurried Pace*, 27–9.
46. Lyndsay A. Farrall, "Quakers in Australia," in *The Encyclopedia of Religion in Australia*, ed. James Jupp (Port Melbourne: Cambridge University Press, 2009), 548; Humphreys and Ward, *Religious Bodies in Australia*, 214.
47. Humphreys and Ward, *Religious Bodies in Australia*, 213; Unwin, *Religion and Biology*, 165, 174.
48. Farrall, "Quakers in Australia," 548.
49. Quakers constituted just 0.02 percent of the Australian population when Harris and Unwin migrated in the early 1920s, dropping to 0.01 percent by the time of the 1933 census: Hilary M. Carey, *Believing in Australia: A Cultural History of Religions* (St. Leonards, NSW: Allen and Unwin, 1996), 200–2.
50. Roger Homan, *The Art of the Sublime: Principles of Christian Art and Architecture* (Aldershot: Ashgate, 2006), 93–5; John Dillenberger, *The Visual Arts and Christianity in America: The Colonial Period through the Nineteenth Century* (Chico, CA: Scholars Press, 1984), 10; Don E. Saliers, "Liturgical Aesthetics: The Travail of Christian Worship," in *Arts, Theology and the Church: New Intersections*, ed. Kimberly Vrudny and Wilson Yates (Cleveland: The Pilgrim Press, 2005), 181.
51. Homan, *Art of the Sublime*, 95.
52. Roger Homan, "The Inward and the Outward Eye: Quaker Attitudes to Visual Culture," *Quaker Studies* 18, no. 2 (March 2014): 139–50.
53. Marcia Pointon, "Quakerism and Visual Culture," *Art History* 20, no. 3 (September 1997): 399.
54. E.g.: Mabel Forrest, "Simple Little Bonnet," *Sunday Times* (Sydney), April 16, 1911; the comic opera, "The Quaker Girl," with libretto by James Tanner, was popularly performed by amateur theater groups around Australia including the Hobart Amateur Opera Company, *Critic* (Hobart), August 31, 1917; advertisements for women's clothing and fashion reviews include mention of the color Quaker grey throughout the early to mid-twentieth centuries, see *Australasian*, August 5, 1905 and *Lithgow Mercury*, December 4, 1951; the prevalence of Quaker grey is noted at a Peace Society afternoon tea where many members of the Religious Society of Friends were in attendance, *Sun* (Sydney), October 8, 1931.
55. Peter Collins, "Quaker Plaining as Critical Aesthetic," *Quaker Studies* 5, no. 2 (2000): 125–7.
56. Homan, "The Inward and the Outward Eye," 139–50.
57. Douglas Gwyn, "Quakers, Eschatology and Time," in *The Oxford Book of Quaker Studies*, ed. Stephen W. Angell and Ben Pink Dandelion (Oxford: Oxford University Press, 2013), 5; Geoffrey Plank, "'The Flame of Life was Kindled in Animal and Sensitive Creatures': One Quaker Colonist's View of Animal Life," *Church History* 76, no. 3 (2007): 585–6. See also Curtis W. Freeman, *Undomesticated Dissent: Democracy and the Public Virtue of Religious Nonconformity* (Waco, TX: Baylor University Press, 2017), 34, 43.
58. Edward Hicks, "The Peaceable Kingdom" *c.* 1833, oil painting. The Worcester Art Museum. Available online: http://www.worcesterart.org/collection/American/1934.65.html (accessed September 26, 2016).

59. Roger Homan, "The Art of Joseph Edward Southall," *Quaker Studies* 5, no. 1 (2000): 73.
60. Ibid., 76; Homan, *Art of the Sublime*, 103–4.
61. Homan, "Southall," 75–6; Homan, *Art of the Sublime*, 102.
62. Design and Art Australia Online. Available online: https://www.daao.org.au (accessed August 14, 2017).
63. William Nicolle Oats, *A Question of Survival: Quakers in Australia in the Nineteenth Century* (St. Lucia, Qld.: University of Queensland Press, 1985), 15–17.
64. Erin E. Zavitz, "Artistic Presence: A Sketch of the History of Art in Quaker Schools," *Quaker History* 94, no. 1 (Spring 2005): 36.
65. Ibid., 24, 26–8.
66. Caroline Miley, *Beautiful and Useful: The Arts and Crafts Movement in Tasmania* (Launceston: Queen Victoria Museum and Art Gallery, 1987), 13.
67. Ibid., 17.
68. Oats, *Friends' School*, 14.
69. Ibid., 36.
70. "Friends' School Report," 10.
71. Ibid.
72. The work of Arts and Crafts movement architect, Augustus Pugin, did not resonate with Quaker values in the same way, not least because of Pugin's Catholicism.
73. Homan, *Art of the Sublime*, 126–7.
74. William Morris, "The Beauty of Life," in *Hopes and Fears for Art* (London: Longmans, Green, 1908), 108, 110. It was based on a lecture in Birmingham, UK, in 1880 and published in *Hopes and Fears for Art* in 1882.
75. Homan notes the similarity between William Morris's ideas and the basis of craftwork among Shakers (a religious group with roots in Quakerism): Homan, *Art of the Sublime*, 126.
76. Miley, *Beautiful and Useful*, 9.
77. Homan, *Art of the Sublime*, 9.
78. Miley, *Beautiful and Useful*, 9.
79. Homan, *Art of the Sublime*, 116, 123.
80. Oats, *Question of Survival*, 26–7.
81. Unwin, "One Hundred Years," 37.
82. William Nicolle Oats, *Backhouse and Walker: A Quaker View of the Australian Colonies, 1832–1838* (Sandy Bay, Tas.: Australian Yearly Meeting of Religious Society of Friends, 1981), 2, 6, 9, 11.
83. Susannah Kay Brindle, *To Learn a New Song: A Contribution to Real Reconciliation with the Earth and Its Peoples* (Armadale North, Vic.: Australia Yearly Meeting Religious Society of Friends, 2000), 9–12, 27.
84. Within Quakerism, the term "concern" has a particular meaning. A "concern" is something that the Spirit has led the believer to consider and which requires the observation of procedures: the individual's "concern" would be shared with the meeting and corporate action may be agreed upon. Oats, *Question of Survival*, 13.
85. Ex-students of the school were also especially prominent in the Field Naturalists' Society of Tasmania when it formed in 1904. Oats, *Friends' School*, 14, 20.
86. Ibid., 16–18, 38, 42.
87. "Friends' School Report," 10.
88. David Jones, "Bush Garden Ethos in South Australia," *Australian Garden History* 13, no. 6 (2002): 10–11; Edwin Ashby, "Australian Native Shrubs," in *Australian Gardening of To-day*, ed. W. A. Shum (Melbourne: Sun-News Pictorial, c. 1940), 83–103.

89. Prominent Quaker botanists included among many others Peter Collinson (1694–1768, London), brothers James and Thomas Backhouse (1792–1845, northeast England), John Gilbert Baker (1834–1920, Keeper at the Kew Gardens Herbarium), and John Bartram (1699–1777, Pennsylvania), whose business associations with Collinson saw a number of American plants imported to England. John Brooke and Geoffrey Cantor, *Reconstructing Nature: The Engagement of Science and Religion* (Edinburgh: T&T Clark, 1998), 289, 304; Geoffrey Cantor, *Quakers, Jews and Science: Religious Responses to Modernity and the Sciences in Britain, 1650–1900* (Oxford: Oxford University Press, 2005), 96, 176–8.
90. Brooke and Cantor, *Reconstructing Nature*, 302.
91. Cantor, "Aesthetics in Science," 3; Geoffrey Cantor, "Quaker Responses to Darwin," *Osiris* 16 (2001): 321–42; Brooke and Cantor, *Reconstructing Nature*, 282–8, 312–13.
92. Cantor, *Quakers, Jews and Science*, 96.
93. Ibid., 278.
94. Ibid., 179; Cantor, "Aesthetics in Science," 7; Oats, *Backhouse and Walker*, 33.
95. Cantor, "Aesthetics in Science," 16.
96. Leonie Norton, *Women of Flowers: Botanical Art in Australia from the 1830s to the 1960s* (Canberra: National Library of Australia, 2009), 2. On women's botanical illustration and collecting, see also Penny Olsen, *Collecting Ladies: Ferdinand von Mueller and Women Botanical Artists* (Canberra: National Library of Australia, 2013). Examples of Quaker artists were not necessarily educated women, however. Alfred and Lewis May were orchardists, and Alison Ashby was largely homeschooled. Ron Kershaw, "May, William Lewis (1861–1925)," *Australian Dictionary of Biography*. Available online: http://adb.anu.edu.au/biography/may-william-lewis-7538/text13149 (accessed July 12, 2016); Enid L. Robertson, foreword, *Alison Ashby's Wildflowers of Southern Australia* (Adelaide: South Australian Museum Board and the Botanic Gardens Board, 1981).
97. Cantor, "Aesthetics in Science," 13.
98. Cantor, "Quaker Responses to Darwin," 328; Cantor, "Aesthetics in Science," 11–13, 15; Cantor, *Quakers, Jews and Science*, 98.
99. E.g.: "Anaspides Tasmaniae (The Mountain Shrimp)," *Friend of Australia and New Zealand*, August 20, 1944; Edwin Ashby, "The Azure Butterflies of Australia," *Friend of Australia and New Zealand*, April 20, 1939, 11.
100. In contrast, the column titled "Peregrination" by Christopher Mudd in *Spectator and Methodist Chronicle* in the 1910s carried natural history description but always made analogies to human religious experience.
101. Richard Jefferies, cited in Unwin, *Religion and Biology*, 122.
102. Ibid., 141–2.
103. John Stenhouse, "Darwinism in New Zealand, 1859–1900," in *Disseminating Darwinism: The Role of Place, Race, Religion and Gender*, ed. Ronald L. Numbers and John Stenhouse (Cambridge: Cambridge University Press, 1999), 61–79; John Stenhouse, "Response by John Stenhouse," in *Science and Theology: Questions at the Interface*, ed. Murray Rae, Hilary Regan, and John Stenhouse (Edinburgh: T&T Clark, 1994), 92.
104. Unwin, *Religion and Biology*, 29.
105. Prince Evgenii Troubetzkoy (Russian philosopher), cited in Unwin, *Religion and Biology*, 29.
106. Ibid., 127.
107. Ibid., 174.

108. Harris, *Cosmic Rhythm*, 22.
109. Unwin, *Religion and Biology*, 138.
110. Harris, *Cosmic Rhythm*, frontispiece; Mary Packer Harris, "Exhibition of Paintings, 9–26 April 1946," exhibition catalogue, State Library of Victoria.
111. Harris, *One Splendour*, opposite dedication page. This work originally appeared in the *Forerunner*, the annual journal of South Australian School of Arts and Crafts, November 1934. See also the malformed kangaroos in illustration with text, "And the leaves of the tree were for the healing of the nations" (Rev. 22:2), another eschatological scene in Harris, *One Splendour*, 103.
112. Christopher Menz, "Mary P. Harris," in *Heritage: The National Women's Art Book, 500 works by 500 Australian Women Artists from Colonial Times to 1955*, ed. Joan Kerr (Sydney: Art and Australia, 1995), image number 388.
113. Francis, "Personal Note on Mary."
114. Unwin, *Religion and Biology*, 136.
115. Unwin, "One Hundred Years," 41.
116. Francis, "Personal Note on Mary." Francis was a student and colleague and great supporter. It is interesting that he uses the word "humbug" as Mary regularly took her art students to be inspired by Mr. Bellchambers's native sanctuary called "Humbug Scrub": Harris, *One Splendour*, 19–22. Thomas Paine Bellchambers is remembered with Bellchambers Crescent, Banks, A.C.T., adjacent to the streets named for Alison Ashby and Olive Pink.
117. Harris, *Art, the Torch of Life*, 129.
118. Harris seems to accept that people may be anonymous Quakers. For example, she reports that when she joined the Quakers her uncle said that really she had been "a Quaker all her life without knowing it." Harris, *One Splendour*, 25.
119. Harris, *Art, the Torch of Life*, 104.
120. Ibid.
121. In comparison with the well-known art textbook by Gombrich, *Story of Art*, Harris consistently preferences portraiture, bucolic scenes, and Australian art.
122. Harris, *Art, the Torch of Life*, 104.
123. Jay Arthur, *The Default Country: A Lexical Cartography of Twentieth-Century Australia* (Sydney: University of New South Wales Press, 2003), 91–5; Eleanor Dark, *The Timeless Land* (London: Collins, 1941), 101.
124. Harris, *Art, the Torch of Life*, 105.
125. Unwin, *Religion and Biology*, 135.
126. Ibid., 136.
127. Ibid., 124, 126.
128. Ibid., 123.
129. Harris, *Art, the Torch of Life*, 104.
130. "Educational Ideals," *Mercury*, November 7, 1930.
131. Unwin, *Religion and Biology*, 148–9.
132. Ibid., 123.
133. Ibid. See also Ernest E. Unwin, "The Society of Friends, Tercentenary of George Fox, Part III—The Message of Quakerism," *Mercury* (Hobart), August 9, 1924. Unwin's thinking preempts the work of David Tacey on the "sacramentality of nature": Wayne Hudson, *Australian Religious Thought* (Clayton, Vic.: Monash University Press, 2016), 223.
134. Harris, *Cosmic Rhythm*, 61.
135. Ibid., 59.

136. Unwin, *Religion and Biology*, 151. Unwin also drew on English mystic, Julian of Norwich, and early proponent of psychology studies in religion, W. Fearon Halliday, *Reconciliation and Reality* (London: Headley, 1919).
137. Unwin, *Religion and Biology*, 153.
138. Ibid., 151.
139. Ibid.
140. Stevenson, *With Unhurried Pace*, 7; Unwin, "One Hundred Years," 38. The Cottons were relatives of the Quaker natural history artists Alfred and Lewis May: their mother was Mary Cotton. See Kershaw, "May, William Lewis (1861–1925)."
141. Unwin, *Religion and Biology*, 138–9.
142. Mary P. Harris, "Editorial," *Forerunner*, November 1932. Margaret Preston, "Away with the Poker-Worked Kookaburras and Gumleaves!," *Daily Telegraph Sunday Pictorial* (Sydney), April 6, 1930, cited in Lesley Harding, *Margaret Preston: Recipes for Food and Art* (Melbourne: Miegunyah Press, 2016), 73.
143. Harris, "Editorial." Chesterton's poem, and many others referred to by Harris, is in D. H. S. Nicholson and A. H. E. Lee, eds., *The Oxford Book of English Mystical Verse* (Oxford: Oxford University Press, 1917).
144. Harris, *Art, the Torch of Life*, 132.
145. Mary Finnin, "Drought" (originally in *Jindyworobak Anthology* 1941) and Rex Ingamells, "Lands of the Gods" (originally in *Jindyworobak Anthology* 1942) are cited in Harris, *Art, the Torch of Life*, 21, 119.
146. Mary P. Harris, "Paintings of Old Walkerville," exhibition catalogue (Walkerville, SA: Walkerville Gallery, December 1963).
147. Ibid.
148. Ibid.
149. Tom Griffiths, *The Art of Time Travel: Historians and their Craft* (Carlton, Vic.: Black, 2016), 148.
150. Harris, *One Splendour*, 51. Harris is vague on the date. The title is taken from a line in Joseph Plunkett's poem, "I See His Blood upon the Rose." See also Harris's painting "Shadow Crucifix" in the 1963 exhibition, "Paintings of Old Walkerville."
151. Harris, *One Splendour*, 53.
152. Ibid.
153. Harris, *Art, the Torch of Life*, 132.
154. Ibid.
155. David Morgan, *The Sacred Gaze: Religious Visual Culture in Theory and Practice* (Berkeley: University of California Press, 2005), 183.
156. Harris, *Art, the Torch of Life*, 22–3.
157. James Frazer on totems cited in Baldwin Spencer, *Guide to the Australian Ethnographical Collection in the National Museum of Victoria* (Melbourne: National Museum of Victoria, 1901), 9.
158. Harris, *Art, the Torch of Life*, 23.
159. Harris, *Cosmic Rhythm*, 181.
160. Dark, *Timeless Land*, 9.
161. Harris, *One Splendour*, 84.
162. Stevenson, "Mary Harris."
163. Harris, *Art, the Torch of Life*, 132.
164. Harris, *One Splendour*, 54–6.

165. Paul Carter, *Lie of the Land* (London: Faber and Faber, 1996), 43. See also Philip Jones, *Ochre and Rust: Artefacts and Encounters on Australian Frontiers* (Kent Town, SA: Wakefield Press, 2007), 312–13.
166. Albert Ludbrook, "Notes of Travel: First Impressions of the Holy City," *Australasian Christian Standard*, November 5, 1896, 300; Carter, *Lie of the Land*, 46.
167. Deborah Edwards, *Margaret Preston* (Sydney: Art Gallery of New South Wales, 2005), 154. The phrase was used by Preston in an issue of *Art in Australia* (1930).
168. Unwin, *Religion and Biology*, 132 and 138.
169. Harris, *One Splendour*, 53.
170. Rita Dunstan, "Follow Me Around," *News* (Adelaide), no date, cited in Harris, *One Splendour*, 56.
171. Harris, *One Splendour*, 53.
172. T. G. H. Strehlow, *An Australian Viewpoint* (Adelaide: Hawthorn Press, 1950), 14.
173. *Advertiser*, July 22, 1956, quoted in Harris, *One Splendour*, 57.
174. Ibid.
175. Harris, *One Splendour*, 54.
176. Dunstan, "Follow Me Around," cited in Harris, *One Splendour*, 56–7.
177. Edwards, *Margaret Preston*, 190–1.
178. In referring to "rhythm" in this instance and in the title of her second book, Harris draws on Leonhard Adam's *Primitive Art* (London: Penguin, 1940). See also Edwards, *Margaret Preston*, 190–1.
179. Harris's four paintings in this exhibition were "The Timeless Time" (purchased by the Quakers for donation to the National Gallery of South Australia, which changed its name in 1967 to Art Gallery of South Australia, with funds going to Olga Fudge's "Aboriginal Hostel"), "Rain Song" (purchased by T. G. H. Strehlow), "Fathers and Sons" (purchased by Hans Heysen), and "Clouds of Wings" (purchased by Iris and Heinz Schulz): Harris, *One Splendour*, 53–5.
180. Edwards, *Margaret Preston*, 240–1. Anthropologist James Frazer argued in *The Golden Bough* that primitive people shared a timeless primordial story before progressing toward scientific thought.
181. Billy Griffiths, Lynette Russell, and Richard "Bert" Roberts, "When Did Australia's Human History Begin?" *Conversation*, November 17, 2017. Available online: https://theconversation.com/friday-essay-when-did-australias-human-history-begin-87251 (accessed January 18, 2021).
182. Francis, "A Personal Note."
183. Wayne Tunnicliffe, *Tradition Today: Indigenous Art in Australia* (Sydney: Art Gallery of New South Wales, 2014), quoted in "Otto Pareroultja," Art Gallery of New South Wales. Available online: https://www.artgallery.nsw.gov.au/collection/artists/pareroultja-otto/ (accessed November 21, 2016).
184. Strehlow, *An Australian Viewpoint*, 24–5.
185. H. Stafford Northcote, *Advertiser*, no date, cited in Harris, *One Splendour*, 54. Strehlow used the simplified phonetic designation Aranda, but Arrernte is the term now used by the Arrernte Council.
186. Strehlow, *An Australian Viewpoint*, 20.
187. Carter, *Lie of the Land*, 109. Strehlow published this information in 1970 in *Songs of Central Australia*, but Harris may have been aware earlier as she and Strehlow were known to one another in Adelaide in the 1950s.
188. Strehlow, *An Australian Viewpoint*, 22.
189. Harris, *One Splendour*, 53–5, 57.

190. Harris, *One Splendour*, 27, 52–8.
191. Edwards, *Margaret Preston*, 240; Harris, *Cosmic Rhythm*, 181.
192. Contemporary expressions of this thinking include David Tacey, *Re-Enchantment: The New Australian Spirituality* (Sydney: HarperCollins, 2000), 93–106.
193. Ivor Francis, *News* (Adelaide), December 9, 1950; Edwards, *Margaret Preston*, 250.
194. Edwards, *Margaret Preston*, 241.
195. Harris, *One Splendour*, 55.
196. Until the late 1930s, Ricketts produced numerous kookaburra-themed homewares, but it was his new work that Harris encountered and embraced. Peter Brady, *Whitefella Dreaming: The Authorised Biography of William Ricketts* (Olinda, Vic.: Preferred Image, 1994), 72, 80, 109; Harris, *One Splendour*, 96; Ivor Francis, "Aboriginal Legends Told in Clay," *News* (Adelaide), May 21, 1947.
197. Brady, *Whitefella Dreaming*, 25.
198. Harris, *One Splendour*, 96.
199. Ibid., 97.
200. Ibid.
201. Mitchell Rolls, "William Ricketts Sanctuary Is a Racist Anachronism but Can It Foster Empathy?" *Conversation*, May 25, 2018. Available online: https://theconversation.com/friday-essay-william-ricketts-sanctuary-is-a-racist-anachronism-but-can-it-foster-empathy-96274 (accessed January 18, 2021); Marcia Langton and Bruno David, "William Ricketts' Sanctuary, Victoria (Australia): Sculpting Nature and Culture in a Primitivist Theme Park," *Journal of Material Culture* 8, no. 2 (2003): 157. Both these critiques might apply to Harris's work also.
202. One work at William Ricketts Sanctuary (Mount Dandenong, Victoria) depicts Ricketts crucified beside an Indigenous man, with the bodies of dead wallabies and possums piled up beneath an armed man wearing a crown of bullets.
203. Mary Packer Harris (writing as "Bundilla"), "The Holy Mountain of a Crusader in Clay," chapter 2, page 7, unpublished manuscript, State Library of South Australia.
204. Ibid., chapter 10, page 3.
205. Brady, *Whitefella Dreaming*, 101.
206. Harris, "The Holy Mountain of a Crusader in Clay," chapter 5, page 2.
207. Brady, *Whitefella Dreaming*, 117. Original emphasis.
208. Harris, "The Holy Mountain of a Crusader in Clay," chapter 9, page 1.
209. William Ricketts, Letter to "Dear Friends," Papers of Mary Packer Harris, State Library of South Australia. Also quoted in Harris, "The Holy Mountain of a Crusader in Clay," chapter 9, page 2.

8 God in the Landscape

1. Malcolm Prentis, "Methodism in New South Wales, 1855–1902," in *Methodism in Australia: A History*, ed. Glen O'Brien and Hilary M. Carey (Farnham: Ashgate, 2015), 44; Graeme Chapman, *One Lord, One Faith, One Baptism: A History of Churches of Christ in Australia* (Melbourne: Vital Publications, 1980), 81, 85.
2. Barbara Bolton, *Booth's Drum: The Salvation Army in Australia 1880–1980* (Sydney: Hodder and Stoughton, 1980), 60.

3. E.g.: F. J. Wilkin, *Baptists in Victoria: Our First Century, 1838–1938* (East Melbourne: Baptist Union of Victoria, 1939); W. L. Blamires and John B. Smith, *The Early Story of the Wesleyan Methodist Church in Victoria* (Melbourne: Wesleyan Book Depot, 1886); A. B. Maston, *Jubilee Pictorial History of Churches of Christ in Australasia* (Melbourne: Austral, 1903); Ern West, *A History of the Christian Brethren Assemblies in Western Australia* (Western Australia: self-published 1993); and The Salvation Army produced a booklet that listed congregational buildings and institutions (with further opportunity for donation), James Hay, *Property Souvenir, Australia: A Record of Progress, 1909–1921* (Melbourne: The Salvation Army, 1922).
4. Cf. Mark McKenna, *Looking for Blackfellas' Point: An Australian History of Place* (Sydney: University of New South Wales Press, 2002), 99.
5. Mary Packer Harris, *The Cosmic Rhythm of Art and Literature* (Adelaide: Frank Cork, 1948), 59.
6. Joseph Bowes, *Jackaroos* (London: Oxford University Press, 1926), 116.
7. Ibid., 70–2, 116–17, 136.
8. Manning Clark, "Heroes," in *Australia: The Daedalus Symposium*, ed. S. Graubard (North Ryde, NSW: Angus and Robertson, 1985), 77–8.
9. Ernest E. Unwin, *Religion and Biology* (London: Swarthmore Press, 1922), 174.
10. David Tacey, *Re-Enchantment: The New Australian Spirituality* (Sydney: HarperCollins, 2000), 80–1.

Bibliography

Primary Sources: Periodicals

Adelaide Observer (SA)
Advertiser (Adelaide, SA)
Advocate (Melbourne, Vic.)
Age (Melbourne, Vic.)
Albury Banner and Wodonga Express (Vic. and NSW)
Areas' Express (Booyoolee, SA)
Argus (Melbourne, Vic.)
Australasian (Melbourne, Vic.)
Australasian Christian Standard (Melbourne, Vic.)
Australian Christian (Melbourne, Vic.)
Australian Friend (Sydney, NSW)
Ballarat Star (Vic.)
Barrier Miner (Broken Hill, NSW)
Bendigo Advertiser (Vic.)
Bendigo Independent (Vic.)
Bird O'Freedom (Sydney, NSW)
Bootham Magazine (UK)
Brighton Southern Cross (Vic.)
Brisbane Courier (Qld.)
Bulletin (Sydney, NSW)
Bunbury Herald (WA)
Bunyip (Gawler, SA)
Camperdown Chronicle (Vic.)
Casterton News and the Merino and Sandford Record (Vic.)
Christian Pioneer (Melbourne, Vic.)
Chronicle (Adelaide, SA)
Cootamundra Herald (NSW)
Critic (Hobart, Tas.)
Daily Herald (Adelaide, SA)
Daily News (Perth, WA)
Daily Northern Argus (Rockhampton, Qld.)
Daily Telegraph (Launceston, Tas.)
Daily Telegraph (Sydney, NSW)
Darling Downs Gazette (Qld.)
Dungog Chronicle: Durham and Gloucester Advertiser (NSW)
Evening Journal (SA)
Examiner (Launceston, Tas.)
Forerunner (Adelaide, SA)
Friend of Australia and New Zealand (Sydney, NSW)

Geelong Advertiser (Vic.)
Goulburn Herald (NSW)
Graphic of Australia (Melbourne, Vic.)
Gympie Times and Mary River Mining Gazette (Qld.)
Hay Standard and Advertiser (NSW)
Horsham Times (Vic.)
Huon Times (Franklin, Tas.)
Independent (Footscray, Vic.)
Kalgoorlie Miner (WA)
Kapunda Herald (SA)
Laura Standard and Crystal Brook Courier (SA)
Lismore, Derrinallum and Cressy Advertiser (Vic.)
Lithgow Mercury (NSW)
McIvor Times and Rodney Advertiser (Heathcote, Vic.)
Mail (Adelaide, SA)
Maitland Daily Mercury (NSW)
Mercury (Hobart, Tas.)
Methodist (Sydney, NSW)
Morning Bulletin (Rockhampton, Qld.)
Mount Alexander Mail (Vic.)
Mudgee Guardian and North-Western Representative (NSW)
Murray Pioneer (Renmark, SA)
Newcastle Morning Herald and Miners' Advocate (NSW)
News (Adelaide, SA)
New South Wales Government Gazette
Northern Herald (Cairns, Qld.)
Northern Miner (Charters Towers, Qld.)
Northern Star (Lismore, NSW)
Northern Territory Times and Gazette
Observer (Adelaide, SA)
Otago Daily Times (New Zealand)
Port Macquarie News (NSW)
Protestant Standard (Sydney, NSW)
Punch (Melbourne, Vic.)
Queenslander
Queensland Figaro
Queensland Times, Ipswich Herald and General Advertiser
Register (Adelaide, SA)
Richmond River Herald and Northern Districts Advertiser (NSW)
Riverina Recorder (Balranald, NSW)
South Australian Advertiser
South Australian Register
South Australian Weekly Chronicle
South Coast Times and Wollongong Argus (NSW)
Southern Cross (Adelaide, SA)
Southern Mail (Bowral, NSW)
Southern Times (Bunbury, WA)
Spectator and Methodist Chronicle (Melbourne, Vic.)
Sun (Sydney, NSW)

Sunday Times (Sydney, NSW)
Sydney Mail and New South Wales Advertiser
Sydney Morning Herald
Sydney Stock and Station Journal
Tasmanian News
Telegraph (Brisbane, Qld.)
Upper Hutt Leader (New Zealand)
Victorian Express (Geraldton, WA)
Victorian Independent (Melbourne, Vic.)
Wagga Wagga Advertiser (NSW)
Wallaroo Times and Mining Journal (SA)
The War Cry (Melbourne, Vic.)
Warwick Argus (Qld.)
Warwick Daily News (Qld.)
Watchman (Sydney, NSW)
Week (Brisbane, Qld.)
Weekly Times (Melbourne, Vic.)
West Australian (Perth, WA)
Windsor and Richmond Gazette (NSW)
Zeehan and Dundas Herald (Tas.)

Primary Sources

Abbott, E. S., ed. *Violet Verses*. Adelaide: E. S. Abbott, 1917.
Alexander, Cecil Frances. "All Things Bright and Beautiful." *Hymns for Little Children*. London: J. Masters, 1848.
Ashby, Edwin. "Australian Native Shrubs." In *Australian Gardening of To-day*, edited by W. A. Shum, 83–103. Melbourne: Sun-News Pictorial, c. 1940.
Aston, Tilly. *The Woolinappers or, Some Tales from the By-ways of Methodism*. Melbourne: Spectator, 1905.
Betts, Margery Ruth. "Brussells Streets." *Victorian Independent*, February 1, 1919.
Betts, Margery Ruth. "Called." *Australasian*, August 19, 1916.
Betts, Margery Ruth. "Communion on the Battlefield." *Victorian Independent*, December 1, 1915.
Betts, Margery Ruth. "The Crowning." *Australasian*, July 24, 1915.
Betts, Margery Ruth. "Earth to the Spring." *Victorian Independent*, June 1, 1918.
Betts, Margery Ruth. "Faith." *Victorian Independent*, January 1, 1916.
Betts, Margery Ruth. "The First Night." *Victorian Independent*, December 1, 1917.
Betts, Margery Ruth. "Gallipoli." *Australasian*, December 25, 1915.
Betts, Margery Ruth. "The Ghost." *Australasian*, August 2, 1919.
Betts, Margery Ruth. "His Wounded Wait." *Lismore, Derrinallum and Cressy Advertiser* (Vic.), January 23, 1918.
Betts, Margery Ruth. "The Kaiser's Boast." *Victorian Independent*, July 1, 1918.
Betts, Margery Ruth. "The Little Brother." *The Australasian*, February 9, 1918.
Betts, Margery Ruth. "The Recall." *The Australasian*, August 14, 1915.
Betts, Margery Ruth. "The Red Brother." *Victorian Independent*, May 1, 1917.
Betts, Margery Ruth. *Remembering and Other Verses*. Melbourne: Australasian Authors' Agency, 1917.
Betts, Margery Ruth. "The Route March." *Victorian Independent*, August 1916.

Betts, Margery Ruth. "The Sacrament." *Victorian Independent*, December 1, 1915.
Betts, Margery Ruth. "We Would Not Have Thee." *Victorian Independent*, June 1, 1916.
Betts, Margery Ruth. "Which Were Buried Together." *Victorian Independent*, October 2, 1916.
Bevan, Beatrice. 'A Tribute to the ANZACS: The Deathless Army.' *Bunyip* (Gawler, SA), April 21, 1933.
Bevan, Beatrice. "Edith Cavell." *Register* (Adelaide), October 22, 1915.
Bevan, Beatrice. "Enlistment." *Register* (Adelaide), May 18, 1915.
Bevan, Beatrice. "Gawler Memorial." *Bunyip* (Gawler, SA), September 16, 1921.
Bevan, Beatrice. "Lord God of Empires." *Register* (Adelaide), May 24, 1917.
Bevan, Beatrice. "Two Songs (Sorrow and Joy)." *Observer* (Adelaide), April 24, 1915.
Bevan, Beatrice. "Under the Hedge." *Observer* (Adelaide), December 18, 1915.
Bevan, Beatrice. "Via Crucis (For 25th April, 1916)." *Victorian Independent*, May 1, 1916.
Bevan, Beatrice. "Wattle Blossom." *Register* (Adelaide). September 7, 1915.
Bevan, Beatrice. "Wattle Blossom and Southern Cross." *Register* (Adelaide), September 6, 1915.
Binyon, Robert Laurence. "Edith Cavell." In *The Cause: Poems of the War*. London: Elkin Matthews, 1917.
Blake, William. "Milton." In *Seven Centuries of English Poetry*, edited by John Leonard, 266. Melbourne: Oxford University Press, 1987.
Blamires, W. L., and John B. Smith, *The Early Story of the Wesleyan Methodist Church in Victoria*. Melbourne: Wesleyan Book Depot, 1886.
Blanch, William Harnett. *Ye Parish of Camberwell: A Brief Account of the Parish of Camberwell; Its History and Antiquities*. London, 1875.
Boake, Barcroft. "Where the Dead Men Lie." In *The Penguin Book of Australian Ballads*, edited by Russel Ward, 111–13. Ringwood, Vic.: Penguin, 1964.
Booth, Catherine. *Papers on Aggressive Christianity*. London: The Salvation Army, 1891.
Booth, Herbert. "Move-On Manifesto." *The War Cry*, November 21, 1896.
Booth, Herbert, and Cornelie Booth. *Heart Melodies*. Melbourne: Salvation Army, 1900.
Booth, Herbert, and Cornelie Booth. "Programme and Songs for the Great Social Salvation Carnival at the Exhibition Building, Melbourne on Monday August 1st, 1898, under the conductorship of Commandant and Mrs Booth." Melbourne: Salvation Army Press, 1898.
Booth, Herbert, and Cornelie Booth. "The Salvation Army Great Carnival to be held in the Exhibition Building, Programme, Tuesday April 3, 1900, under the Conductorship of Commandant and Mrs Booth." Melbourne: Salvation Army Press, 1900.
Booth, Herbert, and Cornelie Booth. *Songs of Peace and War*. England: Salvation Army, 1890.
Booth, William. *In Darkest England, and the Way Out*. London: International Headquarters of The Salvation Army, 1890.
Booth, William. *Salvation Soldiery: A Series of Addresses on the Requirements of Jesus Christ's Service*. London: International Headquarters of The Salvation Army, c.1889.
Bowes, Joseph. "The Australian Aborigine." In A Century in the Pacific, edited by James Colwell, 153–73. London: Charles H. Kelly, 1914.
Bowes, Joseph. *The Jackaroos*. London: Oxford University Press, 1926 [1923].

Bowes, Joseph. *Pals: Young Australians in Sport and Adventure*. London: James Glass, 1910.
Brief History of Jerusalem with description of the Cyclorama, Victoria Parade, Melbourne. Melbourne: Rae Bros., 1902.
Buckingham, Marjorie. *Broad Is the Way*. London: Oliphants, 1953.
Buckingham, Marjorie. *In All These Things*. Melbourne: New Life, 1949; London: Oliphants, 1953.
Buckingham, Marjorie. *Strait Is the Gate*. London: Oliphants, 1956.
Bunyan, John. *The Life and Death of Mr Badman* (originally published 1680). Glasgow: Robert and Thomas Duncan, 1772.
Bunyan, John. *The Pilgrim's Progress* (originally published 1678), edited by Roger Sharrock. Harmondsworth: Penguin, 1965.
Campbell, Alexander. *The Christian System in Reference to the Union of Christians, and a Restoration of Primitive Christianity, as Plead in the Current Reformation*, 2nd ed. Pittsburg, PA: Forrester & Campbell, 1839.
Carmichael, Grace Jennings. "Evening on the Plains." *Australasian*, January 23, 1892.
Carne, Thomas Clement. *Galilee by the Ganges*. Melbourne: Book Depot, 1944.
Cave, H. "A Pioneer Preacher." *Australian Christian*, June 29, 1948.
Cocks, Elizabeth A. "Foreword" to *Australian Songs and Other Poems*, by Nicholas John Cocks. Sydney: Bourne's Book Shop, 1925.
Cocks, Nicholas John. *Australian Songs and Other Poems*. Sydney: Bourne's Book Shop, 1925.
Cocks, Nicholas John. *The Betty Songs*. Sydney: W. Geo. Smith, 1919.
Cocks, Nicholas John, and D. H. Souter. *Songs of the Dardanelles*. Sydney: s.n. 1915.
Congregational Church of South Australia. *Jubilee of Congregationalism in South Australia: Report of the Intercolonial Conference held in Adelaide, September, 1887*. Adelaide: Stow Congregational Church Manse Chambers, 1887.
Daley, Victor J. "The Parson and the Prelate." In *The Penguin Book of Australian Ballads*, edited by Russel Ward, 217–19. Ringwood, Vic.: Penguin, 1964.
Dark, Eleanor. *The Timeless Land*. London: Collins, 1941.
Deane, Wallace. *The Strange Adventures of a Whale's Tooth: A Missionary Story of Fiji for Young People and Others*. Sydney: Methodist Book Depot, 1919.
Duncan, Handasyde. *The Colony of South Australia*. London: T. and W. Boone, 1850.
Dyer, Eldred. "Joseph Bowes: A Minister Beloved." *Methodist*, April 7, 1928.
Farrar, Frederic W. *The Life of Christ*. London: Cassell, Petter and Galpin, 1884.
Farrer, William, and J. Brownbill, eds. "Townships: Torver." In *A History of the County of Lancaster*, vol. 8, 363–5. London: Victoria County History, 1914.
Fenner, Charles. Foreword to *Art, the Torch of Life*, by Mary Packer Harris. Adelaide: Rigby, 1946.
Forrest, Mabel. "Simple Little Bonnet." *Sunday Times* (Sydney), April 16, 1911.
Fowles, J. *Sydney in 1848*. Sydney: J. Fowles, 1848.
Franc, Maud Jeanne. *Golden Gifts: An Australian Tale*. Kapunda, SA: Scandrett and Elliott, 1869.
Franc, Maud Jeanne. *Minnie's Mission: An Australian Temperance Tale*. London: Sampson Low, Son and Marston, 1869.
Franc, Maud Jeanne. *Silken Cords and Iron Fetters*. London: Sampson Low, Son and Marston, 1870.
Francis, Ivor. "A Personal Note on Mary." In *Mary Packer Harris 1891–1978*, by Rachel Biven. Walkerville, SA: Walkerville Town Council, 1986.

Fullerton, William Young. *C. H. Spurgeon: A Biography*. London: Williams and Norgate, 1920.

Gibbs, Philip. "The Hazard of War." *West Australian*, April 15, 1918.

Gilks, Edward (compiler). "Hutchinson's Exhibition Pocket Map of Melbourne." Melbourne: J. Batten, 1880.

Gombrich, E. H. *The Story of Art*. London: Phaidon, 1950.

Gordon, Adam Lindsay. "The Sick Stock-Rider." *Colonial Monthly*, December 1869.

Gordon, Adam Lindsay. "A Dedication." *Bush Ballads and Galloping Rhymes*. Melbourne: Clarson, Massina, 1870.

"Gunby Hall Estate: Monksthorpe Chapel." Available online: https://www.nationaltrust.org.uk/gunby-hall-estate-monksthorpe-chapel (accessed January 18, 2021).

Handasyde, M'Millan and Co.'s Catalogue of Ornamental Trees, Shrubs, Fruit Trees, Herbaceous Plants, and Culinary Plants and Roots. Melbourne: Walker, May, 1864.

Harris, Mary Packer. *Art the Torch of Life*. Adelaide: Rigby, 1946.

Harris, Mary Packer. *The Cosmic Rhythm of Art and Literature*. Adelaide: Frank Cork, 1948.

Harris, Mary Packer. "Exhibition of Paintings, 9–26 April 1946." Exhibition catalogue.

Harris, Mary Packer (writing as "Bundilla"). "The Holy Mountain of a Crusader in Clay." Unpublished manuscript. State Library of South Australia.

Harris, Mary Packer. "The Indian upon God," 1929. Silk and wool embroidery on linen. Art Gallery of South Australia.

Harris, Mary Packer. *In One Splendour Spun: Autobiography of a Quaker Artist*. Walkerville, SA: self-published with Fred and Barbara Whitney, 1971.

Harris, Mary Packer. "Life Is Sweet, Brother," 1946. Watercolor. Source: Harris, Mary Packer. *The Cosmic Rhythm of Art and Literature*. Adelaide: Frank Cork, 1948.

Harris, Mary Packer. "Paintings of Old Walkerville." Walkerville, SA: Walkerville Gallery, December 1963. Exhibition catalogue.

Harris, Mary Packer. "Rain ancestor of Kaporilja," 1956. Charcoal and watercolor on paper. Art Gallery of South Australia.

Harris, Mary Packer. "The Timeless Time," early 1950s. Gouache on paper on board. Art Gallery of South Australia.

Harris, Mary Packer. "Urban Crucifix," no date. Print, woodcut.

Hay, James. *Property Souvenir, Australia: A Record of Progress, 1909–1921*. Melbourne: The Salvation Army, 1922.

Heysen, Hans. "Mystic Morn," 1904. Oil on canvas. Art Gallery of South Australia.

Hicks, Edward. "The Peaceable Kingdom," c. 1833. Source: The Worcester Art Museum.

Hocking, Joseph. "The Story of Andrew Fairfax." *Adelaide Observer*, July 15, 1893.

Holliday, Margaret. *Australian Methodist Idylls*. Sydney: J. A. Packer, 1906.

Holliday, Margaret. *The Day of Reckoning*. Sydney: Epworth Press, 1922.

Holliday, Margaret. "How Sundowner Ned Got on the Right Track." *Methodist*. December 21, 1907.

"Holy Dan." In *Australian Ballads*, edited by Russel Ward, 133–4. Ringwood, Vic.: Penguin, 1964.

"Inauguration of the Commonwealth," 1901. Australian Screen Online.

Isaac, Cyril E. *Annotated Catalogue of Seeds and Plants Supplied to Members of the Victorian State School's Horticultural Society*. Oakleigh: Victorian State School's Horticultural Society, 1917.

Jobson, F. J. *Chapel and School Architecture, as Appropriate to the Buildings of Nonconformists, particularly to those of the Wesleyan Methodists*. London: Hamilton Adams, 1850. Quoted in Binfield, Clyde. "Nonconformist Architecture: A Representative Focus." In *T&T Clark Companion to Nonconformity*, edited by Robert Pope, 257–84. London: Bloomsbury, 2013.

Kearney, James (draughtsman). "Melbourne and Its Suburbs." Melbourne: Andrew Clarke, Surveyor General, 1855.

Kerr, Alan J. "Adieu!" *Victorian Independent*, April 1916.

Kerr, Alan J. "At Sea." *Victorian Independent*, July 1915.

Lawson, Henry. "The Shearers." In *Australian Ballads*, edited by Russel Ward, 140–1. Ringwood, Vic.: Penguin, 1964.

Ling, John K. "Preface" to *Alison Ashby's Wildflowers of Southern Australia*, by Enid L. Robertson. Adelaide: South Australian Museum Board and the Botanic Gardens Board, 1981.

Locke, John. "Letter Concerning Toleration" in Works 2: 235. Cited in Richey, Russell E. *Denominationalism Illustrated and Explained*. Eugene, OR: Cascade, 2013.

Lucerna: The Magic Lantern Web Resource. Available online: http://lucerna.exeter.ac.uk/ (accessed January 17, 2021).

Ludbrook, Albert Milton. "Notes of Travel." *Australasian Christian Standard*, July 16, 1896–January 25, 1897.

McGarvey, J. W. *Lands of the Bible: A Geographical and Topographical Description of Palestine, with Letters of Travel in Egypt, Syria, Asia Minor and Greece*. Cincinnati, OH: Standard, 1880.

McGarvey, J. W. "The River Jordan." In *The Gospel Preacher: A Book of Sermons by Various Writers*, edited by A. B. Maston, 92–107. Melbourne: Austral, 1894.

MacKellar, Dorothea. "My Country." In *My Country: Australian Poetry and Short Stories, Two Hundred Years, Beginnings-1930s*, vol. 1, edited by Leonie Kramer, 472–3. Sydney: Lansdowne Press, 1985.

Maston, Aaron Burr. "Conference Essay: The Church in the Light of History." *Australasian Christian Standard*, April 29, 1897.

Maston, Aaron Burr. "A Horse-Back Ride through Palestine." *Christian Pioneer*, July 9, 1889–October 24, 1889. (Continuation of series, "Letters of Travel," April 2–May 7, 1889.)

Maston, Aaron Burr. *Jubilee Pictorial History of Churches of Christ in Australasia*. Melbourne: Austral, 1903.

Maston, Aaron Burr. "Walks about Palestine." *Australasian Christian Standard*, March 1, 1891–October 1, 1892.

M. C. "Only A Name." *Independent* (Footscray). August 21, 1915.

Melville, Herman. *Journals*. Edited by Howard C. Horsford with Lynn Horth. Evanston, IL: Northwestern University Press, 1989.

"The Modern Plague of London." Museum of London.

Morris, William. *Hopes and Fears for Art*. London: Longmans, Green, 1908.

Mudd, Christopher. "Peregrinations." *Spectator and Methodist Chronicle*. c. 1914–18.

Mudd, Christopher. *Tales and Trails of Austral Bush and Plain*. Melbourne: Spectator, 1912.

Mudd, Christopher. *Whys and Ways of the Bush and Guide to Bush Plants, or In Nature's School*. Melbourne: Spectator, 1914.

Murphy, William S. *In Memoriam: Edith Cavell*. London: Stoneham, 1916.

Nicholson, D. H. S., and A. H. E. Lee, eds. *The Oxford Book of English Mystical Verse*. Oxford: Oxford University Press, 1917.

Paterson, Andrew Barton "Banjo." "A Bush Christening." In *My Country: Australian Poetry and Short Stories, Two Hundred Years, Beginnings-1930s*, vol. 1, edited by Leonie Kramer, 281–2. Sydney: Lansdowne Press, 1985.

Paterson, Andrew Barton "Banjo." "The Man from Ironbark." In *My Country: Australian Poetry and Short Stories, Two Hundred Years, Beginnings-1930s*, vol. 1, edited by Leonie Kramer, 278–80. Sydney: Lansdowne Press, 1985.

Paterson, Andrew Barton "Banjo." "My Religion." In *Old Bush Songs Composed and Sung in the Bushranging, Digging and Overlanding Days*. Melbourne: E. W. Cole, 1905.

Paterson, Andrew Barton "Banjo." "Song of the Future." In *The Works of 'Banjo' Paterson*, 131–5. Ware: Wordsworth Editions, 2008.

Pattison, T. H. "Congregationalism and Aesthetics," in *Religious Republics*. Quoted in Binfield, Clyde. "Nonconformist Architecture: A Representative Focus." In *T&T Clark Companion to Nonconformity*, edited by Robert Pope, 257–84. London: Bloomsbury, 2013.

Payne, George Warren (writing as "Tom Bluegum"). *The Backblock's Parson*. London: Charles H. Kelly, 1899.

Payne, George Warren. *From Bark Hut to Pulpit*. London: Epworth Press, 1924.

Payne, George Warren (writing as "Tom Bluegum"). "The Middle Ridge Appointment." *Methodist*, July 22, 1899.

Pearce, Andrew. *The Land of Sunburnt Babies*. Adelaide: United Aborigines Mission, 1946.

Phillpotts, Eden. "Edith Cavell." *Observer* (Adelaide), December 25, 1915.

Pittman, G. P. *Life of Maston*. Melbourne: Austral, 1909.

Plaque at Wangaratta Church of Christ, Victoria, c. 1990. Photograph. Private collection.

Robert, R. Ambrose, Rev. "War." *Victorian Independent*, December 1, 1934.

Robson, Thomas. Letter in *Bootham Magazine* 11, no. 5 (December 1923).

Roughley, Edna. "Brindoonan." *Queenslander*, April 28, 1932.

Roughley, Edna. "The Crooked Tree." *Queenslander*, December 4, 1930.

Roughley, Edna. "Dream Mother." *Methodist*, July 16–October 15, 1938.

Roughley, Edna. *Ellice of Ainslie*. Sydney: Australasian, 1947.

Roughley, Edna. "Footsteps." *Australian Women's Weekly*, April 13, 1935.

Roughley, Edna. "Laugh, Marienne." *Sydney Morning Herald*, June 29, 1937.

Roughley, Edna. *The Locked Door*. Sydney: Australasian, 1948.

Roughley, Edna. "The Lost Road," serial in 42 parts. *Methodist*, June 6, 1942–April 3, 1943.

Russell, Alex. "For the Lads of Our Church Who Have Fallen." *Spectator and Methodist Chronicle*, August 15, 1917.

"Salvation Army Citadel in Russell Street, Bathurst" (1934). Colorized photographic postcard. National Museum of Australia, Josef Lebovic Gallery Collection.

Sargant, George. *My Inland Island*. Melbourne: Wyatt and Watts, 1921.

Sargant, George. *The Sweet Heart of the Bush*. Melbourne: Lothian, 1915.

Sargant, George. *The Winding Track*. Melbourne: Lothian, 1920.

Scambler, T. H. "Big Enough for God." *Christian Standard*. Cincinnati, OH, 1941.

Scambler, T. H. *Constant Stars*. Melbourne: Book Depot, 1946.

"Science and Salvation." *The Victory: An Illustrated Record of Salvation Army Advances in All Nations*, Supplement – "Four Conquering Years 1896–1901," September 1901: 440–3. In *Cinema in Australia: A Documentary History*, edited by Ina Bertrand, 21–3. Kensington, NSW: University of New South Wales Press, 1989.

Silcock, Thomas H. *Tradeways*. Sydney: Currawong, 1971.

Sinclaire, Frederick. *Conscription and Christianity: Manifesto from Protestant Ministers*. Melbourne: Free Religious Fellowship, 1917.

Smeaton, Thomas Hyland. *The Forest*. Adelaide: Vardon and Sons, 1920.

Smeaton, Thomas Hyland. "Hawthorne Dene." *Register* (Adelaide), June 3, 1922.
Somerville, Phyllis. "The Influence of Cornwall on South Australian Methodism." *The Journal of the South Australian Methodist Historical Society* 4 (October 1972): 1–13.
Somerville, Phyllis. *Not Only in Stone*. Sydney: Angus and Robertson, 1942.
Souvenir Programme of the Jubilee Conference of Churches of Christ in Victoria. Melbourne: Austral, 1903.
Spencer, Baldwin. *Guide to the Australian Ethnographical Collection in the National Museum of Victoria*. Melbourne: National Museum of Victoria, 1901.
Strehlow, T. G. H. *An Australian Viewpoint*. Adelaide: Hawthorn Press, 1950.
Taylor, William George. *Pathfinders of the Great South Land*. London: Epworth Press, c. 1925.
Thornsby, Frederick W., ed. *Dictionary of Organs and Organists*. Bournemouth: H. Logan, 1912.
Turner, Henry Gyles. "Preface" to *The Woolinappers or, Some Tales from the By-ways of Methodism*, by Tilly Aston, i–v. Melbourne: Spectator, 1905.
Unwin, Ernest E. "Kelvedon, Swansea, Tas.," no date. Private collection.
Unwin, Ernest E. "One Hundred Years." In *The Centenary of Australian Quakerism: 1832–1932*, edited by Margaret L. Benson, Frederick Coleman, and Ernest E. Unwin, 35–44. Hobart: General Meeting of Religious Society of Friends, Australia, 1933.
Unwin, Ernest E. *Religion and Biology*. London: Swarthmore Press, 1922.
Unwin, Ernest E. "The Society of Friends, Tercentenary of George Fox, The Message of Quakerism." *Mercury* (Hobart), August 9, 1924.
V. V. H. "Ernest Ewart Unwin." *Papers and Proceedings of the Royal Society of Tasmania*. Hobart: Royal Society of Tasmania, 1944.
Wesley, John. *The Journal of John Wesley*, edited by P. L. Parker. Chicago: Moody Press, 1951.
Wilkin, Frederick J. *Baptists in Victoria: Our First Century, 1838–1938*. East Melbourne: Baptist Union of Victoria, 1939.
Wiltberger, C. "Temperance Map," 1838. Library of Congress.
Wordsworth, William. "Discourse of the Wanderer, and an Evening Visit to the Lake." In *The Excursion: A Poem*, 315–43. London: Edward Moxon, 1836.
Wordsworth, William. "Elegaic Stanzas." In *Norton Anthology of Poetry*, 3rd ed., 559. New York: W. W. Norton, 1983.
Wordsworth, William. "Lines. Composed a Few Miles above Tintern Abbey." In *Norton Anthology of Poetry*, 3rd ed., 523. New York: W. W. Norton, 1983.
Zollars, E. V. *Bible Geography: A Series of Lessons on the Old and New Testament Worlds*. Cincinnati, OH: Standard, 1895.

Secondary Sources

Anderson, Misty G. *Imagining Methodism in Eighteenth-Century Britain: Enthusiasm, Belief, and the Borders of the Self*. Baltimore: Johns Hopkins University Press, 2012.
Armstrong, Karen. *Jerusalem: One City, Three Faiths*. London: Harper Collins, 1996.
Arthur, Jay M. *The Default Country: A Lexical Cartography of Twentieth-Century Australia*. Sydney: University of New South Wales Press, 2003.
Ashcroft, Bill, Frances Devlin-Glass, and Lyn McCredden. *Intimate Horizons: The Post-Colonial Sacred in Australian Literature*. Hindmarsh, SA: Australian Theological Forum Press, 2009.

Atkinson, Alan. *The Europeans in Australia*, vols. 1–3. Sydney: University of New South Wales Press, 2014–16.
Austlit: The Australian Literature Resource. https://www.austlit.edu.au.
Beauman, Nicola. "'It Is Not the Place of Women to Talk of Mud': Some Responses by British Women Novelists to World War I." In *Women and World War I: The Written Response*, edited by Dorothy Goldman, 128–49. London: Macmillan, 1993.
Beaumont, Joan. *Broken Nation: Australians in the Great War*. Sydney: Allen and Unwin, 2013.
Bebbington, David W. "Evangelicalism and British Culture." In *Culture, Spirituality and the Brethren, Studies in Brethren History*, vol. 3, edited by N. T. R. Dickson and T. J. Marinella, 25–38. Troon, Ayrshire: Brethren Archivists and Historians Network, 2014.
Bebbington, David. *Evangelicalism in Modern Britain: History from the 1730s to 1980s*. London: Routledge, 1989.
Bebbington, David. "Methodism and Culture." In *The Oxford Handbook of Methodist Studies*, edited by William J. Abraham and James E. Kirby, 712–29. Oxford: Oxford University Press, 2009.
Bebbington, David. *The Nonconformist Conscience: Chapel and Politics, 1870–1914*. London: Allen and Unwin, 1982.
Bertrand, Ina, ed. *Cinema in Australia: A Documentary History*. Kensington, NSW: University of New South Wales Press, 1989.
Bertrand, Ina. "Perry, Joseph Henry (1863–1943)." *Australian Dictionary of Biography* (1988). Available online: http://adb.anu.edu.au/biography/perry-joseph-henry-8024/text13987 (accessed March 24, 2017).
Binfield, Clyde. "Breadth from Dissent: Ada Ellen Bayly ('Edna Lyall') and her Fiction." In *The Church and Literature (Studies in Church History Volume 48)*, edited by Peter Clarke and Charlotte Methuen, 349–61. Rochester, NY: Published for The Ecclesiastical History Society by The Boydell Press, 2012.
Binfield, Clyde. "Nonconformist Architecture: A Representative Focus." In *T&T Clark Companion to Nonconformity*, edited by Robert Pope, 257–84. London: Bloomsbury, 2013.
Binfield, Clyde. "Strangers and Dissenters: The Architectural Legacy of Twentieth-Century English Nonconformity." In *Protestant Nonconformity in the Twentieth Century*, edited by Alan Sell and Anthony Cross, 132–83. Carlisle: Paternoster, 2003.
Blakeney, Michael. *Australia and the Jewish Refugees 1933–1948*. Sydney: Croom Helm Australia, 2001.
Blowers, Paul. "'Living in a Land of Prophets': James T. Barclay and an Early Disciples of Christ Mission to Jews in the Holy Land." *Church History* 62, no. 4 (1993): 494–513.
Bollenbaugh, Michael W. "Reason, Place of." In *The Encyclopedia of the Stone-Campbell Movement*, edited by Douglas A. Foster, Paul M. Blowers, Anthony L. Dunnavant, and D. Newell Williams, 627–8. Grand Rapids, MI: Wm. B. Eerdmans, 2004.
Bolton, Barbara. *Booth's Drum: The Salvation Army in Australia 1880–1980*. Sydney: Hodder and Stoughton, 1980.
Bongiorno, Frank. "Aboriginality and Historical Consciousness: Bernard O'Dowd and the Creation of an Australian National Imaginary." *Aboriginal History* 24 (2000): 39–61.
Bongiorno, Frank. "In This World and the Next: Political Modernity and Unorthodox Religion in Australia, 1880–1930." *ACH: The Journal of the History of Culture in Australia, Antipodean Modern* 25 (2006): 179–207.
Boyce, James. "Return to Eden: Van Dieman's Land and the Early British Settlement of Australia." *Environment and History* 14, no. 2 (May 2008): 289–307.

Bradshaw, Clare. *Reading Race: Aboriginality in Australian Children's Literature.* Melbourne: Melbourne University Press, 2001.

Brady, Peter. *Whitefella Dreaming: The Authorised Biography of William Ricketts.* Olinda, Vic.: Preferred Image, 1994.

Brady, Veronica. *Caught in the Draught: On Contemporary Australian Culture and Society.* Sydney: Angus and Robertson, 1994.

Brady, Veronica. *A Crucible of Prophets.* Sydney: Australian and New Zealand Studies in Theology and Religion, 1981.

Breward, Ian. "Australasian Church Histories before 1914." In *Re-visioning Australian Colonial Christianity: New Essays in the Australian Christian Experience 1788–1900*, edited by Mark Hutchinson and Edmund Campion, 41–59. Sydney: Centre for the Study of Australian Christianity, 1994.

Breward, Ian. *A History of the Churches in Australasia.* Oxford: Oxford University Press, 2001.

Breward, Ian. "Methodist Reunion in Australasia." In *Methodism in Australia: A History*, edited by Glen O'Brien and Hilary M. Carey, 119–31. Farnham: Ashgate, 2015.

Breward, Ian. "Methodists." In *The Encyclopedia of Religion in Australia*, edited by James Jupp, 404–15. Port Melbourne: Cambridge University Press, 2009.

Breward, Ian. "Presbyterians." In *The Encyclopedia of Religion in Australia*, edited by James Jupp, 523–34. Port Melbourne: Cambridge University Press, 2009.

Briggs, John H. Y. "The Changing Shape of Nonconformity, 1662–2000." In *T&T Clark Companion to Nonconformity*, edited by Robert Pope, 3–26. London: Bloomsbury T&T Clark, 2013.

Brindle, Susannah Kay. *To Learn a New Song: A Contribution to Real Reconciliation with the Earth and its Peoples.* Armadale North, Vic.: Australia Yearly Meeting Religious Society of Friends, 2000.

Brooke, John, and Geoffrey Cantor. *Reconstructing Nature: The Engagement of Science and Religion.* Edinburgh: T&T Clark, 1998.

Brooks, Margaret. "Conscientious Objectors in their Own Words." Imperial War Museums. Available online: http://www.iwm.org.uk/history/conscientious-objectors-in-their-own-words (accessed February 10, 2016).

Bryan, Donna. "First Ecumenical Assembly of Asian Church Women Held in Asia." Australian Church Women Inc, 2020.

Cameron, John. *In Stow's Footsteps: A Chronological History of the Congregational Churches in SA, 1837–1977.* Adelaide: South Australian Congregational History Project Committee, 1987.

Cantor, Geoffrey. "Aesthetics in Science, as Practised by Quakers in the Eighteenth and Nineteenth Centuries." *Quaker Studies* 4, no. 1 (1999): 1–20.

Cantor, Geoffrey. "Quaker Responses to Darwin." *Osiris* 16 (2001): 321–42.

Cantor, Geoffrey. *Quakers, Jews and Science: Religious Responses to Modernity and the Sciences in Britain, 1650–1900.* Oxford: Oxford University Press, 2005.

Carey, Hilary M. *Believing in Australia: A Cultural History of Religions.* St Leonards, NSW: Allen and Unwin, 1996.

Carey, Hilary M. "Bushmen and Bush Parsons: The Shaping of A Rural Myth." *Journal of Australian Colonial History* 14 (2011): 1–26.

Carey, Hilary M. *God's Empire: Religion and Colonialism in the British World, c. 1801–1908.* Cambridge: Cambridge University Press, 2011.

Carey, Hilary M. "Religion and Society." In *Australia's Empire*, edited by Deryck Schreuder and Stuart Ward, 186–210. Oxford: Oxford University Press, 2008.

Carey, Hilary M., Ian Breward, Nicholas Doumanis, Ruth Frappell, David Hilliard, Katharine Massam, Anne O'Brien, and Roger Thompson. "Australian Religion Review, 1980–2000, Part 2: Christian Denominations." *Journal of Religious History* 25, no. 1 (February 2001): 56–82.

Carter, Paul. *The Lie of the Land*. London: Faber and Faber, 1996.

Chapman, Graeme. *One Lord, One Faith, One Baptism: A History of Churches of Christ in Australia*. Melbourne: Vital Publications, 1980.

Childers, Joseph W. "Observation and Representation: Mr Chadwick Writes the Poor." *Victorian Studies* 37, no. 3 (Spring 1994): 405–32.

Clancy, Eric G. "Ecclesiastical Stock Riders: Wesleyan Methodist Ministers in Nineteenth-Century Rural New South Wales." *Church Heritage* 9, no. 3 (March 1996): 143–62.

Clapham, Noel, ed. *Seventh-day Adventists in the South Pacific 1885–1985*. Warburton, Vic.: Signs, 1985.

Clark, Manning. "Heroes." In *Australia: The Daedalus Symposium*, edited by S. R. Graubard. North Ryde, NSW: Angus and Robertson, 1985.

Clark, Manning. *A Short History of Australia*, 6th ed. New York: Mentor, 1969.

Cleary, John. "Australia." In *Brass Bands of the Salvation Army: Their Mission and Music*, vol. 1, edited by Ronald W. Holz, 273–332. Stotfold, UK: Streets, 2006.

Clifford, Herbert, and Noel Clapham. "Hospitals and Healing." In *Seventh-day Adventists in the South Pacific 1885–1985*, edited by Noel Clapham, 76–97. Warburton, Vic.: Signs, 1985.

Coate, Jennifer, Robert Fitzgerald, and Helen Milroy. "Report of Case Study No. 33, The Response of the Salvation Army (Southern Territory) to Allegations of Child Sexual Abuse at Children's Homes that it Operated." *Royal Commission into Institutional Responses to Child Sexual Abuse*. Commonwealth of Australia, July 2016.

Coffey, John. "Church and State, 1550–1750: The Emergence of Dissent." In *T&T Clark Companion to Nonconformity*, edited by Robert Pope, 47–74. London: Bloomsbury T&T Clark, 2013.

Coffey, John. *Persecution and Toleration in Protestant England 1558–1689*. Harlow: Pearson, 2000.

Colligan, Mimi. *Canvas Documentaries: Panoramic Entertainments in Nineteenth-Century Australia and New Zealand*. Melbourne: Melbourne University Press, 2002.

Collins, Mervyn E. *Sounds of the Gospel: 125 Years of the Melbourne Staff Band*. Melbourne: The Salvation Army, Australia Southern Territory, 2015.

Collins, Peter. "Quaker Plaining as Critical Aesthetic." *Quaker Studies* 5, no. 2 (2000): 121–39.

Cooley, Steven D. "Applying the Vagueness of Language: Poetic Strategies and Campmeeting Piety in the Mid-Nineteenth Century." *Church History* 63, no. 4 (December 1994): 570–86.

Cooley, Steven D. "Manna and the Manual: Sacramental and Instrumental Constructions of the Victorian Methodist Camp Meeting during the Mid-Nineteenth Century." *Religion and American Culture: A Journal of Interpretation* 6, no. 2 (Summer 1996): 131–59.

Cox, Gordon. *The Musical Salvationist: The World of Richard Slater (1854–1939), "Father of Salvation Army Music."* Woodbridge, UK: Boydell Press, 2011.

Cox, Lindsay. *The Salvation Army Soldiers of the Cross, 1900–2000: Centenary of the First Screening*. Melbourne: The Salvation Army Archives and Museum, 2000.

Crotty, Martin. "Frontier Fantasies: Boys' Adventure Stories and the Construction of Masculinity in Australia, 1870–1920." *Journal of Australian Colonial History* 3, no. 1 (April 2001): 55–76.
Cummins, D. Duane. *The Disciples: A Struggle for Reformation*. St Louis: Chalice Press, 2008.
Curthoys, Patricia. "Congregationalists." In *The Encyclopedia of Religion in Australia*, edited by James Jupp, 299–304. Port Melbourne: Cambridge University Press, 2009.
Damousi, Joy. *The Labour of Loss: Mourning, Memory and Wartime Bereavement in Australia*. Melbourne: Cambridge University Press, 1999.
Daniel, Esther. "Salvationists." In *The Encyclopedia of Religion in Australia*, edited by James Jupp, 554–60. Port Melbourne: Cambridge University Press, 2009.
Daniel, Esther. "'Solving an Empire Problem': The Salvation Army and British Juvenile Migration to Australia." *History of Education Review* 36, no. 1 (2007): 33–48.
Davis, John. *Landscape of Belief: Encountering the Holy Land in Nineteenth-Century American Art and Culture*. Princeton, NJ: Princeton University Press, 1996.
Davis, Nancy J., and Robert V. Robinson. *Claiming Society for God: Religious Movements and Social Welfare*. Bloomington: Indiana University Press, 2012.
Davison, Graeme. "Christianity and Australian Culture." In *Shaping the Good Society in Australia*, edited by Stuart Piggin, 99–108. Macquarie Centre, NSW: Australian Christian Heritage National Forum, 2006.
Davison, Graeme. *City Dreamers: The Urban Imagination in Australia*. Sydney: NewSouth, 2016.
Davison, Graeme. *The Rise and Fall of Marvellous Melbourne*, 2nd ed. Carlton, Vic.: Melbourne University Press, 2004.
Davison, Graeme, and David Dunstan. "'This Moral Pandemonium': Images of Low Life." In *The Outcasts of Melbourne*, edited by Graeme Davison, David Dunstan, and Chris McConville, 29–57. Sydney: Allen and Unwin, 1985.
De Krey, Gary. "Dissenting Cases for Conscience, 1667–1672." *Historical Journal* 38 (1995): 53–83.
Design and Art Australia Online. https://www.daao.org.au.
Dill, Vicky Schreiber. "Land Relatedness in the Mennonite Novels of Rudy Wiebe." *The Mennonite Quarterly Review* 58 (1984): 50–69.
Dillenberger, John. *The Visual Arts and Christianity in America: The Colonial Period through the Nineteenth Century*. Chico, CA: Scholars Press, 1984.
Dingle, Tony. "Depressions." eMelbourne. Available online: http://www.emelbourne.net.au/biogs/EM00460b.htm (accessed April 5, 2017).
Dixon, Robert. *Writing the Colonial Adventure: Race, Gender and Nation in Anglo-Australian Popular Fiction, 1875–1914*. Cambridge: Cambridge University Press, 1995.
Duncan, Troy. "Methodism and Empire." In *Methodism in Australia: A History*, edited by Glen O'Brien and Hilary Carey, 107–18. Farnham: Ashgate, 2015.
Edwards, Deborah. *Margaret Preston*. Sydney: Art Gallery of New South Wales, 2005.
Eisenberg, Joseph, and Joan Kerr. "Olive Crane." *Design and Art Australia Online*. Available online: https://www.daao.org.au/bio/olive-crane/biography/ (accessed March 30, 2016).
Elias, Ann. "War, Flowers, and Visual Culture: The First World Collection of the Australian War Memorial." *Journal of the Australian War Memorial* 40 (February 2007): 234–50.
Ely, Richard. "Protestantism in Australian History: An Interpretative Sketch." *Lucas: An Evangelical History Review* 5 (March 1989): 11–20.

Emilsen, Susan, Ben Skerman, Patricia Curthoys, and William Emilsen. *Pride of Place: A History of the Pitt Street Congregational Church*. Beaconsfield: Melbourne Publishing Group, 2008.

Engel, Frank. *Conflict and Unity 1788–1926*. Melbourne: Joint Board of Christian Education of Australia and New Zealand, 1984.

Farrall, Lyndsay A. "Quakers in Australia." In *The Encyclopedia of Religion in Australia*, edited by James Jupp, 546–9. Port Melbourne: Cambridge University Press, 2009.

Fitchett, William Henry. *The Commander of the Hirondelle*. London: Smith, Elder, 1904.

Fitchett, William Henry, *The Adventures of an Ensign*. Edinburgh: Blackwood, 1917.

Freeman, Curtis W. *Undomesticated Dissent: Democracy and the Public Virtue of Religious Nonconformity*. Waco, TX: Baylor University Press, 2017.

Garrett, John. "Cocks, Nicholas John (1867–1925)." *Australian Dictionary of Biography*. Available online: http://adb.anu.edu.au/biography/cocks-nicholas-john-5706/text9647 (accessed February 3, 2016).

Garrett, John, and L. W. Farr. *Camden College: A Centenary History*. Sydney: Camden College, 1964.

Gascoigne, John. *The Enlightenment and the Origins of European Australia*. Cambridge: Cambridge University Press, 2002.

Gaynor, Andrea, ed. *George Seddon: Selected Writings*. Carlton: Latrobe University Press, 2019.

Ginzburg, Carlo. "Microhistory: Two or Three Things That I Know about It." Translated by John Tedeschi and Anne C. Tedeschi. *Critical Inquiry* 20, no. 1 (Autumn 1993): 10–35.

Goldman, Dorothy, ed. *Women and World War I: The Written Response*. London: Macmillan, 1993.

Goody, Jack. *The Culture of Flowers*. Cambridge: Cambridge University Press, 1993.

Gorman, James L. "European Roots of Thomas Campbell's *Declaration and Address*: The Evangelical Society of Ulster." *Restoration Quarterly* 51, no. 3 (2009): 129–37.

Gorringe, Timothy. *A Theology of the Built Environment: Justice, Empowerment, Redemption*. Cambridge: Cambridge University Press, 2002.

Gough, Paul. "'Planting' Memory: The Challenge of Remembering the Past on the Somme, Gallipoli and in Melbourne." *Garden History* 42, Suppl.1 (2014).

Graham, William C. *Half Finished Heaven: The Social Gospel in American Literature*. Lanham, MD: University Press of America, 1995.

Green, O. S. "Aston, Matilda Ann (Tilly) (1873–1947)." *Australian Dictionary of Biography*. Available online: http://adb.anu.edu.au/biography/aston-matilda-ann-5078 (accessed August 6, 2015).

Green, Roger J. *The Life and Ministry of William Booth, Founder of the Salvation Army*. Nashville: Abingdon Press, 2005.

Gregory, John Stradbroke. *Church and State: Changing Government Policies Toward Religion in Australia, with Particular Reference to Victoria Since Separation*. North Melbourne: Cassell Australia, 1973.

Griffiths, Billy, Lynette Russell, and Richard "Bert" Roberts. "When Did Australia's Human History Begin?" *Conversation*, November 17, 2017. Available online: https://theconversation.com/friday-essay-when-did-australias-human-history-begin-87251 (accessed January 18, 2021).

Griffiths, Tom. *The Art of Time Travel: Historians and their Craft*. Carlton, Vic.: Black Inc., 2016.

Griffiths, Tom. *Forests of Ash: An Environmental History*. Port Melbourne: Cambridge University Press, 2001.

Gwyn, Douglas. "Quakers, Eschatology and Time." In *The Oxford Book of Quaker Studies*, edited by Stephen W. Angell and Ben Pink Dandelion, 1–12. Oxford: Oxford University Press, 2013.

Handasyde, Kerrie. "Anzac Theology and the Women Poets under the Southern Cross." *Colloquium: The Australia and New Zealand Theological Review* 49, no. 1 (May 2017): 17–30.

Handasyde, Kerrie. "Holy Land Tourism: A Horseback Ride from Public Theology to Private Faith." *Melbourne Historical Journal* 43 (2015): 61–71.

Handasyde, Kerrie. "Mother, Preacher, Press: Women Ministers and the Negotiation of Authority, 1910–1933." In *Contemporary Feminist Theologies: Power, Authority, Love*, edited by Kerrie Handasyde, Cathryn McKinney, and Rebekah Pryor. Abingdon: Routledge, 2021.

Handasyde, Kerrie. "Pioneering Leadership: Historical Myth-Making, Absence and Identity in the Churches of Christ in Victoria." *Journal of Religious History* 41, no. 2 (June 2017): 235–50.

Handasyde, Kerrie. "Religious Dress and the Making of Women Preachers in Australia, 1880–1934." *Lilith: A Feminist History Journal* 26 (2020): 103–19.

Handasyde, Kerrie. "Wattle: 'Symbol of This Nation's Heart.'" *Australian Garden History* 29, no. 3 (January 2018): 12–14.

Hansen, Donald. "The Adventist Press." In *Seventh-day Adventists in the South Pacific 1885–1985*, edited by Noel Clapham, 58–75. Warburton, Vic.: Signs, 1985.

Hapgood, Lynne. "The Reconceiving of Christianity: Secularisation, Realism and the Religious Novel: 1888–1900." *Literature and Theology* 10, no. 4 (December 1996): 334–5.

Harding, Lesley. *Margaret Preston: Recipes for Food and Art*. Melbourne: Miegunyah Press, 2016.

Hay, Michael F. "'Onward Christian Soldiers': The Salvation Army in Milton 1884–1894." In *Building God's Own Country: Historical Essays on Religions in New Zealand*, edited by John Stenhouse and Jane Thomson, 113–23. Dunedin: University of Otago Press, 2004.

Heath, Gordon L. "Passion for Empire: War Poetry Published in the Canadian English Protestant Press during the South African War, 1899–1902." *Literature and Theology* 16, no. 2 (December 2002): 127–47.

Hempton, David. *Methodism: Empire of the Spirit*. New Haven, CT: Yale University Press, 2005.

Herbst, Matthew T. "'The Pernicious Effects of Novel Reading': The Methodist Episcopal Campaign Against American Fiction, 1865–1914." *Journal of Religion and Society* 9 (2007): 1–15.

Hindmarsh, Bruce. "'My Chains Fell Off: My Heart Was Free': Early Methodist Conversion Narrative in England." *Church History* 68, no. 4 (December 1999): 910–29.

Hoffenberg, Peter. "Landscape, Memory and the Australian War Experience, 1915–1918." *Journal of Contemporary History* 36, no. 1 (January 2001): 111–31.

Hogan, Michael. *The Sectarian Strand: Religion in Australian History*. Ringwood, Vic.: Penguin, 1987.

Holloway, David. *Dark Somme Flowing: Australian Verse of the Great War, 1914–18*. Malvern: Robert Anderson and Associates, 1987.

Holmes, Katie. *Between the Leaves: Stories of Australian Women, Writing and Gardens*. Crawley, WA: University of Western Australia, 2011.

Holmes, Katie, and Kylie Mirmohamadi. "Howling Wilderness and Promised Land: Imagining the Victorian Mallee, 1840–1914." *Australian Historical Studies* 46, no. 2 (2015): 191–213.

Holton, Sandra Stanley. *Suffrage Days: Stories from the Women's Suffrage Movement.* London: Routledge, 1996.

Homan, Roger. "The Art of Joseph Edward Southall." *Quaker Studies* 5, no. 1 (2000): 69–83.

Homan, Roger. *The Art of the Sublime: Principles of Christian Art and Architecture.* Aldershot: Ashgate, 2006.

Homan, Roger. "The Inward and the Outward Eye: Quaker Attitudes to Visual Culture." *Quaker Studies* 18, no. 2 (March 2014): 139–50.

Honest History. Available online: http://honesthistory.net.au/ (accessed December 20, 2017).

Howe, Brian, and Renate Howe. "The Influence of Faith-Based Organisations on Australian Social Policy." *Australian Journal of Social Studies* 47, no. 3 (2012): 319–33.

Howe, Renate. "Booth, Herbert Henry (1862–1926)." *Australian Dictionary of Biography.* Available online: http://adb.anu.edu.au/biography/booth-herbert-henry-5290 (accessed March 19, 2017).

Howe, Renate. "'Five Conquering Years': The Leadership of Commandant and Mrs H. Booth of the Salvation Army in Victoria, 1896–1901." *Journal of Religious History* 6, no. 2 (December 1970): 177–97.

Howe, Renate. *A Reappraisal of the Relationship between the Churches and the Working Classes, 1880–1910.* Melbourne: Uniting Church Historical Society, October 1989.

Hudson, Wayne. *Australian Religious Thought.* Clayton, Vic.: Monash University Press, 2016.

Hughes, Philip J., and Darren Cronshaw. *Baptists in Australia: A Church with a Heritage and a Future.* Nunawading, Vic.: Christian Research Association, 2013.

Hughes, Richard T. "Why Restorationists Don't Fit the Evangelical Mold; Why Churches of Christ Increasingly Do." In *Re-forming the Center: American Protestantism 1900 to the Present*, edited by Douglas Jacobsen and William Vance Trollinger, 194–213. Grand Rapids, MI: Wm. B. Eerdmans, 1998.

Hughes, Richard T., and C. Leonard Allen. *Illusions of Innocence: Protestant Primitivism in America 1630–1875.* Chicago, IL: University of Chicago Press, 1988.

Hughes-d'Aeth, Tony. *Like Nothing on This Earth: A Literary History of the Wheatbelt.* Crawley: University of Western Australia, 2017.

Humphreys, Robert, and Rowland Ward. *Religious Bodies in Australia: A Comprehensive Guide*, 3rd ed. Wantirna, Vic.: New Melbourne Press, 1995.

Hunt, Arnold D. *This Side of Heaven: A History of Methodism in South Australia.* Adelaide: Lutheran Publishing House, 1985.

Hyams, B. K. "Smeaton, Thomas Hyland (1857–1927)." *Australian Dictionary of Biography.* Available online: http://adb.anu.edu.au/biography/smeaton-thomas-hyland-8461/text14877 (accessed February 3, 2016).

Hynes, Samuel. *A War Imagined: The First World War and English Culture.* London: Bodley Head, 1990.

Inge, John. *A Christian Theology of Place.* Burlington, VT: Aldershot, 2003.

Inglis, Ken. *Sacred Places: War Memorials in the Australian Landscape.* Carlton, Vic.: Miegunyah Press, 1998.

"Interactive Warlpiri—English Dictionary: with English—Warlpiri finderlist," 2nd ed. Compiled by Stephen M. Swartz. *AuSIL Interactive Dictionary Series* B-3. Edited by

Charles E. Grimes and Maarten Lecompte. Darwin: Australian Society for Indigenous Languages, 2012.
Jasper, David. "The Study of Literature and Theology." In *The Oxford Handbook of English Literature and Theology*, edited by Andrew Hass, David Jasper and Elisabeth Jay, 15–32. Oxford: Oxford University Press, 2007.
Jenkins, Philip. *The Great and Holy War: How World War I Changed Religion Forever*. Oxford: Lion, 2014.
Jones, David. "Bush Garden Ethos in South Australia." *Australian Garden History* 13, no. 6 (2002): 10–11.
Jones, David Ceri. "Evangelicalism." In *T&T Clark Companion to Nonconformity*, edited by Robert Pope, 593–6. London: Bloomsbury T&T Clark, 2013.
Jones, Philip. *Ochre and Rust: Artefacts and Encounters on Australian Frontiers*. Kent Town, SA: Wakefield Press, 2007.
Judd, Stephen, and Anne Robinson. "Christianity and the Social Services in Australia." In *Shaping the Good Society in Australia*, edited by Stuart Piggin, 109–25. Macquarie Centre, NSW: Australian Christian Heritage National Forum, 2006.
Jupp, James. "Seventh Day Adventists." In *The Encyclopedia of Religion in Australia*, edited by James Jupp, 563–6. Port Melbourne: Cambridge University Press, 2009.
Karney, Robyn, ed. *Cinema Year By Year*. London: Dorling Kindersley, 1996.
Karskens, Grace. *People of the River: Lost Worlds of Early Australia*. Sydney: Allen and Unwin, 2020.
Kennedy, Thomas C. *British Quakerism, 1860–1920: The Transformation of a Religious Community*. Oxford: Oxford University Press, 2001.
Kent, Alan M. *Pulp Methodism: The Lives and Literature of Silas, Joseph and Salome Hocking, Three Cornish Novelists*. St Austell, Cornwall: Cornish Hillside Publications, 2002.
Kerr, Joan. "Churches – Our Australian Architectural Heritage." In *The Future of Our Historic Churches: Conflict and Reconciliation*, edited by John Henwood and Tom Hazell, 8–16. Melbourne: National Trust of Australia (Vic.), 1988.
Kerr, Joan, ed. *Heritage: The National Women's Art Book, 500 works by 500 Australian Women Artists from Colonial Times to 1955*. Sydney: Art and Australia, 1995.
Kershaw, Ron. "May, William Lewis (1861–1925)." *Australian Dictionary of Biography*. Available online: http://adb.anu.edu.au/biography/may-william-lewis-7538 (accessed July 12, 2016).
Khan, Nosheen. *Women's Poetry of the First World War*. Lexington: University Press of Kentucky, 1988.
Kingston, Beverley. *Oxford History of Australia: Glad, Confident Morning, 1860–1900*, vol. 3. Oxford: Oxford University Press, 1988.
Knight, Mark, and Emma Mason. *Nineteenth-Century Religion and Literature: An Introduction*. Oxford: Oxford University Press, 2006.
Krause, Gary D. "The Growth of the Seventh-day Adventist Church in Sydney and Melbourne: 1885–1918." In *Seventh-day Adventists in the South Pacific 1885–1985*, edited by Noel Clapham, 118–27. Warburton, Vic.: Signs, 1985.
Langton, Marcia, and Bruno David. "William Ricketts' Sanctuary, Victoria (Australia): Sculpting Nature and Culture in a Primitivist Theme Park." *Journal of Material Culture* 8, no. 2 (2003): 145–68.

Lake, Marilyn, Henry Reynolds, Mark McKenna, and Joy Damousi. *What's Wrong with ANZAC? The Militarisation of Australian History*. Sydney: University of New South Wales Press, 2010.

Lake, Meredith. *The Bible in Australia: A Cultural History*. Randwick, NSW: NewSouth, 2018.

Lane, Belden. *Landscapes of the Sacred: Geography and Narrative in American Spirituality*. New York: Paulist Press, 1988.

Lester, Hiram J. "An Irish Precursor for Thomas Campbell's Declaration and Address." *Encounter* 50, no. 3 (Summer 1989): 247–67.

Lewis, Jack P. "James Turner Barclay: Explorer of Nineteenth-Century Jerusalem." *Biblical Archaeology* 51, no. 3 S (1988): 163–70.

Lewis, Miles, ed. *Victorian Churches*. Melbourne: National Trust, 1991.

Leyerle, Blake. "Landscape as Cartography in Early Christian Pilgrimage Narratives." *Journal of the American Academy of Religion* 64, no. 1 (1996): 119–43.

Lilburne, Geoffrey. *A Sense of Place: A Christian Theology of the Land*. Nashville: Abingdon Press, 1989.

Linder, Robert D. *The Long Tragedy: Australian Evangelical Christians and the Great War 1914–1918*. Adelaide: Openbook, 2000.

Lindley, Susan H. "Women and the Social Gospel Novel." *Church History* 54 (March 1985): 56–73.

Lindsay, Elaine. *Rewriting God: Spirituality in Contemporary Australian Women's Fiction*. Atlanta: Rodopi, 2000.

Lockley, Geoffrey Lindsay. *Congregationalism in Australia*, 2nd ed., edited and updated by Bruce Upham. Melbourne: Uniting Church Press, 2001.

Long, Burke O. *Imagining the Holy Land: Maps, Models and Fantasy Travels*. Bloomington: Indiana University Press, 2003.

Lovegrove, Deryck W. *Established Church, Sectarian People: Itinerancy and the Transformation of English Dissent 1780–1830*. Cambridge: Cambridge University Press, 1988.

McCracken, Victor. "The Restoration of Israel." *Restoration Quarterly* 47, no. 4 (2005), 207–20.

McKenna, Mark. *Looking for Blackfellas' Point: An Australian History of Place*. Sydney: University of New South Wales Press, 2002.

McKernan, Michael. *Australian Churches at War: Attitudes and Activities of the Major Churches 1914–1918*. Sydney: Catholic Theological Faculty; Canberra: Australian War Memorial, 1980.

Mack, Phyllis. *Heart Religion in the British Enlightenment: Gender and Emotion in Early Methodism*. Cambridge: Cambridge University Press, 2008.

Maddox, Randy L. "Holiness of Heart and Life: Lessons from North American Methodism." *Asbury Theological Journal* 51, no. 1 (1996): 151–72.

Manley, Ken R. *From Woolloomooloo to Eternity: A History of Australian Baptists*. Milton Keynes: Paternoster, 2006.

Mansfield, Joan. "Music: A Window on Australian Christian Life." In *Re-Visioning Australian Colonial Christianity: New Essays in the Australian Christian Experience 1788–1900*, edited by Mark Hutchinson and Edmund Campion, 131–52. Sydney: Centre for the Study of Australian Christianity, 1994.

Marks, Lynne. "The 'Hallelujah Lasses': Working-Class Women in The Salvation Army in English Canada, 1882–92." In *Gender Conflicts: New Essays in Women's History*, edited by Franca Iacovetta and Mariana Valverde, 67–117. Toronto: University of Toronto Press, 1992.

Marnin-Distelfeld, Shahar, and Edna Gorney. "Why Draw Flowers? Botanical Art, Nationalism, and Women's Contribution to Israeli Culture." *Anthropology of the Middle East* 14, no. 1 (2019): 44–69.

Matthews, Arnold Gwynne. *Calamy Revised: Being a Revision of Edmund Calamy's Account of the Ministers and Others Ejected and Silenced, 1660–62*. Oxford: Clarendon Press, 1988.

Mayne, Alan. *Representing the Slum: Popular Journalism in a Late Nineteenth-Century City*. Parkville: History Department, University of Melbourne, 1990.

Menz, Christopher. "Mary Packer Harris." Design and Art Australia Online. Available online: https://www.daao.org.au/bio/mary-packer-harris/biography/ (accessed September 29, 2016).

Menz, Christopher. "Mary P. Harris." In *Heritage: The National Women's Art Book, 500 Works by 500 Australian Women Artists from Colonial Times to 1955*, edited by Joan Kerr. Sydney: Art and Australia, 1995.

Miley, Caroline. *Beautiful and Useful: The Arts and Crafts Movement in Tasmania*. Launceston: Queen Victoria Museum and Art Gallery, 1987.

Mills, Alex. "One Nation Under God: The Christian Contribution to Australian Federation." *Church Heritage* 12, no. 1 (March 2001): 2–15.

Montefiore, Janet. "'Shining Pins and Wailing Shells': Women Poets and the Great War." In *Women and World War I: The Written Response*, edited by Dorothy Goldman, 51–72. London: Macmillan, 1993.

"Moonta Mines." *Organ Historical Trust of Australia*. Available online: http://www.ohta.org.au/organs/organs/MoontaMines.html (accessed January 12, 2015).

Morgan, David. "'For Christ and the Republic': Protestant Illustration and the History of Literacy in Nineteenth-Century America." In *The Visual Culture of American Religions*, edited by David Morgan and Sally M. Promey, 49–67. Berkeley: University of California Press, 2001.

Morgan, David. *Protestants and Pictures: Religion, Visual Culture, and the Age of American Mass Production*. New York: Oxford University Press, 1999.

Morgan, David. *The Sacred Gaze: Religious Visual Culture in Theory and Practice*. Berkeley: University of California Press, 2005.

Moses, John A. "Was There an Anzac Theology?" *Colloquium* 35, no. 1 (2003): 3–13.

Moyles, R. G. "William Booth's Dream of an Alberta 'Oversea Colony.'" *Alberta History* (Summer 2016): 21–5.

Munro, Doug, and Brij V. Lal, eds. *Texts and Contexts: Reflections in Pacific Islands Historiography*. Honolulu: University of Hawai'i Press, 2006.

Munro, Marita. *A Struggle for Identity and Direction: A History of Victorian Baptists, c.1960–2000*. Berlin: Peter Lang, forthcoming.

Murdoch, Norman. *Christian Warfare in Rhodesia-Zimbabwe: The Salvation Army and African Liberation, 1891–1991*. London: Lutterworth Press, 2015.

Murdoch, Norman. *Origins of the Salvation Army*. Knoxville: University of Tennessee Press, 1994.

Murphy, John. *A Decent Provision: Australian Welfare Policy, 1870–1949*. Burlington, VT: Ashgate, 2011.

Newton, Ken. *A History of the Brethren in Australia*. Indooroopilly, Qld.: Aberdeen Desktop Publishing, 1999.

Norton, Leonie. *Women of Flowers: Botanical Art in Australia from the 1830s to the 1960s.* Canberra: National Library of Australia, 2009.

Oats, William Nicolle. *Backhouse and Walker: A Quaker View of the Australian Colonies, 1832–1838.* Sandy Bay, Tas.: Australian Yearly Meeting of Religious Society of Friends, 1981.

Oats, William Nicolle. *The Friends' School, 1887–1961: The Seventy-Fifth Anniversary.* Hobart: The Friends' School, 1961.

Oats, William Nicolle. *A Question of Survival: Quakers in Australia in the Nineteenth Century.* St Lucia, Qld.: University of Queensland Press, 1985.

Oats, William Nicolle. "Unwin, Ernest Ewart (1881–1944)." *Australian Dictionary of Biography.* Available online: http://adb.anu.edu.au/biography/unwin-ernest-ewart-8899/text15633 (accessed July 11, 2016).

Obenzinger, Hilton. *American Palestine: Melville, Twain, and the Holy Land Mania.* Princeton, NJ: Princeton University Press, 1999.

O'Brien, Anne. *God's Willing Workers: Women and Religion in Australia.* Sydney: University of New South Wales Press, 2005.

O'Brien, Anne. "Religion." In *The Cambridge History of Australia: Indigenous and Colonial Australia,* vol. 1, edited by Alison Bashford and Stuart Macintyre, 414–37. Melbourne: Cambridge University Press, 2013.

O'Brien, Glen. "Australian Methodist Religious Experience." In *Methodism in Australia: A History,* edited by Glen O'Brien and Hilary M. Carey, 167–80. Farnham: Ashgate, 2015.

O'Dwyer, Patricia, ed. "Early Balwyn and Deepdene Churches." *A Compilation of Newsletter Articles.* Balwyn Historical Society (2010): 3–5.

Olsen, Penny. *Collecting Ladies: Ferdinand von Mueller and Women Botanical Artists.* Canberra: National Library of Australia, 2013.

Parker, David. "Queensland Baptist Churches, 1849–1929, by Date of Commencement with Some Building Erection Dates." Available online: http://www.dparker.net.au/churches1849-1929/index1.html (accessed September 30, 2020).

Parr, Robert. "Sanitarium Health Food Company." In *Seventh-day Adventists in the South Pacific 1885–1985,* edited by Noel Clapham, 98–111. Warburton, Vic.: Signs, 1985.

Patrick, Arthur N. "Doctrine and Deed: Adventism's Encounter with its Society in Nineteenth-Century Australia." In *Adventist History in the South Pacific: 1885–1918,* edited by Arthur J. Ferch, 19–29. Wahroonga, NSW: South Pacific Division of Seventh-day Adventists, 1986.

Phillips, Richard. "Thomas Campbell: A Reappraisal Based on Backgrounds." *Restoration Quarterly* 49, no. 2 (2007): 75–102.

Phillips, Walter. *James Jefferis: Prophet of Federation.* Melbourne: Australian Scholarly, 1993.

Piggin, Stuart, and Robert D. Linder. *Attending to the National Soul: Evangelical Christians in Australian History, 1914–2014.* Melbourne: Monash University Press, 2019.

Piggin, Stuart, and Robert D. Linder. *The Fountain of Public Prosperity: Evangelical Christians in Australian History.* Melbourne: Monash University Press, 2018.

Piggin, Stuart. "Power and Religion in a Modern State: Desecularisation in Australian History." *Journal of Religious History* 38, no. 2 (September 2014): 320–40.

Pike, Douglas. *Paradise of Dissent: South Australia 1829–1857.* Melbourne: Melbourne University Press, 1967.

Plank, Geoffrey. "'The Flame of Life was Kindled in Animal and Sensitive Creatures': One Quaker Colonist's View of Animal Life." *Church History* 76, no. 3 (2007): 569–90.

Pointon, Marcia. "Quakerism and Visual Culture." *Art History* 20, no. 3 (September 1997): 397–431.
Potter, Jane. *Boys in Khaki, Girls in Print: Women's Literary Responses to the Great War*. Oxford: Oxford University Press, 2008.
Prentis, Malcolm. "Methodism in New South Wales, 1855–1902." In *Methodism in Australia: A History*, edited by Glen O'Brien and Hilary M. Carey, 30–44. Farnham: Ashgate, 2015.
Quaker Faith and Practice: The Book of Christian Discipline of the Yearly Meeting of the Religious Society of Friends (Quakers) in Britain (5th ed.). https://qfp.quaker.org.uk/passage/25-05/.
Rae, Murray. *Architecture and Theology: The Art of Place*. Waco, TX: Baylor University Press, 2017.
Ratkowsky, D. A. "A Little-known Scientific Club in Hobart, Tasmania—Its Early Years." *Papers and Proceedings of the Royal Society of Tasmania* 144 (2010): 37–42.
Read, Peter. *Haunted Earth*. Sydney: University of New South Wales Press, 2003.
Reed, Thomas Thornton. *Historic Churches of Australia*. South Melbourne: Macmillan, 1978.
Richey, Russell E. *Denominationalism Illustrated and Explained*. Eugene, OR: Cascade, 2013.
Richey, Russell E. *Early American Methodism*. Bloomington: Indiana University Press, 1991.
Richey, Russell E. *Methodism in the American Forest*. New York: Oxford University Press, 2015.
Rickard, John. *A Family Romance: The Deakins at Home*. Carlton South, Vic.: Melbourne University Press, 1996.
Robbins, Keith. "Nonconformity and the State, ca. 1750–2012." In *T&T Clark Companion to Nonconformity*, edited by Robert Pope, 75–88. London: Bloomsbury T&T Clark, 2013.
Roberts, David Andrew, and Margaret Reeson. "Wesleyan Methodist Missions to Australia and the Pacific." In *Methodism in Australia: A History*, edited by Glen O'Brien and Hilary M. Carey, 197–210. Farnham: Ashgate, 2015.
Roberts, Winsome. "The Churches' Role in Constituting an Australian Citizenry." In *Spirit of Australia II: Religion in Citizenship and National Life*, edited by Brian Howe and Philip Hughes, 64–8. Hindmarsh, SA: Australian Theological Forum Press, 2003.
Robertson, Enid L. *Alison Ashby's Wildflowers of Southern Australia*. Adelaide: South Australian Museum Board and the Botanic Gardens Board, 1981.
Robins, Roger. "Vernacular American Landscape: Methodists, Camp Meetings, and Social Respectability." *Religion and American Culture* 4, no. 2 (Summer 1994): 165–91.
Roe, Michael. *Quest for Authority in Eastern Australia 1835–1851*. Parkville: Melbourne University Press, 1965.
Rogers, Stephanie S. *Inventing the Holy Land: American Protestant Pilgrimage to Palestine, 1865–1941*. Lanham, MD: Lexington Books, 2011.
Rolls, Mitchell. "William Ricketts Sanctuary Is a Racist Anachronism but Can It Foster Empathy?" *Conversation*, May 25, 2018. Available online: https://theconversation.com/friday-essay-william-ricketts-sanctuary-is-a-racist-anachronism-but-can-it-foster-empathy-96274 (accessed January 18, 2021).
Saliers, Don E. "Liturgical Aesthetics: The Travail of Christian Worship." In *Arts, Theology and the Church: New Intersections*, edited by Kimberly Vrudny and Wilson Yates, 179–99. Cleveland: The Pilgrim Press, 2005.

"Sanitarium Factory Complex and Garden." *Victorian Heritage Database*. Available online: http://vhd.heritage.vic.gov.au/search/nattrust_result_detail/ 70262 (accessed January 10, 2015).

Schaffer, Kay. *Women and the Bush*. Sydney: Cambridge University Press, 1988.

Schedvin, C. B. "Rivett, Albert (1855–1934)." *Australian Dictionary of Biography*. Available online: http://adb.anu.edu.au/biography/rivett-albert-8218/text14381.

Sebag-Montefiore, Simon. *Jerusalem: The Biography*. London: Phoenix, 2011.

Seed, John. *Dissenting Histories: Politics, History and Memory in Eighteenth- Century England*. Edinburgh: Edinburgh University Press, 2008.

Serle, Geoffrey. "James Service." *Australian Dictionary of Biography*. Available online: http://adb.anu.edu.au/biography/service-james-4561 (accessed January 18, 2015).

Sharkey, Michael. "'But Who Considers Woman Day by Day?': Australian Women Poets and World War I." *Australian Literary Studies* 23, no. 1 (May 2007): 63–78.

Sheldrake, Philip. *Spaces for the Sacred: Place, Memory, and Identity*. London: SCM Press, 2001.

Silberman, Neil Asher. *Digging for God and Country: Exploration, Archaeology, and the Secret Struggle for the Holy Land, 1799–1917*. New York: Knopf, 1982.

Simpson, James. *Burning to Read: English Fundamentalism and its Reformation Opponents*. Cambridge, MA: Belknap Press, 2007.

Sivasundaram, Sujit. *Nature and the Godly Empire: Science and Evangelical Mission in the Pacific, 1795–1850*. Cambridge: Cambridge University Press, 2005.

Sleight, Simon. "'For the Sake of Effect': Youth on Display and the Politics of Performance." *History Australia* 6, no. 3 (2009): 71.1–71.22.

Smith, Erin A. "'What Would Jesus Do?': The Social Gospel and the Literary Marketplace." *Book History* 10 (2007): 193–221.

Snape, Michael. *God and the British Soldier: Religion and the British Army in the First and Second World Wars*. New York: Routledge, 2005.

Stenhouse, John. "Darwinism in New Zealand, 1859–1900." In *Disseminating Darwinism: The Role of Place, Race, Religion and Gender*, edited by Ronald L. Numbers and John Stenhouse, 61–89. Cambridge: Cambridge University Press, 1999.

Stenhouse, John. "Response by John Stenhouse." In *Science and Theology: Questions at the Interface*, edited by Murray Rae, Hilary Regan, and John Stenhouse, 87–96. Edinburgh: T& T Clark, 1994.

Stevenson, Charles. "Mary Harris (1891–1978)." Quaker Learning Australia. Available online: http://www.qlau.quakers.org.au/resources/quaker-biographies/mary-harris/ (accessed August 1, 2016).

Stevenson, Charles. *With Unhurried Pace: A Brief History of Quakers in Australia*. Toorak, Vic.: The Religious Society of Friends, 1973.

Stewart, Pamela J., and Andrew Strathern, eds. *Landscape, Memory and History: Anthropological Perspectives*. London: Pluto Press, 2005.

Swain, Shurlee. *Constructing the Good Christian Woman*. Melbourne: Uniting Church Historical Society, 1993.

Swain, Shurlee. "The Poor People of Melbourne." In *The Outcasts of Melbourne*, edited by Graeme Davison, David Dunstan and Chris McConville, 91–112. Sydney: Allen and Unwin, 1985.

Swain, Shurlee, with Renate Howe. *Single Mothers and Their Children: Disposal, Punishment and Survival in Australia*. Cambridge: Cambridge University Press, 1995.

Taylor, Dennis. *English Brass Bands and Their Music, 1860–1930*. Newcastle: Cambridge Scholars, 2011.

Taylor, Richard. *How To Read A Church*. London: Rider, 2003.

Thomas, Nicholas. *In Oceania: Visions, Artifacts, Histories*. Durham, NC: Duke University Press, 1997.

Thompson, Roger C. *Religion in Australia: A History*. Melbourne: Oxford University Press, 1994.

Trim, John B. "The Origin and Development of Adventist Health Work." In *Seventh-day Adventists in the South Pacific 1885–1985*, edited by Noel Clapham, 152–63. Warburton, Vic.: Signs, 1985.

Tuck, Ruth. "Harris, Mary Packer (1891–1978)." *Australian Dictionary of Biography*. Available online: http://adb.anu.edu.au/biography/harris-mary-packer-10438/text18507 (accessed July 11, 2016).

Tunnicliffe, Wayne. *Tradition Today: Indigenous Art in Australia*. Sydney: Art Gallery of New South Wales, 2014. Quoted in "Otto Pareroultja." Art Gallery of New South Wales. Available online: https://www.artgallery.nsw.gov.au/collection/artists/pareroultja-otto/ (accessed November 21, 2016).

Turner, Naomi. *Sinews of Sectarian Warfare?: State Aid in New South Wales 1836–1862*. Canberra: Australian National University Press, 1972.

Ussher, Blair. "The Salvation War." In *The Outcasts of Melbourne*, edited by Graeme Davison, David Dunstan, and Chris McConville, 124–39. Sydney: Allen and Unwin, 1985.

Vogel, Lester Irwin. *To See a Promised Land: Americans and the Holy Land in the Nineteenth Century*. University Park, PA: Pennsylvania University Press, 1993.

Wakeling, Chris. "The Nonconformist Traditions: Chapels, Change and Continuity." In *The Victorian Church*, edited by Chris Brooks and Andrew Saint, 82–97. Manchester: Manchester University Press, 1995.

Walker, Pamela. *Pulling the Devil's Kingdom Down: The Salvation Army in Victorian Britain*. London: University of California Press, 2001.

Wallace-Crabbe, Chris. *Melbourne or the Bush: Essays on Australian Literature and Society*. Sydney: Angus and Robertson, 1974.

Walsham, Alexandra. *The Reformation of Landscape: Religion, Identity and Memory in Early Modern Britain and Ireland*. Oxford: Oxford University Press, 2011.

Ward, W. Reginald. *Religion and Society in England, 1790–1850*. London: B. T. Batsford, 1972.

Watts, Michael R. *The Dissenters, Volume I: From the Reformation to the French Revolution*. Oxford: Clarendon Press, 1978.

Watts, Michael R. *The Dissenters, Volume II: The Expansion of Evangelical Nonconformity 1791–1859*. Oxford: Clarendon Press, 1995.

Webb, Robert Kiefer. "The Limits of Religious Liberty: Theology and Criticism in Nineteenth-Century England." In *Freedom and Religion in the Nineteenth Century*, edited by Richard Helmstadter, 120–49. Stanford, CA: Stanford University Press, 1997.

Weiner, Myron. *Sons of the Soil: Migration and Ethnic Conflict in India*. Princeton, NJ: Princeton University Press, 1978.

Weir, Christine. "Deeply Interested in These Children Whom You Have Not Seen." *Journal of Pacific History* 48, no. 1 (2013): 43–62.

Welborn, Suzanne. *Lords of Death: A People, A Place, A Legend*. Fremantle: Fremantle Arts Centre Press, 1982.

"Welcome to Christian Community Churches of Australia." Christian Community Churches of Australia. Available online: http://cccaust.org (accessed July 12, 2017).

Wellings, Martin. "'Pulp Methodism' Revisited: The Literature and Significance of Silas and Joseph Hocking." In *The Church and Literature: Studies in Church History*, vol.

48, edited by Peter Clarke and Charlotte Methuen, 362–73. Rochester, NY: Published for The Ecclesiastical History Society by The Boydell Press, 2012.
West, Ern. *A History of the Christian Brethren Assemblies in Western Australia*. Western Australia: self-published, 1993.
Wilkey, Glaucia Vasconselos. *Worship and Culture: Foreign Country or Homeland*. Grand Rapids, MI: Wm. B. Eerdmans, 2014.
"William Mountford Kinsey Vale." Collingwood Historical Society (Vic.). Available online: http://collingwoodhs.org.au/view/collingwood-notables/entry /177/ (accessed July 19, 2017).
Williams, John. "'Art, War and Agrarian Myths': Australian Reactions to Modernism 1913–1931." In *An Anzac Muster: War and Society in Australia and New Zealand 1914–1918 and 1939–1945*, edited by Judith Smart and Tony Wood, 40–57. Clayton, Vic.: Monash Publications in History, 1992.
Willis, W. Waite. "The Archaeology of Palestine and the Archaeology of Faith: Between a Rock and a Hard Place." In *What Has Archaeology to Do with Faith?* edited by James H. Charlesworth and Walter P. Weaver, 75–111. Philadelphia, PA: Trinity Press, 2002.
Wilson, Elisabeth. "'The Irregularity of Killing People': Tasmanian Brethren Responses to World War I." *Tasmanian Historical Studies* 14 (2009): 25–52.
Winston, Diane. "All The World's a Stage: The Performed Religion of the Salvation Army." In *Practicing Religion in the Age of the Media*, edited by Stewart M. Hoover and Lynn Schofield Clark, 113–37. New York: Columbia University Press, 2002.
Winston, Diane. *Red-Hot and Righteous: The Urban Religion of the Salvation Army*. Cambridge, MA: Harvard University Press, 1999.
Winter, Jay. *Sites of Memory, Sites of Mourning: The Great War in European Cultural History*. Cambridge: Cambridge University Press, 1995.
Winton, Tim. *Island Home: A Landscape Memoir*. Melbourne: Penguin Australia, 2015.
Yates, Nigel. *Buildings, Faith, and Worship: The Liturgical Arrangement of Anglican Churches 1600 –1900*. Oxford: Oxford University Press, 1993.
Yothers, Brian. *The Romance of the Holy Land in American Travel Writing, 1790–1876*. Burlington, VT: Ashgate, 2007.
Zainu'ddin, A. G. Thomson. "Fitchett, William Henry (1841–1928)." *Australian Dictionary of Biography*. Available online: http://adb.anu.edu.au/biography/fitchett-william-henry-6179 (accessed October 26, 2016).
Zavitz, Erin E. "Artistic Presence: A Sketch of the History of Art in Quaker Schools." *Quaker History* 94, no. 1 (Spring 2005): 22–40.

Index

Act of Toleration 14
Act of Uniformity 1, 13–14
Act to Promote the Building of Churches and Chapels. *See* Church Act
Adams, Leonard 127
Adderley, James 95
adventure 67, 89–91, 93–6, 98, 102, 138–9
Anglican Church. *See* Church of England
Arcadia 47, 123, 160 n.69
archaeology 24, 26, 28, 32–33, 38, 133, 137
architecture 2–11, 111, 114
Arminianism 15
Art (formerly National) Gallery of South Australia 113, 127–8
Arts and Crafts Movement 110, 111–12, 115–17, 122, 129, 131.
   See also School of Arts and Crafts
Ashby, Alison 114, 185 n.96
Ashby, Edwin 110, 112, 114
Aston, Tilly 93, 95
atonement theory 74

Backhouse, James 117, 185 n.89
Baker, John Gilbert 112, 185 n.89
Banks, Joseph 114, 117
baptism 25, 30, 76, 121
Baptist churches 5, 7, 9, 10, 14, 16, 26, 93, 115
Barbizon School 122
Barclay, James Turner 24–6, 33
Barker, James 44, 46, 159 n.60
beauty
  aesthetic 2, 36, 101, 116–17
  divine 12, 29, 109–11, 114, 117–24, 126, 131, 134, 139
  ethical 112, 120, 125
  "Testament of Beauty" 112
  wartime 76, 81
Bellchambers, Thomas 186 n.116
belonging

  in Australia 76, 79–80, 83–7, 98, 107, 122, 139
  beyond Australia 27
  and exile 13–14
  in Papuan mission fields 96
  on the road 37–8, 136–7
Benson, George 125, 128
Betts, Margery Ruth
  biography 67
  poetry 68, 72–4, 78, 80–1, 84–6, 136, 138
Betts, Robert Arthur 67
Bevan, Beatrice
  biography 66
  poetry 68, 72–3, 75, 78–85, 136, 138
Bevan, Llewelyn 48, 66, 70, 82
Bevan, Louisa 66
Bevan, Willett 66, 83
Bible
  as authoritative 4, 15, 24–5, 28, 32–3, 38, 94, 98, 139
  interpretation 33, 73, 92, 94, 119
  places named after biblical places 26–7
Bible books
  Acts of the Apostles 25, 32, 44, 98, 121
  Deuteronomy 2
  Exodus 27
  Ezekiel 1, 72–3, 102, 133
  Genesis 105
  Isaiah 89, 115, 119–20, 127, 136
  John 48
  Luke 27, 37, 47, 87, 94
  Micah 119, 133
  Nehemiah 33
  Proverbs 33
  Psalms 4, 80, 105
  Revelation 26
  Song of Solomon 33
birds 28–9, 79–81, 106, 109, 118–19, 122, 129, 153 n.51
Black, Dorrit 125

Blake, William 129
Blake Prize for Religious Art 124
Boake, Barcroft 93
Booth, Catherine 41–2, 47
Booth, Cornelie Schoch 39–40, 54–6, 60–1
Booth, Herbert 19, 40–1, 47–51, 54–6, 58–61, 136
Booth, William 40–2, 45–8, 51, 60
Bourke, Richard 16
botanical art. *See* natural history art
Bowes, Joseph
   biography 90–1
   The Jackaroos 91, 97, 103, 138
   Pals: Young Australians in Sport and Adventure 91, 98–9, 100, 105
Brethren church at Balcatta 7
Bridges, Robert 112, 123
Brooke, Rupert 76
Bruce, Mary Grant 67, 98
Buckingham, Marjorie 93
Bunning, W. C. 26
Bunyan, John 13, 23, 133
   The Pilgrim's Progress 23–4, 31
Burr, Aaron 23
bush myths 65, 76–9, 87, 92–3, 100–1

Calamy, Edmund 44
calling 27, 37, 42, 85–7, 89–90, 94, 101, 105, 136–7
Campbell, Alexander 5, 22, 26, 28, 30
Campbell, Thomas 5, 22
Canaan. *See* Promised Land
Carleton, Caroline 66, 79
Carne, Thomas Clement 93
Catholic Church 11, 16, 18, 24, 27, 30–1, 52, 68, 73, 123
Cavell, Edith 75, 169 n.88
chapel architecture. *See* architecture
Chesterton, Gilbert Keith 123
Christian Community Churches of Australia. *See* Brethren
Christian Zionism 26
Church Act 16–17
church and state. *See* Act of Toleration; Act of Uniformity; Church Act; Dissent; state aid; Voluntary Principle
Church of England (Anglican) 2, 13–16, 19, 32, 34, 46, 51–2, 68, 73, 115–16

Church of the Nativity 31, 34, 136
Churches of Christ
   Australasian Christian Standard 23–4, 31
   belief, origins and practice 22, 25–6
   Christian Pioneer 23–4, 44
   Coolgardie 5–6
   Hobart 23
   Melbourne 23
   Restorationism 22, 25
Churchill, Winston (author) 95
cinematograph. *See* filmmaking
circuit ministry 4, 49, 94–5, 107, 136
Clark, Manning 139
Clarke, George 17
Cocks, Nicholas
   biography 67–8
   poetry 73–4, 76–7, 79–80, 84–5
Communion (Lord's Supper) 5, 72, 78, 121
Congregational Church
   belief, origins and practice 69–70
   Camden College 67
   Congregational College of Victoria 67
   Congregational Union of South Australia 71
   Deepdene 70
   Gawler 66, 83, 85
   Kew 67
   Mount Drummond 70
   Pitt Street, Sydney 67
   Victorian Independent 42, 71, 86
   Whitefield 70
   Wollongong 70
conversion 15, 26, 37, 42, 47, 55, 61, 63, 94, 105–6
Cotton, John 26
Cotton family in Tasmania 122
Crane, Olive 67, 76–7
Creeth, Helen 115
Creeth, May 115
cross 4, 72, 74–5, 84, 114, 124. *See also* atonement theory; Salvation Army "Soldiers of the Cross"; Southern Cross
Cunningham, James 115
Cyclorama 36–7

Dale, Robert William 8–9
Dark, Eleanor 125, 127
Darwin, Charles 118

Deane, Wallace 93
Dickinson, Emily 67
Dissent
　origins 1–2, 13–15
　Paradise of 17, 104, 149 n.44
　See also Act of Toleration; Act of Uniformity; Bible as authoritative; Church Act; state aid; Voluntary Principle
distance 27, 34, 48–9, 60, 65, 68–9, 83–5, 87
drought 2, 40, 79, 93, 187 n.145
Duncan, Handasyde 17

Eden 47, 59–60, 81, 102, 139.
　See also Salvation Army welfare institutions
education 15, 17, 59, 91–2, 110–11, 116–17, 121
Eggleston, Edward 94
empire 12, 27, 45, 49, 70–6, 84
Enlightenment 15, 22, 28, 37, 103, 105, 139
　empiricism 33–4.
　　See also Locke
　reason 100, 103–5, 139
eschatology. See Christian Zionism; heaven; Holy Mountain; Jesus Christ Second Coming; peaceable kingdom; Religious Society of Friends
Eusebius 44
Evans, Matilda Jane 93
Ewers, David 44

fairies 78, 86
Farrar, Frederic 24, 30, 31, 34–7
Federation of Australia 18–20, 50, 70, 82, 93, 134
Fenner, Charles 111
filmmaking 19, 20, 40–1, 43, 55, 58, 60–1, 135
Finnin, Mary 123
fire 9, 50, 79, 83, 89, 103
First Nations
　absence and dispossession 1–2, 12, 18, 51, 78, 90–1, 96–8, 100, 124, 138
　Arrernte 20, 111, 126, 129–31
　art and appropriation 111, 123–31, 138

Kapurn 5, 144 n.41
Kaurna 3, 20, 124
Kulin 9
Mandandanji 97
Muwinina 4
Narungga 3
Native Police 91
Papuan peoples in fiction 96–7, 103, 105–6
Wangkathaa 5, 144 n.41
Whadjuk 7
Wiradjuri 5
"Yellow Billy" 98, 105, 178 n.94
Yuggera 9
See also Hermannsburg School
Fitchett, William Henry 93
Fletcher, Winifred Scott 115
flood 9, 93, 100, 105, 136
flowers
　Australian 28, 109, 122
　British 76, 81
　Palestinian 28–9, 31
　Violet Memory Day 81–2
　wattle 65, 79, 80, 82–4, 86–7, 119, 135, 138
Fox, George 113, 116, 117
Foxe, John 44
Franc, Maud Jeanne. See Evans
Francis, Ivor 120
Frazer, James 91
Freemasonry 83
Friends' School. See Religious Society of Friends
Fudge, Olga 126–8

Gallipoli 72, 74, 76, 78, 84, 112
gardens 52, 75, 78, 81, 83–4, 94, 106, 113–14, 121, 125, 137.
　See also Eden, Arcadia
Gellert, Leon 68–9
Gerome, Jean-Leon 61
Gibbs, Philip 81
Ginzberg, Carlo 11
God
　in Creation 107, 109–10, 119, 122–4, 127, 139–40
　Creator 31, 119
　estrangement from 97, 101
　Kingdom of 2, 15, 32, 47, 95, 110

and nation 18, 27, 69–73, 104
oneness 129, 131
presence in bush 1–2, 101, 103, 105–7, 113, 139
presence in landscape of mission 12, 89, 93, 96, 102, 107
Providence 103–4
and reason 28, 100, 103
See also Jesus Christ; Spirit; supernatural
Gordon, Adam Lindsay 29, 66, 83
Great War. *See* war

Harris, Corra 94–5
Harris, Mary Packer 109
art 119–20, 124, 127–8, 138, 188 n.179
Art, the Torch of Life 111–12, 123–4, 128, 131
biography 111–13
Bundilla Sanctuary 113, 125, 129, 130
The Cosmic Rhythm of Art and Literature 112, 119, 125, 127
Hazelwood, Rex 115
heaven 37, 40, 42, 74, 81, 86
Hermannsburg School 126, 138
Heysen, Hans 111, 120, 131
Hicks, Edward 115, 119
historiography 11, 13, 15, 26, 124, 127, 133–5, 137, 139
omission of women 66, 68
Hocking, Joseph 2, 12, 94
Hocking, Salome 94
Hocking, Silas 94
Holliday, Margaret (pseud. Helen Graham) 93, 174 n.29
Holy Land
Bethlehem 31–2, 34, 136
Emmaus 22, 37, 87
Galilee 29–30, 34–5
Jerusalem 23, 25–8, 31, 33–4, 36, 126
Jordan River 21, 28, 30–1, 33, 35, 37, 139
Palestinian people 30, 32, 34–5
souvenirs 30–1
tourism 21, 24–5, 27–8, 31, 35
See also flowers; lantern (limelight) shows; Ludbrook; Maston; travel writing
Holy Mountain. *See* Religious Society of Friends
Hope Hume, E. 70–1

Imbarndarinja, Lindsay 126
Inauguration of Commonwealth of Australia. *See* Federation of Australia
Indigenous Australians. *See* First Nations
Ingamells, Rex 123
innocence 4, 59, 74, 80–1, 86, 138

Jefferies, John 44–5
Jefferis, James 70
Jekyll, Gertrude 83
Jennings Carmichael, Grace 80
Jesus Christ
absence 73, 93, 97
emulation of 29, 94, 113–14, 133, 136–7
and patriotism 73
presence 22, 25, 30, 35–6, 38, 106, 136, 139
Second Coming 25–7, 160 n.70
walking with 28, 35–8, 136–7
See also God; Spirit
Johnston, Joseph 17

Kerr, Alan J. 73, 84
Keswick Military Hospital 83

landmarks 1, 53, 75, 85, 136
Lang, John Dunmore 9
lantern (limelight) slides 11, 22–3, 26, 36–7, 39–41, 43, 50, 54–5, 59–62, 136–7
Locke, John 14–15
Ludbrook, Albert Milton 22–3, 27–8, 31–8, 136–7

MacKellar, Dorothea 76, 80, 84
McCrae, Dorothy Frances 68
McGarvey, John William 24, 30
Marvell, Andrew 14
Maston, Aaron Burr 21, 23–4, 27–38, 136–7
Mather, Cotton 26
May, Alfred and W. Lewis 114
Melville, Herman 25
memorials 75, 81–2, 85
memory 9, 13, 34, 38, 65, 68, 72, 78–82, 85, 87, 104
Methodism
belief, origins and practice 93–4

Bible Christians 3, 143 n.23, 144 n.32
Bondi 91
Cobar 4
Cornwall 3–4, 94, 104
Epping 91
heart 100–5, 107.
See also Sargant *Sweet Heart of the Bush*
Home Missions 89–91
Johnsonville 4
Moonta 3–4, 104
New Connexion 3
Primitive 3, 5, 143 n.23, 144 n.32
visual imagination 90, 94, 107
Wesleyan 3–4, 16–17, 26, 51, 115, 144 n.32
Milner, Thomas Hughes 22
Milton, John 22, 89, 93, 106
modernity 10, 32, 34, 38, 48, 50, 58–60, 124, 126, 131, 135, 138–9
Moran, Patrick 18
Morland, George 121–2
Morris, William 116
motherhood 34, 54, 65, 68, 73, 78–81, 83, 85–7, 91, 102, 105
Mountford, Charles P. 125, 128
Mudd, Christopher 1–2, 60, 106
music
of birds 28–9
brass bands 4, 45, 54, 136
hymns 4, 40, 58, 67, 104
lullabies 68
services of song 43
of waves 89
See also Salvation Army performance
mysticism 119, 121, 123–4, 126, 128–9, 138–9, 187 n.136

Namatjira, Albert 111, 125–6
natural history 2, 41, 91, 106, 110, 114, 117–18, 137
art and illustration 12, 109, 117–18, 122, 131
Nonconformity. See Dissent

O'Reilly, Maurice J. 68
Orthodox in the Holy Land 24, 30–1
Owen, John 14

pacifism 69–71, 119, 123.
See also Peace Society
Papua
Australian territorial administration 91, 96, 174 n.23
colonialism 96, 101
Methodist missions 136, 177 n.70.
See also Roughley "The Locked Door"
Salvation Army plans 51
paradise. See Eden
Pareroultja, Otto 126, 128
Parkinson, Sydney 117
Paterson, Andrew Barton "Banjo" 76, 92–3, 153 n.51
patriotism 2, 18, 50, 122–3, 133, 135, 138, 140.
in war 65–6, 68–9, 70–4, 77–80, 82–4
See also Federation of Australia
Payne, George Warren 93
Peace Society 70–1, 183 n.54.
See also pacifism
peaceable kingdom. See Religious Society of Friends
Penn, William 14, 115, 117
persecution
Act of Uniformity 14
Salvation Army 19, 44–5, 60
Perry, Joseph 41, 50–1, 60–1, 137
pilgrimage 11, 22, 24, 27, 95–6, 136–7.
See also Bunyan *The Pilgrim's Progress*
Pink, Olive 114
Pitts, Lillian 115
plaining. See Religious Society of Friends
Presbyterian Church 9, 23, 141 n.4
Preston, Margaret 111, 122–4, 126–8
primitivism
anthropology 91, 123–5, 127
religion 6, 11, 26
Promised Land 1, 27, 95, 133
prosperity 3, 10, 24, 66, 139

Quakers. See Religious Society of Friends

Red Cross 82–3
redemption 46, 72–5, 80
religious liberty 12–15, 17–19, 49, 69, 71, 134–5, 140
Religious Society of Friends
Adelaide 3, 112, 131

aesthetics. *See below* plaining
art heritage 114–16
belief, origins and practice 113–14
General Meeting for Australia 114, 116
The Friends' School, Hobart 110, 112, 116–17
Holy Mountain 115, 119, 129–31, 138. *See also* Isaiah 11
Inner Light 111, 113, 120, 122, 138
London Yearly Meeting 3, 114
"Nature Notes" 118
peaceable kingdom 115, 119–22, 129, 131. *See also* Hicks
plaining 113–16, 118, 131
Tasmania 116, 122
See also natural history; pacifism; gardens
Rentoul, Laurence 68
Restorationism. *See* Churches of Christ
reunion 85–6, 134
revelation 36, 90, 95, 113–14, 121, 133, 139–40
Ricketts, William 129–31
Rivett, Albert 70–1, 167 n.47
Robey, Elinor 114
Robinson, Edward 24, 33
Romanticism 30, 65, 72, 106
Roughley, Edna
  biography 91–2
  The Locked Door 89, 91, 96–7, 101–6
  "The Lost Road" 91, 101–3, 105
Ruskin, John 112, 116–17, 131

sacrifice 65, 72–5, 80
Salvation Army, The
  Ballarat 41, 43, 49, 52
  Bathurst 5, 49
  belief, origins and practice 41–2, 45
  Collingwood 52
  Darwin 44–5
  Fiji 51
  Hobart 4–5, 49
  Indonesia (Java, East Indies) 51
  Limelight Department/Biorama Company 19, 41, 43. *See below* performance
  London 40, 43, 45–6, 56
  Melbourne 41, 43–4, 49, 51–2, 61
  Moonta 52
  New York 43, 46, 52
  North Melbourne (Hotham) 52
  performance 39–41, 43–5, 50–2, 54–63, 137
  Prahran 52, 56
  "Social Salvation" 54–60
  "Soldiers of the Cross" 60–2
  War Cry, The 41–3, 47–8, 51–3, 55, 59–61, 134
  welfare institutions 41, 46–7, 51, 55–6, 58–61, 156 n.8
  See also filmmaking; lantern (limelight) slides; persecution
sanctuary 97, 113, 125, 129, 131, 138, 186 n.116
Sargant, George
  biography 90
  The Sweet Heart of the Bush 89, 100–6
Scambler, Thomas Henry 93
School of Arts and Crafts, Adelaide 112–13
science. *See* natural science; Unwin *Religion and Science*
Scudder, Vida Dutton 95
sculpture 112, 129
Sellors, Richard 26
Service, Robert 17
Seventh-day Adventists 10–11, 18
Sheldon, Charles Monroe 95
Singleton, John 46
slum journalism 48, 55–6
Smeaton, Thomas Hyland 71, 78
Smith, William Saumarez 18
Snowden, Rita 93
social gospel 2, 12, 95, 100, 102
"Social Salvation." *See* Salvation Army
"Soldiers of the Cross." *See* Salvation Army
Somerville, Phyllis 104
  Not Only in Stone 103–4, 139
Southall, Joseph 115
Southern Cross 82, 84, 87, 138
Spirit 96, 119, 122, 126, 131, 139. *See also* God; Jesus Christ
Spiritualism 86
Spurgeon, Charles 7
Stanley, Arthur Penrhyn 24, 32
state aid 4, 6, 16–17, 134
Stephens, Alfred George 93

Stevenson, Robert Louis 23
Stone-Campbell Movement. *See* Churches of Christ
Strehlow, Theodor George Henry 126–8, 133
supernatural 86, 101, 105–7, 139
superstition 25, 103

Taylor, William George 52
temperance 15, 52–3, 56
Tennyson, Alfred 106, 133
Thake, Eric 126
Thomson, William 24, 29–30
time. *See* Dark; Harris "The Timeless Time"; travel in time
travel
  bicycle 49, 136
  horse 27, 47, 136
  itinerant ministry 93–4, 136
  marching 18–19, 40–2, 52, 74, 78, 80–1
  in time 25–6, 28, 31, 37, 87
  tourism 21, 24–5, 27–8, 31, 35
  train 27–8
  walking 27–8, 35–7, 106, 136–7
  See also Jesus, walking with; pilgrimage
travel writing 24–5, 27.
  See also Maston; Ludbrook
trees
  in art 124, 128
  blossoming 81, 138–9
  cypress 54, 83
  eucalypt 9, 100, 120, 124, 128, 135
  fig 119
  ghost gum 124, 138
  Tree of Knowledge of Good and Evil 138
  Tree of Life 81, 139
  wattle 79, 82–4, 86–7, 135
Turner, Henry Gyles 95
Twain, Mark 25

United Evangelical Church 9
Uniting Church in Australia 70

Unwin, Ernest Ewart
  art 110–11, 122, 126
  biography 110–11
  on divinity in nature 118–22, 139
  education 109, 117, 119, 121, 131
  Religion and Biology 110, 118–19
urban development 113, 124, 136
urban landscape 7, 41, 44, 51–9, 61, 73–4, 76–7.
  See also Holy Land; Jerusalem

Vale, William Mountford Kinsey and Rachel Lennox 66, 165 n.9
Voluntary Principle 69

Walker, George Washington 117
Walls of Jerusalem National Park 27
war
  Anzac 68, 73–5, 80
  conscription 71–2, 167 n.47, 168 n.54
  enlistment 68, 71, 74–6, 168 n.51
  First World War 12, 20, 65–87, 90, 112, 115, 136, 138
  returned soldiers 74, 84–7
  Second World War 96, 119
  Wilhelm II, Kaiser 68, 70, 72
  women's grief 68, 76, 78, 80–5
  See also Gallipoli; memorials; pacifism
wattle. *See* flowers; trees
Webb, Arch 98–9
Wesley, Charles 104
Wesley, John 7, 93, 104
Weymouth, E. W. 70
Whitefield, George 93
Wiebe, Rudy 95
wilderness 1–2, 11–13, 20, 23, 89, 94–5, 101, 103, 120, 129, 133
Wilton, Raymond and Annie 112
Winthrop Hall, University of Western Australia 125
Wordsworth, William 14, 34–5

Zionism. *See* Christian Zionism

www.ingramcontent.com/pod-product-compliance
Lightning Source LLC
Chambersburg PA
CBHW062218300426
44115CB00012BA/2113